"Islam"
Means Peace

Understanding the Muslim Principle of Nonviolence Today

Amitabh Pal

D0075323

 PRAEGER

AN IMPRINT OF ABC-CLIO, LLC
Santa Barbara, California • Denver, Colorado • Oxford, England

Copyright 2011 by Amitabh Pal

All rights reserved. No part of this publication may be reproduced, stored in a retrieval system, or transmitted, in any form or by any means, electronic, mechanical, photocopying, recording, or otherwise, except for the inclusion of brief quotations in a review, without prior permission in writing from the publisher.

Library of Congress Cataloging-in-Publication Data

Pal, Amitabh.
  Islam means peace : understanding the muslim principle of nonviolence today / Amitabh Pal.
       p. cm.
  Includes bibliographical references and index.
  ISBN 978-0-313-38290-1 (hard copy : alk. paper) — ISBN 978-0-313-38291-8 (ebook)   1. Nonviolence—Religious aspects—Islam.   2. Nonviolence—Islamic countries—History.   I. Title.
  BP190.5.V56P35   2011
  297.5'697—dc22   2011000553

ISBN: 978-0-313-38290-1
EISBN: 978-0-313-38291-8

15 14 13 12 11   1 2 3 4 5

This book is also available on the World Wide Web as an eBook.
Visit www.abc-clio.com for details.

Praeger
An Imprint of ABC-CLIO, LLC

ABC-CLIO, LLC
130 Cremona Drive, P.O. Box 1911
Santa Barbara, California 93116-1911

This book is printed on acid-free paper ∞

Manufactured in the United States of America

This book is dedicated to my family, who believed in me even when I didn't—and to all those around the world advancing peace and social justice.

My reading of the Qur'an has convinced me that the basis of Islam is not violence but is unadulterated peace. It regards forbearance as superior to vengeance. The very word "Islam" means peace, which is nonviolence.
—Mahatma Gandhi

Contents

Acknowledgments

I'd like to acknowledge all the scholars who have done groundbreaking research on Islam and nonviolence. I have drawn a lot on their work and am deeply indebted to them. I am in gratitude, too, to all the people whom I have interviewed over the years. They were generous enough to give me their time and insights, and their perspectives have enlightened the book. I am also grateful to the folks at *The Progressive* who allowed me the time off—and generously took up the slack at the office—that enabled me to complete this assignment. In addition, my articles for the magazine served as the building blocks for this book, and I am thankful to Juleyka Lantigua-Williams for helping me obtain this project. And it is wonderful of Praeger to realize the importance of this subject and commission me to write on it. Thanks to everyone.

CHAPTER 1

Introduction

ISLAM'S IMAGE

I spent much of my childhood in India, where Hindus and Muslims live and work together at numerous levels. The idea of Muslims being inherently violent goes against a lifetime of my observations. I had Muslim neighbors, friends, and classmates, and the notion that they somehow were more disposed toward violence was ridiculous.

During Ramadan, I remember Muslim neighbors bringing generous amounts of food to our house in the city of Lucknow, a city heavily imbued with Muslim culture. My maternal grandfather's Muslim friends used to drop by his house. The Muslim residents of our village came to visit us in our ancestral home. I recall the gentle, protective man ferrying my cousins and me to our elementary schools.

So, after 9/11—and the relentless focus on Osama bin Laden, the September 11 terrorists, and their ilk—I've felt a responsibility to correct the distorted picture that has emerged of Islam. A number of books have been written on the supposed link between Islam and violence, with a good portion of the output unfortunately consisting of crude Islamophobic tracts, such as the best-sellers Mark Steyn's *America Alone: The End of the World as We Know It* and Robert Spencer's *The Politically Incorrect Guide to Islam (and the Crusades)*. Individuals like David Horowitz and Daniel Pipes have made it a full-time crusade to inveigh against Islam, with Horowitz even organizing an Islamo-Fascism Awareness Week on college campuses across the country. Leading evangelists such as Pat Robertson and Franklin Graham have spoken of Islam in the crudest possible terms. Some politicians have pandered subtly—and not so subtly—to the anti-Islam prejudices of many in their base. (President Obama supposedly being Muslim is a political liability he constantly has had to battle during his presidential campaign and his presidency.) Hollywood and television have contributed their share with movies and shows like *The Kingdom* and *24*. The spotlight on Islam and violence has not dimmed because of the Iraq and Afghanistan wars and because of a few subsequent if feeble terrorist attempts in the United States.

The incessant drumbeat of negative news about Muslims has had a deep impact. A September 2007 Pew poll discovered that 35 percent of Americans possessed an "unfavorable" perception of Muslims.[1] An August 2007 *Financial Times/Harris* poll found that 21 percent of Americans consider the presence of Muslims in this country as a national security threat, with another one-fifth "not sure."[2]

Most disturbingly, a 2006 *USA Today*/Gallup poll revealed that 39 percent of Americans wanted Muslims to hold special identification cards.[3] The same poll found that almost half of Americans feel that Muslims are extremists. Nearly one-fourth would not want a Muslim as a neighbor. Less than half think that Muslims would stand the test of loyalty to the United States. (Positive views of Muslims increase if an American knows a Muslim personally.)[4]

These are astonishing numbers and may be understating the problem since the honesty of people with pollsters on such sensitive issues is open to question. And such opinions are not going away. An April 2009 *Washington Post*/ABC poll found that negative views of Islam were highest since the September 11 attacks, with 48 percent holding an unfavorable view of the religion. Nearly 3 in 10 Americans think that Islam encourages violence against non-Muslims, double such an opinion a year after the devastating terrorist attacks. Interestingly, a lack of basic knowledge of Islam is a huge problem, with a majority of Americans admitting they don't know much about Islam or a Muslim.[5]

So, merely reading the Qur'an on the New York subway can provoke a negative reaction, such as verbal abuse, in a way that reading the Bible never would. And the repercussions have sometimes been much more serious. At least four individuals have been murdered in the United States because of anti-Arab and anti-Muslim feelings, with another seven killings possibly due to the same bigotry. Lesser acts of discrimination have ranged from Middle Eastern–looking passengers being denied seats on a commercial flight to Arab and Muslim organizations receiving nasty phone calls and e-mails.[6]

This distrust has been reflected at the official level, with, for example, the Los Angeles Police Department coming up with a plan to create a map detailing areas of the city with Muslim concentrations. (The idea had to be abandoned after a public uproar.)[7] In October 2009, four members of Congress held a press conference to accuse a prominent Muslim organization of placing spies in congressional offices.[8]

Even members of Congress have not been immune from such attacks. Representative Keith Ellison, the first Muslim American to be elected to Congress (and someone I've had the privilege of interviewing), came under fire. The right-wing blogosphere attacked him as a radical in disguise. Glenn Beck asked him to "prove to me that you are not working with our enemies." Conservative commentator Dennis Prager fulminated about Ellison taking an oath on the Qur'an. (In reality, no holy books are used during the actual swearing in, with religious texts being used only during photo-op reenactments. At the reenactment, Ellison used Thomas Jefferson's Qur'an.) Even a couple of Ellison's colleagues derided their new associate. Representative Virgil Goode of Virginia warned in a letter to hundreds of voters that Ellison's election was a threat to the country's traditions. Representative Bill Sali of Idaho opined that having a Muslim member of Congress wasn't what the founding fathers had envisioned.[9]

"It has become much more respectable to assert that the Muslim faith turns people violent," says the *Economist*. "There are political as well as theological reasons why Western debates on the nature of Islam are so charged. If it can be shown that Islam itself is anti-freedom and pro-violence, then it makes less sense to take Muslim opinion into account when deciding policy. If you can prove that 'they hate us whatever we do,' all efforts to assuage Islamic sentiment are futile."[10]

It's never been more important to understand Islam and its followers. According to a recent Pew report, roughly one in four people in the world practices Islam. There are 1.57 billion Muslims around the world, making Islam second only to Christianity as a global religion. Contrary to notions held by many people, two out of three Muslims are Asian, not Arab. An astonishing 38 million are in Europe (the ninth-largest group globally), while 2.5 million Muslims are Americans. "The Pew Forum study depicts the world's second-largest religion as complex and nuanced, challenging the notion that its trajectory is defined by a minority of Islamists," reports the British *Guardian*.[11]

By the very nature of media coverage, the violent acts of a few Muslims have dominated the public space. Too few have asked the question as to whether there are qualities in Islam that make it compatible with nonviolence and whether there are instances in history—and especially the modern world—that show this to be true.

This void needs to be filled. We have to urgently dispel the unfair stereotype that has been attached to Islam: that it is intrinsically violent, and so are its adherents. With the population of Muslims in the United States being relatively small, the impressions most Americans have of Islam is through the mass media, which have provided a distorted image. Most every time Americans hear the word "Islam," it is married to "radical" or "extreme."

As a result, the public has become hostile to Islam. President Obama was so afraid of being tagged a Muslim during his election campaign that he never said that there isn't anything wrong with practicing Islam. He even spurned the offer of Congressman Ellison to campaign for him at mosques. Attempts at introducing a balanced analysis of Islam in school textbooks have been met with hostility around the country. A public middle school in New York established to disseminate Arabic culture, the Khalil Gibran International Academy, has been marred by controversy since its inception, with critics accusing it of being a stalking horse for radical Islam and forcing its principal to resign.[12] Even such an innocuous move as an effort by a union to obtain a Muslim holiday at a Tyson Foods poultry plant in Tennessee has caused an uproar.[13] And then there's the tumult over the proposed Islamic community center near Ground

Zero, which has crystallized anti-Muslim opinion like nothing else has since the September 11 attacks.

My research provides a rebuttal to the general misperceptions of Islam by showing that the tradition of nonviolence within Islam has been rich. These findings will be invaluable for both Muslims and non-Muslims alike. For Muslims, they will reveal an alternative tradition that they can embrace; for non-Muslims, they will show a side of Islam they probably have never seen before.

NONVIOLENCE IS THE RIGHT CHOICE

Nonviolence is the right path to pursue regardless of religious affiliation. Obviously, it occupies the ethical high ground. And a comprehensive study has shown that nonviolent resistance not only is the morally superior choice but also is twice as effective as the violent variety. That's the startling and reassuring discovery by Maria Stephan and Erica Chenoweth, who analyzed an astonishing 323 resistance campaigns from 1900 to 2006.[14]

"Our findings show that major nonviolent campaigns have achieved success 53 percent of the time, compared with 26 percent for violent resistance campaigns," the authors note in the Summer 2008 issue of the journal *International Security*.[15] The result is not that surprising once you listen to the researchers' reasoning.

"First, a campaign's commitment to nonviolent methods enhances its domestic and international legitimacy and encourages more broad-based participation in the resistance, which translates into increased pressure being brought to bear on the target," they state. "Second, whereas governments easily justify violent counterattacks against armed insurgents, regime violence against nonviolent movements is more likely to backfire against the regime."[16]

In some sense, the authors have subjected to statistical analysis the theories of Gene Sharp, an influential Boston-based proponent of nonviolent change. In his work, Sharp stresses the practical utility of nonviolence, deemphasizing the moral aspects of it. He even asserts that for Gandhi, nonviolence was more of a pragmatic tool than a matter of principle, painting a picture that's at variance with much of Gandhian scholarship. In an interview with me in 2006, Sharp declared that he derives his precepts from Gandhi himself.

Gandhi's use of nonviolence "was pure pragmatism," Sharp told me. "At the end of his life, he defends himself. He was accused of holding on to nonviolent means because of his religious belief. He says, 'No.' He says, 'I presented this as a political means of action, and that's what I'm saying today. And it's a misrepresentation to say that I presented this as a purely religious approach.' He was very upset about that."[17]

The reason for choosing nonviolence hence becomes easier: it is much more successful than its violent counterpart as a means of social change, apart from being the honorable choice.

Obviously, for Muslims, too, nonviolence would be the best way to go. But have adherents of Islam chosen to take that route? The debate begins with the very name of the religion itself. Does Islam mean submission to peace, as defenders of the religion claim? Or is it the attainment of peace through submission to the will of God, surely a different thing? The standard Muslim greeting is *Salaam ale-kum*, or "peace be upon you." Does the conduct of the religion live up to its catchphrase?

THE SOURCES OF ISLAM

My journey of exploration starts with the founder of the religion, the Prophet Muhammad, and Islam's holy book, the Qur'an. The prophet is a role model for devout Muslims. In support of the fact that Islam places an emphasis on nonviolence, scholars point to the conduct of the Prophet Muhammad in Mecca. For 12 long years, he endured persecution in that city without fighting back, emphasizing instead the virtues of forbearance (*sabr*) and patience.

Famed Egyptian writer Alaa Al Aswany cites repeated stories of Muhammad's compassion toward children. "How can anyone use the same prophet's name to kill?" asks Al Aswany. "You can see clearly there has been a terrible interpretation of Islam."[18]

The notion of emigration as a form of nonviolent protest is central to Islam and is hallowed among Muslims since they believe that by doing so they are following in the footsteps of Muhammad and his companions. The flight, or *hijrah*, of the prophet and his followers from Mecca to Medina constitutes a pivotal moment in the religion. As early as the eighth century, Muslims like those of the Khawarij community took this concept to heart, emigrating from their homeland to avoid being annihilated. Many centuries later, those Muslims who went to Pakistan from India during the partition of the subcontinent were called *muhajir* since they believed they had engaged in the act of *hijrah*, or emigration, to preserve their faith.

Even after his emigration to Medina, Muhammad often used skillful diplomacy instead of warfare to placate his enemies. And when he triumphantly reentered Mecca, he forgave the inhabitants instead of taking revenge. There are other instances in his life that have him engaged in peacemaking and conflict arbitration, important episodes to build on. The founder of Islam—the most venerated figure in Muslim history—provides a guide map to embark on the path of nonviolence.

As for Islam's holy book, we enter into the realm of endless debate about its contents and about which particular passages take precedence. The Qur'an clearly contains, however, several verses forbidding aggression. And there are strict rules of conduct for warfare, with, for example, restrictions on harming children, women, and old men. The first caliphs are said to have conducted themselves according to these rules.

Islam stresses values such as compassion, benevolence, wisdom, and justice, which are compatible with the practice of nonviolence. The Qur'an also underscores that forgiveness for an ill deed is a much nobler quality than revenge. A corollary to this is the emphasis on performing good deeds toward everyone, not just Muslims.

Muslims consider the Hadith, the preachings and deeds of Muhammad that have been passed down over time, second to the Qur'an in importance. There are many commendations of nonviolence within Hadith literature, too. Such references in the Qur'an and the Hadith demonstrate the place of nonviolence within Islam.

THE SPREAD OF ISLAM

The nature of the spread of Islam has also generated controversy. Critics charge that even if the actual conversion of people to the religion wasn't at the point of a sword, at least it was made possible through the conquest of lands in the Middle East and beyond.

Reality was more complicated, however. Contrary to stereotype, the message of Islam was often extended peacefully by Sufi orders. Scholars like Khalid Kishtainy assert that even the supposed military prowess of the Arabs and their achievements of conquest immediately after the advent of Islam are exaggerated. The empires they defeated and conquered, such as the Persian and the Byzantine, were already exhausted. The Arabs never had a military class, unlike the Prussians in Germany, the Samurais in Japan, or the Rajputs in India. Instead, the elite was of a merchant nature. And even the behavior of the Arabs after their conquest was not that of a militaristic people. Instead, Baghdad became known as a center of learning and the finer arts.[19]

My work will uncover lesser-known facets of Muslim history that are at variance with conventional wisdom. But I am not engaging in a remote historical examination of the role of nonviolence in Islam—far from it, especially when there is such a rich tradition of nonviolence available in modern Muslim societies.

PACIFIST MUSLIM SECTS

Several Muslim sects have exhibited a pacifist bent. The most famous of these are the Sufis, whose pacifism and tolerance are acknowledged by even many critics of Islam.

Sufism has played a big part in the Islam of South, Southeast, and Central Asia, and hence I am baffled that this aspect of the religion has been almost completely ignored in the United States. Either it has not been acknowledged to exist, or, if it has, it's been treated as something that is extraneous to the religion.

This is completely erroneous. Sufism has been an integral part of Islam since its founding, and Sufis are responsible for the spread of Islam, for instance, among one of the largest concentrations of Muslims in the world, Bengali Muslims—those in current Bangladesh plus the Indian state of West Bengal. Sufi preachers went into the forests of the region and disseminated Islam's message.

The impact of Sufism can be seen everywhere in South Asia. Shrines of Sufi saints, equally popular among Hindus and Muslims alike, dot the Indian subcontinent. (In fact, perhaps the most revered Sufi shrine in India is in the city of my boarding school.) These shrines are an amazing testament to religious harmony, with people from all faiths and walks of life visiting them in an act of nonsectarian piety. The fact that the guardians of the tombs—as well as those buried within—are Muslims is irrelevant to the legions who come to pay their respect and offer decorative cloth as a mark of reverence.

Sufi influence can be also seen in the distinctly South Asian syncretic art forms that are extremely popular in the region. One prominent example is the devotional music *qawwali*, the most famous exponent of which in the West was the late Nusrat Fateh Ali Khan, who collaborated with the likes of Peter Gabriel and Eddie Vedder. On a kitschier level, Indian Bollywood movies have generally projected a secular, vaguely Sufi outlook, with Muslims playing important roles at all levels and the films themselves most often preaching religious harmony.

The Sufis don't have different principles from other Muslims; they just differ in their emphasis. For instance, a central concept for Sufis is *tawhid*, or unity, which can be taken to mean the unity of mankind and of existence, not just of Muslims. An extension of this outlook is the Sufi emphasis on peace.

There are other lesser-known Muslim sects, too, such as the Ahmadiyyas (controversial among Muslims for other reasons, as we shall see), that have concentrated on the pacifist aspects of the religion. These groups deserve to be better known to an American audience that often reflexively pictures violence when thinking about Islam.

JIHAD AND ISLAM

The notion of jihad in Islam is an extremely controversial one and is something that has to be grappled with. There is no denying the fact that religiously inspired violence has captured the headlines when it comes to Islam. I'm filled with sadness every time I see mention of a suicide bombing in Iraq or in Pakistan and Afghanistan. The most distressing aspect is the enormous toll that these jihadists inflict. But what also dies a small death each time is the reputation of Islam.

There is a big debate within Islam about whether jihad mainly connotes the internal struggle within a believer or is chiefly about externally directed violence. And, if it is externally directed violence, is jihad meant to be used as a last resort, when Muslims are in grave danger, or is it justified to use jihad for the expansion of the faith? We have to deal with this issue without getting lost in theological thickets.

There is a vicious self-perpetuating cycle going on in Islam when it comes to jihad. Intense media coverage of jihadist violence gives rise to more young Muslims going on this path, which, in turn, leads to further media-grabbing headlines. We have to emphasize instead the alternative tradition of nonviolence within the religion. Even if a few who would otherwise have strayed over to the dark side are prevented from doing so by works such as mine, I will have considered my project successful.

THE PASHTUN PACIFISTS

One of the most remarkable examples of nonviolent resistance in history that has been almost completely ignored in the West is that of Khan Abdul Ghaffar "Badshah" Khan and his movement. Khan, a Pashtun friend of Gandhi, founded a peace force of more than 100,000 Pashtuns dedicated to social reform and non-violent protest in the area of the world currently most closely associated with terrorism—the Pakistan–Afghanistan border. Nicknamed the "Frontier Gandhi" for his association with the Mahatma, Khan, who had the same ethnicity (and grew up in the same area) as the Taliban, nevertheless drew much more inspiration from the Qur'an and the Prophet Muhammad than from Mohandas. In spite of massive repression by the British, Khan and his followers kept to their creed. The movement had as its bedrock principles nonviolence, societal reform, religious tolerance, social justice, and women's rights.

I first heard of Khan when he died in January 1988. His death was marked in India as the last remaining link to the leaders of the Indian independence struggle and to Gandhi himself. In an act of supreme condescension, much of the Indian media treated Khan's movement as a curious anomaly formed because of the influence of Gandhi. What got little mention was that Khan's campaign was very rooted in the heritage of Islam and the Pashtuns and derived much more from both than from Gandhi.

For Khan, Islam's core was nonviolence. When I spoke to Khan's daughter-in-law and grandson a few years ago for an article for *The Progressive*, both of them stressed the importance of Islam in Khan's worldview and mentioned Gandhi only in passing. (Some scholars have also suggested that Gandhi himself drew inspiration from Islam, a tantalizing assertion that I will look into.)

Khan's obscurity partly stems from the fact that after independence, the Pakistani government viewed him with suspicion because of his bond with Gandhi and his demand for Pashtun self-rule and repressed and marginalized him. In addition, unlike Gandhi, he left behind little written material, except for an autobiography dictated to an associate. Jailed by the British and Pakistanis for a total of almost three decades, this remarkable man never lost his faith in nonviolence. (His political heirs have made an amazing political comeback in recent elections in Pakistan and currently govern his home state.) Sadly, Americans have barely heard of him. Going by the overwhelmingly positive response to my *Progressive* article on him some years ago, there is a hankering for accounts like his. I aim in my book to offer them.

GANDHIAN MUSLIMS

Khan was far from the only Muslim to be associated with the Gandhian struggle for Indian freedom. There were several others. The most prominent of these was Maulana Abul Kalam Azad, a highly respected scholar and theologian who headed Gandhi's Congress Party for a number of years. In sovereign India, he rose to the highest ranks of government, being appointed by Jawaharlal Nehru as education minister. Another Gandhian Muslim, Zakir Husain, earned such stature as an educationist that he was chosen as the third president of independent India. Both Azad and Husain were devout Muslims who saw no contradiction between their faith and pluralism and nonviolence. And they were just the most prominent ones. There were several others who joined with Gandhi and remained faithful to Gandhian principles. Such life stories are completely unknown outside India and will add another wrinkle to the notion of Islam being inextricably tied to violence.

THE KOSOVO MASSIVE CIVIL DISOBEDIENCE MOVEMENT

But why go back decades? Another notable exercise in nonviolence in a Muslim society took place in a more recent era: the 1990s. When the Serb regime of Slobodan Milosevic started repressing the Kosovar Albanians and denying them basic educational and health care facilities, the Kosovars launched a vibrant, extensive nonviolent movement. Headed by Ibrahim Rugova (the "Gandhi of the Balkans"), they instituted a parallel social system to educate and heal themselves and coupled this with social reform.

The Albanian response in the face of repression was remarkable. Two separate and parallel societies were set up. This endeavor extended to the sports and the cultural realm. Houses, cafés, and restaurants became the venue for schools, arts exhibitions, and sporting venues.

The Albanians set up a new health network. After the Serbs ejected Albanian medical personnel from state hospitals, the Kosovars established a system of dispensaries run on private premises, supplementing a chain of Albanian Catholic clinics, and Albanian babies were delivered at home. Interestingly, Catholic priests and Muslim imams worked together to coordinate these activities. And a Christian Democratic Party, comprising Christian and Muslim personalities, worked alongside Rugova's organization.

Because of several slipups, Rugova was not able to realize the full potential of his nonviolent strategy, nor was he able to reach out to his adversaries in a Gandhi-like manner. The fact, however, that he managed to sustain a nonviolent campaign for years in extremely difficult circumstances is a huge achievement. Even with all its flaws of personality and tactics, the Rugova path was far preferable to that of other leaders in the Balkans, past and present. And in the end, his efforts did bear fruit, albeit accompanied by many zigzags, with Kosovo declaring independence and attaining recognition from dozens of countries just a couple of years after Rugova's death from lung cancer.

NONVIOLENCE IN THE MIDDLE EAST

Nonviolence has been tried even in a part of the Muslim world that has seemed to be perhaps the most impervious to this perspective in recent times: the Middle East. One such example is Egypt in the early part of the 20th century, when mass agitation in the form of strikes, boycotts, and petitions forced the British to abandon the protectorate arrangement and grant Egypt limited self-independence in 1922. An obsequious 1948 treaty signed by Iraqi prime minister Salih Jabr with the British led to a predominantly nonviolent uprising that brought about the government's resignation. Another little-known instance of a successful modern nonviolent movement in the Arab region is a 1985 mass revolt in Sudan that toppled the government of Jafar Numeiri.

The 1979 Iranian Revolution that ousted the shah was, contrary to popular notions, almost completely a nonviolent one, with nearly all the violence coming from the shah's security forces. The anti-shah forces comprised a broad spectrum of society, ranging from workers and students to intellectuals and clerics (that the mullahs hijacked the movement later is another matter) and engaged in a vast array of devices to topple the king, including strikes, civil disobedience, and massive rallies.

"A month later, at the end of the fasting month of Ramadan, one hundred thousand people poured into the streets, the first of the grand marches against the Shah," writes Nobel Peace laureate Shirin Ebadi (whom I've had the privilege of interviewing) in her memoir *Iran Awakening*. "An ocean of Iranians as far as the eye could see filled the wide boulevards of Tehran and raised their voices against the Shah."[20]

Beleaguered from all sides, a nonviolent resistant movement also formed in Iraq to resist the U.S. occupation. This nascent coalition was composed of a loose network of civil society organizations, unions in the oil sector, women's groups, and students. Despite being outgunned and largely ignored in the U.S. media, such entities persisted in their peaceful resistance to the U.S. presence in Iraq.

The most inspirational prodemocracy movement in the recent past has been in Iran, with a mass nonviolent uprising—the Green Movement—daring to take on the government after a questionable presidential election in 2009. While the movement has not emerged victorious, it has managed to persist in the face of intense repression, changing the Iranian political landscape and earning admiration from around the world in the process.

PALESTINIAN NONVIOLENCE

The nonviolent aspect of the First Palestinian Intifada has been all but forgotten because of the extensive violence of the second one. But the Palestinian uprising in the late 1980s and the early 1990s was predominantly nonviolent, with the significant and controversial exception of stone throwing at Israeli security forces.

Several groups were responsible for coordinating and putting into effect the nonviolent strategies that marked this phase. Perhaps most remarkable in a highly patriarchal society was the pivotal role played by women's groups, which engaged in much-needed organizing, even though women were denied leadership positions. Several other civil society organizations also played important functions. All these various segments of society got together and engaged in a

gamut of actions—ranging all the way from noncooperation and boycott of Israeli goods to tax resistance, mock funerals, demonstrations, road blocking, and
graffiti campaigns.

In constructing their program, the Palestinians were helped by some remarkable individuals. Two of the most prominent were Mubarak Awad and Gene
Sharp, both of whom I've interviewed. Awad has been the most prominent Palestinian proponent of nonviolence, helping set up a center for the propagation
of his views in East Jerusalem, conducting regular workshops on the importance
and efficacy of nonviolence, and engaging in direct action. The Israeli authorities, however, deported him in 1988. Awad collaborated and built on the work
of the nonviolent strategist Sharp—whose ideas have had global influence—
and widely disseminated his writings in Arabic. Awad also drew on the legacy of
Abdul Ghaffar Khan.

Professor Mohammed Abu-Nimer contends that even though the movement was nationalist in character, Islam played an important role in various
ways. Palestinians drew on the religion to make sacrifices for the movement.
The leadership of the Intifada used religious symbols to inspire its workers.
Mosques were utilized as sites of mobilization. And the movement took inspiration from the egalitarian nature of Islam to fashion a nonhierarchical grassroots
movement.[21]

The spirit of nonviolence continues today. In the most significant example,
Palestinian protesters in the village of Bilin have been engaging in weekly demonstrations against the Israel–Palestine separation barrier. They won an Israeli
Supreme Court decision in September 2007 that ordered a partial rerouting of
the barrier to hand back confiscated farmland. When the Israeli government
dragged its feet on implementing the judgment, the protests continued.

SOUTH ASIAN MOVEMENTS

Modern South Asia also provides several examples of predominantly nonviolent uprisings successfully toppling dictators. One occurred back in 1969, when
a popular movement in Pakistan forced military ruler Ayub Khan to step down.
Another one, in Bangladesh in 1990, caused dictator Muhammad Ershad to ab-
dicate and democracy to be restored.

But the most incredible instances have taken place in the recent past. An
amazingly brave nonviolent movement occurred in Pakistan. It was precipitated
by military ruler Pervez Musharraf's wanton dismissal in 2007 of the Supreme
Court Chief Justice Iftikhar Mohammed Chaudhry. In response, lawyers' groups
and other segments of Pakistani civil society mounted a sustained peaceful agitation. The results were impressive, even in the face of the murders of dozens of
protesters by Musharraf's allies (in the city of Karachi) and a massive bomb blast
at a site where Chaudhry was due to give a speech. Musharraf was initially forced
to accept a Supreme Court's ruling when it reinstated Chaudhry as the chief justice but then decided to dig in and crack down. He declared emergency rule and
arrested thousands of lawyers, judges, and their allies in civil society. In fact, he

reserved a fury for them that he didn't show toward religious fundamentalist parties, subjecting the lawyers to massive detentions, beatings, and teargassing.

But domestic and international pressure forced Musharraf to hold elections. The results vindicated the protesters, with Musharraf's party being decimated. The game was up. Musharraf held on to the presidency for a few more months but eventually gave up the ghost in August 2008 and fled to England. Democracy was restored, and the protesters triumphed.

When Benazir Bhutto's widower, Asif Ali Zardari, procrastinated on restoring some of the top judges, the lawyers came out again in force in early 2009 and forced him to reinstall them. Such a victory, twice over, may be unprecedented in recent times. And Pakistan is not the only Muslim country even in South Asia to have an inspirational ending in the past few years. In late 2008, in a little-known instance, the people of the small Indian Ocean island nation of Maldives brought down a tyrant, Maumoon Abdul Gayoom, after 30 years of his autocratic rule, the longest in Asia at that point in time. Mass peaceful mobilization by the opposition candidate, former political prisoner Mohamed Nasheed, helped ensure that Gayoom finally conceded when he lost the presidential election to Nasheed in October. Gayoom was no slouch in the repression department. Demonstrators were badly beaten by the police, and critics were sentenced to long years in prison. Nasheed himself was brutally tortured before being forced into exile.

My work will tell of several such episodes—both in the modern era and further back in time. It will be a journey of personal exploration for me as well as for the reader. I will introduce the reader to fascinating, courageous leaders of nonviolent movements in the Muslim world. The treatment that Islam has received in the recent past has been a source of despair to me but also bewilderment since it didn't fit with the religion I've known since I was a child. The media coverage of Islam in the West has given rise to grotesque oversimplifications and stereotypes. If my book can play even a small part in correcting this, it will have fulfilled its objective.

Gandhi, the ultimate icon of nonviolence, said, "My reading of the Qur'an has convinced me that the basis of Islam is not violence, but is unadulterated peace. It regards forbearance as a superior to vengeance. The very word 'Islam' means peace, which is nonviolence."[22]

Islam, just like any other religion, has had its share of positives and negatives. A focus on just the negative is not fair to the religion at all. What we need in an open society is balanced information on each other so that there is ample room for dialogue. My book is an attempt to initiate the conversation.

CHAPTER 2

Inspiration at the Roots: Sources of Nonviolence in Islam

A RELIGION OF PEACE?

In its source texts and the conduct of its prophet, is Islam a religion of peace? The answer would be a qualified yes.

Islam has never abjured the notion of war, and the Qur'an allows self-protection. Similarly, there are a number of instances of the Prophet Muhammad taking up arms. But the wars sanctioned by the religion and its texts are of a defensive nature when the religion and its followers are under attack. The primacy of peace is emphasized.

Comparative religion expert J. Patout Burns asserts that there is nothing in Islam holding back its adherents from taking the path of nonviolence.[1] "Every religion can foster either violence or nonviolence," affirms nonviolence proponent Professor Muhammad Abu-Nimer. "It is the responsibility of those who follow a particular faith to cull those resources for nonviolence from their religious scriptures."[2]

Muslim nonviolence scholar K.G. Saiyidain asserts that the core of Islam is nonviolence and that even if there are circumstances in which Islam contemplates the possibility of war, the essential thing in life according to Islam is peace.[3]

Abu-Nimer contends that Islam does not need to be thought of as an "absolute pacifist" religion for Muslims to engage in nonviolent resistance campaigns and activities since there are abundant signposts within Islam that can provide ample guidance.[4]

"Does Islam 'mean peace'?," asks scholar John Kelsay, "or is it a 'very evil and wicked religion?'" Islam "commands its followers to strive for peace," he answers. "It does not, of course, understand peace as a simple matter of the absence of conflict. Rather, Islam is associated with the idea that peace requires justice, and that these terms signify a condition best served when human societies are ordered in ways that may be described as legitimate."[5]

Seeing the possibilities of peace in Islam starts with examining the religion's language. The word "Islam" is derived from the word *silm*, which "means reconciliation, peace, submission, and deliverance." Indian progressive activist and scholar Asghar Ali Engineer (recipient of the "Alternative Nobel" prize) takes the most positive reading of the word, stating that it means peace and surrendering to the will of Allah. Since one of the names of Allah is *Salaam* (peace) and Muslims are servants of Allah, he says that de facto they are servants of peace.[6] Another of Allah's name is *Rabb*, one who takes mankind step-by-step to perfection. Surely, this perfection includes peace, and those who believe in him have to follow peace.[7] Engineer asserts that Islam is at its roots a religion of peace since it repeatedly uses the terms *adl* (justice), *rahmah* (compassion), and *ihsan* (benevolence).[8]

Paradise in Islam is described as a place of peace and security. The central greeting among Muslims is *Salaam ale-kum*: "Peace be upon you," which is derived from the Qur'an: "And their greeting shall be Peace" (10:10).

A Qur'anic verse says, "God invites people to the abode of peace" (10:25). Another verse goes, "And 'the servants of (Allah)' most Gracious are those who walk on the Earth in humility, and when the ignorant address them, they say, 'Peace!'" (25:63). And the Qur'an says about Muhammad, the messenger of the religion, "We have sent you but as a mercy to the worlds" (21:107).

"Life in Islam is sacred and to be respected," Bangladeshi author Tamizul Haque says. "Islam therefore advocates peace as a fundamental principle of life, and it not only takes all the necessary measures to secure it but also to maintain it."[9]

Another of the names of God in Islam is *al-Wadud*—the most loving, the most affectionate—and there are several such references in the Qur'an, such as "He is the all-forgiving, all-loving" (85: 14) and "Surely my lord is all-merciful, all-love" (11:90). Even one of the titles of Muhammad is *Habib Allah*—the friend or beloved of God—and the Qur'an says to him, "If ye love God, follow me. Allah will love you and forgive you your sins. For Allah is oft-forgiving, most merciful" (3:31). The view that many westerners have of the Muslim God not containing love within him is mistaken. The medieval Jewish poet and saint Abraham ibn Ezra stated, "The Muslims sing of love and passion, the Christians of war and revenge."[10]

"[In Islam] love runs through the vein of the universe and, like compassion, is inseparable from existence," Iranian intellectual Seyyed Hossein Nasr writes. "There is no realm of existence where love does not manifest itself in some way."[11]

Love in Islam is meant to be centered on God. But it can manifest itself on several planes at once, best seen in Sufism (a later chapter in this book deals with this) in the poetry of women such as Rabia al-Adawiyya: "Two ways I love Thee: selfishly, And next, as worthy is of thee. . . . Tis purest love when Thou dost raise the veil to my adoring gaze." The Sufi spiritual school of Khurasan in Persia was especially identified with love, yielding among its adherents none other than Rumi.[12]

"The very presence of this vast literature on Divine Love in nearly every Islamic language from Arabic and Persian to Turkish and Swahili, as well as most of the local languages of India and Southeast Asia, is the best eternal sign of the significance of the dimension of love in the inner life of Islam," writes Nasr. "This outpouring was so extensive and powerful in expression that it even influenced Jewish, Christian and Hindu writers and spiritual practitioners."[13]

And such poetry is neither limited to Sufi mystics nor marginal to Muslims at large. Nasr describes a visit to Lahore in Pakistan, where his carriage driver, on learning that Nasr was from Iran, began reciting numerous love poems by Persian mystics such as Rumi and Hafiz.[14]

But because of groups like Al Qaeda, Islam has been hampered by a negative image that has impeded study of the possibilities of nonviolent action in Muslim societies. This has led to the widespread assumption that the Islam is hostile to any notion of peace. And this stereotype has been so widely purveyed in the Western media that it has gained traction not only among the public but among policymakers, too.

Or, as Professor John Esposito of Georgetown University, one of the most renowned American scholars on Islam, puts it, "A combination of ignorance, stereotyping, history, and experience, as well as religio-cultural chauvinism, too often blinds even the best-intentioned when dealing with the Arab and Muslim world."[15]

There has been as a consequence an almost complete lack of study of the tradition of nonviolence in Islam. When Professor Abu-Nimer searched the Library of Congress catalog some years ago for "Islam and violence," he was bombarded with thousands of entries. By contrast, when he searched for "Islam and nonviolence," he came up with a sum total of fewer than five items. There are many reasons for this dismal state of affairs, but a few major ones are lack of research into nonviolence in Muslim societies and the failure of Muslims to convey an alternative narrative to violence.[16] The result is that "Islam and the Muslim world still remain, to a considerable extent, rather neglected areas of peace studies and peace research," says scholar Syed Sikandar Mehdi.[17]

PEACEFUL QUALITIES OF ISLAM

But there are Islamic precepts that can wonderfully be used in the service of peace. Thai Muslim nonviolence proponent Chaiwat Satha-Anand traces interesting similarities between the notions of Mahatma Gandhi, the very symbol of nonviolence, and the foundations of Islam, a comparison that deserves to be quoted at some length.

"Belief in nonviolence is based on the assumption that human nature in its essence is one and therefore unfailingly responds to the advances of love," Gandhi said. "A nonviolent resister depends on the unfailing assistance of God, which sustains him throughout difficulties that could otherwise be considered insurmountable."[18] This conforms very well to the Muslim notion of humanity as one and created by God.

Gandhi also said, "Truth and nonviolence are not possible without a living belief in God, meaning a self-existent, all-knowing, living force which inheres in every other force known to the world and which depends on none, and which will live when all other forces may conceivably perish or cease to act."

This, Satha-Anand points out, is very close to the beliefs of devout Muslims. "A Muslim following Gandhi's teaching would not feel estranged," Satha-Anand writes. "In fact, it may be possible to trace the Islamic influence on Gandhi concerning the omnipotent and incomparable God."[19]

Satha-Anand also draws an intriguing parallel between the basic theory of eminent nonviolent theorist Gene Sharp—power depends on the consent of the governed—and Islamic thought. After all, "For Muslims, this so-called modern theory of power simply embodies the basic Islamic principle that a person should submit to the Will of God," writes Satha-Anand. "As a result, a Muslim is not bound to obey anyone whose power has been used unjustly."[20] The Qur'an commands people to leave the domain of an unjust ruler: "Was not the Earth of Allah spacious enough for you to move yourselves away?" (4:97).

Professor Abu-Nimer says that the positions of Western nonviolent resisters and just war theorists would actually be quite close and compatible with Islam in that all these agree that the use of force always needs justification. The conduct of the Prophet Muhammad reflected these rules (as will be discussed later in the chapter). In this sense, the Qur'an and Muhammad reflect very much a version of the "just war" theory.

"Islam as a religion and tradition privileges and embodies values that facilitate nonviolence and peace building," even if force is permitted as a last resort, contends Abu-Nimer, saying that this can readily be evidenced in the Qur'an, the Hadith texts, and Muslim traditions.[21]

Satha-Anand's interpretation of the five pillars of Islam segues very well into nonviolent activism. The vow of obedience to God (*shahadat*) enables a Muslim to resist injustice. The pillar of *salat* (prayer) offers discipline when offered in a gathering and helps build community. The *zakat* (tax) makes Muslims more conscious about the needs and obligations of the larger community and urges them to do something to rectify social shortcomings like injustice and poverty. Ramadan (fasting) fosters both sacrifice and empathy for others, developing qualities like patience that enabled movements like, Satha-Anand says, that of Ghaffar Khan (the pacifist leader who is dealt with at length later in this book) to become successful. And the haj reaffirms the notion of brotherhood among Muslims and mankind.[22]

We can see then that there are a number of basic principles in Islam on which nonviolent movements can easily be built. Satha-Anand proposes five pillars of Muslim nonviolent action (in parallel with the five pillars of Islam). First, Muslims are willing to disobey injustice since they obey only Allah. Second, Muslims are courageous since they fear only Allah. Third, Muslims possess enormous self-discipline because of their rituals like Ramadan. This can come in very handy in nonviolent protest. Fourth, the concept of a Muslim community is very strong ("Hold fast all together by the rope which God stretches out for you and be not divided among yourselves," says the Qur'an 3:103). This can enable them to resist oppression together. And, fifth, Islam is action oriented, which can be channeled into nonviolent action.[23]

From all this, Satha-Anand prescribes his eight theses on Muslim nonviolent action:

1. Violence in Islam is a central moral question.
2. If violence has to be used, it should be governed by the rules of the Qur'an and Hadith.
3. And if it cannot distinguish between combatants and noncombatants, then it can't be used.
4. Modern technology, indiscriminate in its use, makes the use of violence in Islam virtually unacceptable.
5. So, in the modern world, use of violence by Muslims is unacceptable.
6. The notion of the fight for justice in Islam is intertwined with the sacredness of life.
7. Hence to be true Muslims, followers of Islam should engage only in nonviolent action.
8. And Islam, due to its qualities (such as discipline and sacrifice) described above offers a lot of rich material for nonviolent action.[24]

The Qur'an says, "Peace! A word (of salutation) from the Lord most merciful!" (36:58). Similarly, Abu-Nimer lists seven principles in Islam that support coexistence and tolerance and hence, by extension, the existence of nonviolence:

1. Human dignity is an absolute, regardless of a person's religion or other background (Qur'an 17:70).
2. All human beings have sprung from a common source and hence are part of one large family (Qur'an 4:1, 5:32, 6:98).
3. And so the differences between people are part of a grand design (Qur'an 10:99, 11:188–199, 30:22).
4. Islam recognizes other religions (Qur'an 2:136, 42:13).
5. Muslims have the freedom of choice (Qur'an 2:256, 17:107, 18:29, 109:4–6).
6. Only God has the right to judge, and on Judgment Day (Qur'an 16:124, 31:23, 42:48, 88:25–26).
7. Muslims have a duty to be nice, just and equitable toward all human beings (Qur'an 4:135, 5:8, 60:8).

One of the main virtues that Islam encourages and that nonviolence proponents over the years have used as a foundation is patience (*sabr*). In Arabic, *sabr* has multiple shades of meaning: patience in not being hasty, patience through perseverance, and patience in a cheerful attitude in the face of suffering.[25]

O ye who believe! Seek help with patient perseverance and prayer: for
Allah is with those who patiently persevere. (Qur'an 2:153)

If ye persevere patiently, and guard against evil—then that will be a
determining factor in all affairs. (Qur'an 3:186)

O ye who believe! Persevere in patience and constancy; vie in such
perseverance; strengthen each other; and fear Allah; that ye may prosper.
(Qur'an 3:200)

There are at least 15 other Qur'anic verses that encourage patience and steadfastness. Such qualities can easily be used toward peace (as will be seen in the
chapter on pacifist Abdul Ghaffar Khan), in addition to giving Muslims the advantage in conflicts. It also fosters peaceful coexistence.[26] And this patience is
active, not passive, a form of resistance in tandem with prayer. "Power resides not
in being able to strike another, but in being able to keep the self under control
when anger arises," said Muhammad.

"If ye show patience, that is indeed the best (course) for those who are patient. And do thou be patient, for thy patience is but from Allah; nor grieve over
them: and distress not thyself because of their plots. For Allah is with those who
restrain themselves. And those who do good" (Qur'an 16:126–128). "The words
are wide enough to cover all human struggles, disputes and fights," says commentator Yusuf Ali about these verses.[27]

Yet another activity encouraged by Islam is group activity or collaboration.
"God's hand is with the group," it is said. Nonviolent movements in Muslim societies will naturally be most effective if they are based on notions of solidarity:

O mankind! Reverence your Guardian-Lord, who created you from a single
person, created, of like nature, his mate, and from them twain scattered
(like seeds) countless men and women. (Qur'an 4:1)

Help your brother, whether he is an oppressor or he is an oppressed one.
People asked: "How should we help him if he is an oppressor?" The prophet
replied, "By preventing him from oppressing others."[28]

The notion of the Muslim community being one is a very strong one. This
concept can be a very strong one in building nonviolence within Muslims—
since if all Muslims are a part of a greater whole, then they should not be willing
to inflict violence on each other. And scholars like Farid Esack argue that the
ummah—community—can be expanded to include non-Muslims. "The universal
community under God has always been a significant element in Muslim discourse
against tribalism and racism," says Esack. Other scholars have built on this to say
that the ummah is at the very least meant to include other "People of the Book"—
Jews and Christians. This sense of solidarity can be used adeptly in peace efforts.[29]
"The idea of a Muslim community has proved a powerful tool of social mobilization and selflessness and thus has enormous potential for contributing to peaceful
conflict resolution," says Abu-Nimer.[30]

Islamic ethics emphasize compassion, mercy, and forgiveness toward everyone (especially the poor, the infirm, and the disadvantaged). This circle of kindness starts with family but then radiates outward to one's neighbors and community. But it doesn't stop there. "Beyond one's neighborhood there is society at large, in which the same attitude of compassion and kindness must exist even beyond the boundary of one's religion," writes Nasr. This has even extended to animals and plants in Muslim societies. For instance, Muhammad is said to have been gentle with animals, and a number of Hadith references emphasize the importance of kindness to other living creatures. So, in the medieval era, a number of Muslim cities had animal hospitals, and there were shelters for old and past-their-prime animals.[31]

The notion of compassion is integral to Islam. There are four key words that are repeated the most in the Qur'an: compassion, benevolence, justice, and wisdom. *Rahman* and *Rahim* (Compassionate and Merciful) are among the names of Allah, and observant Muslims start things by reciting *Bismillah al-Rahman al-Rahim*—beginning in the name of Allah who is Compassionate and Merciful. The opening verses of the Qur'an describe Allah as *Al-Rahman Al-Rahim* and *Rabb al-Alamin* (sustainer of the whole world). Muhammad is said to be a manifestation of his mercy—the mercy of the world. This shows, Engineer asserts, that anyone who follows Muhammad has to be merciful and compassionate.[32]

Another fundamental Islamic value on which nonviolence can easily be built is the universality and dignity of mankind. The three major types of responsibilities in Islam are responsibility toward Allah, responsibility toward oneself by living in harmony with yourself, and responsibility toward other human by living in harmony and peace with them.

"Human beings are a manifestation of God's will on Earth, and part of a larger, divine plan," writes Abu-Nimer. "Thus, protecting human life and respecting human dignity is sacred in Islam."[33]

In addition, dignity and honor for all human beings is inherent to Islam. "We have honored the sons of Adam; provided them with transport on land and sea; given them for sustenance things good and pure; and conferred on them special favors, above a greater part of our creation," says the Qur'an (17:170). And at another place, it says, "We have indeed created man in the best of molds" (95:4).

It's a logical extension to perform every act in Islam so as to protect the dignity and honor of each and every human being, not just all Muslims. "In Islam, every person has human sacredness," writes Egyptian exegete Mohammad Abdullah Daraz. "Due to this human dignity, Islam protects its enemies."[34]

Professor Abu-Nimer asserts that tolerance of non-Muslims is an integral part of Islam, and the religion asks its followers not to differentiate between people of different faiths, except for their good deeds and piety. It also discourages violence between Islam and other religions:[35]

> Those who believe [in the Qur'an], those who follow the Jewish scriptures
> and Sabians and the Christians—any people who believe in God, the Day

of Judgment, and do good deeds, on them shall be no fear nor shall they grieve. (Qur'an 5:68–69)

The Medina charter, drawn up by Muhammad, showed the tolerance of Islam since the covenant respected the customs and traditions of all the tribes involved—both Muslim and Jewish.[36] Abdulaziz Sachedina, a prominent Muslim nonviolence advocate, has even reinterpreted the notion of salvation in Islam to reject the notion that it applies only to Muslims. He says that all people who believe in one God and are in good relations with Muslims. Sachedina says that the Qur'an stresses the oneness of mankind, not just of Muslims.[37]

So, Allah's mercy can be said to extend to everyone. One story has the Prophet Abraham not eating since there was no guest at his table. He finally found an old man who told him that he was an atheist. Angry, Abraham canceled his invitation. He is said to have heard a voice from God that said, "O Abraham, we tolerated him for seventy years despite his disbelief, and you could not tolerate him for seven minutes." Abraham repented and took the old man home.[38]

Another Islamic concept that can be used quite fruitfully is *fitrah*: the notion that all human beings are innately capable of righteousness. This can be quite well used on a global scale for affirming the worth of every person and for avoiding conflict on that basis since this is "based on a positive view of human nature that makes a nonadversarial, collaborative conception of human freedom viable," says scholar Meena Sharify-Funk.[39]

In addition, a lot of emphasis in the Qur'an is placed on good deeds:

If you do good, it will be for your own self; if you do evil it will react on you. (17:7)

He that doeth good shall have ten times as much to his credit: He that doeth evil shall only be recompensed according to his evil. (6:160)

Whoever works righteousness, man or woman, and has faith, verily, to him will we give a new life, and life that is good and pure, and we will bestow on such their reward according to the best of their actions. (16:97)

Forgiveness is a prized virtue in Islam, especially when Muslims are angry. Muhammad, when he reentered Mecca, set an example by declaring the whole of the city a sanctuary: "There is no censure from me today on you (for what happened is done with), may God, who is the greatest amongst forgivers, forgive you." During the Mecca period, he always prayed while being persecuted and, in an uncanny biblical echo, said, "Forgive them, Lord, for they know not what they do." "God fills with peace and faith the heart of one who swallows his anger, even though he is in a position to give vent to it," he also said.[40]

And the Qur'an also urged him to stay on this path. "Keep to forgiveness [O Muhammad] and enjoin kindness, and turn away from the ignorant" (7:199). "The most gracious act of forgiving an enemy is his who has the power to take revenge," states an interpretation of the Qur'an.

A related prized quality in Islam is mercy: God is "the most merciful of the merciful ones," states the Qur'an (7:151). "He is oft-forgiving, most merciful" (39:53). When Muhammad was asked by his followers to ask God to wreak havoc on Meccans for persecuting Muslims, he replied, "I have not be sent to curse anyone but to be a source of *rahmah* [compassion and mercy] to all." Hence, retribution in Islam should be subordinate to forgiveness, which, in turn, leads to a restorative outcome. This is in clear contrast with pre-Islamic Arab society, which placed a central emphasis on revenge.[41]

An intriguing, extremely overlooked facet of Islam that can be utilized in the service of peace is its feminine aspect. Scholars have pointed out many feminine qualities of God, such as compassion, beauty, and love. "Efforts to decipher and reinterpret these qualities is not an exclusively theological and philosophical exercise, for reinterpretation of Islamic texts can become a basis for peacefully empowering Muslim women while contributing to nonviolent reform in the Islamic world," writes feminist scholar Sharify-Funk.[42]

What's happened instead is that the male qualities of God—of his dual nature—have been emphasized over his feminine ones, with the result that Muslim societies have a heavily patriarchal culture. Scholars have noted a difference between the orthodox interpretation of Islam—heavily biased toward the patriarchal—and the Sufi notion—leaning toward the feminine.[43]

For regular Muslim jurists, "His attributes are those of a strict and authoritarian father," states comparative religion scholar Sachiko Murata. "In contrast, those authorities who are more concerned with Islam's spiritual dimensions constantly remind the community of the Prophetic saying, 'God's mercy is greater than His wrath.' They maintain that mercy, love, and gentleness are the overriding reality of existence and that these will win out in the end. God is not primarily a stern and forbidding father, but a warm and loving mother."[44]

But it is not too difficult to point out the feminine qualities of Islam. Every verse of the Qur'an (except one that is grammatically feminine) starts with an invocation to the "most compassionate and merciful God." God's presence itself is said to be the "breath of the merciful." God is said to have remarked, "I am the *al-Rahman* (most compassionate) and you are *al-Rahim* (merciful and compassionate). I have derived thy name from my name." Relatedly, it is the presence of compassion within human beings that causes them to completely accept—be receptive to—God, a feminine quality.[45]

Some Muslim thinkers have gone so far to stress the feminine qualities of God so as to say that it would be appropriate to contemplate God in a woman. "This is because of the spiritual, essentially divine quality of the feminine Being in her," writes scholar Henry Corbin. "It is she who creates love in us all, and then leads us beyond herself, toward that which she alone can manifest and show to us."[46]

And the Sufis (more on them later in the book) have been in the forefront of grasping the centrality of love and beauty in spirituality. "Beauty, the Sufis have recognized, inspires love, and from love comes more beauty," Corbin says. Unfortunately, such qualities of Islam have been neglected. However, some contemporary Muslim scholars are attempting to reclaim this tradition.[47]

The centrality of love in the Qur'an is found in verses such as the following, from which Sufis have taken particular inspiration: "And He has united their hearts in Love. If you had spent all that is in the Earth, You could not have put love between their hearts, but God has put love between them. Surely, He is powerful, wise" (8:63). Even the notion of soul is feminine in Islam since the stages of transformation and the perfected soul is feminine. Not surprisingly, the Sufi notion of a "soul at peace" is taken from here.[48]

Yet another value Islam cherishes that can be put into the good service of nonviolence is rationality and reason.[49] The values of wisdom and rationality are major Islamic values, cited in the Qur'an and the Hadith literature again and again:

Invite (all) to the way of thy Lord with wisdom and beautiful preaching; and argue with them in ways that are best and most gracious. (Qur'an 16:125)

"This verse clearly encourages the faith-based use of reason, dialogue, and courtesy in dealing with the others," asserts Abu-Nimer.[50]

Contrary to stereotypes of Islam, there is a major philosophical school that places rationality at the center—the Muatazilite school. A number of verses in the Qur'an encourage such thinking. "Islam is a rational religion: Islam calls on man to use reason; and whoever employs reason to study the natural world will grow stronger in faith," says scholar Jamal al-Din Al-Qasimi.[51]

Related to this is the tradition of *ijtihad*, or independent judgment and reasoning. Muslims can use this tradition to reinterpret the religion in a more progressive and peaceful way. The methods employed by traditional scholars to close off discussion and debate has stopped the religion from progressing.[52] The skills required in *ijtihad* are the same as in peace-building efforts—creativity, flexibility, and a willingness to face new challenges.[53]

ROLE OF VIOLENCE IN ISLAM

Then we come to the important question of violence in Islam. Islam unfairly gets tainted as the "religion of the sword" when there are more passages in the Old Testament dealing with war than in the Qur'an, and the Hinduism holy book the Bhagavad Gita is set in a battlefield. People also fail to distinguish between conflicts that use the name of Islam and those that actually have much to do with the religion.

"In the Islamic world, because religion remains a powerful force, its name is still used in support of whatever causes arise that lead to contention and conflict, although the Qur'an emphasizes that war must be only for defense of one's homeland and religion and not be offensive and aggressive," writes Nasr.[54]

"Some countries bomb other countries in the name of democracy and human rights, while some Muslims commit acts of violence and terror in the name of Islam," Engineer emphasizes. "We must try to differentiate between ideals and their misuse by some vested interests of frustrated people."[55]

According to a number of Muslim scholars, the only justified cause of war is an attack on Muslims, and even then there should be strict proportionality and obedience of the humanitarian laws of combat. (Interestingly, Islam has considered rape a war crime right from the start, even in retaliation for such an atrocity from the other side. In contrast, international law has recognized rape as a war crime only recently.)[56]

Peace is a natural state in Islam, and war is unnatural or situational, as stated in both the Qur'an and Hadith literature. Islam does not tolerate aggressive war, even with humanitarian restrictions. "In Islam, war is restricted to the purpose of defense," Turkish scholar Ergun Capan writes.[57]

"The principle in Islam is peace," writes Turkish Professor Ahmet Gunes. "According to the law, the permission to kill—no matter what faith a person believes in—is restricted to combatants actively participating in an active war, to combatants who are determined to inflict harm. Thus assaults on civilian targets are not in agreement with the principles of Islam, even during wartime, and this includes suicide attacks." These rules have been laid down by the Qur'an and the Prophet Muhammad and were followed by the first caliphs.[58]

"Muslims are commanded to exercise self-restraint as much as possible," states Abdullah Yusuf Ali, author of a respected translation of the Qur'an. "Force is a dangerous weapon. It may have to be used for self-defense or self-preservation, but we must always remember that self-restraint is pleasing in the eyes of God. Even when we are fighting, it should be for a principle, not out of passion."[59]

An entire group of progressive scholars have attempted to make Islam completely congruous with nonviolence. They argue that since times have changed so drastically from the time of Muhammad, even the limited use of force is not acceptable now for settling differences. Furthermore, the presence of small Muslim minority communities around the world makes even this impractical, and the presence of weapons of mass destruction far beyond the conception of the seventh century renders any war abhorrent today.

"As a minor element in the life of the prophet and the scripture, violence should be of no greater importance to Muslims today than it was then," Abu-Nimer writes, summarizing their position. "The Hadiths and Islamic tradition are rich sources of peace-building values and if applied in Muslims' daily lives will lead only to nonviolence and peace."[60]

In this age of a democracy, the notion of war is said to be outdated. "In today's conditions, when democracy prevails, even if Muslims are persecuted anywhere, democratic remedies will have top priority," asserts Engineer. "Terrorism can never be elevated to the category of jihad, in any sense of the Qur'anic term."

"Peace is far more fundamental to Islam than war," he adds. "War, at best, could be an instrument of establishing peace in some exceptional circumstances or for defending against aggression."[61]

So, it is asserted that even though violence in keeping with the teachings of the Qur'an and the Hadith are permissible in theory, in the modern world, Muslims cannot use violence. Muslims can be true to Islam only by hewing to

nonviolence and utilizing qualities in the religion such as social justice, perseverance, self-sacrifice, and the beliefs in the unity of Muslims and of mankind.[62]

And Islamic traditions emphasize that those who work for social justice are as
good as warriors. Abu Hurayrah, a companion of Muhammad and a major narra-
tor of the Hadith, states, "The prophet said, 'The one who looks after and works
for a widow and for a poor person, is like a warrior fighting for Allah's cause or
like a person who fasts during the day and prays all the night.'"[63]

Some scholars have interpreted the notion of nonviolence in Islam as being
subordinate to that of justice. Justice in Islam does get precedence before pacifism, and the duty of Muslims is to work for it. So, several Qur'anic verses prohibit
the taking of life—except in just cause: "Nor take life—which Allah has made
sacred—except for just cause" (17:33). "Take not life, which Allah hath made
sacred, except by way of justice and law" (6:151). But proponents of nonviolence
within Islam say that even if the ultimate goal is justice, not peace, the best way
to attain that goal is nonviolence.[64]

Satha-Anand also tries to solve the paradox of how Muslims are meant to fight
tumult and oppression and still hold all human life to sacred. His answer: to fight
by nonviolent means. He goes so far as to assert that since modern modes of warfare make the death of innocents pretty much impossible to avoid, it is incumbent
on Muslims to be nonviolent even when fighting for justice and righteousness.
And, he says, Islam provides a strong basis for that with its belief in discipline,
social responsibility, perseverance, and the notion of the oneness of Muslims and
the unity of mankind. "That such theses of Muslim nonviolent action are essential to peace in this world and the true meaning of Islam is evident from the
Qur'an: 'Peace!—a word (of salutation) from the Lord most merciful!'"[65]

In fact, Islam encourages arbitration and negotiation to settle disputes. There
are several Qur'anic verses promoting this. An example: "And obey Allah and
his messenger; and fall into no disputes, lest ye lose heart and your power depart,
and be patient and persevering; for Allah is with those who patiently persevere"
(8:46).

"In accordance with the injunctions, 'If they incline to peace, incline thou to
it as well,' [Qur'an 8:61] and 'If they desist, then all hostility should cease' [Qur'an
2:193], the believers are obliged to make peace with an enemy who makes it clear
that he wants to come to an equitable understanding; similarly, they must show
every consideration to individual persons from among the enemies who do not
actively participate in the hostilities," writes commentator Muhammad Asad.[66]

The Prophet Muhammad himself encouraged mediation and negotiation, and
we'll deal with these instances later in the chapter. "In short, Islamic values shun
aggression, violent confrontation and bigotry, and favor the methods of peace-
building and nonviolence for resolving conflicts," says Abu-Nimer.[67]

The Qur'an was recognizing the then-prevalent culture in the area when it
sanctioned the use of force under certain limited circumstances. It was also bowing to the complexity of human nature. But this has been misinterpreted over
time to justify offensive war.

"All the fighting injunctions in the Qur'an are, in the first place, only in self-defense," Moulavi Cheragh Ali, a prominent 19th-century Indian scholar, stated. "In the second place, it is to be particularly noted that they were transitory in their nature."[68]

Many Muslim preachers and scholars stress that, in Islam, peace is the norm and that violence is only a last option. Fetullah Gulen, a very prominent Turkish Muslim preacher, says that the whole notion of killing for Islam is totally contrary to the true tenets of the faith. "God's approval cannot be won by killing people," he says. So, he asserts that individuals and random groups can never declare war; only states can under exigent circumstances. He goes on to condemn Osama bin Laden in the strongest possible terms, stating that bin Laden is "one of the people whom I hate most in the world. . . . Even if we were to try our best to fix the terrible damage that has been done, it would take years to repair."[69]

Indian activist Engineer even contends that to term Al Qaeda's activities as "Islamic" is misleading since not one of the founders or main members is a theologian and that the organization is the creation of disgruntled Muslims from some Arab countries with grievances against American policies who are trying to express their anger against America through violence. Since there is no churchlike structure in Islam, no act of such an organization can be said to have religious sanction.[70]

"The jihadi groups among Muslims today are also doing great injustice to Islam," he states. "Their urge for violence has nothing to do with Islamic teachings. It is either their impatience or their personal interests, which make them take up guns even where problems could be resolved peacefully and democratically. . . . Islam is, and remains, a religion of peace. It wants its followers to devote themselves to peace and worship of Allah."[71]

THE HOLY TEXTS

We now look at the prospects for peace in the Qur'an.

> And those who believe and do good are made to enter gardens (jannah), wherein flow rivers, abiding by their Lord's permission. Their greeting therein is peace! (14:23)
> Enter it (paradise) in peace and security. (15:46)
> God guideth him who seeketh His good pleasures unto paths of peace. (5:16)
> In paradise there is not idle chatter but only the invocation of peace. (19:62)
> Peace—such is the greeting from the Lord All-Compassionate. (36:58)

Violence in the Qur'an is an aberration. The verses permitting it by and large have a qualifier in the spirit of "if they commit violence against you." Furthermore, violence is prohibited for revenge. Engineer cites the story of Ali, Muhammad's son-in-law, who refrained himself from doing further damage to an opponent after the opponent had spat on him since it would have been in the spirit of vengeance.[72] A person who suppresses anger (kazim al-ghayz) is a person of great merit, says the Qur'an. "Those who restrain anger and pardon men. And Allah loves the doers of good" (3:133).

"O you who believe, enter into complete peace and follow not the footsteps of the devil" (Qur'an 2:208). Engineer says that here although entering into peace means surrendering to Allah, it also denotes entering into peace wholeheartedly. "Acceptance of violence, as the other part of the verse says, is like following in the footsteps of the devil," he writes.[73]

And Muslims always invoke peace for all their prophets and write "peace be upon him" after all their names, most prominently Muhammad. "They hear therein [paradise] no vain or sinful talk but only the saying Peace! Peace" (Qur'an 56:25–26).

The word "mercy" (rahm) and its derivatives have been used more than 300 times in the Qur'an. Rahmah is said to be used in the sense of softening your heart toward someone and getting induced toward doing good toward that person. (Interestingly, the word has a feminine connotation since the word for "womb" in Arabic is also rahm.)[74]

Relatedly, only Allah qualifies for the title of Rahman—someone whose mercy encompasses all. But since Allah is the role model for all his servants, all human beings should aspire toward the same notion and attempt to love all human beings equally.

"The term rahmah, which means both 'mercy' and 'compassion,' is related to the two divine names al-Rahman, the Infinitely Good, and al-Rahim, the All-Merciful, with which every chapter of the Qur'an except one commences," Professor Nasr writes. "They are also the names with which daily human acts are consecrated. Because these names are interwoven into every aspect of the life of Muslims, life is thereby wrapped in divine goodness, mercy and compassion, which are inextricably associated with the Arabic word al-rahmah."[75]

There are many verses in the Qur'an that command believers to be nice with others, scholars have observed. Among the recommended qualities are love, kindness, affection, forgiveness, and mercy.[76] "When evil is done to you, it is better not to reply with evil, 'but to do what best repels the evil,'" a commentator on the Qur'an has observed.[77]

So, there are several passages in the Qur'an enjoining aggression. One such verse says, "You will continue to uncover treachery from all but a few of them, but be forgiving and pardon, for God loves the kindly" (5:13).

Another says, "Only argue nicely with the People of the Book, except with the oppressors among them. Say: We believe in what has been revealed to us and revealed to you. Our God and your God is one, and it is Him to whom we surrender" (29:46).

Yet another verse with a similar sentiment is "Say: I believe in what God has revealed from a book and have been commanded to be just among you. Allah is our Lord and your Lord. We have our works and you have yours. There is no argument between us and you. God will bring us together, for the journey is to Him" (42:15).

"The attitude of these verses toward opponents to Muhammad's program, whether idolaters or Jews and whether at the earliest period of his mission in Mecca or after the transition to Medina, remains constant," writes Professor Reuven Firestone. "Muhammad is commanded to argue with his opponents kindly but effectively and to have patience. Hints are provided suggesting that his opponents might receive punishment at the hand of God, but it was not the role of Muhammad or the Muslim community to inflict punishment or to escalate the conflict."[78]

The Qur'an preaches at three levels—realistic, reformative and moral—and Muslims do the religion a disservice by ignoring the two latter levels. "It was Qur'an that gave mankind values such as equality, justice, benevolence, compassion, wisdom, tolerance toward other faiths, human dignity, love and truth," argues Engineer. "These values were meant to elevate human behavior to a much higher moral plane."[79]

Engineer says the Qur'an repeatedly emphasizes that Allah is forgiving, Allah is compassionate, and Allah is benevolent and asserts that even though there is a bit of tension in the Qur'an between the moral and the real, the moral gets precedence:[80]

> Whenever the [People of the Book] kindle the fire of war, God extinguishes it. They strive to create disorder on Earth and God loves not those who create disorder. (5:64)
> God commands you to treat [everyone] justly, generously, and with kindness. (16:90)
> Cast not yourselves to perdition with your own hands, and do good [to others]; surely God loves the doers of good. (2:195)

Such verses reveal that the Qur'an can be a guiding light for nonviolence.

There is a wonderful Qur'anic passage placing primacy on the sanctity of life: "If anyone kills another without a just cause . . . it is as if he has killed the whole of mankind. And whosoever saves a life, it is as if he has saved the whole of mankind" (5:32).

A Hadith quotation clearly states, "I am the enemy of any who injures non-Muslims. And whomever I am the enemy to, I will reckon with him on Judgment Day," while another Hadith quote says, "Whenever violence enters into something, it disgraces it, and whenever 'gentle-civility' enters into something it graces it. Truly, God bestows on account of gentle conduct what he does not bestow on account of violent conduct."[81]

And then there is the famous verse in the Qur'an urging tolerance toward other faiths: "There is no compulsion in the name of religion. Right and wrong have become distinct. Those who wish so may believe and those who may wish otherwise may disbelieve. Do you want to compel people to become believers?" (2:256).

"The Qur'an is adamantly opposed to the use of force in religious matters," writes renowned comparative scholar Karen Armstrong. "Its vision is inclusive, it recognizes the validity of all rightly guided religion, and praises all the great prophets of the past."[82]

A tale in the Qur'an that illustrates the superiority of nonviolence is the story of Abel and Cain, well known in the West: "Recite to them the truth of the story of the two sons of Adam. Behold! They each presented a sacrifice: It was accepted from one, but not from the other. Said the latter: 'Be sure I will slay thee.' 'Surely,' said the former. 'Allah doth accept the sacrifice of those who are righteous. If thou dost stretch thy hand against me to slay me, it is not for me to stretch my hand against thee to slay thee: For I do fear Allah, the Cherisher of the World'" (5:27–28).

Scholar Jawdat Said says of this remarkable parable, "I don't see anyone in the world who has clearly explained when it is incumbent upon a Muslim to behave like [Abel] the son of Adam!" Said also narrates a number of instances when Muhammad cited Abel's example. For instance, he told his companion Sa'd Ibn Abi Waqqas, "Be as the son of Adam!" when talking to him about infighting within Muslims. He also told another companion, Abu Musa al-As'hari, "Break your bows, sever your strings, beat stones on your swords; and when infringed upon by one of the perpetrators, be as the best of Adam's two sons."[83]

One of the best-known Hadith quotations says, "Verily, My Mercy and Compassion precede my Wrath." This shows as dubious the notion often held in the West that the Muslim God does not contain mercy, compassion, or love. This idea is also made questionable by the fact that "God's mercy, compassion, forgiveness, and love are mentioned more times in the Qur'an than are His justice and retribution."[84]

The Sufis grasp best such aspects of the Qur'an since for them the cosmic existence is made up of the "breath of the compassionate." The legendary medieval poet Rumi has a poem with the line "Mustafa [Muhammad] came to bring about intimacy and compassion." Muhammad is often called *rahmah* to all the worlds. Other names for God are *al-Karim* (the all-merciful), *al-Ghafur* (the all-forgiver), and *al-Latif* (the all-kind). "It is impossible for a Muslim to pray to God or to even think of God without awareness of this essential dimension of compassion and mercy," writes Nasr. He says that during his visit to Muslim shrines, the invocation he has heard most often besides Allah is *Rahmah* or *Rahim*.[85] The Qur'an itself has lines like "And who despaireth of the mercy of his Lord save those who go astray" (15:56) and "Do not despair of God's mercy" (39:53).

Similarly, there are numerous verses in the Qur'an recommending forbearance (*sabr*), a quality used through the ages by nonviolent activists of all stripes and religions. For instance, "If any show patience and forgive, it would be an exercise of courageous will and resolution in the conduct of affairs" (42:43). A Qur'anic phrase that is often hung at Muslim homes says, "God is with those who are patient." Another popular Qur'anic phrase is "beautiful patience." Muhammad exemplified this. Once, while he was saying his prayers, his opponents pelted him with dung. He stopped his followers from chasing down the perpetrators, saying,

"God, I leave them to you." Since patience and forbearance can be utilized very effectively for nonviolence and have been by pacifist stalwarts such as Ghaffar Khan, such Qur'anic injunctions are invaluable guideposts.[86]

In the face of insults and calumny, the Qur'an preaches, "Profess openly what you have been commanded, and turn away from the idolaters, for we are sufficient for you against the scoffers" (15:94–95). And this is the advice that Muhammad followed at Mecca. (In fact, for two years, Muhammad did not preach at all.) Commenting on this, an early exegesis says, "When [Muhammad] gave an account of his Lord, the Meccan unbelievers confronted him with annoyance and accused him openly of lying. Therefore, the words 'and turn away from the idolaters.' God commanded him to avoid [them] and [to have] patience in the face of insult."[87]

Another Qur'anic verse is important because it gave Muhammad guidance in the face of a personal tragedy that had deeply angered him. This happened 12 or 13 years after the initial revelation to Muhammad, making the verse doubly significant since it blows a hole in many people's notion that the latter, more warlike verses of the Qur'an supersede the earlier, more peaceful ones. Muhammad's uncle Hamza Abd al-Muttalib had been killed in the Battle of Uhud in March 625, with his body being horribly mutilated. Muhammad was so incensed that he threatened to kill scores of the enemy. It was then that the Qur'an says, "Invite [all] to the way of your Lord with wisdom and beautiful preaching; and argue with them in ways that are best and most gracious: For your Lord knows best who has strayed from His path, and who receives guidance. If you punish, then punish with the like of that with which you were afflicted. But if you endure patiently, that is better for the patient. Your patience is only through God" (16:125–127).

"The actual message of 16:125, that verbal argument and not physical violence against Muhammad's detractors is called for, tends to have been largely disregarded," writes Firestone. "Despite the exegetes' claims that scholars consider it abrogated, not a single tradition is actually cited to this effect. In short, this verse, which prescribes a nonmilitant approach to the spread of Islam was not formally abrogated but rather ignored."[88]

A Hadith line gives Muhammad's response when his wife Aisha cursed back people who wished death on him: "Gently O Aisha! Be courteous, and keep yourself away from roughness."[89]

Another universal quality of the Qur'an is that it asserts the oneness of mankind:

Behold the Lord said to the angels, "I will create a vicegerent on Earth. When I have fashioned him in due proportion and breathed into him of my spirit. Fall ye down in obeisance unto him." (15:28–29)

This verse suggests that all human life is sacred since God's spirit is residing in every human body. By extension, it can be said to imply that mankind is one, amplified by the following Qur'anic verses: "Mankind was one single nation, and

God sent messengers with glad tidings and warnings" (2:213) and "Mankind was but one nation but differed later" (10:19).

"The foundational idea in the Qur'an is that people are one community," Abu-Nimer writes.[90] This is taken a step above in Islam with the notion that all human beings are equal, with privileges given only by faith and good deeds:

> O mankind! We created you from a single (pair) of a male and female, and made you into nations and tribes, that ye may know each other (not that ye may despise each other). (Qur'an 49:13)

"All people are equal, as equal as the teeth of a comb," says a Hadith line. "There is no claim of merit of an Arab over a Persian, or of a white over a black person, or of male over female. Only God-fearing people merit a preference with God."[91] And when talking about weaker sections, the Qur'an doesn't qualify it with Muslim—there are just orphans, widows, and slaves.

"A real Muslim is one who despite being firm in his/her faith, shows equal love and compassion for all human beings, whatever faith tradition they belong to," says Engineer. "The Qur'an itself declares that all human beings, all children of Adam, have been honored equally. Thus, there is no justification in showing any discrimination on the basis of faith, as far as the Qur'an is concerned."[92]

Arabia had a culture of revenge that the Qur'an helped modify. It was the first moral code that made *afw* (pardon) morally superior to *qisas* (revenge), so much so that even when the Prophet was dying, he asked for forgiveness from his followers if he had done any wrong. "Ali and Fazl on either side to hold him up, and he raises his feeble voice and cries: 'Muslims! If I have wronged any one of you, here I am to answer for it; if I owe aught to anyone, all I may happened to possess belongs to you.' One man says that he owes him three Dirhams and the coins are paid, the last debt to be discharged on Earth."[93]

The Qur'an exhorts that revenge should be proportional to the wrong inflicted and that patience (*sabr*) is always superior to revenge: "If ye take vengeance on any, take a vengeance proportional to the wrong which hath been done to you; but if ye suffer wrong patiently, verily this will be better for the patient" (16:125–128).

"Those who restrain anger and pardon men" have the qualities of a good behavior, says the Qur'an. "And Allah loves doers of good" (3:133). One of Allah's names is *Ghafur*—one who pardons. "Therefore, one can conclude from a closer study of the Qur'an and Hadith that compassion is the best human quality and no one deserves to be human unless he is compassionate," Engineer writes.[94]

The Hadith specifically has a saying that prohibits revenge. A Hadith story narrates the incident of Miqdad ibn Amr al-Kindi and the prophet. Al-Kindi asks Muhammad what he should do to a person who cuts off one of his hands and then says, "I surrender to Allah." Muhammad says that Al-Kindi should not harm him because he would be placing himself in the same position that his attacker had initially.[95]

Even in the matter of murder, the Qur'an prescribes forgiveness if the victim's family agrees: "If remission is made to one by his aggrieved brother, prosecution should be according to usage and payment to him in a good manner. This is alleviation from your Lord and a mercy" (2:278).

The Qur'an exhorts Muhammad not to exert pressure in the realm of religion: "Therefore do remind, for you are only a reminder. You are not a watcher over them" (88:22). Another verse exhorts him to be gentle in his dealings with others: "That it is due to mercy from God that you deal with them gently, and had you been rough, hard-hearted, they would certainly have dispersed from around you" (3:159):

O you who believe! Be upright for God, bearers of witness with justice, and let not hatred of a people incite you to act unjustly; act justly, which is nearer to piety, and be careful of (your duty to God); surely God is aware of what you do. (5:8)

What about the Qur'an's attitude toward the commencement of warfare? Sir Syed Ahmed Khan, an eminent 19th-century Indian scholar, emphasizes that while the Qur'an gives permission to fight, its transcendent vision is of peace and it is this vision which is more important than what is permitted.[96]

The Qur'an clearly states repeatedly that fighting is justified as a defensive measure and that, too, in a proportionate manner:

Fight in the way of God those who fight you, but do not begin hostilities; God does not like the aggressor. (2:190)

Permission to fight is given only to those who have been oppressed . . . who have been driven from their homes for saying, "God is our Lord." (22:39)

God forbids you to fight those who fight not your faith and who do not drive you out. Be just and kind to them for God loves the just. (60: 8)

"The words in which the permission is granted [to fight] show clearly that war was first made on the Muslims by their opponents; and secondly, that the Muslims had already suffered great oppression at the hands of their persecutors," says theologian Maulvi Cheragh Ali.[97] And even when the Qur'an gave permission to fight, for instance, for the rights of old people, women, and children, it was in a context of the absence of democracy and debate. "In those days, when the Holy Qur'an was being revealed, such possibilities did not exist," Engineer says. "Today, we will have to creatively reinterpret such provisions as above."[98] Many scholars reject the notion that the later Qur'anic verses supersede the earlier ones. Egyptian exegete Mahmud Shaltut says that the notion of temporal abrogation—where the later, more warlike verses abrogate the earlier ones—is a false one and that anyway the verses are not incompatible.

"There is no contradiction or incompatibility between the different verses of fighting and no room for opinions that some of them have been abrogated by others, since abrogation may only be applied when there is a contradiction," writes Shaltut. "These verses are therefore fixed and unassailable. They all amount to the same thing and establish one and the same rule, one and the same reason and one and the same end."[99]

From all this, some scholars have concluded that Muslims should establish peace with non-Muslim communities if Islam is allowed to be practiced and does not engage in aggression. Muslims are permitted only peaceful methods of preaching and spreading their religion.

And there is no disputing that the Mecca period verses of the Qur'an have a decidedly nonviolent approach, with the central emphasis being on resisting persecution by patience and forbearance. "I am not ordered to fight! I am not ordered to fight!" Muhammad says when enduring the wrath of his tormentors.[100]

Firestone goes into a detailed analysis of a pivotal verse in the Qur'an, the one that first gives authorization to take up arms: "Permission is given to those who fight because they have been wronged—God is most powerful for their aid—those who have been unjustly expelled from their homes only because they say: 'Our Lord is God'" (22:39–40). This verse was revealed a full ten years after the initial verses, showing a full decade when forbearance and patience were God's prescribed options to Muhammad and his followers.

Another similarly nonbelligerent verse is "Fight in the path of God those who fight you, but do not transgress limits, for God does not love transgressors" (2:190). This was revealed at the time of the Hudaybiya agreement that allowed Muhammad and his followers to enter Mecca the following year.[101]

And the Qur'an encourages living in harmony and negotiating for peace:

Do not kill those of the pagans with whom you made an agreement, then they have not failed you in anything and have not backed up with anyone against you. (9:4)

A number of Qur'anic verses urge negotiations and settlement with the enemy, as long as the adversary is not prone to breaking agreements:

It may be that Allah will bring about friendship between you and those of them whom you hold as enemies. (60:7)
      Allah forbids you not respecting those who fight you not for religion, nor drive you forth from your homes, that you show them kindness and deal with them justly. Surely Allah loves the doers of justice. (60:8)

And it urges Muslims not to refuse any proposal for peace: "And if they incline to peace, incline thou also to it, and trust in Allah, Surely he is the Hearer, the Knower" (8:61).

Islam also stresses the absolute right of neutral parties to be unharmed:

[But the treaties] are not dissolved with those pagans with whom ye have entered into an alliance and who have not subsequently failed you in aught nor aided anyone against you. So fulfill your engagements with them to the end of their term. For God loveth the righteous. (9:4)

But if the enemy inclines toward peace do thou (also) incline toward peace, and trust in God: For He is the One that heareth and knoweth. (8: 61)

Such instances reveal that the Qur'an sanctions war only in self-defense.

The Qur'an also teaches clemency:

If one amongst the pagans asks thee for asylum, grant it to him so that he nay hear the word of God; and then escort him to where he can be secure. (9:6)

But if they desist, then surely Allah is forgiving and merciful. . . . If they desist, there should be no hostility except against the oppressors. (2:192–193)

Among the code of ethics in the Qur'an is to treat prisoners well:

And they feed, for the love of God, the indigent, the orphan and the captive. (76:8)

We feed you for the sake of God alone; No reward do we desire from you, nor thanks. (76:9)

Islam attempts to tackle the root causes of violence by emphasizing social justice and charity. It states that the amount above what you need to minimally need to spend on your personal needs should be treated as "surplus" and given away (2:219). It admonishes against wealth circulating only among the wealthy (59:7) and warns of punishment for those who do not share their wealth (9:34).

"Thus, the Qur'an wants to establish peace, not superficially, but by trying to tackle the very socioeconomic roots of conflict," Engineer writes. "If few people or countries grab the largest part of the resources of the world and live in all comfort while denying other people even their basic needs, violence and conflict will result, whatever the pleadings of peace. . . . The Qur'an is opposed to an unjust order and domination by a few powerful, who persecute the weak."[102]

The Qur'an often draws attention to the conflict between the arrogant and powerful and the weak and the oppressed in stories such as those of Abraham and Moses liberating by nonviolent struggle their people from rulers like Nimrod and the Pharaoh.

What's very important in the Qur'an is the notion of injustice, and that sometimes supersedes the desire for peace. "If Muslims are put in a particular situation which is unjust (not only for them but for humanity as such), they may have to struggle peacefully (and if violence is thrust on them, reluctantly through that) to remove the cause of injustice," Engineer writes. He claims that since the Arabic words for "arrogant" and the "oppressed" are found throughout the Qur'an without reference to religion, it doesn't matter which of these is Muslim or non-Muslim; believers in Islam will have to side with the oppressed regardless.[103]

Among the most troublesome lines in the Qur'an is the following one: "Kill the idolaters wherever you may find them" (9:5). But even this is placed in context a few verses later, when the Qur'an explains when it would be appropriate to mete out harsh justice: "They respect neither ties nor covenant in case of a believer. . . . If they break their oaths after their agreement and revile your religion, then fight the leaders of disbelief—surely their oaths are nothing—so that they may desist. Will you not fight a people who broke their oaths and aimed at the expulsion of the Messenger, and they attacked you first?" (9:10–13).

Another similar verse is the following:

Permission is given to those who fight because they have been wronged—God is most powerful for their aid—those who have been unjustly expelled from their homes only because they say: "Our Lord is God." If God had not warded off some people by means of others, then monasteries and churches and synagogues and mosques in which the name of God is often cited would have been destroyed. God most certainly helps those who help him. God is strong, mighty. (22:39–40)

The most interesting thing about this verse is the length to which it goes to justify fighting, which clearly reflects deeply mixed feelings about the violent path.

"It certainly does not support the classic view that Islam has been an extremely aggressive and militant religious expression almost from the outset," writes Firestone. "On the contrary, it expresses a strong reticence toward fighting and may very well articulate the nonmilitant view of a faction within the community paralleling nonmilitant positions of early Christianity and Rabbinic Judaism."[104]

Professor Firestone considers the most problematic of the Qur'anic verses, the so-called Sword Verses, which command fighting and are supposed to have superseded the earlier ones. He shows with an intricate discussion that there are conflicting opinions even among early Muslim scholars.

"The fact is that the conflicting Qur'anic verses cannot prove an evolution of the concept or sanction for religiously authorized warring in Islam from a nonaggressive to a more militant stance," writes Firestone. "To suggest that they do is nothing more than an interpretation applied to the obvious problem of disparity in the Qur'anic revelations treating war."[105]

THE LIFE AND CONDUCT OF THE PROPHET

The life of the Prophet Muhammad does contain some violent incidents since, uniquely for a prophet, he was a commander of chief, too. However, the battles he fought were defensive in nature and were of a limited type.

"His military triumphs awakened no pride nor vain glory, as they would have done had they been effected for selfish purposes," American intellectual and author Washington Irving (creator of Rip Van Winkle) said. "In the time of his greatest power, he maintained the same simplicity of manners and appearance as in the days of his adversity."[106] Scholar Muhammad Ali asserts that Muhammad had "no inclination for war" and "was peace-loving by nature," while biographer Martin Forward states that "the prophet was a reluctant warrior."[107]

"The traditional biographies make it clear that even though the first *ummah* had to fight in order to survive, Muhammad did not achieve victory by the sword but by a creative and ingenious policy of nonviolence," writes esteemed comparative scholar Armstrong. "The last time Muhammad preached to the community before his death, he urged Muslims to use their religion to reach out to others in understanding, since all human beings were brothers: 'O men: behold we have created you all out of a male and a female, and have made you into nations and tribes so that you may know one another.'"[108]

In one instance, a companion, Abu Dharr al-Ghifari, asked him what to do if someone entered into his house to kill him. He replied, "If you fear to look upon the gleam of the sword raised to strike you, then cover your face with your robe. Thus will he bear the sin of killing you as well as his own sin." Muhammad also famously said that the battle (jihad) against one's enemies within oneself were much more difficult than the physical battle against external enemies.[109]

The image of Muhammad as a ruthless warrior is contradicted by the record. During his decade-plus stay at Mecca, Muhammad and his followers endured torture, trash, stones, and a murder plot, but instead of retaliating, Muhammad first asked his followers to emigrate and then famously did so himself, an act of migration (called *hejira*) that is a defining moment in Islam. In Medina, he arrived at agreements between the various tribes to run the affairs of the city. And he crafted the constitution of Medina, which allowed the religious minorities of the area to practice their religion as long as they pledged to support the Muslims in any conflict situation.[110]

Scholars point out the completely nonviolent conduct of the prophet during his more than a decade in Mecca, a period of several years when he didn't use violence even in self-defense. Instead, he preached the value of patience and steadfastness in resisting oppression.[111]

Muhammad's response to all the taunting and criticism he received during his days in Mecca was quite benign. "Although [Muhammad] is harshly criticized by his Meccan opponents for insulting their idolatrous way of life, he is described even during the most heated argument as refraining from any kind of physical violence," writes Professor Firestone. "This description is significant, given the fact that all the available accounts of Muhammad's career were written and redacted by the winning Muslims, whose very success was predicated by their willingness (or desire) to engage actively in war. Muhammad is invariably portrayed as steadfast in his refusal to respond to insult with violence."[112]

The early Muslims were beaten and even tortured in Mecca by their opponents (with at least one death) but even then refrained from retaliation. For instance, Abdallah ibn Masud, a companion of Muhammad and a famed early

Qur'an reciter, narrated some of Muhammad's revelations to the Quraysh tribe and, in spite of being badly beaten, refused to retaliate.[113]

The harassment and bullying was ceaseless until the first emigration in Muslim history, that of a large number of followers to current-day Ethiopia. A poem that Professor Firestone reproduces by one of the early Muslims, Ibn Ishaq, provides a lot of insight into the mentality of early Muslims:

> My heart refuses, I will not lie, to fight them.
> So too, refuse my fingertips [to fight].
> How can I fight a group of people who educated you
> About truth, that you not mix it with falsehood.[114]

And when they were brought before the ruler of Ethiopia, their representative said, "God commanded us to be truthful in speech, trustworthy, to honor ties of kinship, be hospitable, and refrain from forbidden things and bloodshed."

"The distinctions made in this monologue between the ways of Islam and those of the *jahiliyya* are revealing, for it considers the early ways to be full of lies and violent behavior in association with idolatry," writes Firestone. "Muslims, as opposed to Meccans of *jahiliyya*, honored kinship ties but refrained from violence."[115]

Other scholars also emphasize the peacefulness and patience of Muhammad during his long years in Mecca. Even when faced with oppression in various forms, he never engaged in physical or even verbal retaliatory violence.[116]

Instead, the prophet preached steadfastness (*sabr*) and patience, values that were taken to heart by Muslim proponents of nonviolence in modern times, such as Abdul Ghaffar Khan (as we shall see later in this book). Here he relied on his spiritual inspiration in the Qur'an to deal with the aggression and confrontation. And when Muhammad finally did take action in response to the oppression, it was with the nonviolent act of emigration (*hijrah*), an act held in reverence by Muslims.

Although there was a change in emphasis after the emigration to Medina because of the exigencies of circumstances, it can still be said that Muhammad was an essentially nonviolent person who most often applied skillful diplomacy rather than force to win over enemies.

"Despite all the battles Muhammad had to fight, he remained inherently a nonviolent leader, even in difficult circumstances," Kishtainy writes. "He often had to restrain his followers from violence."[117]

A number of times, Muhammad forswore the use of force. When three months before the Battle of Badr, a follower, Abbas ibn Ubada, told Muhammad, "If you should ask me, we shall put all the people in Mina to the sword," for continually harassing Muhammad, he replied, "This is not what we have been ordered to do; now return to your goods."[118] Similarly, Muhammad abandoned the siege of Taif because of the fear that women and children would be at the receiving end of the catapults used as weapons. His tactics paid off when the people of Taif voluntarily converted to Islam.[119]

When during the march to Mecca, one of Muhammad's followers shouted that "today is the day of fighting," Muhammad corrected him and said, "No, today is the day of mercy."[120] Time and again, Muhammad showed his distaste for war and violence.

In 629 CE, Muhammad sent Khalid ibn Walid to face off against the tribe of Bani Jazima. He gave him an important instruction—not to fight unless attacked first. When that happened, ibn Walid retaliated. During the battle, a widow of a fallen soldier on the other side died of heartbreak. When informed of this, Muhammad cried, "Was there no one who had mercy among you?" Similarly, when he was informed that ibn Walid had killed some prisoners, he wailed, "Dear God! I swear to you that I am in no way involved in what Khalid has done. I did not order him to do so!"[121]

When a woman named Safiyya binti Huyay and her cousin were passing by corpses, the cousin started to wail and strike her head on seeing the bodies of her dead relatives. Muhammad admonished Bilal, his close associate: "O Bilal! Has the feeling of mercy so abandoned your heart that you have led these women to where the corpses were?"[122]

Irish intellectual and activist Annie Besant says of the initial instance that Muhammad took up arms: "This is Muhammad's first bloodshed repelling an attack. He had ever been tender, compassionate, 'the womanish,' as his enemies called him. But now he is no longer a private individual, free to forgive all wrongs done to himself; he is ruler of a state, the general of an army, with duties to his followers who trust him."[123]

The wars that Muhammad fought should be placed in the context of his times and the situation he was up against. His enemies constantly tried to kill him, and even then he tried to avoid conflict as much as possible, as exemplified by the Treaty of Hudaibiya, one of the most famous agreements he signed.

"If one takes note of all the battles the Prophet had to fight, it will be obvious that all were forced on the Muslims," Engineer writes. "Various Islamic scholars an historians have given details of these battles to show that Muslims were not the aggressors."[124]

"It is clear that in every case [involving violence], he acted under provocation," concurs Indian scholar Rafiq Zakaria. "His general attitude was that of reconciliation. He did not approve of aggression because the Qur'an has warned the faithful that 'God does not love the aggressors.'"[125]

Besides, a notion that is as important in Islam as peace is justice, and much of the conflict between early Muslims and non-Muslims was because Muslims were trying to establish a more just, less stratified society (with mandatory almsgiving by the rich, for instance). This brought the Muslims into conflict with the traditional hierarchies.[126]

Each prophet has to be judged according to his times. Muhammad had to fight battles because he was constantly under attack and had to take up arms in order not to perish. And the battles he fought were most often no more than skirmishes. Citing historical sources, Zakaria says that between 622 and 632 CE, no more than 500 people died on both sides in the conflicts that Muhammad participated.

"In the Middle Ages, when wars devoured thousands of men on either side, these figures indicate the restraint, compassion and consideration for human life that Muhammad exercised," Zakaria writes. "He cannot, therefore, be termed a warrior. He held every life sacred, and he abhorred the shedding of blood unless for a just cause. His life was dedicated to peace."[127]

The battles that Muhammad did fight were defensive in nature. One of the biggest, for instance, was the Battle of Badr. Zakaria asserts that this battle was forced on Muhammad by the Quraysh tribe, and he was an unwilling combatant. He says that it doesn't make any sense that Muhammad would have taken on a vastly powerful army 85 miles from Medina with a ragtag band of 300 followers. That he managed to win the battle was incredible. Similarly, the Battle of Uhud, another famous battle, was initiated by the Quraysh as a way of avenging their defeat at Badr. This time, the Quraysh won but were unable to press their advantage home because they were too disorganized to mount an invasion of Medina.[128]

And, interestingly, at the Battle of Badr, he was reluctant to go into the field, waiting instead for a sign from God. Finally, one of his closest companions, Abu Bakr, got him off his knees by saying, "O Prophet of God, do not call upon your Lord so much; for God will assuredly fulfill what he has promised you."[129]

"Almost all the military campaigns in which the prophet fought were intended to repel the attacks of the great armies ranged against the Muslims, or in order to prevent the battle preparations of the enemy," Turkish Professor Ibrahim Canan writes. "The Battle of Khaybar, the Battle of Bani Mustaliq, the Tabuk Campaign and many other serious battles and also the battles of Badr, Uhud and Trench were all battles of one of the two types mentioned here."[130]

Indian progressive activist Engineer contextualizes the violence in Muhammad's life by comparing his life with the Buddha. The Buddha did not have to face violent persecution during his preachings, only having to debate those who opposed him. Hence, he did not have to reflect on the place of violence in self-defense.

Muhammad, on the other hand, faced immense violence at the hands of the tribal elites whose status was threatened by his message, as the use of violence for political purposes was quite common at that time in that region. After their persuasion efforts failed to make an impression on him, they started using brutality.[131]

"Now please to disabuse your mind of the impression . . . that Muhammad was fanatical or harsh in war or ever in his life played the aggressor," writes Muhammad Marmaduke Pickthall, author of a classic translation of the Qur'an in English. "For many years, he was patient under cruel persecutions. . . . It was only when his enemies were on the road with a great army, meaning to hound him out of that retreat and make an end of the community that he proclaimed to his disciples the command to fight."[132]

The doctrine of war developed under Muhammad was far more just than anything the region had seen: it forbade the killing of women, children, clergy, and other noncombatants. It also laid down other ground rules that were advanced for their time, such as no torture, no random destruction of property, and a pro-hibition on destroying religious or medical institutions.[133]

Contemporary literature and accounts of Muhammad's military campaigns have again and again chronicled the strict rules of combat that his army followed, such as not harming civilians. After the Battle of Hunayn against the Hawazin, Muhammad saw the body of a dead woman and said, "Run to Khalid! Tell him that the Messenger of God forbids him to kill children, women and servants." One of his followers said, "Dear Messenger of God! Are they not the children of pagans?" Muhammad answered, "Were not the best of you, too, once the children of pagans? All children are born with their true nature and are innocent."[134]

Similarly, when the Northern Arabs, in league with the Byzantines, were preparing to attack, Muhammad asked Usama ibn Zayd to prepare a force but instructed, "Do not be cruel to people. Do not cut down fruit-bearing trees. Do not slaughter livestock. Do not kill the pious who are secluded in monasteries, engaged in worship, children or women. Do not wish to encounter the enemy. You may not be aware of it, but you face a test with them." He echoed these instructions to other commanders several times. Before the Battle of Muta, he told Abu Qutada, "Do not kill women and children!" To commander Abd al-Rahman ibn al-Awf, he said, "Do not amputate the organs of the corpses. Do not kill children. This is the covenant you have made with God and it is the way of His Prophet."[135]

The most controversial of Muhammad's actions in this realm was his treat-ment of Banu Qurayza, a Jewish tribe of the area, whose menfolk were said to have been killed and the women and children held captive.

Iranian American scholar Reza Aslan has a good summary of differing research among scholars regarding this episode. He cites experts who say that the massacre never happened, or at least not the way in which it has been portrayed. Others, like Armstrong, contend that while the massacre may be revolting to modern sensibilities, it was very much in keeping with the ethos of the period.[136]

Zakaria analyzes this incident in detail. He says that the tribe had been very treacherous in its behavior. In fact, it tried to poison him at a feast after he agreed to peace with the tribe. After the tribe's defeat a second time, an arbiter from a tribe allied with it was appointed, and he recommended the punishment that was supposedly meted out to them—the beheading of all the adult males, involving hundreds.

But more important, Zakaria points out that the historicity of the entire epi-sode is dubious. A number of contemporary accounts—both Jewish and Arab—fail to mention the episode. Scholar Barakat Ahmad in his book *Muhammad and the Jews* did extensive research on the event and says that the stories of the killings are quite certainly baseless. Besides, says Zakaria, if the prophet were that bloodthirsty, he would have taken brutal revenge for the initial failed poisoning attempt.[137]

And, contends Zakaria, to take the episode as "proof" that Muhammad hated Jews is calumny of the worst sort. For instance, when Muhammad once found that his troops had taken with them copies of the Torah as spoils of war, he apologized to the local rabbi and ordered all copies of the Jewish holy book returned and apologized for the behavior of his troops.

"The event shows what a high regard the prophet had for their scriptures," Israel Welphenson, a Jewish scholar, is quoted as saying by Zakaria. "His tolerant and considerate behavior impressed the Jews, who could never forget that the Prophet did nothing which trifled with their sacred scriptures."[138] Welphenson contrasts this behavior with that of Romans and Christians previously, who had burned and trampled the scriptures: "This is the great difference we find between these conquerors and the Prophet of Islam."[139]

One example of the primacy that Islam places on peace and negotiations is the skill that Muhammad had in this realm. Muhammad was welcomed in Medina when he entered there because he had already developed a reputation as a peacemaker because of his mediation between the Aus and Khazraj tribes.

In Medina, Muhammad also had to face lots of distrust and conspiracy. Again, he acted as a peacemaker, managing to unite the tribes in Medina. That Muhammad was not interested in warfare, Engineer says, is proven by the Treaty of Hudaibiya (the most famous treaty he signed), which he agreed to with the Meccans. His own followers thought the terms to be humiliating and were against the accord. But Muhammad preferred the peaceful option wherever possible.[140]

After the Treaty of Hudaibiya, there was an interesting exchange between Muhammad and his followers, as narrated in a Muslim text by Abu Wa'il: "Umar ibn al-Hattab came and said, 'O Allah's messenger! Aren't we in the right and our opponents in the wrong?' Allah's messenger said, 'Yes.' Umar said, 'Then why should we accept hard terms in matters concerning our religion? Shall we return before Allah judges between us and them?' Allah's messenger said, 'O ibn al-Hattab! I am the messenger of Allah, and Allah will never degrade me.'"[141]

"The prophet accepted the treaty all the same, as he was never for war," says Canan. "He was on the side of peace." Besides, Muhammad's perspective was that the treaty gave Islam's opponents an opportunity to know the religion and its followers firsthand, paving the way for its acceptance among its detractors. Muhammad was proven right in his assessment.[142]

And Muhammad was happy to keep the peace with nonbelievers who honored peace agreements with him: "The pagans were of two kinds as regards their relationship to the prophet and the believers," writes Engineer. "Some of them were those with whom the prophet was at war and used to fight against, and they used to fight him; the others were those with whom the prophet made a treaty, and neither did the prophet fight them, nor did they fight him."[143]

So, Muhammad is said to have signed several peace treaties in his lifetime. As soon as he came to Medina, he signed a peace treaty with the Jewish inhabitants of the city, for instance. "The prophet tried to find diplomatic solutions—to whatever extent possible—when relations became hostile," writes Turkish scholar Gunes. Even before the initiation of hostilities with the Quraysh, Muhammad sent a peace emissary.[144]

For example, Muhammad's terms in a treaty that he signed with Christians from a place called Najran were very generous. Canan quotes from there: "No bishop will be sent outside his region of service, no priest will be sent out of his parish, no monk will be taken out of the monastery where he lives and sent elsewhere . . . they will not be allowed to oppress others, nor will they themselves be oppressed."[145]

"He who makes peace between the people is not a liar," he is said to have stated. Among his most famous successful mediation attempts was at the holiest shrine of Islam. When two clans disputed over where to put the black stone at Kaaba, Muhammad came up with the ingenious solution of having both the clans pick up jointly a cloak with the stone and lift it to a commonly desired height.[146]

"The resolution of this problem implies a repudiation of violence and competition, and an appreciation of the creative possibilities of joint problem solving," writes Abu-Nimer. "In fact, there are many accounts of interventions by the prophet in which he utilized such skills and principles in arbitrating or mediating disputes; these examples serve as powerful referents and resources for conflict resolution efforts."[147]

There are several other examples of Muhammad's arbitration. He mediated an end to the enmity of the Aws and Khazraj tribes. He also agreed to third-party mediation in the dispute between his people and the Banu Qurayza tribe.

When a tribe sued for peace during Muhammad's army's march from Medina to Mecca, Muhammad treated them quite generously. Every person (except three or four men accused of treason) was pardoned, and no home was looted. A promise of equal treatment was made. Even the Meccans who had emigrated to Medina were not allowed to take back their houses from those who occupied them. The chief, Abu Sufiyan, and his wife, Hind, were also spared.[148]

The most significant episode in this regard (and one of the pivotal moments in Islam) was Muhammad's reentry into Mecca. It was unprecedented for its time in that the city was not wrecked, the people were not butchered or driven out, and no revenge or blood feuds were engaged in. And with a handful of exceptions, there was a general amnesty for the people of Mecca.[149]

Similarly, after the defeat of the Banu Qaynuqa tribe, Muhammad exiled them, allowing them to take their property, instead of killing them and selling their women and children into slavery, as was the Arab norm then. Again, when Muhammad defeated the clan of Banu Nadir, he let them leave Medina unharmed, much to the consternation of many of his soldiers.[150] In doing all this, Muhammad was following the Qur'anic injunction "When, with God's help, victory comes, and you see men in hordes accepting His way, then glorify the Lord and ask for His forgiveness and proclaim His grace and mercy" (110:1–3).

"Never a wrong done to him that he did not forgive; never an injury that he was not ready to pardon," stated Besant. "Judge a religion by its noblest, not by its worst, then we shall learn to love one another as brothers, and not hate one another as bigots and as fanatics."[151]

And Muhammad was squarely against torture. Suhayl ibn Amr, a prime tormentor of Muhammad, was taken prisoner and then tried to escape. Umar, a follower, suggested to the prophet that ibn Amr's two front teeth be taken out.

"No, I will not have him tortured," replied Muhammad. "If I did, God would punish me. Moreover, we should always have the hope that one day he will act in a way that will not seem unsympathetic to you." (Ibn Amr later became an ardent proponent of Islam.)

When Nabbash ibn Qays, a member of the Bani Qurayza tribe who had been sentenced to death for treachery, was brought before Muhammad, he remonstrated his guard for breaking Qays's nose. In another incident, when people who pretended to seek asylum betrayed Muhammad's trust by torturing a shepherd to death, Muhammad forbade the use of torture in retaliation, no matter what the reason.[152]

Muhammad did lose his cool when he saw his uncle Hamza's body disemboweled and defiled by the other side and vowed to do the same to 30 bodies in revenge. In response, as mentioned previously, the following Quran'ic verse was revealed to him: "And if you have to respond to any wrong, respond to the extent done to you; but if you endure patiently this is indeed better for he who endures" (16:126). Muhammad was so chastened that he took back his oath and did the appropriate rites for atonement. To one of his followers who was about to defile bodies in revenge, he said, "Wish for the reward you will get from God! The dead of the Qurayshi pagans are entrusted to our care. . . . Would you rather your name was remembered with what you did and resented with what they have done?"[153]

Muhammad actually gave humanitarian aid when his enemies needed it. He sent gold to Mecca after his emigration to Medina so that his antagonists there could buy food. This helped lessen the hatred of him. Even though some of his enemies did not want to accept the aid, his uncle expressed his gratitude: "May God reward the son of my brother with favors, for he has taken into consideration the dues of his kinship." In a subsequent incident, Sumama, a Muslim, cut off the food supply to Mecca after being almost killed. When Muhammad found out about this, he sent a written order asking Sumama to lift the blockade.[154]

Muhammad set an example for his followers on other fronts. He freed his slave Zaid and adopted him as his son. So strong was the bond between them that when Zaid's biological father came to take him away, Zaid refused to leave and opted to stay with the prophet. Muhammad later got him married to a relative, Zainab. Another slave, Bilal (said to be the first black Muslim), was given the honor of issuing the call the prayer.[155]

Muhammad is reputed to have treated prisoners of war well—providing them with sufficient food and water—before most often setting them free. He is recorded to have spoken well even of his enemies: "O God, they are your servants as well; just like us, your servants."[156] After the Battle of Badr, only two people were executed, and prisoners were treated with kindness, being given dates by the prophet's followers who had bread only for themselves.[157]

Muhammad is also said to have been very compassionate toward animals. He embraced the entirety of creation as being the family of Allah (ayal Allah) and urged compassion toward all living creatures. When a woman of dubious reputation came to him and told him that she had saved a thirsty cat from dying by fetching it water from a pit with her socks, Muhammad reportedly said, "Allah will pardon all your sins and you will go to paradise." Additionally, there is a Hadith incident in which Muhammad narrates the story of Allah reprimanding a previous prophet who burnt an anthill because an ant bit him. These ants, Allah said, also sang my praises. In another narrated incident, Muhammad was grooming his horse and, when asked why, said that Allah had chastised him for neglecting it.[158]

"A large number of the prophet's traditions dealing with kindness and compassion to animals are included in the authentic Hadith literature," states scholar Iqbal Ansari. Cruelty to and torturing of animals, even the obnoxious ones, in any form, is forbidden. "This criterion is so absolute that even when for valid reasons man is permitted to kill any animal for food or to save himself from its venom or other harm, he is enjoined to do so without causing avoidable pain or torture."[159]

Muhammad had a robust sense of humor and loved exchanging jokes. "Othman will enter paradise laughing because he makes me laugh," he is said to have remarked about the third caliph.[160] And he had the reputation until the very end of being a patient and a humble man. "When thousands were bowing to him as Prophet—and gentle all around. "Ten years,' said Anas his servant, 'was I about the Prophet, and he never said so much as *uff* to me.'"[161]

Now that we have explored the seeds of peace in Islam's holy book and its prophet, we can examine how the religion has held up in its conduct in history.

CHAPTER 3

At the Point of a Sword? How Islam Actually Spread

IMAGES OF ISLAM'S HISTORY

The history of Islam has been caricatured as one of bloodthirsty warfare and conversion by the sword. This has been a trope in the West since medieval times. However, reality was much more complicated, and violence has played a much lesser role in the formation and spread of Islam than is commonly imagined.

The Middle East has suffered from a surfeit of stereotypes. Included in this is ever-present bloodshed, fed to people in the West through biblical stories and movies since childhood. But, in actuality, the Middle East has not been any more violent than other regions, and, in fact, it has been less so. Historian Quincy Wright, who compiled a list of wars fought from 1484 to 1945, found that 187 were in Europe and a sum total of 91 were everywhere else.[1]

One reason Islam has been the subject of attack is because for centuries it outshone Christianity in its achievements in the scientific, cultural, and artistic fields. This led to a backlash in the Christian world that continues today. Ordinary Americans' images of Muslim history are suffused with "images of medieval violence: of fierce warriors on horseback wielding broad scimitars, or of caliphs delivering swift and arbitrary justice via the executioner," writes historian Richard Eaton. Or there is "some hazy notion of Islam as a religious heresy or of Muhammad as a false prophet."[2] The problem here is that unlike Hinduism and Buddhism, which were far away and much less of a threat, Islam was next door and destined to be the main historical rival to Christianity, hence the lurid imagery since the medieval era.

So, a typical Western account was that of Scottish historian William Muir in 1898: "It was the scent of war that now turned the sullen temper of Arab tribes into eager loyalty. . . . Warrior after warrior, column after column. . . . Fresh tribes arose and went. Onward and still onward, like swarms from the hive, or flights of locusts darkening the land, tribe after tribe issued forth and hastening northward, spread in great masses to the East and to the West."[3] The imagery may look overripe now, but the basic notions have not gone away in the minds of westerners: that Islam is a religion of violence.

Never mind that Islam is a faith with a long history and in a huge number of countries, with a multitude of events enclosed inside it. "Like all religions, [Islam] contains within it both the deep and the simple, the sublime and the cruel, the exalted and the ignoble," writes Professor Firestone. "Like Judaism and Christianity, Islam is multifaceted, offering a variety of responses to the questions and perplexities of the human condition. It cannot be fairly forced into a single wrapping."[4]

And there are nonviolent aspects of Islam that its followers have adhered to through history. So, there is the notion of migration or *hejira*—a singularly nonviolent foundational act of the religion—that has hallowed status in the Muslim world as a way of escaping persecution because of the prophet and his followers' flight from Mecca to Medina. The Muslim calendar begins with this act. And, in fact, in early Muslim history, a number of Muslim sects, such as the Khawarij, engaged in migration to disperse and survive.[5] Alas, it is only the few episodes of conflict that we remember today, forgetting all the rest.

"For centuries after the initial [Arab] conquests, coexistence was the norm," writes historian Zachary Karabell, contending that the violent episodes are centrally remembered, while those of peaceful harmony—such as, say, Andalusia—are on the margins of history.[6]

Religion, while an integral part of people's lives, did not historically create barriers to interaction, including that most intimate of interchanges—marriage. In Muslim Spain, legendary for its civilizational achievements, the fabled dynamism was the product of all the multiple cultures present and most often in a peaceful way.[7]

Ironically, in both the West and the Muslim world, this tradition of coexistence (and often decadence) has been forgotten. In actuality, the caliphs were a lot like the Chinese and Byzantine emperors, "cosmopolitan, erudite and attached to the pleasures of wealth," Karabell states. Singers and poets—often irreverent and immersed in alcohol—filled the courts. And then there were the Sufis, who very often used wine-filled and lovelorn imagery to describe God and their passionate attachment to him. Of course, it wasn't all sunny, with smaller spans of intolerance punctuating longer periods of coexistence and harmony. These periods of intolerance were often launched by exogenous factors, such as desperate attempts by rulers to preserve the empire by pandering to the traditionalists.[8] One can either highlight the story of mostly coexistence and harmony or the sporadic episodes of violence and discord. Such is the story of Islam.

ARAB HISTORY

Much of Arab military history was one of blunders, not surprising when you consider the fact that many of their commanders were merchants, poets, or tribal chieftains. The Arabs never had a social group dedicated to fighting, unlike the

Spartans in Greece, the Prussians in Germany, or the Rajputs in India. Instead, the Arabs looked on warfare with a mix of contempt and fear. It isn't astonishing that there is no Carthage, Gallipoli, Troy, or Stalingrad in Arab history. And even the battles fought around the time and shortly after the Prophet Muhammad were mere skirmishes with little loss of life. In Islam, the paramount concern is saving your life. So, suicide is forbidden, and Islam even condones the practice of avoidance, where you are allowed to conceal being a Muslim to avoid death. In Arab culture, war is something ugly and to be detested.[9]

Let us take the Arab conquest of much of the then known world, cited as prime proof of the violent history of Muslims. But this is far from the truth. A large reason that these military conquests were successful was not so much the military prowess of the Arabs but the exhaustion of their opponents. Byzantine and Persia (the two most famous instances), led by tired rulers and riven by internal conflicts, made no serious attempts to push back the conquerors. The Arabs entered Jerusalem and Egypt without resistance, too, and took advantage of the infighting among Spaniards to annex much of Spain. So, the first time that they faced serious resistance, the Arabs received a shock. This was when the Europeans gathered together their forces under Charles Martel at Poitiers in France, dealing the Arabs such a decisive blow that they had to draw back to central Spain.[10]

Historians confirm that the fall of the Persian and the Byzantine empires was due not so much to the Arab military prowess as to the internal state of exhaustion of these two entities. "In history, as in life, timing is everything," Karabell states. Both had just finished a debilitating war against each other. The Byzantines were simultaneously staving off Slavic tribes. Even with the Byzantines' triumphal conquest of Jerusalem, both empires were enervated. So, when the Arabs attacked soon after, it was a particularly opportune time.[11]

And a number of the Arab victories were accomplished without bloodshed since the populations were disillusioned with their current rulers. So, for instance, the bishops in Damascus had a bitter doctrinal dispute with the higher clerical authorities in Constantinople, and when the Arabs surrounded the city, the disenchanted population barely put up a fight. The bishops entered into secret negotiations with the Arab commander Khalid ibn al-Walid, who promised not to harm the residents or their properties as long as they paid a tax. These assurances being taken, the bishops opened the gates, and the Byzantine garrison in the city was quickly defeated.[12]

Similarly, the residents of Hims, north of Damascus, were so upset with their emperor Heraclius that they actually offered to join with the Arabs in repelling their emperor's army. Even the Jews participated: "We swear by the Torah that no governor of Heraclius shall enter the city of Hims unless we are first vanquished and exhausted."[13]

Likewise, the Christians of Egypt were severely disillusioned with Constantinople. According to lore, the Arab commander of the area, Amr ibn al-As, had once saved the life of a Christian deacon and had started a large business with the money he received in gratitude. He was the one who asked the caliph to invade

Egypt since there was a bitter doctrinal dispute that the Coptic Christians had over the nature of Christ that seems abstruse now but was the source of much fighting then. Later Arab historians claim that the Coptic Christians even aided the conquerors, solving the conundrum as to how a small army of 5,000 soldiers was able to win so easily. The Coptic Christians were not too unhappy since they knew that they ironically had a better chance of practicing their faith undisturbed under the Muslims than their fellow Christians of Byzantine.[14]

Very interestingly, the Jews of the region were so dissatisfied under the Byzantine Empire that they were quite pleased with the Muslim invaders. "Most of the Jewish population was discontented with their persecuted status within the Byzantine Empire and welcomed the Muslim armies, whose rule would turn out to facilitate a new flowering of Jewish culture," writes scholar Graham Fuller.[15] And in practice such good faith was rewarded.

"Why were the Muslim conquerors relatively benign?" asks Karabell. "The Qur'an instructed the Muslims to respect the People of the Book, and that is precisely what they did. The early history of Islam, therefore, unfolded against the backdrop of toleration for the religions of the conquered."[16]

In addition, with the conquering Arab Muslims constituting just a tiny percentage of the overall population, it would have been impossible to govern without the consent of the governed. So, the collection of taxes was left to the local administrators instead of imposing officials from above, and large-scale pillaging of the conquered cities was a rarity. Instead, the strategy was to create garrison cities and maintain a light touch in the large urban centers such as Damascus and Jerusalem. "In that sense, religious toleration was a pragmatic component of an overall strategy of staying separate from the conquered peoples," states Karabell.[17]

Even though Muslim armies swept over the region, the effect was felt largely by the elite, with the people at the ground level being very vaguely aware of the fact, even if they had to pay a different type of tax. A Christian monk in the Mosul region of Iraq seemed in the late seventh century very dimly aware of Islam while at the same time praising the Muslim treatment of Christian monks.[18]

So, if you were away from the large urban centers, the differences between the new and the old rulers were almost imperceptible. Initially, taxes had to paid, just like under the previous regime. Then a few Muslim soldiers might have appeared. Finally, over time, an administrative apparatus tied to Islam sprang up, having more and more impact on daily lives as time went on.

Professor Eaton says that recent scholarship has shown that the conventional notion of an expansion of Islam—with its warlike imagery—is quite mistaken. "The dominant trend among scholars studying the Islamization process appears to be the effort to see it not as an expansion of force, an old European stereotype; but rather to view it as an assimilation," writes Eaton. "One adopts the perspective of someone standing in a remote and dusty village, incorporating into his existing religious system elements considered useful or meaningful that drift in from beyond the ocean, from over the mountains, or simply from the neighboring village."[19]

In actuality, there was a lot of continuity between the pre-Arab, pre-Muslim regimes and the Arab conquerors, including the attitude toward minority religions. So, in Egypt they continued appointing church patriarchs, and in Iraq they resolved disputes among the Nestorian Christians, just like before. And the Arabs in Persia continued a lot of the Persian practices, such as minting coins for the first half a century with the portrait of the Persian shah on one side and appropriating a number of the titles of the Persian kings.[20] "Scholars have long since disposed of the image of Islam being spread by the sword, but that has not altered popular imagination," writes Karabell.[21]

The conversion to Islam came about most often gradually and peacefully over time because of shared features between the pre-Islamic religions and Islam. "How Islam actually expanded says a lot about the complex process of religious conversion and civilizational change," writes Fuller. "It also tells us something about the nature of religious accommodation and coexistence; here Samuel Huntington's facile term 'bloody borders of Islam' is little more than a caricature of the complex political and social interactions that took place."[22]

For instance, there was a free mixing and matching of festivals between the religions. Many Muslims persisted in their old practices. The conversion process itself often took several generations.[23] So, the Arab Abbasid Empire integrated components of Byzantine, Christian, Jewish, and Persian cultures. And in North Africa and Spain, the influences were even more diverse since Berber and Roman cultures were also assimilated.[24]

Professor Eaton catalogs some of the pre-Islamic customs that continued and helped make the process of conversion much smoother. "For example, the Muslims shared animal sacrifice with pagans and Zoroastrians and ritual slaughter with Jews; they shared circumcision with Jews and Christians; they institutionalized charity, like Jews and Christians; they covered their heads during worship like Jews; they had a month-long fast followed by a festival, like many other groups; they practiced ritual ablutions, as did Zoroastrians; and their ritual prayer resembled that of Nestorian Christians," writes Eaton.[25] So, several studies have shown that the hackneyed stereotypes of Islam being spread by coercion and violence widely miss the mark.

"We see an important process of fusion here as Islamic culture gradually absorbed ambient cultures, traditions, languages, arts, histories, and experiences, making Islam part of the region rather than merely an Arabian import imposed on the area," writes Fuller. "It is this deep integration of Islamic culture into the most ancient region of civilizations in the world that suggests in many ways a continuum, a continuity of large numbers of values, attitudes, and attributes."[26] Of course, this goes against the notions of Islam in the West. But, in actuality, even though the Arabs were propelled in some measure by religion, "they were also tribal, and tribals rarely admit converts," writes Karabell.[27]

The conquering Arabs were not really interested in proselytizing among the subject populations, taking the attitude that while the message of Islam was correct, it was not their duty to save everyone's souls. In fact, non-Arab converts were generally not treated better than the unconverted and may have sometimes been treated worse. "The early Arab conquerors were still strongly ethnically oriented and perceived Islam to be an Arab religion of which they were the privileged recipients," writes Fuller. This wasn't surprising since the origins of the religion, the holy book, and the prophet were all Arab. This made the Arabs even less eager to get their subject populations to embrace Islam.[28]

Certainly, the areas ruled by the Arab conquerors did eventually become Muslim. But this was a process that "took centuries, and happened peacefully and organically," as Karabell states. "Only by conflating centuries can it be said that Islam was spread by force, and it simply cannot be said that initial conquests imposed Islam on the conquered."[29]

Professor Ira Lapidus has chronicled a multilayered, fascinatingly complex long process of conversion to Islam in the Middle East. The animists and polytheists in the desert regions became Muslim because of their desire to be a part of a grand, culturally rich civilization. The urban elites became absorbed as part of the administrative apparatus of the new rulers. Slowly, minorities started becoming assimilated with visions of personal advancement, riches, and social mobility. Even then, the process of conversion was remarkably gradual. Under the Umayyad caliphate (seventh to eighth centuries), for example, only 10 percent of the population was Muslim.[30] Arab soldiers and merchants came into more and more contact with the broader society and had more and more of an influence, resulting in a culture that was a hybrid of Islam, Christianity, Judaism, and Zoroastrianism.[31]

The Muslim tolerance came from secure confidence. Unlike in Muhammad's time (who felt threatened by the Jewish tribes of Medina), the Muslims knew that the Christian populations were not inclined to be a threat. "The Muslims adopted a policy of tolerance that was both sublime and mundane, sublime because it was grounded in the Qur'an and mundane because it allowed them to rule an empire with minimal manpower," Karabell states.[32]

In addition, "conversion of the conquered citizenry to Islam was not at all the immediate goal of the Arab conquerors; the extension of Muslim power and authority was," writes Fuller. Besides, as Fuller points out, if their subjects became Muslim, this reduced revenue since it lessened the number of people on whom a tax (the *jizya*) could be levied in place of military service and for guarantees of protection. "We can discount the tendency—which has been popular in Christendom—to overestimate the extent of the use of force in the propagation of Islam," Fuller quotes famed historian Arnold Toynbee.[33]

And after their conquests, the Arabs did not seem duly perturbed when provinces broke off from the empire and made no serious attempt to subjugate them. Instead, they devoted their time to the finer pursuit of life, such as art, music, poetry, literature, and cuisine. What was left untouched was the science and art of warfare. Not a single breakthrough in this field—from gunpowder to the use of the horse or the formation of artillery—can be attributed to the Arabs. Instead, the Arabs taught the Europeans everything from how to upholster furniture to wear silk and apply makeup and perfume.[34]

Another aspect in which history has been misrepresented is in overstating the extent and nature of the caliph's power, making it seem that he had absolute authority over both spiritual and temporal realms.[35] The notion that the Western world has had a separation between church and state for a long time and the Islamic world has never had it is a fallacy. The Byzantine emperor was also the head of church, as were kings in several other parts of Europe. In contrast, the Ottoman emperors almost never pretended to have complete religious authority, even if they later added the title of caliph to give themselves legitimacy. The Muslim clerical authorities were pretty much always deferred to.[36] With the exception of Shiite Iran, Islam had no central governing authority, Karabell points out.[37]

And the attitude of Arab leaders toward violence was often of repulsion. Once, officials during the reign of Caliph Abu Bakr caught a person who had been singing satirical poems about him and amputated her hand. Abu Bakr was deeply shocked when he came to know about this and wrote a letter to the particular person who had done this: "Try to be considerate and sympathetic in your attitude toward others in the future. Never mutilate, because it is a great offense. God purified Islam and the Muslims from rashness and excessive wrath. You are well aware of the fact that those enemies fell into the hands of the Messenger of Allah who had been recklessly abusing him; who had turned him out of his home; and who fought against him, but he never permitted their mutilation."[38]

As an example of the negative feelings of Arabs toward combat, Kishtainy quotes Caliph Imam Ali as saying to his men, "If I order you to march on them on warm days, you say, 'This is the fire of summer. Give us time until the heat is over.' If I ask you to march on them in winter, you say, 'This is the bite of frost. Give us time until the cold is over.' All this, and you fleeing from the heat and the cold but, by God, you are more in flight from the sword."[39]

There was a cultural renaissance during Arab rule that included free inquiry, the preservation of knowledge, and the giant strides that were attained in all fields of inquiry. All this was accomplished in an atmosphere where Muslim rulers were very indulgent toward People of the Book, "igniting a cultural renaissance," as Karabell puts it.[40]

In Baghdad, the hallmark of tolerance and coexistence continued. This spanned the range from just tolerating minorities to actually engaging in dialogue and collaboration. And Islam borrowed liberally from other religions, such as Judaism, Christianity, and Zoroastrianism. Stemming from a deep-rooted pragmatism, the caliphs even studied ancient Greece and Persia to adapt workable models. And non-Muslims held high office. (For instance, an extremely prominent tax collector was Jewish, and many prime ministers in the ninth century were Nestorian Christians.)[41]

What made Baghdad under the caliphs so unique was not only that all these people lived in peace but also that the boundaries between the categories and cultures were so blurred. Muslims attended Christian observances and vice versa. A similar situation existed in Spain under the Muslims. "In the middle of the ninth century, Muslims were nowhere near a majority of the population," writes

Karabell. "Both Christians and Jews occupied prominent positions in society, and they shared the rewards of Cordoba's increasing power and wealth."[42]

The Jewish community especially benefited, enjoying more liberty and riches than their coreligionists in any other part of the world until the 19th century.[43] Their particular strength was in establishing trade networks that were truly multinational in nature, spanning the entire Mediterranean region, encompassing a variety of kingdoms that the Jewish merchants were able to uniquely connect. With all the intra- and intertensions between the Christian and Muslim kingdoms, they were able to build a bridge between all of them. They were also prominent in other spheres. Hasdai ibn Sharput served as the chief physician for two Cordoban caliphs and also as an emissary and diplomat to other countries, including with the Byzantine Empire. In fact, relations between Cordoba and the Byzantine Empire remained cordial at least partly because of the Jewish community acting as facilitators and translators.[44]

There is the fascinating story of a Turkish Khazar tribe that had converted to Judaism when the king invited representatives from Islam and Christianity, and even they admitted that they thought Judaism to be the better faith, an incredible episode that teaches a lot about the reality—as opposed to the myth—of religion at the time.[45]

And both the internal and the external policies of the caliphs were most often marked by pragmatism. Even when they fought against certain non-Muslim entities, they made alliances with other non-Muslim kingdoms. So, Caliph Harun al-Rashid took up arms against the Byzantines, couching the battle in religious terms, but reached out to Charlemagne with multiple overtures and gifts, including an elephant transported all the way from North Africa. Similarly al-Rashid's son al-Mamun alternated between attacking the Byzantines and asking them for the works of Aristotle.[46]

In sum, relations between the religions and Islam's conduct spanned the gamut, with violence at one end occupying a small part and respect and active cooperation, most often in the pursuit of knowledge, occupying a much larger portion. But there was cooperation even at a more mundane, albeit touching, level. Muslims and Christians prayed with each other, side by side, for the simple reason that they needed all the help they could get for successful harvests and a bountiful life. And it's not like battles among adherents of the same religion were any less violent. When the Berbers conquered Cordoba, they were ruthless toward the city's inhabitants and prized monuments. Even when wars took place across religious lines and were couched in religious terms, most often they were fought for very earthly reasons.[47]

And when the Muslims did fight, for example in the Crusades, they were often quite a bit less ruthless than the armies sent by the pope. Of course, the best-known Muslim warrior was Saladin, and his exemplary conduct is remembered even today. His conquest of Jerusalem on October 2, 1187, is an excellent case in point since it was so swift so as to be almost without bloodshed. The conduct of the troops toward the conquered was exemplary.[48]

This wasn't surprising since all that it shows is that Saladin took the Qur'anic notions seriously about being kind toward the People of the Book. And on Saladin's retaking of the Al-Aqsa mosque, the benediction given by the chief cleric of Aleppo invoked both Abraham and "the Word which entered into Mary and Jesus," linking Islam to both Judaism and Christianity rather than pitting it against them.[49]

Even though Saladin was on a jihad, it was a very different type of jihad since it was not a war of conquest but rather a war for restoration of the status quo in the holy lands. And much of the time, Saladin fought against Islamic extremists, such as the cult of the Assassins.[50]

THE OTTOMAN EMPIRE

A worthy successor to Saladin was Mehmed, the Ottoman emperor to whom Constantinople finally fell in 1453, marking the end of the Byzantine Empire. "No matter how psychologically devastating, the physical damage was relatively mild, both to property and to people," writes Karabell. And Mehmed quickly established a hands-off policy toward the religion of the conquered (with the exception of converting Hagia Sophia church into a mosque). He appointed Gennadius, by all accounts a very worthy man, as the patriarch of the Greek Orthodox Church and left the matters of the community in his hands.[51] "Gennadius was more than the spiritual guide of the Greek Orthodox," writes Karabell. "He was in many ways their king, with power to tax and judge and the authority to appoint local representatives throughout the empire."[52]

Emperors like Mehmed had a hands-off attitude toward the Christians. And the Christians reciprocated with enthusiasm by participating in the rebuilding of Constantinople, including the legendary Grand Bazaar of Istanbul and many of the walls and fortifications. But what remains in the West are memories of the Ottomans as being belligerent fanatics. Certainly, the Ottomans styled themselves as *ghazis* (holy warriors) and fought frequently against the Christian West. What is forgotten is that they were generally indifferent to the religions of the conquered, with the majority of the population in conquered European areas (such as Greece and Cyprus) remaining Christian until the end.[53] And while the Ottomans did battle against Christian kingdoms, they also waged war with a passion against the Muslim rulers of Iran. For them, religion was an instrument, which explained why in the interest of pragmatism they were willing to leave alone their minority populations.

The Jews fared much better under the Ottomans, in spite of their various whims, than under Christian Europe until the mid-18th century. And Christian Europe's anti-Semitism reached its culmination, of course, with the horrors of the Holocaust in the 20th century.[54] This explains why few Christians and Jews converted to Islam in Europe during Ottoman rule. The Ottoman state adopted a hands-off policy toward its minorities that permitted Jews, Greek Orthodox, Armenians, Catholics, Copts, and others to continue to practice their religion without hindrance. Even if the Ottoman emperors had a medieval mentality, fundamentalist Islam was not one of their mainstays. In fact, they exhibited a streak of pragmatism that included "marrying Christians, employing Jews, and forging alliances with Catholic states—none of which were held to be incompatible with orthodox Islam as then understood," writes Karabell. And so the Turkish court and administration was until a very late stage in its history not very Turkish, instead being made up of a "crazy quilt" of Tartars, Serbs, Greeks, Arabs, Berbers, Copts, Armenians, Jews, Nubians, Slavs, and Bulgars as well as Venetians, Genoese, Florentines, and Romans and many, many others.[55]

The relative tolerance of the Ottoman Empire was so much in contrast to Western Europe that the French philosopher Jean Bodin wrote that the emperor "permits every man to live according to his conscience . . . and suffers four diverse religions: that of the Jews, that of the Christians, that of the Greeks, and that of the Mahometans." This, to Bodin, was very much contrary to the intolerance and strife he had seen in his part of the world.[56]

The biggest black mark on the Ottoman Empire has been the Armenian Genocide, starkly in contrast with its treatment of the Armenians and other minorities in earlier times. And this era marked the worst treatment of all minorities by the Ottomans, as it moved away from the decentralized system of treating minorities that had been around for centuries and moved to a more centralized and heavy-handed system. Accompanying this was a terribly destructive force—nationalism—in this case Turkish nationalism. It was this Turkish variant of nationalism that had such horrible consequences for the Armenians, much in deviation from the security that minorities had felt in previous times under the Ottomans. So, throughout the earlier centuries, minorities felt so secure that there was little conversion, forced or otherwise, in Cyprus and Greece, and they continue to be Christian nations to this day since being Muslim wasn't a prerequisite for fully participating in the running of the Ottoman Empire.[57]

This fostered a diversity that was quite unique for its era. "The fact that Istanbul contained Janissaries, Ottoman princes, Armenian and Greek merchants and craftsmen, and Jewish doctors, to name a few, contributed to its greatness," writes Karabell.[58] And this diversity—religious and cultural—was a source of amazement to the Europeans. The wife of a British ambassador to the Ottoman Empire, Lady Mary Wortley Montagu, commented awestruck, "My grooms are Arabs, my footmen French, English and German, my nurse an Armenian, my housemaids Russian, half a dozen other servants Greeks; my steward an Italian; my Janissaries Turks, [and] I live in the perpetual hearing of this medley of sounds."[59]

But, alas, as the empire crumbled, this multiculturalism became more and more tenuous, and intolerance increased, culminating with the intense persecution of the Armenians in the dying days of Ottoman rule and a crackdown on Christians in general. "But these events should not stand as an indictment of earlier centuries," says Karabell. "Tolerance and coexistence were real, even if they dissipated at the end."[60]

"Muslims, Christians, and Jews are entwined, but their history is as varied as the story of the human race," he adds. "If conflict is what we want to see, there is conflict. But if peace is what we are looking for, then peace is there to be found."[61]

It is anyway reductive and overly simplistic to attribute the troubles in the Middle East to Islam. "It is hard to argue that Islam represented some kind of new and aggressive force that suddenly changed the character of Middle East geopolitics or established some kind of new precedent of anti-Western impulses," writes Fuller. "Traditional cultures, attitudes, and geopolitics continued to exist, but under an Islamic patina."[62]

ISLAM IN OTHER REGIONS

An interesting process took place in South Asia—the region with the largest concentration of Muslims globally—at the ground level. The more lightly Hindu regions on the western and eastern flanks—where the notions of religion and caste had infiltrated less—were the most easily persuaded. And the process of conversion to Islam corresponded with the growth of settled farming. On the western edge, in the Punjab and Sind regions, Sufi saints formed alliances with clan leaders and were granted tracts of lands by kings to build shrines. At the other end, in the Bengal area, Sufi saints went along on the drive to clear forests and convert land into rice-farming land. They built mosques along the way. On both flanks, Muslims became numerous, much more so than in the heartland, where established practices and religious customs held sway. (The Sufis are dealt with extensively in a separate chapter.)[63]

In superb research on the largest concentration of Muslims in South Asia and among the largest concentration of Muslims anywhere in the world—the Bengali Muslims—Professor Eaton has shown that the process of conversion was a slow, peaceful process that took centuries. This was initiated when Sufi pioneers accompanied the clearing of the land in the Bengal deltaic region. These individuals were granted land to help push the conversion of the land from forests to agriculture. This was meant to foster progress in the area.

"Because they mobilized local labor for these purposes, these men played decisive roles in the socioeconomic development of the eastern delta," writes Eaton. "Through their agency, much of this region witnessed either the introduction or an intensification of wet rice cultivation, which local communities formerly engaged mainly in hunting, fishing or shifting agriculture began devoting more time to full-time wet-rice peasant agriculture."[64]

These pioneers could be either Hindu or Muslim, and if they were Hindu, the focal point of the local community became a temple. "Since most pioneers were Muslims, however, mosques comprised the majority of institutions established, with the result that the dominant mode of piety that evolved on East Bengal's economic frontier was Islamic," says Eaton. And even though they were humble structures, these mosques continued to have a profound impact even after the pioneers' death, propagating Islam for perpetuity. The acceptance of Islam was also helped by the fact that area was only nominally Hindu, with the hierarchy and rigidity of the caste system not yet in place. In addition, the spread of the printed matter granted the Qur'an almost magical powers. "In the east, then, Islam came to be understood as a religion, not only of the ax and the plough, but also of the book," writes Eaton.[65]

This process of conversion to Islam took centuries. In fact, Eaton writes, "This 'seepage' occurred over such a long period of time that one can at no point identify a specific moment of 'conversion' or any single moment when peoples saw themselves as having made a dramatic break with the past." It would be inappropriate to speak of even conversion of Hindus to Islam in Bengal. "What one find, rather, is an expanding agrarian civilization, whose cultural counterpart was the growth of the cult of Allah," writes Eaton. There were several simultaneous processes going on: eastward expansion of agriculture, tribal people becoming assimilated into settled civilization, and the processes accompanying all this. "It is testimony to the vitality of Islam—and one of the clues to its successes as a world religion—that its adherents in Bengal were so creative in accommodating local sociocultural realities with the norms of religion," Eaton writes.[66]

The reputation that Islam has for violence is also due to the extreme magnification of the episodes of violence in the religion. A good example is India. If you talk to a lot of Hindus, the widespread notion is that Muslim invaders destroyed hundreds, if not thousands, of temples and engaged in a cultural, if not literal, genocide. The British were eager to propagate such myths as part of their divide-and-rule policies. Historians with an anti-Muslim bias have spread such falsehoods by selectively reading and distorting documents and history from that period. Such notions, which extend far beyond the right-wing fringes, have poisoned Hindu–Muslim relations in the country. The reality is quite different.

"One often hears that between the thirteenth and the eighteenth centuries, Indo-Muslim states, driven by a Judeo-Islamic 'theology of iconoclasm,' by fanaticism or by sheer lust for plunder, wantonly and indiscriminately indulged in the desecration of Hindu temples," writes Eaton. "Had instances of temple desecration been driven by a 'theology of iconoclasm,' as some have claimed, such a theology would have committed Muslims in India to destroying all temples everywhere."[67] Instead, what happened infrequently (80 times over more than 500 years) was driven by a desire to punish kings by desecrating the temple most closely associated with the ruling deity. In doing this, Muslim conquerors were extending a practice that was carried out by Hindu kings in the centuries prior.

"Contemporary royal temples were understood to be highly charged political monuments, a circumstance that rendered them fatally vulnerable to outside attack," writes Eaton. "Therefore, by targeting for desecration those temples that were associated with defeated kings, conquering Turks, when they made their own bid for sovereign domain in India, were subscribing to—even while they were exploiting—indigenous notions of royal legitimacy."[68]

On the southwestern extremity of India, a different—and peaceful—process of Islamization happened. The Malabar subregion of Kerala became an important trading post. Arab traders came there in large numbers. "Eventually, a sizeable Muslim community emerged through Arab intermarriage with the local population," writes Eaton. And Kerala has one of the largest Muslim concentrations currently in India, famed for its high socioeconomic development and for the relative harmony in which the various religions coexist (Muslims and Christians form roughly 20–25 percent each, with the majority Hindus making up almost all the rest).[69]

The process of the spreading of Islam in Southeast Asia was analogous to that of Kerala, with the region becoming a focal point in the international spice-trading network. Along with the growth of trade and trading communities—accompanied by a fusion with the broader world—came the spread of Islam. Often, the Arab merchants were accompanied by Muslim clerics and Sufi saints who spread the word and gradually expanded Islam into the hinterlands. And even later on, when Muslim kings defeated Hindu–Buddhist kingdoms, the key figures were Javanese Sufis called *kiyayis* who "cultivated forms of Islamic mysticism that were heavily tinged with Hindu-Buddhist and native Javanese conceptions" that served to "connect Hindu Java with Muslim Java," Eaton writes.[70]

An interesting story in the *New York Times* shows us the reality—as opposed to the stereotype—of how Islam spread in Southeast Asia. When a prominent university in Indonesia decided to construct a library, it found ruins of a Hindu temple that it is proudly preserving. What is interesting is what this revealed about the previous religions in the country and how Islam spread in the world's largest Muslim nation. Many early mosques in the country had Hindu temple roofs. And they often faced west or east like temples rather than in the direction of Mecca. "Things didn't change all of a sudden," archaeology Professor Timbul Haryono told the newspaper. "Islam was adopted through a process of acculturation."[71] So, be it the shadow puppetry dramatizing Hindu epics or the incense and flowers at Muslim funerals, traces of previous religions still survive in the Islam practiced in the country.

Similarly, the growth of Islam in sub-Saharan Africa was intimately tied to trade. Arab and Berber merchants established trade routes that linked fabled cities in North Africa, such as Cairo and Tunis, to Mali, Ghana, and Chad in the south. As formerly isolated tribes and communities were drawn into these trading networks, they abandoned their local gods and became enamored of a larger worldview linked to Islam. (In fact, on some occasions, the reverse process happened.) Merchants got kings to convert to Islam, and then, through the introduction of paper, scholars solidified a religion that was, after all, centered on a book. "Networks of teachers and students, together with the corps of literate jurists and judges they produced, came to provide the sturdy scaffolding that would hold together a permanent Muslim community," writes Eaton. The fabled city of Timbuktu was the main center of Islamic learning. "So in West Africa it was not Sufis who played the initial role in Islamization—they appeared in the eighteenth century with reformist movements—but mercantile and scholar classes," writes Eaton. "Nonetheless, in West Africa, as in Bengal and much of Southeast Asia, the Islamic religion was accepted and assimilated as part and parcel of the broader world civilization into which Islam had evolved by the thirteenth century."[72]

Even in China, Islam first arrived by peaceful contact as early as 651 C.E. through an envoy of Caliph Umar less than two decades after Muhammad's

death. This led to the establishment of the first mosque in China and the process of formation of a distinct Chinese community called the Hui Muslims, currently numbering roughly 10 million. A remarkable feature of Hui Muslims has
been the constant attempt by many intellectual leaders among them to synthe-
size Islam and Confucianism. "They used Confucian language and Confucian
ideas systematically to study, arrange, and summarize Islamic religious doctrine;
they constructed a complete Chinese Islamic intellectual system, writing a set of
Chinese-language Islamic works with a uniquely Chinese style," writes scholar
Jonathan Lipman. So, the mosques of the community are constructed in Chinese
temple and pagoda style, and a unique script has been created to fuse the Chinese
and Arabic languages.[73]

By the medieval era, Islam had formed a global network, the difference here
being that the connections were based not on moneymaking. "It was, rather, a
world system linking men and women through informal networks of scholars and
saints, built on shared understandings of how to see the world and structure one's
relationship to it," writes Eaton. "Above all, it was a world system constructed
around a book, the Qur'an, and of humanity's attempt to respond to its message
by fulfilling both its external project of building a righteous social order and its
internal project of drawing humans nearer their Maker."[74]

When Ibn Batuta, the famous 13th-century Moroccan traveler, went on his
world travels, he hence found Muslim communities in the vastly different regions
he visited—from Central Asia and India to Southeast Asia and China—over a
course of 73,000 miles. Many of his 30 years away from home were spent as a
Muslim jurist in the various communities he resided in.[75]

One unfortunate result of the September 11 attacks has been the tendency of
a lot of people to see the past in a similar, conflict-laden ways. But, in doing so,
"people have magnified the role of fundamentalism and the prevalence of historical conflict and minimized those aspects of the past that don't fit the mold of the
present," writes Karabell.[76]

"Throughout history, there has been active cooperation," Karabell adds.
"There has been tolerance, and there has been indifference. The only way to
describe the arc of fourteen hundred years as primarily a history of conflict is to
forget and ignore not only the stories told here, but countless others that have
been lost to history."[77]

We would do well to keep that in mind.

CHAPTER 4

Ignored for No Fault of Theirs: The Sufis and Other Pacifist Muslim Sects

SUFISM AS ISLAM?

Sufism occupies a unique position in the Western conception of Islam. It has generally enjoyed a positive reputation across the political spectrum. "For its message of tolerance, Sufism has long been fashionable outside the Muslim world," says the *Economist*. "Events since the September 11 attacks have caused Western analysts to look at Sufism more closely as a counterweight to militant Islam. In fact, a report by the RAND Corporation has recommended encouraging Sufism, since it is an 'open, intellectual interpretation of Islam.'"[1]

At the same time, outsiders often see Sufism as a curious anomaly, not given much accordance by average Muslims, or perceive it as almost extraneous to the religion, an accretion that has little to do with the core beliefs of Islam. But such notions are quite at odds with reality. "Most of the 450 million Muslims in Pakistan, India and Bangladesh—nearly a third of the Islamic world—practice a gentler, more tolerant faith," states the *Economist*. "It is strongly influenced by Sufism, an esoteric and, in theory, nonsectarian Muslim tradition, which is strictly followed by a much smaller number of disciplined initiates. In its popular form, Sufism is expressed mainly through the veneration of saints, including self-styled mystics like those in Lahore, canonized by their followers."[2]

At the core of Sufism is a message of peace, love and tolerance. "My brothers, you must . . . try to heal the sufferings of the world," said M. R. Bawa Muhaiyaddeen, a Sufi mystic who died in 1986 but whose preachings still have a global following. "We should not carry a sword in our hands; we should hold patience in our hearts. We should not arm ourselves with guns; we should be armed with contentment. We should not put our trust in battles; we should have trust in God. . . . These are the true weapons of Islam."[3]

Even a conservative such as Stephen Schwartz has acknowledged the merits of Sufism, as can be seen in his personal journey. Schwartz is of Jewish background and converted to the Sufi strain of Islam. He has since been engaged in a battle with Wahhabi Islam, considering it a threat both to the world and to Islam itself. "If, at one end of the continuum, we find the fanatical creed of Wahhabism, cruel and arbitrary . . . at the other end we find the enlightened traditions of Sufism," writes Schwartz in the conservative *Weekly Standard*. "Sufis emphasize, above all, their commitment to mutual civility, interaction, and cooperation among believers, regardless of sect."[4]

Schwartz points out that the further you travel from the epicenter of Wahhabism—Saudi Arabia—the more Sufism has an influence on Islam, with the impact being the strongest in Southeast Asia, the Balkans, Central Asia, and Turkey. He elucidates instances from the Balkans and Turkey (where Sufi shrines coexist with Christian sites), Central Asia (where Sufis still practice shamanistic and Buddhist rites), and Chinese East Turkestan (where there is liberal borrowing from Confucianism and Taoism as well as martial arts)—all under the leadership of spiritual masters. These places are well known for their tolerant, harmonious brand of Islam, whether it is in Indonesia or Bosnia or Turkey.[5]

And in South Asia, home to the world's largest Muslim population, the influence of Sufis has been immense. "Muslims mystics or Sufis have made a highly important and enduring contribution to the development of a composite, syncretistic ethos" in India, writes scholar A.R. Momin. The Sufi saints drew on essential Islamic precepts, "especially the Islamic tenets of equality and brotherhood of humankind, compassion and tolerance, and service to humanity," he states. (Early Western scholars, refusing to believe that such a pluralistic stream of thought as Sufism had its roots in Islam, sought to credit its origins to Buddhism, Hindu Vedantic philosophy, or neo-Platonism.) "Sufi saints drew Muslims and non-Muslims alike to their fold through their simplicity and sincerity, their broadmindedness, tolerance and compassion, and built bridges of understanding, amity and conciliation between people of different religious and ethnic backgrounds," writes Momin.[6]

Schwartz also delves into the nonviolent nature of Sufism, pointing out that it has resorted to violence only rarely in the face of oppression, and even then it has taken care to spare civilians. "The Sufi always prefers peace to war, and nonviolence to violence. But Sufis are also fighters against injustice," he writes. "As the dean of Western historians of Islam, Bernard Lewis, puts it, Sufism is 'peaceful but not pacifist.'"[7]

One thing to keep in mind is how much Sufism is embedded in Islam and how much it is a legitimate expression of the religion rather than some far-out offshoot. "Sufism traces its origins back to the Prophet of Islam and takes inspiration from the divine word as revealed through him in the Qur'an," writes acclaimed scholar of Sufism Professor Annemarie Schimmel.

Indeed, Muhammad is the central figure in Sufism. "Muhammad is the first link in the spiritual chain of Sufism, and his ascension through the heavens into the divine presence . . . became the prototype of the mystic's spiritual ascension into the intimate presence of God," writes Schimmel. This may seem incongruous to many westerners, who often regard him as much more of a warrior figure. But Sufis see him as the ideal spiritual leader, with his constant exhortations to prayer and his piousness.

Certain of the prophet's followers also have a venerated status in Sufism, such as Salman al-Farisi, a Persian barber and a member of Muhammad's household, and Uways al-Qarani, a Yemeni mystic who the prophet never met but referenced with the famous words "The breath of the Merciful comes to me from Yemen."[8]

For Sufi preacher Muhaiyaddeen, Muhammad is the true role model for peace (even taking into account his role as a warrior). "The prophet had no warlike qualities," he said. "He had only the qualities of patience, contentment, trust in God, and praise of God. If those qualities are reestablished in each heart, if they flourish and grow there, then Islam will become a vast, protective canopy for the world."[9]

"If everyone in the community of Islam understood this and tried to establish peace, tolerance, and patience, that alone would bring peace to the world," he adds. "The weapons of peace and tranquility will grant us victory no matter what enmity, what hostility threatens us."[10]

To the two major aspects of Islam delineated in the Qur'an—islam or surrender to God and iman or faith—the Sufis have attached a third dimension, said to be added by Muhammad himself. This is ihsan: the notion of doing beautiful things through the constant awareness of the presence of God.[11] "The mysticism of love and suffering—which teaches man to live and to die for a goal outside himself—is perhaps the most important message of Sufism today," writes Schimmel.[12]

For Sufis, the way to God is the "path." The notion of love is one of the final way stations on this path. "The whole complex of love was so inexhaustible that the mystics invented different stages and used different terms to classify it," writes Schimmel. One mystic gave it four branches while another thought it to have nine aspects. The notion of love transcends for Sufis pretty much everything else.

"The mystics felt that the love they experienced was not their own work but was called into existence by God's activity," writes Schimmel. And love for the Sufis is the only way to elevate one's faculties. Here, the notion of fanaa become really important: to annihilate yourself in the love of the Supreme Being.[13]

"Love for God is a defining feature of Sufism," writes Yoginder Sikand, an expert on Indian syncretism. "Many Sufis believed that divine love was inseparable from love for all of God's creatures—animals and humans, Muslims and non-Muslims."[14]

The concept of the "heart" is of central importance in Sufism because that is where God resides: "Heaven and Earth contain Me not, but the heart of my faithful servant contains Me." Sufi mystic Nuri actually divided the heart into four aspects, with the "breast" containing Islam, the "heart" the seat of faith, the "heart" being connected with the Gnostic godhead and the "innermost heart," the seat of the oneness of mankind.[15]

In contrast to orthodox Islam, the expression of love in Sufism is through dance and music, though this has caused controversy. In the West, the most famous manifestation are the Whirling Dervishes, the followers of legendary Sufi mystic Jalaluddin Rumi. "The House of Love is made completely of music, of verses and songs," said Rumi, calling music the sound of the doors of paradise. The notion of the liberating force of music gained a huge following among the Sufi orders of the Indian subcontinent, too.[16]

The Sufis were also much more progressive in their approach toward womanhood, with their veneration of many women as the ideal, most interestingly Mary, or Maryam, as they called her. "She is often taken as the symbol of the spirit that receives divine inspiration and thus becomes pregnant with the divine light," states Schimmel.[17]

A good example of the portrayal of women would be the story of Laila-Majnu, a legendary tale in the Indian subcontinent, where the love of Majnu for Laila is symbolic of his love for God. "In the [Pakistani] province of Sind, as well as Punjab, a special aspect of mystical appreciation of women can be observed, i.e., the representation of the longing soul in the form of a woman," writes Schimmel. "The tragic heroines of the Sindhi and Punjabi folk tales represent the human soul in search of the beloved, a beloved to whom she can be united only by endless suffering, and eventually through death on the Path."[18]

So, often the soul is the bride and God (or Muhammad) the bridegroom. "This symbolism allows the poet to give delicate expression to those sentiments of love, yearning, fear and hope that constitute the main topics of classical Sufi poetry in a language that overflows with tenderness and intense, genuine longing," states Schimmel.[19]

Sufi saints like Rabia al-Adawiyya and Muhyiddin Ibn Arabi, a 12th-century mystic, were really prominent in bringing to the forefront the feminine, softer aspect of Islam. "Ibn Arabi's inner vision of the underlying and overriding Oneness of Being allows to us a profound and subtle view of divine self-revelation in feminine mode and opens up to the human religious mind a vision of the Eternal Feminine perhaps even more exalted than that afforded to us by the Christian Madonna," writes scholar Ralph Austin. Not surprisingly, two of Ibn Arabi's earliest influences were Sufi women saints, Shams (dubbed the "mother of the poor") and Nunah Fatimah Bint Ibn Al-Muthanna. As a result, he said that women were capable of the highest spiritual state. And, incredibly, 14 of the 15 students in his mystical inner circle were women. He proclaimed that "woman was the perfect form which enters into existence" and that "the perfect kind of witnessing God has given to a human being is in a woman." He even went further, suggesting that the reason for the repeated male point of view in religion was as a reaction to the natural power of women.[20]

Ibn Arabi embarked on a project to reinterpret the notion that "men have a degree above" women. He composed a number of books with the feminine as the center, with the *Tarjuman Al-Ashwaq*, inspired by a Persian woman, Nizam, being the most prominent. And in the final chapter of *Fusus al-Hikam*, he highlighted the Hadith passage in which the Prophet Muhammad extolled the feminine: "Three things have been beloved to me in this world of yours: women, perfume, and the contentment of my eyes in prayer." Ibn Arabi said that this showed Muhammad's love for women, and that to love the prophet, you have to love women, too.[21]

All this can be tied in to a larger project of peace. "This process of 'implementing' the feminine principle begins by reconsidering the meaning of power," writes feminist scholar Sharify-Funk. "Does power derive from instilling fear in others, or is it a presence of peace, love and integration? The Sufi school of thought has made possible the latter perception of power, linked to an understanding of Islamic precepts in which feminine and masculine qualities are of equal importance."[22]

The Sufi idea of peace is very much grounded in the Islamic concept of *tawhid*, or unity. Here, the Sufis embrace an all-encompassing notion of *tawhid*, interpreting it to mean the unity of God, the unity of humanity, and, ultimately, the unity of all existence. They derive their inspiration from the Qur'an: "To Allah belongs the East and the West: whithersoever ye turn, there is Allah's face. For Allah is all-embracing, all-knowing" (2:115).

"The Islamic understanding of peace suggests an ecology of the spirit predicated on *tawhid*, the fundamental unity of God and of all existence," write scholars Abdul Aziz Said and Nathan C. Funk. "In the consciousness of *tawhid*, humans are at one and at peace with one another and with nature. When *tawhid* is forgotten, relationships become unpeaceful."[23]

Sufism brings to the fore the Islamic message of unity, peace, and reconciliation. So, it has as a fundamental belief the unity of all life, a notion at odds with the exclusiveness or superior status of just Muslims. Sufis base this on the Qur'an: "Oh mankind! We created you from a single (pair) of a male and a female, and made you peoples and tribes that you may know one another" (49:13).

"At the heart of this message of universalistic Islam is a respect for cultural pluralism that is inextricably linked to a recognition of the fundamental solidarity and connectedness of all human beings," write Said and Funk. "If as the Qur'an says, 'To every people (was sent) a Messenger' (10:47), humankind is ultimately one community; comparative evaluation of prophets is discouraged, for all are deemed messengers of God."[24]

Sufis are the most ardent proponents of such beliefs. "For centuries, the Sufis have been among the most rigorous practitioners of Islam in its affirmation of pluralism, its prescription of respect in interreligious relations, and in its condemnation of racial and ethnic discrimination," state Said and Funk.[25]

Islam here is based on the unity of God and "the Islamic ideal of the fundamental unity of all humankind and of all life." The Sufi saints were just building on and extending these notions.[26]

"For Sufis, the real basis of peace in Islam is the transformative knowledge of unity," write Said and Funk. "Islam does not exist to impose an idealized pattern upon the world, but rather to establish *tawhid*, and to promote harmony and justice through right relationships, moderation, and holistic integration of human personality."[27]

Peace is something that human beings need to actively strive for, believe the Sufis, and is firmly rooted in Islam since peace (*al-Salam*) is one of the 99 names of God in the Qur'an (59:23–24). So, peace requires a multifaceted effort: purification of the self, piousness, and the right attitude toward relationship with all human beings. They aim to aspire for the peace to be found in the Qur'anic paradise through constant work in the aim of peace. Even jihad for them is the inner struggle toward this goal. The one distinct area in which they differ from a Western conception is that for them the highest aim is not individual freedom but service to others in the interest of the larger community and in keeping with the Divine mandate.[28]

"True freedom is found in service, for 'doing what is beautiful' (*ihsan*) ennobles human character," write Said and Funk. "The servant becomes creative, fulfilling a human dispensation to contribute to the work of peace."[29]

The Sufis take very seriously the Qur'anic injunction that there is no compulsion in the name of faith and believe very strongly that love is a much more effective path than fear. The Qur'an refers to God as "al-Rahman, al-Rahim," the merciful and the compassionate. And the Qur'an said to Muhammad, "We sent thee not, but as a Mercy for all creatures" (21:107). So, for Sufis, Islam is also a religion of beauty and love. A Hadith passage states, "God has inscribed beauty upon all things." Sufis imbibe such injunctions very deeply and take these as commands to do what is beautiful for their religion. Their interpretation of Islam highlights pluralism, inclusion, and harmony with nature. They also emphasize the Islamic qualities for nonviolence and forgiveness.[30]

From an emphasis on peace is derived a strong ecological consciousness. Since human beings are creations of God like everyone else, they are at harmony with nature: "It is He who has spread out the Earth for (His) creatures; therein is fruit and date-palms, producing spathes (enclosing dates); also corn, with (its) leaves and stalk for fodder, and sweet-smelling plants. Then which of the favors of your Lord will ye deny?" (Qur'an 55:1–13).

So, human beings are granted the role of a vicegerent to fulfill a covenant with God in which the goal is to preserve and enhance nature. If a human doesn't complete this role, he falls to a status lower than an animal. Animals, in fact, form their own communities that will all ultimately return to heaven: "There is not an animal on the Earth, nor a being that flies on its wings, but (forms parts of) communities like you. Nothing have we omitted from the book, and they (all) shall be gathered to their Lord in the end" (Qur'an 6:38). And all of nature is a celebration of God: "The seven heavens and the Earth, and all beings therein, declare His glory: There is not a thing but celebrates his praise" (Qur'an 17:46).

Spirituality is just a byway to peace for the Sufis. Even Islam—in its aspect as an institutionalized religion—has to be reconciled with this. So, Sufis try to live by the Qur'anic injunction for Muslims to be a "Middle People" (2:143), which for them includes being universal and supremely tolerant. Sufis believe diversity to be divinely ordained and actively appreciated rather than just tolerated.

"[Sufi] understanding points to the . . . realization of peace as an ecology of the spirit," write Said and Funk. "Islam offers the stimulus and strength for performing deeds which are distinctively human in the deepest sense, to bring the human being nearer to God and to respecting the sanctity of human and ecological relationships, in which must be mirrored a glimmer of Divine attributes."[31]

The hallmark of Sufi poetry is, not surprisingly, love—which can be interpreted as worldly or spiritual. "The great masters of love mysticism . . . have regarded this worldly love as a pedagogical experience, a training in obedience toward God, since the human beloved, like God, has to be obeyed absolutely," writes Schimmel. Mystic Nizami claims that "the heaven has no *mihrab* [prayer niche] save love," while for legendary Sufi master Rumi the entire creation is a manifestation of love since "it is only for the sake of lovers that the sky revolves," writes Schimmel. Love for Rumi is the thing that changes everything for the better since "from love bitterness becomes sweet, from love copper becomes gold, from love the dregs become pure, from love the pains become medicine."[32]

Sufis found justification for all their exaltation of love in the Qur'an itself, such as in the story of Yusuf and Zulaikha, where the Prophet Yusuf (the Muslim equivalent of Joseph) is united in the end with his beloved Zulaikha after a series of trials and tribulations. The journey is meant to be from human love to divine love, with all the attributes of the lover said to be metaphors or allegories.[33]

An interesting feature of Sufism in the Indian subcontinent has been the incorporation of old love stories (analogous to *Romeo and Juliet*) into the Sufi pantheon, recast as parables of undying love (for the beloved or for God, depending on your perspective). The best-known example is Hir-Ranjha, where this story of star-crossed lovers has been recast as a parable, with Hir, the woman, becoming the soul, and Ranjha, the man, becoming the body. The regions of Punjab (currently divided between India and Pakistan) and Sindh (in present-day Pakistan) have provided fertile soil. "The mystical works center around the endless yearning of the soul, burning love, longing for pain, which is the very blessing of God," writes Schimmel. And much of this was a rebellion against the dry, passionless version of Islam served up by the clergy.

Sufism practiced a startling religious ecumenism. This attitude indeed led some Hindus to conclude that Hindu thought had won over Islam in spite of the constant veneration of Muhammad by the Sufis. Perhaps the foremost example, still revered today, is the Punjabi mystic Bulleh Shah. "He found peace in the inner world of love and surrender, singing his mystical songs in order to console himself and his friends in the times of external sufferings and afflictions," Schimmel writes. (A good corpus of Sufi mystical poetry is also found historically among the Pashtuns in present-day Afghanistan–Pakistan and among Bengalis in present-day Bangladesh–India.)[34]

The notion of forgiveness also loomed large in Sufism. Shaikh Nizammudin Auliya, a legendary Sufi mystic, said that evil should be countered with forbearance, forgiveness, and kindness, a truly Gandhian notion. So, he said, if someone placed a thorn in your path and you did the same to him, the whole landscape would be strewn with thorns. Auliya used to recite a verse by another Sufi saint Shaikh Abu Said Abul Khayr:

He who is not my friend—
May God be his friend
And he who causes me distress—
May his joy increase.
He who places thorns in my path—
With malice in his heart,
May every flower the blooms
In the garden of his life
Be without a single thorn.[35]

The Sufis became well known for their social service. In charting the creation of Sufi charitable institutions in India, scholar Nishat Manzar says that a major part of their mission became to foster "forbearance, service to humanity, and peaceful relations among people." These, she contends, made a significant impact in South Asia during the medieval era. As part of their mission, many Sufis translated Hindu philosophical works from Sanskrit and wrote comparative treatises on Hindu and Muslim saints and their practices and principles. Hanging over all their efforts was an attachment to love and equality and union with God.[36]

At that time, Indian society was massively unequal—segmented by a caste system and by a division between the Muslim elite and the indigenous Muslims. The Sufis proved their allegiance to humanity by working in the most disadvantaged segments of society. So, Shaikh Hamiduddin Nagauri lived like a peasant among the common folk. One Sufi saint said that there were "as many paths to reach God as there are grains of sand, but none of them is more effective in attaining divine recognition than bringing happiness and comfort to the human heart." He observed that there were two kinds of devotion to God: the obligatory—consisting of the traditional Muslim practices—and the elevated—consisting of affection, charity, and compassion—with the latter being far superior to the former.[37]

And Sufi orders played a huge role in disseminating Islam. As Professor Eaton reveals, the seeds of Islam in remote rural communities was most often laid by wandering Muslim mystics whom the local population got enamored of because of their reputations for being miracle doers. Typical was what happened in medieval Bengal (now Bangladesh plus the Indian state of West Bengal, home of one of the largest Muslim populations in the world), as described by J. S. Trimingham in a 1971 book: "There came a Muslim pir [Sufi] to the village. He built a mosque in its outskirts, and for the whole day sat under a fig tree. . . . His fame soon spread far and wide. Everybody talked of the occult powers he possessed." And when the Sufi departed, the mosque remained behind, turning the community over time into a Muslim one.[38]

A key instrument that the Sufis had in attracting the common folk to Islam in South Asia was folk poetry. Professor Eaton has shown, for instance, how this poetry helped popularize Islam in the Deccan plateau region of South India. "This literature employed indigenous themes and imagery for the propagation not of complex mystical doctrines, but of a simpler level of Sufi and also of Islamic precepts," writes Eaton.[39]

The Sufis very ably melded Sufi doctrine and folk imagery and adapted it for the local languages. Along with the propagation of Sufi essentials among village people by word of mouth came the propagation of Islam. And, Eaton argues, to speak of "conversion" misses the point since this was a very slow process of adaptation to Islam over several generations. In addition, there was no conscious effort of the Sufis to gain converts and to guide them to Islam. Nonetheless, they did spread the word and laid the groundwork for the deep-rooted acceptance of Islam among the common people.[40]

THE SUFI MYSTICS

One early Sufi mystic who deserves special mention is Rabia al-Adawiyya, a female saint in Basra, Iraq, in the eighth century. She is meant to have been in ecstatic rapture because of her love of God and is "generally regarded as the person who introduced the element of selfless love into the austere teachings of the early ascetics and gave Sufism the hue of true mysticism," writes Schimmel. A slave girl set free, she is said in a story to have tried to dispel the notion of paradise or hell so that people followed God out of a genuine sense of love. "This love for love's sake has become the central topic of Sufism: almost every mystical poet in Islam has expressed the idea that 'the lover must be in the way of love so that he does not remember hell or paradise,'" writes Schimmel. Rabia is said to have been so lost in her love that she didn't care to notice the world or even include the Prophet Muhammad in her adoration. Indeed, her God was jealous: He didn't want to share her love with anyone else that was due his alone. "If Thou wants to drive me from Thy door, yet would I not forsake it, for the love that I bear in my heart toward Thee," said Rabia. This prayer has become a role model for Sufis since. Rabia wasn't the only early female mystic; there were others, too. "Because of her intense feelings, Rabia was accepted as the model of selfless love even by those who otherwise despised women," Schimmel writes.[41]

Later Sufi mystics built on the notion of love. "O God! Publicly I call Thee 'My Lord,' but in solitude I call Thee 'O my beloved'!" said Dhun-Nun, an Egyptian mystic of the ninth century. Scholar Edward G. Browne goes so far as to say that he was the "first to give to the earlier asceticism the definitely pantheistic bent and quasi-erotic expression which we recognize as the chief characteristics of Sufism." This was carried forward by other Sufi spiritual leaders, often in face of disapproval of the orthodox Muslim clergy. When one of the mystics, Hallaj, was executed in Iraq, his final words are said to have been, "It is enough for the lover that he should make the One single"—letting himself be consumed by God's love, in other words. The ironic thing is that Hallaj created ecstatic descriptions in praise of Muhammad. "All the lights of the prophets proceeded from his light; he was before all, his name the first in the book of Fate; he was known before all things, all being, and will endure after the end of all," he stated. He compared the consuming love of man for God to that of a moth that is attracted to his death in a flame (common imagery since in the Middle East and South Asia for passion and love). For Hallaj, *ishq*—passionate, overflowing love for God—was the essence of piety. Hallaj went in the pantheistic direction in affirming the unity of all of God's creation, ending in his formulation "I am God." Hallaj has been venerated all over the region (often as Mansur) in ballads and plays.[42]

Sufis in South Asia played a positive role in the region's history. Not all Sufis were filled with love and tolerance. Professor Eaton has studied the Sufis of the Bijapur region in India, some of who were quite militant in their own way. "However, by and large, the attitude of the Sufis toward Hindus and their beliefs and cultural traditions reflected openness tolerance and accommodation," writes Momin. Their commitment to harmonious living and coexistence was so strong that one saint is said to have refused to accept the gift of a knife on the grounds of what it symbolized, saying, "Give me a needle instead, for I do not cut, I join." On several occasions, Indian Sufi saints expressed immense respect for Hinduism, saying that it wasn't for Muslims to cast judgment against another's religion. This warmth and affection was reciprocated, with Hindu mystics paying cordial visits to Sufi saints. Some of the saints did not even insist on conversion of Hindus to Islam before admitting them as followers. Momin gives a number of instances, such as the following one: "The Lingayat community, among the Hindus, formed a significant component of the outer circle of disciples and devotees of the Sufi of Bijapur. Even today, Lingayat priests preside over the annual *urs* ceremony at the mausoleum of Shah Ahmad Wali in Bidar." There are numerous stories of Sufi saints conferring blessings and giving amulets to Hindu followers.[43]

A number of Sufi mystics became famous for their devotional poetry to Hindu icons. Saiyyed Ibrahim, better known as Ras Khan, was a 16th-century poet who has become a legend for his poetry dedicated to Hindu God Krishna (more on him later). Another, Malik Mohammad Jaisi, wrote an epic poem, *Padmavat*, about two Hindu lovers, with the story being a parable about divine love. A Muslim mystic and scholar, Mir Abdul Wahid Bilgrami, wrote a comparative dictionary where Hindu terminology was translated into Islamic imagery: Lord Krishna was akin to the Prophet Muhammad, his companions were like angels, and his flute conjured the appearance of existence. A Sanskrit yoga text was first translated into Persian and then into Arabic by a Sufi mystic. Sheikh Abdul Quddus did a comparative treatise on religion and philosophy, with quotations from the Qur'an and Hindu texts interspersed. Another saint, Abdur Rahman Chishti, went even further, finding in the Hindu holy book, the Bhagavad Gita, the notion of the Islamic unity of God. He advised Sufis to embrace the good points of all religions. Dara Shikoh, a Mughal prince who should have become the emperor by right, is renowned in India for his embrace of Hindu philosophy (more on him later). A contemporary of Shikoh also authored a comparative religion study. "In their personal lives, the Sufis remained adherents of Islam; in public, their concern for humanity was all-pervasive," writes Manzar.[44]

On the Indian subcontinent, a lot of people were attracted to the Sufis' compassionate and egalitarian worldview. Muinuddin Chishti, one of the most famous Sufis ever in the subcontinent (whose shrine is in the town of my boarding school), said that a Sufi should have a "generosity like that of the ocean, a mildness like that of the sun, and a modesty like that of the Earth." For mystic Fakhruddin Iraqi, "love is the only thing existing in the world and lover, beloved, and love are one—union and separation no longer pertain." Iraqi saw God as an eternally beautiful beloved, everywhere and in love with all of its creation.[45]

The tolerant and pluralistic spirit of the Sufis most profoundly had an impact on the great Mughal emperor Akbar, two of whose closest friends were the children of a Sufi saint. The arts and poetry under Akbar became heavily influenced by Sufism, and Akbar was a devout follower of Chishti. Akbar's reign is still regarded in India as a high point of religious coexistence and harmony, with modern-day intellectuals such as Nobel laureate Amartya Sen citing him as a role model for posterity. Akbar adopted the Sufi notion of peace and tolerance toward all as his reigning creed and went beyond by conceptualizing Din-I-Ilahi, a syncretic moral code that sought to incorporate the best from the region's religions. Akbar is to this date remembered as one of the best rulers in South Asia, if not the world, an emperor remarkably enlightened for his time.[46]

The attempt at finding a union of Hinduism and Islam (a softer, more lovelorn version of the religion) reached its acme under Dara Shikoh, the eldest son of Mughal Emperor Shah Jahan and the great-grandson of Akbar. He became influenced by Sufi thought quite early on in life and soon started compiling biographical studies of the early Sufi masters (one of which was translated into Arabic in his lifetime). He wrote mystical poetry and tried to find common ground between Hinduism and Islam. He even translated one of the great Hindu philosophical treatises, the Upanishads, into Persian. (This, in turn, was translated into Latin by a Frenchman in 1801 and was one of the major reasons for European fascination with Indian philosophy.) In his inner circle were a Jew and a Hindu. Shikoh aroused huge opposition among the orthodoxy. He facilitated the translation of Hindu holy books and compiled a treatise *Majma ul-Bahrain*: the mingling of two oceans (Islam and Hinduism). He said that the two religions were like twin sisters or two columns, both equally valid as a path to salvation. Sadly, his own brother Aurangzeb was pitted against him and after defeating Shikoh in battle executed him and launched a reign of intolerance. (Interestingly, Aurangzeb's sister, Jahan Ara, and daughter, Zeb-un-Nissa, were Sufis who penned works of literature and poetry, but he seemed to be more indulgent toward them.)[47]

A noteworthy associate of Shikoh was Sarmad Shahid. Although Shikoh was already a Sufi, he also came under the influence of Shahid. "Sarmad's universal vision, based on the love of God and all his creatures, as opposed to a mechanical adherence to religious law, was one with which Dara could readily identify," writes Sikand.[48]

Shikoh spent hours at a time with Sarmad, discussing religion and philosophy with him. This was also the cause of Sarmad's death at the hands of Shikoh's narrow-minded brother Aurangzeb after the defeat and murder of Shikoh. Aurangzeb was one day walking to his prayers at the main mosque in Delhi, the Jama Masjid, when he saw Sarmad in the nude. When he demanded to know why, legend has it that Sarmad replied, "To those with sins to hide, God gave clothes to wear. And upon the pure, He bestowed the robe of nakedness." He asked the emperor to pick up a blanket to cover him with. When Aurangzeb did so, the tale goes, out tumbled the bloody severed heads of the men he had killed. "Now tell me, should I hide your sins or my own nakedness?" Sarmad is said to have asked. For the emperor, this was too much to bear, and he asked his chief cleric to find Sarmad guilty of apostasy, punishable by death.[49] "To the cleric, Islam was a bundle of stern, inflexible laws, but for Sarmad it was, above all, a message of love," writes Sikand.[50]

When the cleric asked him to recite the Islamic profession of faith, Sarmad refused to recite the second portion ("Muhammad is the messenger") since he said he was still seeking God. He was executed for his blasphemy, but lore has it that in his death, head in hand, he did recite the entire profession because he had finally found God. And, it is said, Aurangzeb, with Sarmad's blood on his hands, was cursed from there on, watching the Mughal Empire disintegrate before his very own eyes.[51]

Yoginder Sikand, an Indian scholar of Islam, has embarked on a wonderful project where he has traveled all around India highlighting shared interreligious heritages, particularly in the Sufi tradition. The result has been, among other things, a book titled *Sacred Spaces: Exploring Traditions of Shared Faith in India*. As he points out, the Islam that the Sufis spread was a very capacious, tolerant one. "The lingering presence of pre-Islamic customs and traditions among the 'neo-Muslims' was also evidence of a pragmatic missionary strategy adopted by the Sufis, the principal agents of Islam in the region," writes Sikand. "Too deeply rooted to be completely effaced, these customs were grudgingly accepted or else given a thin 'Islamic' veneer by the Sufis."[52]

At the same time, the Sufis provided solace to lower-caste Hindus who escaped the oppression of their upper-caste brethren by flocking to the abodes or graves of Sufi leaders who welcomed them with open arms and harshly criticized religious oppression by both the Hindu and the Muslim hierarchy. "Appealing for a new vision for humankind that transcended man-made differences of caste and community, they challenged the thesis of 'Hindu-Muslim' rivalry and ushered in a new cultural synthesis," writes Sikand. "By refusing to acknowledge narrowly inscribed boundaries, they pointed to a universal humanism grounded in a simple faith in God and good works, which, they insisted, were all one needed for salvation."[53]

A legend in India is a Sufi saint by the name of Sai Baba of Shirdi. His memorial in the state of Maharashtra is a destination to which legions of non-Muslims flock every year (including my mother, who has been there several times). He is held up as a model of religious tolerance, peace, and love (and someone who could perform miracles, to top it all). Throughout his home city, the slogan "Everyone's God is One" is plastered as a shorthand for his life and message. To make the Baba more palatable to non-Muslims, his Muslim characteristics have been effaced over time, including recasting him as a Hindu raised by a Muslim mendicant.[54]

But, in fact, he was born a Muslim in the mid-19th century and at the age of eight joined a wandering group led by a Muslim mystic (whose identity is still not completely clear), crisscrossing the region for years. He ensconced himself in an abandoned mosque, which he renamed with a Hindu–Muslim title, and his legend grew, even among the local Hindus. His notion of the unity of all mankind that appealed to everyone was very congruous with Sufi Islam. "God being one and the master of all also meant that all his creatures were part of one big family," writes Sikand. "This belief was entirely in keeping with . . . the teachings of Sufis, who believed that the light of God exists in every creature, indeed in every particle of His creation."[55]

Sai Baba urged his Hindu followers to read their holy books and find their own path. For him, all paths were equally valid, "Ishwar" (the Hindu God) and "Allah" being synonymous. People coming to his abode were so taken aback to see Hindus, Muslims, and others living together so peacefully that in many instances it changed their entire lives and belief systems. "When I came to Shirdi, I regarded Hindus as enemies of mine," a Muslim Pashtun wrote. "After remaining about three years with Baba, this feeling of animosity passed away, and I was viewing Hindus as my brethren."[56]

Yet Sai Baba was a Muslim, something not very well known to most of his Hindu followers. A disciple of his said, "The ideas which Baba [was] thoroughly soaked up in to the last were in no way distinguishable from Sufism." So, there were no Hindu deities in his mosque, even though Hindus used to perform some rituals there in his honor. Sai Baba would offer Muslim prayer, albeit only on one day of the week, and often repeat the Muslim profession of faith. To foster religious harmony, Sai Baba instituted an annual Sufi festival, combining it with an important Hindu observance so that Hindus and Muslims worshipped together. In this, he exemplified the Sufi notion of harmony and tolerance at its best. He and a local Hindu priest would felicitate each other, and then prayer would be held in the mosque and the Qur'an read out.[57]

Another remarkable Sufi mystic was Saiyyed Ibrahim, who has passed into folklore as Ras Khan, a passionate composer of hymns of praise to the Hindu Lord Krishna. He composed books of poetry of praise of Lord Krishna, especially his playfully romantic relationship with the belles (gopis) of the village. He had long discursions on the nature of love: "Everybody says: 'Love! Love!' but nobody knows love. If a person knows love, why would the world weep?" Ras Khan then goes on to describe love as "inaccessible, incomparable, immeasurable," astonishingly invoking Hindu gods such as Shiva to prove his point: "Because he drank poison out of love, the Lord of the Mountain [Shiva] is worshipped." Ras Khan scorns the Hindu priests and the Muslim mullahs for being useless because they don't understand the essence of love and says the ultimate goal of life is to turn into a vessel of love once you see the "beauty of Premadava, the God of Love."[58]

Yet another subcontinental Sufi saint who has been swallowed by legend but whose appropriation and narration by Hindus and by Sikhs tells us something about the amazing expansiveness of Sufis is Baba Rattan, a medieval-era mystic. What gives his life story a special twist is that he was meant to have been alive in the time of Prophet Muhammad, making him live an astounding 700 years. (Some stories have him as a teenager during Muhammad's time, blessed by him to have a long life, while others have him born before the prophet.) He attained worldwide controversy because of his claim, with the Muslim world split over whether he was truly blessed or a complete fraud. What's of interest to us here was that he was claimed by a Hindu sect of mystics (the Nath Yogis), who asserted that Baba Rattan's life mission was to seek commonality between Hindu and Muslim philosophy and spread such a syncretic culture.[59] "Nonviolence is the highest form of religion," a master Hindu saint (the head of the Nath Yogis) is supposed to have told him. "You should think of every living being as your own self."[60]

Baba Rattan is then said to have built a huge Hindu temple that is still a major attraction in the region of India where my family village is located. The Naths say that Baba Rattan wrote several books and treatises, among which the most prominent are *The First Sufi Path* and *The Wisdom of the Unbeliever*. Both of these are said to be full of syncretic, universalistic preachings and criticism of religious orthodoxy:

> I roam the world barefoot.
> In peace, contentment and mercy.
> I have devoted myself to the welfare of all.
> I harm no soul, big or small.
> I am a mystic, and not an infidel.
> An infidel is he who walks on the path of sin.
> And does not fear the justice of Allah Paramatma
> [the Hindu name for God].[61]

"The remarkably fluid identity of Rattan, who was credited with being both a [Hindu saint] and a Muslim at the same time, is hardly surprising," writes Sikand. "The worship of the one formless God and a fierce opposition to empty ritualism brought antinomian Sufis and [Hindu mystics] into a shared universe of discourse, allowing for multiple identities and challenging the logic of sharply defined boundaries between Hindus and Muslims."[62]

Similarly, the followers of the Sikh religion have also appropriated Baba Rattan, astonishingly reimagining him as a hero of their religion who aided in the fight against Muslim rulers. The shrine of Baba Rattan in the Indian state of Punjab is dominated by an adjacent Sikh temple. A young Sikh that Sikand met there claimed that the primary role of Baba Rattan was to assist the Sikh gurus in their fight against the Muslims and that he was blessed by a Sikh guru with his long life.[63]

The Sufi mystics were remarkable in their devotion to the commonality of religions. So, Farid, a renowned Sufi spiritual master, emphasized the existence of a single God who is known by different names in different cultures. He even visualized himself as a female companion of the Hindu God Krishna, singing and dancing in ecstasy in the presence of his Lord.[64]

A mystic like Bulleh Shah, perhaps the most famous ever of the Punjab region, divided between current-day India and Pakistan, said that his religious heritage consisting of Muslim and Hindu saints. He adopted as his creed the notion of Sulhekul (peace with all): "Neither Hindu nor Musalman, neither a Sunni nor a Shia, I have adopted the path of peace with all."[65]

The sermons of Sufi saints were attended by Hindus and Muslims alike. A certain mystic, Shaikh Muhammad Sulayman Tonsvi, believed so much in peaceful coexistence that his favorite couplet was the following:

> If you desire union (with God)
> Make peace with all and sundry, O Hafiz!
> Saying "Allah, Allah" to Muslims,
> And, "Ram, Ram" to Brahmins!

In a spirit of true coexistence, many Sufi saints showed remarkable deference to the sensibilities of Hindus. One mystic, Shaikh Hamiduddin Nagauri, became a vegetarian. Another, Ruknuddin Tola, said that anyone wishing to visit his shrine should desist from eating meat from the day before the visit, a ritual that followers continue to practice to this day. The warmth was returned. A Hindu king reportedly ordered a translation of the preachings of Nizamuddin Auliya, a legendary Sufi saint, so that he could appreciate them and for good luck. Numerous ordinary Hindus did this, too.[66]

Some Sufi saints went even further, drawing on Hindu and Sanskrit terminology to express Sufi thought. Burhanuddin Janam described God as *Shudhdha Brahma* (Pure Being) and the world as *maya* (illusion), very Hindu terms, and used the imagery of Krishna very evocatively. Pantheistic imagery from Hinduism also crept into their vocabulary, with prominent saints variously describing God as a banyan tree, a jasmine tree, and Mount Sinai. A saint, Mirza Mazhar Jan-e-Jahan, said that the Vedas (ancient Hindu scriptures) were divinely inspired and that the Hindus were monotheists. He even considered Lord Krishna as a saint. Another mystic took to describing God in the Hindu phrasing of *Parmeshwar*, *Manmohan*, and *Maha Thakur*. One saint was raised by a Brahmin lady and performed all the Hindu rituals at her funeral. Another saint lived like a Hindu mystic for years and acquired so much firsthand knowledge that he wrote books on techniques practiced by Hindu yogis.[67]

"The Sufi saints made highly significant and enduring contributions to the evolution and development of India's composite, syncretistic legacy of civilization," writes Momin. "They made a direct contribution through their message of love, compassion, tolerance, kindness and service to mankind, by building bridges of understanding, amity and harmony between Hindus and Muslims in particular, and among various ethnic groups and religious communities in general, and by bringing about rapprochement between Islamic and indigenous cultural traditions."[68]

In turn, they influence a whole array of Indian nationalist leaders, including Nobel-winning author Rabindranath Tagore. The influence of saints extended in other directions and continues today. The foundation of Golden Temple, the Vatican of the Sikh religion, was laid by a Sufi saint. To this day, the celebration of the main festival at a Sufi shrine in Gulbarga in southern India is started by the placement of a bouquet of flowers on the dome of the tomb jointly by a Hindu and a Muslim. A Western commentator has observed that "while the mosque distinguishes and separates Muslims and Hindus, the dargah [Sufi shrine] tends to bring them together."[69]

Scholar Paul Jackson talks of the amazing current impact of Sharafuddin Maneri, a medieval mystic, in the Indian state of Bihar. His tomb still draws throngs, and his interpretation of Islam—with its emphasis on service, nonviolence, and religious tolerance—has had a huge impact on the Muslims of the region.

"Maneri's legacy touches hearts and minds and opens them up so that people can appreciate truth and goodness wherever they can find it, particularly among the followers of other religions," writes Jackson. "Such sentiments act as a powerful catalyst capable of producing real unity of hearts and minds among people. The importance of such unity of hearts and minds, not only for the people of India, but also for the world in general, can scarcely be overemphasized."[70]

SUFISM IN KASHMIR

The Kashmir region in South Asia has traditionally had a very broad and syncretic version of Islam flourishing in its culture, something that may be very difficult to imagine because of the turmoil that has engulfed the region since an insurgency started against the Indian government two decades ago. (Interestingly, one of the projects of some of the insurgent groups has been to replace Kashmiri Islam with a puritanical, Wahhabi version, which has met with pushback from the area's inhabitants.) The type of Islam followed by Kashmiris is no surprise when you trace its antecedents. The disseminators of Islam here were Sufi saints, revered by both Hindus and Muslims alike. Their influence was so strong that they were advisers to the Muslim kings, impressing on them the notion that a ruler is a "shadow of God, and God's mercy embraces all, including non-Muslims."[71]

In Kashmir "as elsewhere in India, Islam attracted a large number of followers principally through the missionary endeavors of Sufi mystics," writes Sikand. "Scores of 'low' castes, victims of an inhuman caste system, sought to escape Brahminical tyranny by embracing Islam."[72]

The most incredible Sufi figure in Kashmir history is Nund Rishi (or Hazrat Nooruddin Noorani to Muslims), revered with a passion by both the Muslims and the Hindus of the region. In fact, he is often referred as the patron saint of Kashmir. Lore has the Kashmiri population converting to Islam to escape from the oppression of traditional Hinduism, with the religion being spread there by wandering Sufis. "Gradually, owing to the influence of these Sufis, a unique Kashmiri culture—an amalgam of Iranian, Arabic, Tibetan, Indic and indigenous traditions—began to evolve," writes Sikand.[73]

Islam dug deep roots in Kashmir because of the Rishi (saint) movement, which was uniquely syncretic in its character even beyond that of regular Sufis. "They did not claim any Sufi ancestry and did not hesitate to borrow the ideas and practices of the Hindu ascetics," writes scholar A.Q. Rafiqi. "Many Rishi practices such as renunciation of the world, strict adherence to vegetarianism, celibacy, and above all, consuming ashes for food, resembled more the ways of Hindu ascetics of Kashmir than the Sufis of other orders."[74]

Nund Rishi is held in so high a regard in Kashmir for converting people to Islam through his critique of both Hindu priests and Muslim clerics that he is known as "The Teacher of the World" and "The Flag-bearer of Kashmir." He was born in the late 14th century. He came under the influence of a female mystic, Lal Ded, who was steeped in Hindu mysticism but was of indeterminate religion, with the difference being that Rishi was immersed in the Sufi idiom. "As far as their statement of the love for God is concerned, they both shared the same goal," a Kashmiri Muslim writer has written. "Till this day, both the Hindus and Muslims of Kashmir hold both of them in great esteem." He completely redefined the Rishi movement as a movement against injustice and rigid traditionalism. At the same time, he took care to incorporate from Hinduism the best the religion had to offer. For this, he and his followers were often condemned by the traditional Muslim clerics.[75]

"Nund Rishi's expansive understanding of Islam enabled Rishism to take Islam to the Kashmiri countryside by making the new religion intelligible to the populace," writes Sikand. "Inculturating itself to the Kashmiri milieu, Islam, as presented by the Rishis, readily appealed to the Kashmiris, for it did not appear to them as an alien and radically new religion, but one firmly rooted in their own traditional view of the world."[76]

This included preaching vegetarianism and celibacy, a carryover from Hindu mysticism. It also incorporated hymns in the local Kashmiri language. But it also criticized Hindu Brahmin priests for their casteism as well as the local Muslim ruler for his intolerant and heavy-handed interpretation of Islam. At the center of it all was a remarkably holistic worldview: "Children of the same parents, When will Hindus and Muslims cut down the tree of dualism? When will God be pleased with them and grant them His grace?"[77]

The Rishis thought the battle (jihad) against baser desires to be a really important holy war. The Rishis were also famous for their preachings about love, mutual tolerance, and coexistence. "They were not narrow-minded zealots but upholders of a syncretic universal creed," writes Rafiqi. Shaikh Nooruddin famously said,

> We belong to the same parents
> Then why this difference?
> Let Hindus and Muslims (together)
> Worship God alone
> We came to the world like partners
> We should share our joys and sorrows together.

"Kashmir's humanitarianism, love, broadmindedness, sympathy and warmth—all emanate from this source," states Rafiqi.[78]

And like elsewhere in India, Sufis saints had a huge following among non-Muslims, too. They were revered as beings with powers and added into the Hindu pantheon of multitudes. And this reverence continues today, with otherwise orthodox Hindus accepting Sufis as their spiritual masters, happily going to their shrines and sharing food with people of all backgrounds. The Sufis, in reciprocation, adopted Hindu meditational practices and even wrote (as cited elsewhere) Hindu devotional poetry.[79]

One representative figure would be Baba Budhan Ali Shah, who, born into a family of chieftains, left everything to become a Sufi mystic. He met up with Guru Nanak, the founder of Sikhism, and was blessed by him with a long life. Not surprisingly, to this date, his shrine is as popular, if not more, with Sikhs as it is with Muslims.[80] Another such incredible personage is that of a Sufi saint named Pir Mittha, whose shrine is so jointly revered by Hindus and Muslims that a temple and a Sufi shrine exist side by side in harmony at his resting place.[81]

In an amazing example of syncretism, there is a cult of the Panj Pirs, the five pious elders, in the Kashmir region, that is so religiously ambiguous that no one is certain of its religious origin. "Some historians believe that the origin of the cult lies in the worship of the five Pandavas of the [Hindu] epic *Mahabharata*," writes Sikand. "Others argue that it grew out of the popular veneration of the Panjatan Pak, the Holy Family of the Five,' Muhammad, his daughters Fatima and her husband Imam Ali, and their two sons, Hassan and Hussein. In some places, the five holies consist of Hindu heroes, in others of Muslim saints, and in yet others of a curious mélange of the two."[82] Sikand describes an incredible scene at one such shrine in the Jammu region of Kashmir, where the custodian of a Sufi Panj Pir shrine is a Hindu Rajput. Inside the shrine are pictures of Mecca and Medina and a Sufi saint.[83]

Yet another revered shrine in the Kashmir region is of Baba Jiwan Shah, who lived in the 19th and early 20th centuries. The annual grand festival at his tomb was attended by more Hindus than Muslims, the Muslim caretaker proudly informed Sikand. Indeed, buried a short distance from the shrine was one of Shah's most famous disciples, Sain Chhup, the Silent Saint, who is said not to have spoken for 20 years in compliance with his master's wishes. The grave of Sain Chhup is flanked by that of two of his own Hindu followers, showing the expansive nature of the Sufi saints in that time.[84]

A Sufi shrine that Sikand visited in Kashmir (interestingly just a stone's throw from the border with Pakistan) was striking in its eclecticism. "Inside, a Muslim-style grave was draped in a green and ochre silk sheet with a heavy gold border," writes Sikand. "On the tiled walls were posters, not of Mecca and Medina as I had expected, but, and much to my surprise, of various Hindu gods and goddesses. A little pot of red powder and a conch [mainstays of Hindu temples] lay at the foot of the grave."[85] The Sufi shrine "was now, for all practical purposes, a Hindu temple," writes Sikand.

In spite of all the turmoil, Sufi ideals still have a place in the minds of Kashmiris. When the Pakistani Sufi rock band Junoon performed in Kashmir in 2008 (the first major public concert since the start of the militancy), the response was ecstatic. "Sufism is true Islam, Sufism is the path of love," a Kashmiri student tells Sikand. "But for militant Islamists, love is a hated word. In the place of love for all, which the Sufis have taught, they insist that we should hate all those who disagree with us. I think they are the greatest enemies of the faith."[86]

THE AHMADIYYA MOVEMENT

The Ahmadiyya movement is a controversial one in Islam on many levels. Many devout Muslims don't consider them true coreligionists, mainly since their founder Mirza Ghulam Ahmad proclaimed himself a prophet, hence negating the notion in Islam that Muhammad is the final prophet. This has led to a serious rift with other branches of Islam and has even led to their persecution, most notably in Pakistan. (Ironically, both Pakistan's first foreign minister, Muhammad Zafrulla Khan, and the country's only Nobel laureate, physicist Abdus Salam, were members of the community.) However, they are considered Muslims in India, and in Indonesia, the world's largest Muslim country, and in Bangladesh, they are still recognized as Muslims in spite of curbs on some of their activities. (They have tiny communities in the Arab world, where they often live in a legally nebulous zone.) The organization claims to have a presence in 195 countries and tens of millions of followers, a claim that is hard to independently verify because of their fraught status. (Incidentally, they are said to have historically had a huge presence among African American Muslims.) In spite of (and because of) their ambiguous status, the group's views on nonviolence and jihad are worth looking into.[87]

"The Ahmadi have established themselves as a vibrant Islamic reform group in Britain, and throughout Europe, America, Africa and many other localities around the world," writes scholar Simon Ross Valentine in one of the few book-length works on the Ahmadiyyas. "With its message of 'Love for all, hatred for none,' and its presentation of jihad 'through dialogue based on logical and rational arguments,' the Ahmadi present a peaceful Islam, an Islam in sharp contrast to the stereotype of war and militancy often generated by the Western media."[88]

Now, the primary reason for the animus toward Ahmadiyya Muslims among many other Muslims is the claim to prophethood of the sect's founder. However, there are some other areas of theological differences (such as, curiously, the status and fate of Jesus, considered a prophet by all Muslims). One of these is the notion and meaning of jihad. "The fundamental revision of the idea of jihad is a central element in the Ahmadi worldview," writes Israeli Professor Yohanan Friedmann in another book on the community. "This revision amounts to the virtual renunciation of military jihad in the modern period, though jihad in the sense of spreading Islam by means of peaceful persuasion remains, of course, an important part of Ahmadi thought."[89]

The Ahmadiyyas hold up Muhammad as a role model for nonviolence, citing his behavior in Mecca and his migration to Medina as a mark of nonviolent protest. Despite continued torment by their opponents, Muhammad and his followers "raised no cry." The prophet was "repeatedly made the target of stoners that drew his blood; yet that mountain of truth and steadfastness bore all these torments with a cheerful and loving heart," states Ahmadiyya scholar Zafrulla Khan. But then the persecution transgressed all limits, and God finally gave permission to fight. The Ahmadiyyas say that the verse—the foundation of jihad—that he received permitting him to fight set strict limits. "It should also be remembered that Islam permits the taking up of the sword only in opposition to people who themselves take it up first, and it permits the slaughter only of those who embark upon slaughter first," says Khan. The Ahmadiyyas point to the multiple treaties and agreements that Muhammad negotiated as proof of his peaceful nature, particularly with the Meccans. "Much is seen [by the Ahmadiyyas] in Muhammad's 'reconciliation of hearts,' his policy of appeasement on his return to Mecca, in which he issued a general amnesty to all people," writes Valentine.[90] But the fact that Mirza Ghulam Ahmad felt that his interpretation was the one based on the only correct interpretation of the Islamic texts—and that he arrogated to himself in the role of the *mahdi*, or the messiah, the only person capable of a proper reading—made the Ahmadiyya doctrine divergent from the rest of Islam.[91]

The Ahmadiyya interpretation of jihad makes sense in this context. They believe that when the messiah reappears, he will abolish war. A canonical commentary in this tradition has the messiah "restore the peace and transform the swords into sickles. The venom of every scorpion will disappear until a boy will play with a snake without being harmed." And then, according to another commentator, "The earth will be filled with peace like a vessel with water. . . . War will come to an end." It is such unorthodox views of jihad that the Ahmadiyyas embrace.[92]

The historical context for the Ahmadiyyas' embrace of a pacifist interpretation of jihad is useful here. Mirza Ghulam Ahmad lived in British India in the late 19th and early 20th centuries. He was trying to engage in debate on two fronts. The first was whether it was justifiable to engage in violent revolt against British rule. People like Ahmad (and he wasn't the only one) argued that Muslims couldn't wage jihad against the British because they enjoyed full religious freedom under them. Alas, this set the stage for opponents to call Ahmad a British lackey. Some others at the time envisioned a messiah who would conquer Jerusalem and Spain and defeat a big Christian army. "Ghulam Ahmad set out to undermine messianic expectations of this kind when he transformed the *mahdi* into a totally peaceful figure performing this task without recourse to any violent means," writes Friedmann.[93]

The second was the image propagated by Hindu ideologues and Christian missionaries alike of Islam as a violent religion. Ahmad's reinterpretation of jihad was part of his project to recast Islam as a peaceful entity. "The reinterpretation of the idea of jihad is one of the main themes of Ahmadi religious thought," writes Friedmann. "Ghulam Ahmad was convinced that . . . especially those who propagate the traditions about the 'bloody *mahdi*' expected to come and eradicate the infidels, supply the enemies of Islam with an effective weapon. He was convinced that Allah entrusted him with the task of restoring the idea to its original form in order to defend Islam against their attacks."[94]

Now, here things get interesting (and heretical in the eyes of many other Muslims), as Ahmad thought of himself as the Jesus-like messiah sent to save the Earth. Since Jesus didn't use military force in spite of being under attack, so, obviously, wouldn't a messiah like Ghulam Ahmad. Ahmad also used a teleological view of history regarding warfare and bloodshed. During Moses' time, warfare was so rampant that even children were killed. During the Christian period, there was widespread violence. Allah forbade the killing of women and children and endorsed only limited war. "The development of human civilization reached its peak with the emergence of Ghulam Ahmad, after whose time jihad must be abolished forever," writes Friedmann.[95]

So, as with Muslim reformists before and after, Ahmad insisted that God commanded Muhammad not to fight back for years when he was being persecuted in Mecca. It was only when there was no other recourse that Allah gave permission and the first Qur'anic verse allowing jihad was transmitted. Even here, Ahmad's interpretation differed slightly. Reformists prefer the passive "permission [to fight] is given to those who are fought against" instead of "those who fight were given permission [to do so]" for obvious reasons. But Ahmad went further. He translated the verse as "those who are being killed" instead of "those who are fought against," making violence the absolutely last resort in extreme circumstances. And Ahmad said that the verse was applicable only to its era, not for all times. All this provides the most defensive interpretation to the notion of jihad. Ahmad also tackled artfully the subject of abrogation in the Qur'an, the claim that the earlier, peaceful verses are overruled by the later, more violent ones. Ahmad stated that the notion of abrogation applies only to Islam abrogating earlier texts and not to any verses in the Qur'an, all of which have equal legitimacy.[96] "This idea is in keeping with the emphasis laid by the Ahmadis on the unsurpassable beauty and unquestionable validity of the Qur'an, which is, in their view, the only heavenly book that suffered no interpolation," writes Friedmann. "The commandment of jihad was promulgated when nascent Islam was in grave danger and is therefore valid only when similar circumstances occur again."[97]

But Islam was still under difficult circumstances, and so Ahmad proposed a new weapon: the pen. So, in Ahmadiyya thought, "there is no sword except the sword of arguments and proofs," writes Friedmann. "We have killed the infidels with a sword of arguments, and the one who wants to kill us has no hope of success,' Ahmad said. The jihad for Ahmad was metaphorical, remarkably similar to Sufi thought: 'From now on, jihad with the sword has come to an end, but jihad for the cleansing of the souls remains in existence.'"[98]

Ahmad's notion was "to convince the world that Islam, as its name showed, was the religion of peace, and that it could bring about a revolution in the world without the use of physical force." Ahmad arrogated to himself the role of correcting "the fallacious interpretation of jihad which is current amongst some naïve Muslims." In fact, he denounced the notion of jihad prevalent among many clerics as being "utterly incorrect [and] totally contrary to the Qur'anic injunctions." So, Ahmadiyyas almost completely reject the justification of violence in any form, and though they do recognize the legitimacy of fighting in special circumstances (such as self-defense and freedom of conscience), this is also to be only as a very last resort. Ahmad condemned those who sought to spread the religion violently or who hewed to an aggressive interpretation of Islam, calling them "wild beasts" who were not truly aware of the nature of the Qur'an and who were committing "murder in the name of Allah."[99]

Ahmad told his followers, "I have come to you with the message that from now on all armed jihad has come to an end, and only the jihad to purify your souls remains." He, in fact, said that, with its multiple meanings, jihad is similar to the Christian word "crusade." There were emphases placed on other jihads: *jihadi Akbar* (the greater, internal jihad), *jihad al-shaifan* (the struggle against the lower self), *jihad-e-kabir* (propagating Islam), and *jihad al-tarbiyyat* (educational jihad). He summed up, "Propagation of Islam, response to criticism by opponents, spreading the magnificence and merits of the Islamic faith, demonstrating the truth of the Holy Prophet in the world, is jihad in this era." Since Islam "will capture the hearts of people by the sheer beauty of its teaching," Ahmad said, his followers would "strive hard to spread the message of Islam peacefully and not by force."[100]

Ahmad also completely dismissed as false the notion held by some Muslims of a messiah who will come and spread Islam by aid of force. He called this "brimful of all types of error and mischief" and "an invention of the impostors . . . utterly opposed to the Holy Qur'an." Instead, the messiah will "spread Islam, not with the sword, but by heavenly signs and arguments." Ahmad wrote, "His only instrument will be his supplications, and his only weapon will be his firm determination." He concluded, "From now on, anyone who lifts a sword against the unbelievers . . . will be considered to oppose the prophet, the prophet who had informed 1,300 years ago that jihad with the sword will be abrogated in the time of the promised messiah. Thus now after my arrival, there is no jihad." Unfortunately, the fact that he claimed for himself the role of the messiah, as the previous line shows, limited the broader appeal of his message to the Muslim community at large.[101]

Still, the Ahmadi message that "the Holy Qur'an teaches respect for the sanctity of life and adherence to peace" is an invaluable one. Ahmadis point to Qur'anic verses such as "And good and evil are not alike. Repel evil with that which is best. And, lo, he, between whom and thyself was enmity, will become as though he were a warm friend" (41:34). Ahmadis also point to the phrase "reconciliation is best" (4:128), "who so saved a life, it shall be as if he had saved the life of all mankind" (5:32), and "the recompense of an injury is an injury the like thereof; but whoso forgives and thereby brings about an improvement, his reward is with Allah" (42:40).[102]

In keeping with this outlook, the Ahmadiyyas condemn those like Al Qaeda who claim to be carrying out a holy war, saying that they are just utilizing violence "to further their own political aspirations and objectives." They point out the strict rules of engagement that Islam offers (no targeting of civilians or even trees, for instance) that extremist groups flout wantonly. They also point out that only a highly exalted prophet or emissary of God can legitimately declare jihad, something that Osama bin Laden isn't, pointedly condemning him in a leaflet as a "self-proclaimed leader of the Islamic world" and maintain that "the call to jihad by an ignorant mullah holds no value, nor should it be entertained by a true believer."[103]

Similarly, the Ahmadiyyas are unequivocal in their condemnation of suicide bombing: "a double crime because firstly the person kills themselves and secondly because he kills others. Both are violations of the principles of Islam." The *Ahmadi Bulletin* states that suicide bombing is a "clear breach of the simple unambiguous Qur'anic injunction: 'And kill not yourselves, for Allah has been merciful to you.'" The Ahmadiyyas declare that "the concept of suicide in Islam does not exist and anyone practicing this is in violation of the doctrine of preservation of life." In support of this, they cite various sayings and instances from the life of Muhammad. In one instance, he said of a man who had taken his life after a terrible wound: "My servant has hurried his own death. I will not allow him in paradise." And Muhammad is said to have refused to officiate at the burial of a person who committed suicide. "The modern-day suicide bombers who in their ignorance give up their own lives and that of numerous innocent civilians for the presumed cause of Allah are fooled into this action by the unholy Muslim clerics motivated by political agendas and objectives," states the *Ahmadi Bulletin*. "The actions of suicide bombers are prompted by feelings of frustration, desperation, and pessimism, all traits which are declared by the Holy Prophet to be outside the hallmarks of a true believer."[104]

Valentine heard a sermon by an Ahmadiyya preacher barely five weeks after the September 11 attacks in which he reminded his listeners the sanctity of life in the Qur'an, the abhorrence of the taking of innocence life, and the condemnation of suicide. Drawing from Ahmadiyya teachings, he said that jihad was concerned with striving in the way of God, struggling for the purification of one's soul, and winning people over by preaching and discussing. Valentine said that the preacher's teachings were very similar to what he had heard from Ahmadiyya clerics in India, Pakistan, and the rest of the world.[105]

SUFISM'S CONTINUING IMPACT

The continuing impact of Sufism can be seen from a *New York Times* story on a huge Sufi festival in Lahore in Pakistan. "For those who think Pakistan is all hard-liners, all the time, three activities at an annual festival here may come as a surprise," the story begins. "Thousands of Muslim worshipers paid tribute to the patron saint of this eastern Pakistani city this month by dancing, drumming and smoking pot."[106]

The piece goes on to describe how Sufis spread Islam in South Asia by appealing to the disadvantaged and how even today they allow women free access.

The majority of Pakistanis are Sufis, a Pakistani explained to the reporter, and they are as much the victims of fundamentalist terrorists as anyone else. He added, "We are condemning the violence, but no one is listening to us."[107]

The immense popularity and continued relevance of Sufism can also be seen from three incredibly famous musical acts—one from Pakistan, one from Africa, and the third from India. From Pakistan, the rock band Junoon has attained megaphenomenon status, selling tens of millions of albums and attaining a devoted following throughout South Asia and in the global Diaspora. The band has used its success to chart a project of peace and coexistence on the Indian subcontinent and between the Islamic world and the West. To this end, it has used Sufism as a touchstone belief, frequently referencing Sufi giants such as Rumi and Hafiz in its music and weaving songs around the poetry of Bulleh Shah.

"Why Sufism attracts me is that it is a search for knowledge—seeking who you are," the band's lead composer Salman Ahmad, who currently teaches at Queens College, told me. "The whole message of Sufi mystics was knowing yourself, and through knowing yourself, knowing God. When you really see with the heart and connect with God, love for humanity comes automatically."[108]

From Senegal in West Africa has come a titan of world music: Youssou N'Dour. N'Dour has performed and collaborated with the likes of Peter Gabriel, Bruce Springsteen, and Sting. Again, Sufism has been a guiding star for him. In tribute to Sufi mystics, he composed an album, *Egypt*, in 2001, which bagged a Grammy. "I'd like people to understand my life's work better—my music and especially what Islam means to me," he told *The Progressive*. "Islam is a religion of peace and tolerance."[109]

Someone who has become at least as well known as Junoon and N'Dour globally is Allah Rakha Rahman, the Oscar-winning composer of the *Slumdog Millionaire* soundtrack. Rahman has been a living legend in India, and his newfound international fame is just a capstone. What's interesting about Rahman is that he and his entire family converted to Islam after meeting a Sufi saint, Karimullah Shah Kadiri. Ever since then, Sufism has been a major part of Rahman's life and work, so much so that he considers himself merely God's instrument.

"I was really intrigued by the whole Sufi thing and had gone very deeply into it, putting aside three hours every day to learn Arabic," Rahman told an interviewer. "I was drawn to Sufism because they have no regulation, no rules, no distinction between Hindu-Muslim—they just look straight into your heart and see your love for the *auliyas* (Sufi saints), the *noor* (light) of the Prophet."[110]

And Rahman has taken the best lessons from the worldview that Sufism has to offer—our mission in life is to overcome barriers and unite the world in love and peace. "Love can transcend all these segmental issues," he said. "You need to find a larger perspective which bridges all these worlds—West and East, Muslim and non-Muslim, or whatever else divides us."[111]

Performers like Junoon, N'Dour, and Rahman—and ordinary Muslims worldwide—are keeping Sufism's flame alive.

CHAPTER 5

Jihad Is Not War: Grappling with the Most Controversial Aspect of Islam

JIHAD AND ITS MISCONCEPTIONS

The term "jihad" has generated widespread misconceptions in the Western world. Even though the common understanding of the expression is sometimes fuzzy, it most often elicits a very negative reaction. "Generally translated as 'holy war,' the term jihad connotes to non-Muslims desperate acts of irrational and fanatical people who want to impose their worldview on others," Thai peace activist Satha-Anand says. "But that imposition is virtually impossible because the Qur'an says, 'Let there be no compulsion in the name of religion.'"[1]

In actuality, the notion of jihad has much more complex overtones, with the word "jihad" meaning to strive or to struggle. This may be a struggle against your own evil proclivities or for the sake of Islam, nonviolently or violently.[2] "The Arabic word, *jihada*, found throughout the Qur'an, basically means 'striving,' 'effort' or 'to try one's utmost,'" writes scholar Simon Ross Valentine.[3]

The major subtext of jihad is to do with social justice, scholars have contended, and stripped of its violent overgrowth, the term has a lot of positive things to offer. "Jihad has come to mean the advocacy of social justice in a widening circle that also includes economic participation and prosperity for Muslims," Duke University Professor Bruce Lawrence says, and goes so far as to assert that "the future may yet belong to those who learn to wage economic jihad in English."[4]

"Jihad is a verbal noun of the third Arabic form of the root *jahada*, which is defined classically as 'exerting one's utmost power, efforts, endeavors, or ability in contending with an object of disapprobation,'" states Professor Firestone. "Such an object is often categorized in the literature as deriving from one of three sources: a visible enemy, the evil, and aspects of one's own self. There are, therefore, many kinds of jihad, and most have nothing to do with warfare."[5]

As examples, he cites "jihad of the heart," which involves struggles against
your own sinful inclinations, and "jihad of the tongue," which requires speaking
good and banishing evil. And what will astonish a lot of people is that the term
jihad is used in Arabic to describe the best-known nonviolent movement in history: the Gandhi-led Indian independence struggle.[6]

Roland E. Miller, a Lutheran minister and Islamic scholar, compares "jihad"
to the word "crusade." Many Muslims realize that it has a disturbing connotation
for non-Muslims in spite of its many innocuous undertones. But similarly, many
Christians use "crusade," even if they comprehend the enormous negative bag-
gage it carries in the Middle East.[7]

So, there are multiple meanings here, too. As you can launch a crusade against
poverty, you can also wage a jihad for, say, affordable housing. In fact, there is an
Iranian organization called jihad-i-sazandigi—a campaign for housing. Professor
Nasr asserts that the West has carried out more wars in the nature of crusades—
either the "civilizing mission" of the French in the past or the war against communism more recently—than Muslim countries have carried out sanctioned or
unsanctioned jihad.[8]

Scholar Karen Armstrong, one of the world's foremost comparative religionists, has a very illuminating passage on jihad: "The root JHD . . . signifies a physical, moral, spiritual and intellectual effort. There are plenty of Arabic words
denoting armed combat, such as *harb* (war), *siras* (combat), *maaraka* (battle) or
qital (killing), which the Qur'an could easily have used. Instead, it chose a vaguer,
richer word with a wide range of connotations."[9]

Externally directed violence is just a small aspect of jihad. The word means ex-
ertion and relates much more to enhancing the faith through charity, avoidance
of sin, and propagating the religion or protecting it. Lebanese academic Yusuf
Ibish says that the greater jihad is about fighting one's internal base tendencies.
Commenting on the lesser jihad, Ibish says that it is a duty of a Muslim if he is
attacked since a man has the right to defend himself and his property.[10]

So, in Islam, there is a distinction between *jihadi akbar* (the greater jihad) and
jihadi asghar (the lesser jihad). *Jihadi akbar* incorporates the struggle against the
baser instincts within oneself, such as the temptations of worldliness, and the
pursuit of righteousness through elevating the consciousness of God within oneself. It encompasses a whole range of things, from the dissemination of knowledge
and wisdom to the establishment of what's right to the removal of evil and fighting against social negatives such as injustice, poverty, and illiteracy.

Jihadi asghar is the one that is better known globally and is the way of fighting.
But even here, there are rules. Islam and its jurists have very often allowed only
defensive warfare: "Permission to take up arms is given to those against whom
war is made because they have been wronged" (Qur'an 22:39). The Qur'an says
that Muslims should defend themselves against those who have "driven you out
from your homes, but kindness must be shown to those who have not attacked
first" (60:8). And then there are the rules of war: It can only be declared by a legitimate authority, the enemy must refuse to reach a truce or to accept Islam, no
non-combatants can be attacked, and plants and wildlife can't be harmed. Plus,
no sites of worship—including churches and synagogues—can be attacked.[11]

Muslims generally regard jihad in a metaphorical form, as interpreted "to work together towards what is right and keep away from what is evil" and a "joint effort to root out evil and establish truth" or "to try one's utmost to see truth prevail and falsehood vanish from society."[12] "The perpetual inner and greater jihad guide the conduct of lesser jihad in both its objectives and its conduct," says Satha-Anand. "This requirement in Islamic teaching raises the question of whether a lesser jihad can ever be practiced in an age of mass warfare and nuclear weapons."[13]

The open-ended and ambiguous notion of jihad can be seen in the way that respondents in nine Muslim countries recently responded to what jihad meant for them. Interestingly, the most pacifist interpretation of jihad came from the four Arab nations (Lebanon, Kuwait, Jordan, and Morocco), where the most frequent responses to jihad were "duty toward God," "divine duty," and "worship of God." Mention of warfare was pretty much nonexistent. In three non-Arab nations (Pakistan, Iran, and Turkey), however, significant proportions (not a majority though) stated that jihad meant "sacrificing one's life for the sake of Islam or God or a just cause" and "fighting against the opponents of Islam." The only country where a majority interpreted jihad in an aggressive way was Indonesia, generally thought to have a very relaxed version of Islam. In addition to these dominant understandings of jihad, there were many others, such as "a commitment to hard work" and "achieving one's goals in life," "struggling to achieve a noble cause," "promoting peace, harmony or cooperation and assisting others," and "living the principles of Islam." As can be seen, the interpretations of jihad are really multi-faceted and almost as varied as the number of people responding.[14]

"It is important to note that for Muslims, whether jihad means a struggle of the soul or one of the sword, it is in both cases a just and ethical struggle," write Professor John Esposito and Dalia Mogahed. "The word jihad has only positive connotations. This mean that calling acts of terrorism jihad risks not only offending many Muslims, but also inadvertently handing radicals the moral advantage they so deeply desire."[15]

Professor Nasr claims that no word from Islam has been as distorted as jihad, both in the West and by extremist Muslims. "To wake up in the morning with the name of God on one's lips, to perform the prayers, to live righteously and justly throughout the day, to be kind and generous to people and even animals and plants one encounters during the day, to do one's job well, and to take care of one's family and of one's own health and well-being all require jihad," Nasr writes.[16]

Life and making a living in the Middle East is so hard that often many ordinary Arabs—such as taxi drivers—consider everyday living to be a jihad that they have to carry out to provide for their families. The highest kind of jihad, many believe, is the attempt to attain knowledge.

The Prophet Muhammad himself preached a multifaceted notion of jihad. Very famously, he is said to have stated, "We return from the minor jihad to the major jihad," on leaving a battlefield and resuming normal life. Here, the greater jihad was meant to be an internal battle within the soul against evil tendencies of the self, such as selfishness and greed. This is the sense in which the Sufis (and numerous other Muslims) have understood jihad.

He also gave many other connotations to jihad. "After [true prophets] came successors who preached what they did not practice and practiced what they were not commanded," the Prophet Muhammad is quoted by Professor Firestone. "Whoever strives (*jahada*) against them with one's hand is a believer, whoever strives against them with one's tongue is a believer, whoever strives against them with one's heart is a believer."[17] He is also reported to have said, "Pilgrimage is one of the highest forms of jihad." (Muhammad also said in a Hadith quotation that "the ink of the scholar is more precious than the blood of the martyr.")[18]

Professor Abd al-Hafiz Abd Rabboh of Cairo's Al-Azhar University, one of the most important seminaries in the Muslim world, concludes, "None of the meanings discussed implies that jihad is a synonym for war or fighting."[19] So, there is a whole span of activities that is encompassed under the notion of jihad. This ranges from being ethical and speaking well to defending Islam and/or spreading the faith. Even under this last category, taking up arms is just one way. "Jihad cannot be equated semantically with holy war, for its meaning is much broader," explains Professor Firestone. "Even 'jihad of the sword' is not quite equivalent to the common Western understanding of holy war."[20]

Abdulaziz Sachedina, a Muslim scholar educated in India and Iran currently a professor at the University of Virginia, has an understanding of jihad that he claims is firmly grounded in Islamic texts and sources. He says that in certain special circumstances when security cannot be guaranteed to Muslims for the free practice of their religion, Muslims can take up jihad as a defensive measure. Here the key notion is security, however, and it includes the rights of followers of other faiths—and nonbelievers alike—to practice their faith. As long as the rights of Muslims and other believers are respected, there is no justification for jihad, Sachedina says.[21]

Professor Abdullahi an-Naim at Emory University also has an interesting interpretation of jihad. Sudan born, he has followed in the footsteps of Mahmud Muhammad Taha, who was executed by the Sudanese regime on charges of apostasy (but which had much more to do with his political opposition). Taha had argued that Prophet Muhammad's Meccan period provided lessons for all times, with its notions of forbearance and high moral qualities. In fact, even the unbelief of the surrounding tribes is treated with endurance. By contrast, the Medinan period is said to be contextual, with the fighting meant to be limited to the specific enemies of the time. "These are not timeless characters; they are flesh and blood, bound up with a particular social and political context," says Professor Kelsay, explaining Taha's thinking.[22]

Traditionally, Muslim jurists have demarcated the world into *Darul-harb* and *Darul-Islam*. *Darul-harb* is the abode of war, meant to be hostile of Islam. *Darul-Islam* is the abode of Islam, where Islam prevails. But what is little known is that there's also the notion of *Darul-sulh*: the house of truce, a non-Muslim country that is in a state of peace with the world of Islam. *Jihadi asghar* is only allowed in *Darul-harb*, a region or country that is actively hostile to Islam. And even Sunni doctrine, more amenable to launching jihad than Shiite thought, has curtailments. Historically, any Muslim regime is said to be legitimate as long as it allows

Islam to be practiced. In fact, the thought goes most often in the direction of quiescence, with the notion that even a bad ruler is better than disorder (*fitna*). A prominent ninth-century thinker, Ibn Hanbal, commented, "You should obey the government and not rebel against it. If the ruler orders something which implies *masiya* [sin against God] you should neither obey nor rebel. Do not support *fitna*, neither by hand nor by your tongue."[23]

The defensive nature of jihad can be seen by the context of the first permission to fight, which came shortly after Muhammad and his people performed the emigration to Medina. The Qur'an gave this injunction: "Leave is given to those who fight because they were wronged—surely God is able to help them—who were expelled from their homes wrongfully for saying, 'Our Lord is God'" (22:39–40). This notion is emphasized in the verse: "And fight in the way of God with those who fight you, but aggress not: God loves not the aggressors" (2:190).

In a number of instances, the Qur'an enjoins Muslims not to use force against nonbelievers, saying that any corrective action is up to God:

If it had been God's will, they would not have practiced idolatry so. We have not made you their keeper, nor are you responsible for what they do. (6:107)

We know best what the disbelievers say. You are not there to force them. (50:45)

And if it distresses you that those who deny the truth turn their back on you . . . [remember that] if God had so willed, He could bring them all to guidance. So do not join the ignorant. (6:35)

The most problematic verses of the Qur'an are often cited out of context: "And fight them until persecution is no more and religion is all for Allah." Here the following line is, however, "But if they desist, then surely Allah is the Seer of what they do" (8:39). And the context of the Medina verses is what is important here. "These passages stress self-defense—in the widest sense of the word—as the only justification of war," says scholar Muhammad Asad in a commentary on the Qur'an.[24]

Similarly, the full verse of 2:190 is "And fight for the cause of God against those who fight against you: but commit not the injustice of attacking them first; verily God loveth not the unjust." And "Kill them wherever ye shall find them" is followed in the next verse by "But if they desist, then verily God is gracious, merciful" (2:191-92). "It is not difficult to appreciate how a wholly false impression can be created by isolating a single verse and by quoting it out of context," writes Indian intellectual Noorani, and blames Islamic extremists as much as jaundiced critics of the religion.[25]

Another verse often misquoted is "Then, when sacred months have passed, slay the idolaters wherever ye find them, and take them (captive) and besiege them, and prepare for them each ambush. But if they repent and establish worship and pay the poor dues then leave their way free. Lo! Allah is forgiving, merciful" (9:5). Professor Clinton Bennett, a chaplain and Islamic scholar, shows how the verse is often misinterpreted. "This verse has indeed been so used but this is to remove the verse both from the context of what the Qur'an says about war (defensive, or to right a wrong) and from the context of Qur'anic exegesis," writes Bennett. "Scholars point out that the words 'but if they repent . . . leave their way free,' contained in the same verse . . . clearly indicate that the 'unbelievers' must have initiated some type of attack against the Muslims. Indeed the verse probably refers to the existing conflict between the Muslims and their opponents, thus giving Muslims permission to reengage after the religious truce had ended."[26]

The verse in question "relates to warfare already in progress with people who have become guilty of a breach of treaty obligations and of aggression," concurs Asad. "As I have pointed out on more than one occasion, every verse of the Qur'an must be read and interpreted against the background of the Qur'an as a whole." Asad then goes on the discuss the contextualizing verses, such as "there should be no compulsion in faith" (2:256), "God does not love aggressors" (2:190), "if they desist—behold, God is much-forgiving, a dispenser of grace," (2:192), and "if they desist, then all hostilities shall cease" (2:193).[27]

The notion of jihad is inextricably linked in the Qur'an with oppression. "The Qur'an is replete with references to protection of the oppressed and to forbearance from aggression," writes Noorani. So, the Qur'an says, "But what hath come to you that ye fight not on the path of God, and for the weak among men, women and children, who say, 'O our Lord: bring us forth from this city whose inhabitants are oppressors; give us a champion from thy presence; and give us from thy presence a defender?'" (4:75). And, "Permission (to fight) is given to those on whom war is made because they are oppressed. And surely Allah is also to help them" (22:39).

Even here, the unbeliever is meant to be granted protection: "If any one of those who join gods with Allah ask an asylum of thee, grant him an asylum, in order that he hear the word of God, then let him reach his place of safety. This, for that they are people devoid of knowledge" (9:6). The overriding principle is that there should be no coercion in religion.

ORIGINS AND HISTORY OF JIHAD

Sachedina, a leading Muslim peace scholar, is convinced that the notion of jihad, as currently perceived, arose from the needs and circumstances of the early Muslim community rather than any religious sources. "Consequently, these scholars had to formulate terminological stratagems that could reconcile the apparently tolerant tone of the Qur'an with the use of the jihad as a means of 'calling' people to the divine path," he writes. These devices include abrogating those verses in the Qur'an that stress tolerance in favor of those that encourage (defensive) jihad, he notes. To do this, he says, scholars have had to elide several distinctions: that between jihad as a way to make God's cause succeed and the trivialization of this as a way to increase the domain of Islam. There is further a distinction between moral justifications for jihad, preferred in the Qur'an, and religious justifications that scholars most often proffer. Most important was the concept of jihad in the Qur'an as a defensive war to counter aggression and the scholars' notion of a holy war to spread Islam. The confusion between these demarcations was, he says, understandable (because of the blurred lines between state and religion in Islam) but, still, often deliberate.[28]

The Qur'an itself, as indicated previously, draws a clear distinction between jihad and fighting. The term "jihad" connotes struggle or striving, while the Arabic word *qital* is used for fighting. "In a sense, jihad is seen as a method of 'bringing religion into practice,'" writes Sachedina. "In the Qur'anic usage, specifically military activity is consistently identified by terms other than jihad (e.g., *qital*), whereas jihad is reserved for the overall religious struggle, whether in the form of personal purification or the collective effort to establish an Islamic social order."[29]

But scholars began using the term "jihad" in the seventh century to justify the military action engaged in by Arabs. This was reinforced in the eighth century as an ex post facto way of legitimizing the conquests of the previous century. By the 10th century, the notion of jihad had acquired some of the contours of its currently misunderstood meaning. Scholars interpreted the notion of the prophet being sent on a universalizing mission as justifying the notion of jihad. The Qur'an does give the Prophet Muhammad permission to control discord and establish a just order. However, this permission was granted, as Sachedina points out, in the Mecca period as a way to retaliate against the "folk who broke their solemn pledges" by attacking first and by not willing to be ready for peace. This is defensive jihad.

The question is, Does the Qur'an go further in allowing for offensive jihad? Sachedina maintains that the Qur'an has been misinterpreted to justify mere territorial conquests. (Besides, the Qur'an necessitates the presence of a "divinely guided leadership," which the Shiites have taken so literally throughout history so as to pretty much negate the concept for them.)[30]

There is a preoccupation in the Qur'an, Sachedina points out, with the failure of people to respond to the divine call. But the use of force, Sachedina says, is given only to those who initiate fighting: "Fight in the way of God against those who fight against you, but begin not hostilities. Lo! God loveth not aggressors" (Qur'an 2:190).

"It is not unbelievers as such who are the object of force, but unbelievers who demonstrate their hostility to Islam, by, for example, persecution of the Muslims," writes Sachedina. "Nonetheless, in the context of the historical development of Islam, the jurists regarded this principle of the Qur'an as abrogated."[31] Here, Sachedina says, the onus of the burden is on the Muslim clergy to show that a particular military action is justified according to the canon of the Qur'an and is not just a territorial or personal war of aggrandizement. In the case of Shiites, the requirement is much more strict since only a just, infallible imam can initiate hostilities, a personage not present since the 10th century. (Of course, Shiite clergy think it fit to engage in defensive jihad to save Muslims when they're being attacked as outlined in the Qur'an.)[32]

The world into which Muhammad was born was a strife-torn Arabia. He was in danger for years before he fought back. "Muhammad and the first Muslims were fighting for their lives and they had also undertaken a project in which violence is inevitable," Armstrong writes. The whole notion of jihad is traced back to the Prophet Muhammad and existing norms. War was quite a prevalent notion then but was tied to old modes of chivalry. It is such modes of thinking that formed the foundation of jihad.[33]

The earliest instances of jihad were in the Arabian Peninsula against a very degraded form of pagan idolatry and have not been generally applied since. "During Islamic history, some rulers invaded non-Muslim lands and even spoke of jihad, but rarely was a juridical edict given by the ulama that such battles were a jihad to convert people to Islam," writes Professor Nasr. He contends that "all Shiite and most Sunni jurists, especially in modern times, believe that jihad is legitimate only as defense and cannot be originated as aggression." Although in Sunni Islam historically some scholars have called for aggressive jihad with the notion that "offense is the best defense," an edict in the 1950s by the mufti of Al-Azhar in Egypt, the most reputable Sunni seminary in the world, put an end to this notion.[34] (Incidentally, the head cleric of Al-Azhar unequivocally condemned the September 11 attacks, an event curiously little reported in the U.S. media.)

Classical and medieval scholars have leaned more toward a militant interpretation of jihad, while modernist scholars have had a much broader and more tempered approach. Modernists like Chiragh Ali have taken classical Muslim scholars to task for misinterpreting the Qur'an in an aggressive way by quoting disjointedly without context. The really early jurists in the two centuries after never condoned aggressive war, and it was only after that such errors crept in, Ali says. "All these early legists held that the fighting was not religiously incumbent, and that it was only a voluntary act, and that only those were to be fought against who attacked the Muslims," he writes.[35]

Modernist thinkers have sharply differed from the classical expansionist notions of jihad. Syed Ahmed Khan, a very prominent 19th-century Indian reformer and educationist, said that jihad was incumbent on Muslims only in the case of "positive oppression or obstruction in the exercise of their faith . . . impairing the foundation of some pillars of Islam." And, he said, since the British were not engaged in such impediments, jihad could not be declared against them.

Khan was far from the only Muslim modernist to express such views. "Not only did they assert that jihad was essentially defensive, but they also limited this to defense against religious oppression impairing the pillars of Islam, i.e., the five ritual obligations of Muslims, thereby excluding from it all other kinds of political oppression," writes Peters. One of the main reasons for South Asian modernists to do this was to remove the suspicion surrounding their community since the British saw them as primarily responsible for the revolt of 1857. Other early modernist Muslim thinkers also said that jihad was clearly a defensive measure against aggression (but that, since colonialism was an aggressive venture, it was justified in that case). Still others have interpreted jihad as an early exposition of international law. (Of course, there are the most militant interpretations of jihad by groups such as Al Qaeda, and these are the ones that have unfortunately gotten the most attention.)[36]

Modernists underline that jihad is derived from *jahada* meaning exerting or striving, and if the notion was just merely to fight, then the word in Arabic would be *qital*, which necessarily connotes fighting and killing. They point out the different meanings of jihad, such as *jihad-al-nafs*—the struggle against oneself—and *jihad-al-shaitan*—the struggle against the devil. All this constitutes what the Prophet Muhammad famously called the greater jihad. The notion of jihad also includes the struggle against corruption and decadence in society, with one commentator saying that all Muslims need to "work with all their intellectual and material abilities for the realization of justice and equality between the people and for the spreading of security and human understanding, both among individuals and groups." This can be applied to fields as diverse as education (the educational jihad) or the economy (as in Tunisia, where President Habib Bourguiba declared a jihad to overcome economic backwardness). Related to all this is the notion of spreading Islam by peaceful means—*jihad al-dawa*—also known as *jihad al-lisan* (jihad of the tongue) or *jihad al-qalam* (jihad of the pen). To support this, modernists quote the Qur'an: "Call thou to the way of thy Lord with wisdom and good admonition and dispute with them in the better way" (16:125). They argue that in the early era of Islam, there weren't many effective means of communication to spread Islam peacefully, very much contrary to the reality today. Even some other commentators who don't want to completely negate the fighting aspect of jihad argue that spiritual and moral jihads are necessary prerequisites.[37]

The modernist interpreters have challenged traditionalist interpretations of jihad as an offensive campaign and say that the Qur'an has instructed to have peaceful relations with other nations: "If they withdraw from you, and do not fight you, and offer you peace, then God assigns not any way to you against them" (4:90) and "Do not say to him who offers you a greeting, 'Thou art not a believer'" (4:94), and "If they incline to peace, do thou incline to it; and put thy trust in God" (8:61). "The classical interpretation that the fundamental relation between the Islamic and the other states is war, is, according to modernist authors, due to the situation prevalent during the first centuries of Islam, as the Islamic state was then surrounded by bitter enemies," writes Professor Peters.[38]

Not surprisingly, the modernists have also interpreted the early history as that of a defensive campaign forced on Muhammad and his followers by a vicious enemy. The claim is that the early Muslims endured persecution for a long time and then started fighting back. In addition, they attacked tribes that had broken their pledges to remain peaceful. "It appears clearly that the Messenger only fought those who fought him, and that his fighting had no other aims than repelling oppression, warding off rebellion and aggression and putting an end to persecution for the sake of religion," Al-Azhar head cleric (1958–1963) Mahmud Shaltut said.[39]

Shaltut's interpretation of jihad is a good example of how modernists have attempted to come to grips with and reinterpret in a more benign way the notion of jihad. Shaltut dismissed the notion of abrogation, by which the earlier Qur'anic verses were abrogated by the later, more warlike ones. Instead, he encouraged a more topical, subject-based interpretation of the Qur'an, which, he said, leads to a more holistic, deep approach worthy of the holy book. "People would do well to learn the Qur'anic rules with regard to fighting, its causes and its ends, and so come to recognize the wisdom of the Qur'an in this respect: Its desire for peace and its aversion against bloodshed and killing for the sake of the vanities of this world and out of sheer greediness and lust," wrote Shaltut.[40]

Modernists also see the concept of jihad as analogous to "just war" in Christian thought. They point to 14th-century Arab historian Ibn Khaldun and his distinction between "wars of jihad and justice" and "wars of sedition and persecution." One can perhaps detect the seed of a just war notion in the exposition of jihad in classical Islam.[41]

The notion of war and its justness—both in its cause and in its application—reveals a lot of commonality in the Islamic and the Western tradition. "Both the just war tradition and the Islamic tradition reflect a moral concern," writes reformist intellectual Khaled Abou El Fadl. "Indeed the essential question in both traditions relates to the justice of the end pursued and the justice of the means used to serve the end."[42]

Islam "forbids to kill and fight the wounded, it forbids to fight those who have shed their weapons, it forbids to fight those who have shed their weapons, it forbids to kill monks and religious dignitaries and to destroy their cells and churches," writes a modernist Muslim scholar. "Islam forbids sabotage, whereas international law allows the destruction of highways, bridges and anything that can be of any use to the enemy."[43]

Even to date, the textbooks in Egypt, the most important Arab country, depict jihad as a defensive measure. "Everything that is mentioned in the Qur'an with regard to the rules of fighting, is intended as defense against enemies that fight Muslims because of their religion," states Muhammad Rashid Rida. Included here, Professor Peters says, are direct attacks on and oppression of Muslims. They cite several Qur'anic verses to support their interpretation.[44]

Even the most problematic verses of the Qur'an are cast in a new light in the modernist interpretation. So, the "slay the idolaters" verse, they say, should be read in context of the Meccans, whom it is directed against, and not all unbelievers. Again, "fight those who believe not in God and the last day" is interpreted as giving sanction against those Jews and Christians who violated their pledges, and not all non-Muslims. And when the renowned Caliph Abu Bakr is supposed to have said (not in the Qur'an), "I have been ordered to fight the people until they profess that there is no god but God and that Muhammad is the messenger of God," the modernists state that here "the people" is meant as a reference to polytheist Arabs living in the region who had committed aggression against Muslims, and not to all non-Muslims generally.[45]

"[The modernists] have adopted the Western liberal values that became current in the Islamic world as a result of economic and political penetration," states Peters. "Their attempts to reform Islam aimed at incorporating these values in their religion. The modernists' acceptance of such values has included an acceptance of nation-states and the notion of jihad as defensive."[46]

And scholars do not generally see Islam as condoning conversion by violence since the Qur'an talks about no compulsion in religion and since Islam forbids the killing of women, children, and the aged even when they are unbelievers, which doesn't make sense if the aim of the religion is to force conversion. In addition, they see Islam as a natural, divine mission that people will naturally be drawn to instead of having to accept it by force and then secretly not believing in it.

Reformist Iranian president Mohammad Khatami (1997–2005) has also condemned the retrograde interpretation of jihad by violent extremists. "Vicious terrorists who concoct weapons out of religion are superficial literalists clinging to simplistic ideas," Khatami has said. "In the Holy Qur'an, human beings are invited to join their efforts in taawon, and taawon means solidarity, which can be translates into: co-operation to do good."[47]

RULES OF JIHAD

A look at the primary guidance for war in Islam—the instructions received from God by Muhammad—reveals several things: war is not meant to be the primary means for pursuing goals; it is the last resort. "The tradition of Sharia reasoning already provides an equivalent to the just-war criteria of legitimate authority, just cause, righteous intention, and (at least) 'timely' resort," writes Kelsay.[48]

There are also criteria for fighting the war, such as the forbidding of "cheating, treachery, mutilation, and the killing of children," writes Kelsay. This, Kelsay says, is also analogous to the just war tradition. So, an eighth-century Muslim theologian specifically cited Muhammad's injunction to always spare women, children, and old men.[49]

Then we come to the question of who is entitled to declare jihad. At the least, it is Sunni clerics who are authorized to do that. In the case of violent Islamist movements raging around the world (including Al Qaeda), virtually not a single one has been blessed by a renowned cleric having legitimacy. And then, even when jihad is carried out, it can't be done in the spirit of blind hatred, which the Qur'an forbids: "Let not hatred of a people cause you to be unjust" (5:8). In contrast, a person should "repel the evil deed with one which is better, then verily he, between whom and thee there was enmity (will become) as though he were a bosom friend" (41:34). "Traditionally, even external jihad has been associated in the Muslim mind with magnanimity, generosity and detachment, with all the virtues associated with chivalry," asserts Nasr. Such qualities can be seen in Muslim warriors down the ages, he says, starting from Saladin all the way down to Ahmad Shah Masud.[50]

Jihad is meant to be only in self-defense. The Qur'an does speak about fighting one's enemies, as would be expected in a time of strife, but says that Muslims should battle their foes "except those who seek refuge with people between whom and you there is a covenant, or (those who) come unto you because their hearts forbid them to make war on you. . . . So, if they hold aloof from you and wage not war against you and offer you peace, God alloweth you no way against then" (4:90). And the Qur'an offers forgiveness. "Whoso foregoes [revenge] it shall be expiation for him" (5:45). And the moment the enemy ceases fighting, so should you: "If they desist, then let there be no hostility" (2:192).

And then there are the rules under which jihad or wars have to be fought. Certainly, no innocent life can be taken. Women and children and animals and trees are explicitly ruled out. Muhammad's generous behavior on reentering Mecca is a role model for Muslims, as is Caliph Umar's magnanimity toward Christians on conquering Jerusalem. Of course, Nasr says, a number of Muslims are violating such precepts. "But it is essential here not only for Western observers but also for many Muslims who, having lost hope, have fallen into despair and commit desperate acts to remember what the teachings of Islam as a religion are on these matters," writes Nasr.[51]

"The regulations of warfare, especially the protection of the innocent, that is, nonaggression against noncombatants, and dealing with the enemy in justice, also remain part and parcel of the religion and essential to it; they cannot be set aside with the excuse that one is responding to a grievance or injustice," Nasr adds. "If one does so, one is no longer speaking or acting in the name of Islam and is in fact in danger of defiling the religion more than its enemies ever could."[52]

Regarding the rules of war, the Qur'an advises giving clear warning and not attacking the enemy by stealth: "Surely, God loves not the treacherous" (8:58). Similarly, the Qur'an advises to accept truces and peace treaties: "And if they incline to peace, do thou incline to it; and put thy trust in God" (8:61–62). And, "Fulfill God's covenant when you make covenant, and break not the oaths after they have been confirmed, and you have made God your surety" (16:91–92).

This makes the acts of those extremists who claim to wage jihad in the name of Islam even more surprising and incongruous. "The acts of those who kill civilians, women, children and the elderly . . . cannot be seen as being jihad and these people cannot be seen as being mujahids," Turkish scholar Aken writes. "There is no foundation for these acts in either the Qur'an or the Sunna. . . . No Muslim can be a true Muslim and at the same time diverge from or go against the path that God and His Prophet have established."[53]

Scholar Tamara Sonn says that guerrilla warfare and terrorism are "almost uniformly condemned in Islamic literature." Sonn does add that because of the era in which most of Islamic discourse was written, the notion of nation-states and modern warfare was underdeveloped then and that Sunni jurisprudence is so behind the times that it has not even grappled with the meaning of a modern geographically defined nation-state.

But in early Muslim history, two sects—the Kharijis and Nizari Ismailis— who encouraged violence and assassinations against the state were the subject of widespread condemnation and resentment, including by Muslim clergy, for two reasons. "In the first place, the spirit of Islam holds that human life is sacred," writes Sonn. "This is consistent with its Arab heritage." Even in pre-Islamic Arabia, killing was considered the highest crime, consistent with acclaimed scholar Maxine Rodinson's assessment that in Arab ethics, "Man was the highest value for man." In reality, though, this was often limited by considerations of clan or tribe.[54] "It was one of the chief accomplishments of Islam that it introduced a universalizing tendency into Arab ethics," writes Sonn. "Islam thus extended concern about unjust killing by inculcating concern for human life as such."[55]

The second reason for condemnation of the violent sects in early Muslim history was the mayhem caused by their indiscriminate tactics. "Instances of revolutionary behavior involving assassinations and other 'irregular' tactics, while obviously present in the Islamic tradition, were not usually supported by the Muslim community at large," writes Sonn. "They were deviations from the accepted norms. [Renowned scholar] Fazlur Rahman claims that the general antirevolutionary tendency of Islamic law is a direct result of the terror sown by Khariji activity in the first century of Islam."[56]

Of course, the Qur'an does offer scenarios where it would be justified to take up arms: "Men, women and children whose cry is 'Our Lord! Rescue us from this town, whose people are oppressors; and raise for us from you one who will protect . . . one who will help!'" (4:75). But the primary goal is to resist injustice and to restore order. The first step here is to give a public and clear justification for resorting to armed action. Then the group engaging in armed action should be representative of the population at large and not be a group engaging in a private or personal feud. Following this, it is the imperative of the authorities in charge to try to end the feud by engaging in good-faith negotiations. If such attempts fail, then the authorities are justified in putting down the rebellion, albeit with a gentle hand, where prisoners are treated well, noncombatants are spared, and the rebel's property is restored once hostilities end. What about the conduct of the rebels? Although Islamic law does give them latitude since they are a guerrilla force, "This latitude cannot be, and is not, absolute," and right conduct is very important. By this interpretation—consonant with Muslim progressives—both the cause and conduct of extremist groups is wrong.[57]

"Their reasoning suggests that militants not only violate norms governing the conduct of war," Kelsay writes. "They also call Muslims to kill and die in the service of a cause that is not authorized by the practice of Sharia reasoning. The call to jihad stipulated in [Al Qaeda's] and other militant texts is not simply unwise. It is unjust."[58]

To this day, "there remain strong antirevolutionary tendencies in Islamic thought, leading one scholar to claim that the Islamic tradition has a 'clear tendency toward an almost unconditional submission to the authorities, a theologically justified quietism,'" Sonn writes. Sonn says that even though there's been rise in insurrectionary activity and rhetoric in the Muslim word, "it is in opposition to the spirit of Islam, which holds human life sacred and personal culpability a matter for God alone to determine. . . . Terrorist tactics are condemned by scholars of Islamic religious law and are generally viewed by Muslims as repugnant."[59]

"It is difficult to find support for the use of irregular or terrorist tactics in the Islamic tradition," concludes Sonn. "Both are condemned under the rubric of Islam's general reticence concerning revolution, its respect for life, and its insistence that God has exclusive rights in judging the piety of believers. . . . Irregular and terrorist tactics have generally been rejected in Islamic religious law and by Islamic popular opinion." Sonn does acknowledge the rise of jihadist movements in the Muslim world but says that this is an outgrowth of the stagnation of Muslim societies and that, once the process of regeneration has been done, "jihad's more militant connotations will lose their pride of place."[60]

On a side note, Nasr deals with the notion of martyrdom in Islam, which has been famously distorted for suicide bombings. As he says, "Christianity relies particularly on martyrdom and celebrates its martyrs as saints more than Islam does, especially Islam in its Sunni form. It is particularly strange to see some observers in the West speak of martyrdom as if it were a peculiar, solely Islamic concept." The root meaning of martyr and "shahid" is the same—bearing witness. (Even Judaism has a famous martyr, Samson, who killed thousands of Philistines along with himself.)[61]

And the whole notion of martyrdom in Islam through suicide bombing is an oxymoron since suicide is forbidden in Islam. Of course, there is a debate about when suicide bombings may be permissible as a tactic against oppression, but that doesn't alter the fact of the basic prohibition. "Even in such cases the Islamic injunction that one cannot kill innocent people even in war must of necessity hold," Nasr writes. (Nasr add that the irony is that modern technology is what makes this possible in a way that hasn't been available in history.)[62]

Kelsay says that the attempts by Muslim democrats and progressives to recast the notion of jihad is a brave and worthy one and one that addresses one of the central dilemmas of the religion. And the understanding of Islam by groups like Al Qaeda is centrally flawed. "The most important weakness in the militant claim to represent true Islam is the contradiction between the end professed and the means employed," writes Kelsay. "Those who seek rule by the Sharia should themselves be ruled by its norms. If they fail in this regard, their claim to represent the cause of justice and right is placed in doubt. Militants, it appears, are their own worst enemy."[63]

Commenting on the appropriation of jihad by extremist groups, Pastor Miller states, "The so-called 'Islamic Jihad' groups have no right to take this authority to themselves. In addition, their extremist methods that involve violence against the innocent have no basis in Islamic law. In the moderate view, jihad is still necessary, but it must now be directed toward social issues: the individual's struggle for piety, and society's struggle for justice."[64]

It is an erroneous interpretation of jihad that extremist groups have propagated and practiced. Unfortunately, it is this interpretation of jihad that has become the most famous around the world. A better, fuller understanding of the term in the West would go a long way in correcting this misperception—as well as stereotypes about Islam.

CHAPTER 6

A Most Improbable Tale: Nonviolence among the Pashtuns of Pakistan

INTRODUCTION

The Afghanistan–Pakistan border region has become one of the most infamous in the world—synonymous with lawlessness, violence, and terrorist plots. This makes even more remarkable and urgent the story of a person and a movement that arose in the very same area with the bedrock principles of nonviolence, religious tolerance, social justice, and women's rights.

The man was a Pashtun Muslim just like members of the Taliban and grew up in the same portion of Pakistan that many of them did. His name was Abdul Ghaffar (or Badshah—leader or king) Khan, affectionately known as the "Frontier Gandhi," and he helped create one of the most remarkable social and political experiments in modern history.

Khan, a friend and contemporary of the Mahatma, founded in 1929 a nonviolent movement of more than 100,000 Pashtuns called the Khudai Khidmatgar—the Servants of God. This movement was dedicated to social reform and to ending the rule of the British in then-undivided India. For the next many decades—both during and after British rule—he incessantly worked to spread his ideals in the region.

"As we have seen with Gandhi, the leadership of Ghaffar Khan was, above all, creative," writes nonviolence scholar Joan Bondurant. "He used Islamic precepts to communicate to his people the need for changes in the traditional. The effect which the Khudai Khidmatgar had on Frontier society is incalculable."[1]

Khan's calls for reform, social justice, including a more equitable land distribution, and religious harmony threatened some religious leaders and big landlords. His campaign for Pashtun self-rule angered both the British and the Pakistani governments. His movement was brutally repressed, with hundreds of his followers

killed. He was the target of at least two assassination attempts by his fellow Pashtuns. And he spent nearly three decades in prison. But he persevered in his efforts
until he died at the age of 98 in 1988.

Professor Satti Khanna of Duke University met Khan when he visited India in
1985 for the centennial celebrations of the Congress Party, with which Khan and
Gandhi were associated. Khanna interviewed him for a documentary he made on
India's partition, *Division of Hearts*.

"For today's children and the world, my thoughts are that only if they accept
nonviolence they can escape destruction, with all this talk of the atom bomb, and
live a life of peace," Khan told Khanna. "If this doesn't happen, then the world
will be in ruins." "He was a presence rather than a person," Khanna remembered.
"He had an emanation of profound integrity."[2]

Khan used nonviolence as much as a tool of social reform—to end the en-
demic violence among the Pashtuns—as much as to gain freedom from the British. "Gandhi himself remarked that Badshah Khan had a more difficult job than
him, since he made a violent people nonviolent," stated Begum Nasim Wali
Khan, Ghaffar Khan's daughter-in-law. "By doing this, Gandhi said, he showed
the world the true meaning of nonviolence."[3]

Even some of his most famous colleagues held simplistic notions about the Pashtuns, stereotypes that increased their admiration for Khan's work. "That such
men," Gandhi said, "who would have killed a human being with no more thought
than they would kill a sheep or a hen should at the bidding of one man have laid
down their arms and accepted nonviolence as the superior weapon sounds almost
like a fairy tale."

"The man who loved his gun better than his child or his brother, who val-
ued life cheaply and cared nothing for death, who avenged the slightest insult
with the thrust of a dagger, had suddenly become the bravest and most enduring of India's nonviolent soldiers," India's first prime minister, Jawaharlal
Nehru, stated. "That was due undoubtedly to the influence of one man—Abdul
Ghaffar Khan."[4]

EARLY LIFE

Khan was the son of a tribal chief with considerable influence. His father defied
religious orthodoxy and sent him to a British school in the region. One of Khan's
teachers at school was a British pastor, E.F.E. Wigram, whose brother was a doctor. They had devoted themselves to serving the people of the area, and the sight
of foreigners doing this so sincerely had a profound and lasting impact on Khan.
"When a melon sees another melon, it takes on its color," Khan wrote in his autobiography, referring to a Persian proverb. "So the color of service and dedication
that I saw in Mr. Wigram and his brother must have fallen on me, too."[5]

As a young man, Khan planned to go to England to learn engineering, where
his brother was studying to be a doctor. But his mother, devastated that her
younger son would abandon her, became distraught: "I loved my mother very
much, and she was extremely fond of me. How could I go to England without

her consent? So I gave up the idea of going abroad and decided that henceforth I would devote myself to the service of my country and my people—the service of God and humanity."[6]

In an astonishing case of "what if," Khan was recruited into the Frontier Guides, an adjunct of the British armed forces. But while he was visiting a friend, also a guide, a British subordinate showed up and berated the friend for having the temerity to part his hair British style. Khan could not tolerate the insult and instantly changed his mind. "Allah had willed otherwise," he later said.[7]

He came under the influence of a progressive religious figure, Haji Saheb of Turangzai, who was fighting for freedom from the British. Under his guidance, Khan first founded a college and then several schools throughout the region. He started coming into contact with progressive and nationalist Muslim figures from all over the country and attended the Muslim League national conference in Agra in 1913. (He also started subscribing to Al Hilal, a nationalist Muslim publication founded by Maulana Abul Kalam Azad, also profiled in this book.)[8] On April 6, 1919, at a meeting at Utmanzai of more than 100,000 people, Khan was given the title of "Badshah" by the khans (chiefs) of Hashatnagar. The British surrounded the village, took away 60 khans as hostages and forced them to conduct a sham jirga (tribal council meeting) that sentenced Khan and his father to jail.[9]

In 1920, he got involved with the Khilafat movement to protest the end of the caliphate in Turkey and briefly emigrated to Afghanistan as a gesture (an interesting example of the use of emigration as a form of nonviolent protest in emulation of the Prophet Muhammad's journey from Mecca to Medina). After coming back to home, he renewed his commitment to establishing schools and fighting for freedom, for which the British jailed him repeatedly. Inspired by Haji Saheb, he set up a school in his home district of Utmanzai in 1921, much before he came into contact with Gandhi. By 1924, he had become quite famous, and when he was released from jail, a huge crowd awaited him and greeted him with Fakhr-e-Afghan (Pride of the Afghans), one of the many titles bestowed on him.[10]

So, Ghaffar Khan came to the Indian nationalist struggle not through Gandhi but through a different route. His first instance of imprisonment was in April 1919, before he even attended one meeting of Gandhi's Congress Party. In 1921, after another stint in prison, he went on a tour of the Middle East, and this made him determined to work for the upliftment and independence of his people.

FOUNDING OF THE KHUDAI KHIDMATGAR

Paradoxically, the Khudai Khidmatgar was formed in November 1929 in Utmanzai at a pan-Pashtun meeting to celebrate a violent countercoup that brought Nadir Khan to power in Afghanistan. The organization was founded as a nonpolitical organization for socioeconomic reform among the Pashtuns. Members were asked to take an oath swearing to be nonviolent and to lead an ethical life. "Our motive for choosing that name [translated into English as Servants of God] was that we wanted to awaken in the Pathans the idea of service and their people in the name of God, an idea and a desire which was sadly lacking among them," Khan states.[11]

Another main objective, Khan says, was to stop the culture of revenge that had become an integral part of Pashtun society. The Khidmatgar oath made members promise to serve humanity, to abjure from revenge and antisocial practices, and to lead a simple life.[12]

"[The movement] had, first of all, a religious basis," writes Bondurant. "It took as its objective both local socioeconomic reform and political independence. . . . Its adoption of nonviolence was more thorough than that of the Indian National Congress inasmuch as the Khudai Khidmatgar pledged themselves to nonviolence not only as a policy, but as a creed, a way of life. And, finally, the Khudai Khidmatgar required of its members complete devotion."[13]

Khan set up two parallel structures in his home region. On the broader level, he encouraged democracy. There was a network of *jirgas* (councils) set up at the village level, which were democratically elected. These, in turn, elected committees for a cluster of villages, which had the *tahsil* (grouping of villages) committees and the district committees above them. Finally, there was a provincial *jirga*, which acted as an unofficial parliament. Within the Khidmatgar, however, Khan exercised top-down control, with the appointment of the commander in chief being in his hands. The commander in chief appointed officers at the lower levels. All these officers were volunteers and had to pay themselves for even their uniforms. They had a flag—first red and then the Congress Party tricolor—and bands complete with bagpipes and drums. The men wore red and the women black.[14]

Khan visited numerous villages in the area, and young men flocked to put on the red shirt (hence the name Red Shirts). As a critic of the organization, M. S. Korejo, points out, the organization was beset with contradictions from the outset since its devotion to Islam, its homogeneous ethnic identity, nonviolence, and a supposedly nonpolitical mission—as well as its top-down, quasi-militaristic structure devoted to Ghaffar Khan—were to all come into conflict.[15]

Members of the Khidmatgar were drilled and instructed to march long marches in military formation, even though they never carried even a stick. Their uniform was the red shirt since white would get easily dirty and the red dye was easily available in the area. They were pledged to nonviolence, religious harmony, personal integrity, and the socioeconomic upliftment of the Pathans. Until April 1930, the numbers were not more than 500; by 1938, the membership had increased to more than 100,000.[16]

Khan went from village to village, traveling incessantly from one end of the region to the other, promoting social reform—such as an end to blood feuds and education—and political freedom. When Khan ventured into villages, he often found volunteers already doing good work. He toured the area incessantly throughout his life, traveling 25 miles in a day, going from village to village, speaking about social reforms, and having his movement members stage dramas depicting the value of nonviolence.

"I visited a really remote village recently and was taking pride in the fact that I was the first outsider to be there," said Asfandiyar Wali Khan, his grandson and the central president of the Awami National Party, which claims to carry on Ghaffar Khan's work. "However, I learned that Badshah Khan had been there in 1942. Imagine the conditions at the time. He must have had to walk ten to twelve hours to get there."

Asfandiyar remembered the two years he spent in exile with his grandfather in Afghanistan in the late 1960s. "We used to get up early in the morning and start walking after our prayers," Asfandiyar said. "We used to have no lunch and just go from village to village. I used to think to myself if a man of eighty can do it, why can't I?"[17]

Mukulika Banerjee, a lecturer in anthropology at University College London and the author of *The Pathan Unarmed*, a study of the Khudai Khidmatgar, spent months in the frontier region with Khan's family in the early 1990s and interviewed 70 surviving Khidmatgar members for her book. She says that while people initially joined the organization because of Khan's charisma and persuasiveness, later on it was because of the excitement of becoming part of something larger than themselves.[18]

And their commitment to nonviolence was stronger than their allegiance to Khan. When Gandhi asked some of them in 1938 whether they would take up violence if asked by Ghaffar Khan, they famously replied with an emphatic no.[19]

KHAN AND NONVIOLENCE

In his autobiography, Khan spends a bit of time emphasizing the centrality of nonviolence to his movement and how it represented a new phase for Pashtun society.

"There were two freedom movements in our province, one believed in violence and the other in nonviolence," he states. "The violent movement had preached hatred, but the nonviolent movement preached love and brotherhood. It was through nonviolence that the country would be freed, through nonviolence that the British would be driven out."

He goes on to stress the broader significance of his group: "But the Khudai Khidmatgar movement was not just a political movement. Apart from being the political party of the Pashtuns, it was also a spiritual movement that taught the Pashtuns love and brotherhood, that inspired them with a sense of unity, patriotism and the desire to service."[20]

Asfandiyar remembers that his grandfather gave him two basic lessons about the superiority of nonviolence. "He said that violence needs less courage than nonviolence, since with nonviolence you can hit back and then don't," recalls Asfandiyar. "Second, violence will always breed hatred. Nonviolence breeds love."[21]

"To me, nonviolence has come to represent a panacea for all the evils that surround my people, and therefore I am devoting all my energies toward the establishment of a society that should be based on its principles of truth and peace," Khan wrote in the preface to his nephew Mohammad Yunus's book on the Pashtuns.[22]

Some writers even assert that Khan surpassed Gandhi in his devotion to non-violence. Scholar Attar Chand states, "It would indeed not be wrong to say that even as Mahatma Gandhi was the master of the practice of nonviolence at the personal level, Ghaffar Khan proved to be its more successful practitioner at the group or societal level."[23]

KHAN AND ISLAM

For Khan, Islam's core was nonviolence and tolerance. "I cited chapter and verse from the Qur'an to show the great emphasis that Islam had laid on peace, which is its coping stone," Ghaffar Khan recounted to Gandhi an argument he had with a Punjabi Muslim about the compatibility of Islam with nonviolence. "I also showed to him how the greatest figures in Islamic history were known more for their forbearance and self-restraint than for their fierceness. The reply rendered him speechless."[24]

Khan's views on Islam were matched by the Mahatma: "Though the sword has been wielded in the history of Islam and that too in the name of religion, Islam was not founded by the sword, nor was its spread due to it."[25] One of the main values that Khan derived from Islam and the Prophet Muhammad was *sabr* (patience) in the face of oppression. "Great troubles were given to the disciples [of Muhammad]," he told his people. "They were made to lie on the hot sand: A rope was put on their necks and they were dragged in the streets. Because of patience, the Muslims succeeded."[26]

"He said, 'If you are struck on one cheek, then turn the other to your enemy,'" one Khidmatgar member told Banerjee. Another said, "He told us that we were at war against the British, for our independence; but we have no weapons. Our only weapon is patience."[27]

Khan's religious outlook was remarkably broad. Bondurant quotes writer Halide Edib on Ghaffar Khan: "Although he based his simple ideology on religion, his interpretation of it was so universal that instead of separating the Muslims from the rest of the world, he tried to make them so that they could cooperate with their fellowmen for the good of all."[28]

"Remember this also that the Musalmans (Muslims) alone are not the creatures of God," Khan said at a public meeting in January 1931. "The Hindus, Sikhs, Musalmans, Jews, Christians and Parsis, in short, all the creatures that live in this world, are the creatures of God. The mission of Khudai Khidmatgar is to give comfort to all creatures of God."[29]

Khan reminisces in his autobiography about the multidenominational prayer meeting that Gandhi used to have every morning, with Khan reciting verses from the Qur'an. Khan also expresses in his autobiography a wish to learn more about Buddhism and Zoroaster (the founder of Zoroastrianism) since the Pathans were Buddhists before becoming Muslims and Zoroaster was from Afghanistan. "My religion is truth, love, and service to God and humanity," he says. "Every religion that has come into the world has brought the message of love and brotherhood."[30]

When he was in prison for defying the British, he initiated Gita and Qur'an classes for people of the other religion, which unfortunately had to be discontinued because there was just one student each in these classes. "I think at the back of our quarrels is the failure to recognize that all faiths contain enough inspiration for their adherents," he once said. "The Holy Qur'an says in so many words that God sends messengers and warners for all nations and all peoples and they are their respective prophets . . . I would even go further and say that the fundamental principles of all religions are the same, though details differ because each faith takes the flavor of the soil from which it springs."[31] "Badshah Khan told people that Islam operates on a simple principle—never hurt anyone by tongue, by gun or by hand," said Khan's daughter-in-law Nasim Wali. "Not to lie, steal and harm is true Islam."[32]

This Islamic character of the movement, plus the low number of religious minorities in the province, ensured that few non-Muslims were attracted to the movement. But the movement was nonsectarian. When Hindus and Sikhs were attacked in Peshawar, 10,000 Khidmatgar members helped protect their lives and property. And when riots broke out in the state of Bihar in 1946 and 1947, Khan toured with Gandhi to bring about peace. Even Khan's autobiography was narrated by him to a non-Muslim Khidmatgar member. "Although the character of the movement was intensely Islamic, it was also consistently noncommunal [nonsectarian], and one of the objectives of the organization was the promotion of Hindu-Muslim unity," Bondurant observes.[33]

In a biography written by Gandhi's secretary Pyarelal, Khan offers a wonderful interpretation of Islam that deserves to be quoted at length:

Even after the Prophet's exodus from Mecca into Medina his opponents did not leave him in peace. They sent after him a big force to annihilate him. He tried hard to avert a clash but in vain. It was only when he was attacked that he took up arms in self-defense. In Islam that man is considered to be worthy of the highest praise who leads a good life, keeps close to God, and does not return a blow for blow or evil for evil. The Qur'an exalts both justice and generosity, but place generosity above justice. If a man answers a blow with a blow and no more, he practices justice. But if a man is slapped in the face and forgives the injury, he is generous. He is a great and good man, worthy of the highest praise.[34]

"He derives his *ahimsa* (nonviolence) from the Holy Qur'an," Gandhi said about Khan. "He is a devout Muslim. . . . But his devotion to Islam does not mean disrespect for other faiths."[35] His followers, in turn, saw him as blessed, thinking of him as a saint, seer, or prophet. They even attributed miracles to him, such as divining water and having an opponent suffer a stroke.[36]

Mubarak Awad, a Palestinian American who is the executive director of Nonviolence International, has derived inspiration from Ghaffar Khan and has translated his speeches and work into Arabic. (He is profiled in this book, too.) "When I was in India in the early 1980s, I was interested in a Muslim who joined Gandhi not because of his faith in Gandhi but because of his faith in Islam," Awad told me. "I was so happy to learn about him and meet some of his followers."

Awad, who uses Khan's example often, says that he was an eye-opener for a lot of Muslims. "The message of Ghaffar Khan is that people of faith can be strong," Awad says. "He was a soldier of Islam but in a nonviolent way. He showed that even a strong person could be nonviolent."[37]

KHAN'S SOCIAL PROJECT

Ghaffar Khan also astutely took elements of *Pakhtunwali*, the Pashtun tribal code, and made them fit in with his principles. For instance, he told the Pashtuns that true honor—a major part of the code—was best exemplified through the dignified practice of nonviolence. Another notion he used was that of refuge, whereby he turned it around and said that the entire Pashtun population had a duty to give refuge to those campaigning against the British.[38] "My nonviolence has almost become a matter of faith with me. I believed in Gandhiji's *ahimsa* long before," Khan stated. "But the unparalleled success of the experiment in my province has made me a confirmed champion of nonviolence."[39]

For Khan, nonviolence was just a part of a larger social project. Asfandiyar says that his grandfather used to deal with a variety of social problems, including encouraging female education, trying to put a stop to blood feuds, and promoting civic hygiene. He often used to take a broom in his hand and start sweeping the floor, startling his audience, which was not accustomed to seeing such a venerated old man doing this sort of thing. His campaign had a hugely transformative effect on the Pashtuns of the region.

"He was very emphatic about female education," Asfandiyar says. Khan set up a number of schools, including for girls.[40] "In the Pashtun land, whose beautiful daughter gather fuels in the hills and carry it on their heads, reap the harvest and walk through the battlefield," an article said in the *Pakhtun*, a publication established by Khan, "there is no place for *purdah* [gender seclusion]."[41] "If we achieve success and liberate the motherland, we solemnly promise you that you will get your rights," Khan pledged to women. "In the Holy Qur'an, you have an equal share with men. You are today oppressed because we man have ignored the commands of God and the prophet."[42]

The movement encouraged equal participation of women from the start. "Pashtun women participating in nonviolent action campaigns would frequently take their stand facing the police or would lie down in orderly lines holding copies of the Qur'an," Bondurant writes.[43]

Banerjee, much to her disappointment, was able to find only one female Khidmatgar member to interview. The woman, Grana, told her of her prominent role in Khidmatgar activities: "I used to lead processions with a flag in my hand;

3,000 to 4,000 people used to follow me. These were very large processions. . . . I led several men's demonstrations as well."[44]

Banerjee's male interviewees confirmed the prominent role of women in the Khidmatgar movement: "Before Badshah Khan came on the scene, there was the custom of *purdah* in our society. But he talked about educating Pashtuns, even women. When Badshah Khan went to any village to hold a meeting and discuss his ideas, women flocked to meet him and lined the streets to greet him. And the men didn't mind."[45] Khan's family led by example. When a demonstration came under fire, his sister's daughter went to the front to face down the bullets.[46]

KHAN'S LIFESTYLE

Khan lived a simple life and, because of his extensive political activities and lengthy bouts of imprisonment, often neglected his family. "He was a person who denied the luxuries of life first to himself and then wanted you to deny them," Asfandiyar says.

Hiro Shroff, an Indian journalist who met Ghaffar Khan in the 1950s, observed in an article that "his total belongings did not weigh more than a few pounds. His belongings consisted of a bed sheet, a towel and, I think, a spare set of salwar and kameez (clothing). That was all."[47] "He was a very simple man," remembers Begum Nasim. "He had no interest in his family. He dedicated his life to his people."[48]

"His personality seems to act like magic among [the Pashtuns]," wrote Gandhi's son Devdas after a visit to the frontier. "The simplicity of his character and the deep sympathy he evinces for the poor and the oppressed have created for him an abiding place in the hearts of people."[49]

KHAN AND GANDHI

The relationship between Khan and Gandhi is a really interesting one. Khan first saw Gandhi in 1920 but only from a distance. In 1928, at a meeting in Calcutta, Khan first encountered Gandhi and was very impressed with the way he calmly handled a heckler in the audience, in sharp contrast to the boorish attitude that Khan felt that a leading Muslim figure of the time, Mohammed Ali, had. "I found that there was no divergence in the goals that Gandhi was seeking and that I was trying to follow," he said. "Our goals were service of the people and there was no better model or person than Gandhi, who exemplified great virtues any society or nation would cherish."[50]

He first met Gandhi in Lucknow in 1929 at a session of the Congress Party and joined the party in 1930. Khan was completely mesmerized by Gandhi when he heard him assert in 1929 that nonviolence was inherent in all religions, including Islam. Khan, who was quite devout himself, was extremely impressed. From this time on, Khan had an unflinching confidence in Gandhi. During the 1931 Congress session in the city of Karachi, Khan said from the podium that he was a soldier in the command of Gandhi. The Pashtuns, he said, had immense faith in Gandhi, and it was only because of him that they felt Indian. Khan was even invited to be the president of the Congress Party in 1934 but declined, saying that "I am a soldier, a Khudai Khidmatgar, I shall only render service."[51]

His meeting with Gandhi in mid-1929 and his attendance of the Lahore session of the Congress (which asked for complete independence) represented, Gandhian scholar B.R. Nanda says, "a turning point in his life." He even toned down the fire of his speeches after that. He had no more than six months between the founding of the Khidmatgar organization and the start of Gandhi's civil disobedience movement to impart his message of nonviolence to the supposedly violent Pashtuns, but he did so with amazing élan. Gandhi's secretary Pyarelal says that Khan liked Gandhi because he found him a "kindred spirit, a man of faith and prayer dedicated to a pure and ascetic life." But the social project he envisioned pre-dated Gandhi, and he aligned himself with the Congress Party because he knew that in the absence of such backing, the British would not let him go ahead with his plans.[52]

"When they met together, both of them had by then, acquired pre-eminence in public life," writes Gandhian Dr. N. Radhakrishnan. "The unique similarity in their outlook and approach made him believe that in Gandhi he found the one whom he was searching for."[53]

The problem in assessing the size of Gandhi's impact on Khan is that it was so simultaneous with that of Islam that it is hard to know where one ended and the other began. Khan had studied the Qur'an and the life of the early caliphs to derive inspiration for his agenda; Gandhi gave him motivation to apply it on a mass scale. As Nanda point out, "The inspiration for the oath which he prescribed for the Khudai Khidmatgar members came from the Islamic scriptures, but its text was such that Gandhi could have adopted it in toto for members of his ashram."[54]

The term "Frontier Gandhi" was first applied to Khan around 1930, when he was in jail in the Punjab. Khan read Gandhi's autobiography during this period, with a critical eye, and decided to learn from it.[55] Khan had a very ambivalent attitude toward the title bestowed on him. In 1934, addressing a gathering convened to honor him and his brother, Khan said, "Mahatma Gandhi is our general and there should be one general only. So do not add the name of Gandhi to my name."[56]

Khan had unquestioning faith in Gandhi and regarded him as an instrument of God. "Whenever a question of great pith and moment arises in Gandhi's life and Gandhi takes an important decision, I instinctively say to myself, this is the decision of one who has surrendered himself to God, and God never guides ill," Khan once said.[57]

Khan used to meet Gandhi regularly. When he was released from prison in 1945, he first stayed with his son Devdas Gandhi in Delhi, with whom, he says, "I never had the feeling that I was a visitor or a guest." When he went to Bombay, he engaged Gandhi in a conversation about nonviolence, asking how was it that nonviolence was so effective among the Pashtuns, even though he had taught it to them only for a short while. "Nonviolence is not for cowards," Gandhi replied. "It is for the brave and courageous."[58]

Even in the late 1960s, Khan remembered Gandhian precepts with affection. "The message of *khadi* (spun cloth) and *gramodyog* (village industries) that Gandhiji gave us alone can bring deliverance to our suffering people."[59]

KHAN'S NONVIOLENCE IN THE FACE OF BRITISH REPRESSION

In parallel with Gandhi, Khan started a paper, *Pakhtun*, in May 1928 to spread news and information in the Pashto language, which Khan felt strongly attached to. The paper intermittently continued publication from several cities until it was banned, first by the British and then by the Pakistani government. (It has been revived in recent times by the Awami National Party.)

In 1931 in Bombay, the Khidmatgar formally merged with the Congress Party. Some of his colleagues did not take too kindly to this since they thought that Khan had made a bad, unilateral decision to subsume the identity of the Khidmatgar, and two of his colleagues, including the president of the Khidmatgar, Khan Abdul Akbar Khan, left in a huff.[60]

Khan relates that when he came to know of the repression unleashed in the frontier region, he sought the help of the Muslim League (the party that helped establish Pakistan) in combating the British. The League let it be known, however, that it was more interested in fighting Hindus rather than the British. Khan decided to throw in his lot with the Congress. A provincial *jirga* (council) of the Khidmatgar was convened, and it unanimously decided to go with Congress. When the British came to know of this, they were alarmed, and they offered Khan all sorts of inducements and concessions. Khan was firm in his position, however.[61]

The British government desperately tried to link the Khidmatgar to communism. In a communiqué sent to tribal leaders in the area, the chief commissioner stated, "They wear the dress of Bolsheviks and they are nothing but Bolsheviks. They will create the same atmosphere as you have heard of in Bolshevik domination."[62]

And, puzzled by the nonviolence of the Khidmatgar, the British inflicted multiple atrocities on its members. This included stripping them naked, forcing them to bathe in ice-cold water, starving them, and whipping them. The British treated Khan and his movement members with a barbarity that they did not often afflict on other adherents of nonviolence in India because they were so brainwashed by their own stereotypes that they thought the Khidmatgar movement was a ruse by the Pashtuns to deceive them. "The brutes must be ruled brutally and by brutes," a 1930 British report stated. To them, "a nonviolent Pashtun was unthinkable, a fraud that masked something cunning and darkly treacherous," Eknath Easwaran writes in *Nonviolent Soldier of Islam: Badshah Khan, a Man to Match His Mountains*.[63]

After the Gandhi-Irwin Pact of 1931, all political prisoners were released except Khan because the commissioner of the province loathed him, and Gandhi had to personally intervene with the Viceroy Lord Irwin. "Do you mean to say that he, a Pashtun, believes in nonviolence?" Irwin asked Gandhi. "Impossible. No Pashtun does. If they say they do, they are lying. You should go the Frontier Province and see for yourself how nonviolent the Pashtuns are." (Irwin did, however, finally release Khan.)[64]

The British were also comforted by the fact that news from the remote frontier region often did not reach the rest of India. They thus reacted with a singular ferocity, subjecting Khidmatgar members throughout the 1930s and early 1940s to mass killings, torture, and destruction of their homes and fields, transferring large amount of forces from the rest of India and lessening the pressure on Gandhi's movement elsewhere. Khan himself spent more than a decade in prison under the British, often sentenced to hard labor. But the Pashtuns refused to give up their adherence to nonviolence even in the face of this severe repression. In one of the worst incidents, the British killed at least 200 Khidmatgar members in Peshawar on April 23, 1930.

A report of the scene on that day appeared in Gandhi's *Young India* newspaper:

> When those in front fell down wounded by the shots, those behind came forward with their breasts bared and exposed themselves to the fire, so much so that some people got as many as 21 bullet wounds in their bodies, and all the people stood their ground without getting into a panic. . . . The Anglo-Indian paper of Lahore, which represents the official view, itself wrote to the effect that the people came forward one after another to face the firing and when they fell wounded they were dragged back and others came forward to be shot at. This state of things continued from 11 till 5 o'clock in the evening. When the number of corpses became too many, the ambulance cars of the government took them away.[65]

A British military officer writing in the British-edited *Indian Daily Mail* said, "You may take it from me that shooting went on for much longer than has been stated in the newspapers. We taught the blighter a lesson which they won't forget. . . . Our fellows stood there shooting down the agitators and leaders who were pointed out to them by the police. It was not a case of few volleys, it was a case of continuous shooting."[66] The carnage stopped only because a regiment of Indian soldiers finally refused to continue firing on the unarmed protesters, an impertinence for which they were severely punished.

"The two years that followed," writes Yunus, nephew of Ghaffar Khan, "formed an astounding period of darkness for the province. Shooting, beating and other acts of provocation were perpetrated against these people, who had never suffered before without avenging themselves. 'Gunning the Red Shirt' [the Khidmatgar uniform] was a popular sport and pastime of the British forces in the province, observed an American tourist. . . . But the Pashtuns, notwithstanding the fact that they had been brought up in an atmosphere of violence and bloodshed, stood unmoved by such provocations and died peacefully in large numbers for the attainment of their goal."[67]

In just one incident, on August 24, 1930, British troops killed 70 Khidmatgar members in a firing on a crowd of demonstrators. In another, in December 1931, the British killed 50 demonstrators. Gandhi was moved to remark, "Last year, we faced *lathis* (batons). But this time, we must be prepared to face bullets. I do not wish that the Pashtuns in the frontier alone should court bullets." In yet another episode in 1932, British troops killed as many 300 (injuring a thousand more) at a protest against Khan's arrest.[68]

A delegation led by legendary philosopher and activist Bertrand Russell went to the frontier and reported that "the severity of repression has produced something like a war on the Frontier Province. . . . That nonviolence against the persons of British officials still remains the strictly observed rule of the nationalist movement in an area where arms are so readily available and in fact are so openly and usually owned by the villagers is a tribute to the sincerity with which the creed has been embraced."[69]

Gandhi asked a famous anthropologist, Verrier Elwin, to go to the region and prepare a report on the Khidmatgar and the British response. "National activities in this province are largely associated with the name of Khan Abdul Ghaffar Khan," Elwin wrote. "This splendid and heroic figure has captured the imagination of the Pashtuns. Abdul Ghaffar Khan is a great man—great in body, great in heart, great in his possessions, and now truly great in a spiritual outlook on life akin to that of Mahatma Gandhi. . . . The very spirit of nonviolence shines in his face."[70]

Elwin gave remarkable examples of the British repression in the region and how the Khidmatgar remained nonviolent even in the face of such repression. These included mass arrests and collective fines, severe beatings, dousing in the cold waters of rivers, and denial of food. And yet, he said, the "Red Shirts" stuck to their nonviolence. "'We shall do everything we can, even to the giving of our lives, but to bear this *zulum* (repression) without retaliation is indeed hard,'" Elwin reported people telling him. "'But will violence help you?' 'Certainly not.' 'Do you then believe in nonviolence?' 'With all our hearts.'"[71]

The policing methods of the British in the region were so unique that the British government created an uproar when it sought an exemption at the 1933 Air Disarmament Conference to the abolition of air bombing, arguing for an exception for "certain outlying districts," a clear reference to the frontier region.[72] And yet the Khidmatgar remained nonviolent. "The British crushed the violent movement in no time, but the nonviolent movement, in spite of intense repression, flourished," said Khan. "If a Britisher was killed, not only the culprit was punished, but the whole village and entire region suffered for it. In the nonviolent movement, we courted suffering."[73]

The British repeatedly jailed Khan. For instance, after being free for 100 days, Khan was rearrested on December 7, 1934. His four children were left in the care of Gandhi at Wardha ashram in Gujarat. He was sentenced to two years of rigorous imprisonment.[74] "It was . . . faith," his son Ghani Khan said later, when asked how his father endured jail. "The feeling that you are doing the right thing, that even by being in jail you are serving your country, you are giving an example."[75]

When the government of India requested that Khan be moved to the Central Provinces, where Gandhi was already serving time, the government of that state replied, "This government has always shown itself willing to give whatever assistance it could to the government of India in disposing of political prisoners, but that both the Gandhis should be housed within its borders seems to it to be not only undesirable on general grounds but also an undue tax upon its hospitality."[76]

POLITICAL SUCCESS AND GANDHI'S VISITS

In 1931, the Khidmatgar achieved a huge early success by forcing the British to introduce electoral representation in the frontier region, getting them to reverse their earlier reluctance based on security concerns. In 1936, the Khudai Khidmatgar won the provincial elections in the frontier province, and in 1937, after some attempted maneuvering by the opposition party, Khan's brother Abdul Jabbar Khan (or Dr. Khan Saheb as he was called by almost everyone in recognition of his medical degree and stature) was elected the chief minister (the head of the state). The ministry tried to work for the welfare of the people, writes Khan, but was hampered by the fact that much of the power was vested in the British governor. After six years of exile from his home, Khan was allowed to reenter the province in August.[77]

In October, Gandhi's closest confidante and India's future Prime Minister Jawaharlal Nehru paid his first visit to the region and was welcomed by hundreds of thousands. In a rally in Peshawar, Nehru said that Khan was not only "Fakhr-e-Afghan" (pride of the Afghan people) but also "Fakhr-e-Hind" (pride of India). Nehru was so impressed that he came back in January 1937, this time with Khan accompanying him for almost the whole trip. "The province has produced one great man in whom all India took pride," Nehru said. "He has lifted the Frontier people out of the morass, changing the whole atmosphere. He created the great army of Khudai Khidmatgar and mobilized such an arms-loving race for a heroic nonviolent struggle for freedom. It is a miracle that he has performed."[78]

After sending his secretary, Mahadev Desai, to assess the feasibility of a visit, Gandhi made his first trip to the region in 1938, much to the Khan brothers' delight. "You have inspired the greatest man among us—Khan Abdul Ghaffar Khan," said the person giving the address at Islamia College in Peshawar. "You have lifted this great struggle of freedom to the highest moral plane." Gandhi replied, "If, therefore, you really know the essential nature of nonviolence and appreciate Khan Saheb's work, you will have to pledge yourself to nonviolence."[79]

Gandhi traveled as much of the province as his health would permit him, visiting villages and being greeted by enthusiastic Khidmatgar, who, as Gandhi noted, outnumbered nonviolence volunteers in the rest of India. A few months later, Gandhi visited the frontier again, and the climate proved very conducive to his health. Throughout the visit, he kept asking and testing the commitment of

Khidmatgar members to nonviolence, and he kept getting affirmative replies. Khan posted some armed guards to protect Gandhi, and when Gandhi came to know of this, he strenuously objected, citing a parable about how the snake has been attacked for millennia because of its hiss. Khan substituted unarmed guards for armed ones, to which Gandhi reluctantly agreed. Gandhi urged the Khidmatgar to stop bandit raids from the tribal areas, insisting that this would be a true test of their faith in nonviolence. He suggested that batches be sent to Wardha, Gujarat, for training, and that they establish a disciplined and rigorous regimen.[80]

"Even as the rose fills with its sweet fragrance all the air around, when one lakh [100,000] of the Khudai Khidmatgar become truly nonviolent, their fragrance will permeate the entire length and breadth of the country and cure the evil of slavery with which we are afflicted," Gandhi remarked during his travels.[81]

Gandhi toured the region incessantly, traveling a lot and addressing a number of public meetings. In a place called Manshera, there was an address by the inhabitants of the town. They congratulated Gandhi and Khan, "the Pride of the Afghans," for reminding them of the centrality of nonviolence in Islam, which they said they has forgotten.[82]

Gandhi and Khan visited the ruins of Takshila—one of the greatest Buddhist monasteries of its era—at the end of his journey. They reluctantly parted ways, with Gandhi promising to visit again next year. On the train journey back, Gandhi wrote on Khan and the Khidmatgar for *Harijan*, his newspaper, "He wants the Pashtun to become braver than he is and wants him to add true knowledge to his bravery. This, he thinks, can only be achieved through nonviolence."[83] Still, Gandhi knew that Khan had a difficult task ahead of him, even though he expressed his full confidence in his abilities to guide the Pashtuns on the nonviolent path.[84]

In 1939, Khan became involved with a scheme that he thought of in conjunction with Gandhi. It involved trying to get resettled those Hindus and Sikhs who had fled the rural areas in the border region because of repeated tribal raids. Khan and Khidmatgar members gave personal assurances to many displaced and persuaded some of them to return to their homes. At the same time, Khan tried to get more women to participate in the movement. He got Gandhi to send him two prominent Gandhian women, Mirabehn and Bibi Abtus Salam, to help and urged women to contribute more articles to the *Pakhtun* newspaper. "The community in which the women are not well trained can never enjoy freedom," he stated. "The civilization and culture of a community depend to a large extent on the help rendered to it by its womenfolk."[85] Gandhi came to the frontier region for another visit in 1939 but had to curtail his visit because of ill health. He was confined to the hill station of Abbotabad.[86]

WORLD WAR II AND PARTITION

When World War II broke out, the Khidmatgar-led state government, along with all the other state Congress governments, resigned. When the Congress Party decided to give conditional support to the British for the war effort, Gandhi and

Khan stepped down from the Congress Working Committee since they felt that this stance was tantamount to condoning violence.[87]

In a statement, Khan declared, "Because the Pashtuns were previously addicted to violence far more than others, they have profited by nonviolence much more. We shall never really and effectively defend ourselves except through nonviolence. The Khudai Khidmatgar must, therefore, be what our name implies—servants of God and humanity—by laying down our own lives and never taking any life." Gandhi praised his position in the *Harijan*, writing that "it is worthy of Khan Saheb and all he has stood for during the past twenty years."[88]

When the Congress Party changed its stance and launched the "Quit India" movement in 1942, Khan was put in charge of coordinating civil disobedience in the province. Khan founded a Khudai Khidmatgar center on the bank of the Sardaryab River, called Markaz-e-Ala-e-Khudai Khidmatgar, to teach the people of the region the efficacy and rationale of nonviolence. The Khidmatgar came under severe attack on several occasions not only from the British but also from villages and tribes loyal to the British. Undeterred, he held camps for nonviolent training, got sanitation work organized in villages, and taught how to weave cloth on the spinning wheel.

"In the midst of inhuman conflagration which envelopes the world powers who believe in the strength of their arms, little knowing what in reality they are fighting for, it is healthy and uplifting to contemplate what a man like Badshah Khan, the first among the Khudai Khidmatgars, is doing for the cause of peace," Gandhi approvingly noted.[89]

Khan and the Khidmatgar also joined in the campaign of civil disobedience, courting arrest and holding large demonstrations at government buildings. The British responded with predictable fury, beating and arresting large numbers of demonstrators. Khan had two ribs broken while being arrested and was incarcerated in a number of jails. The disturbances were intense for a number of months and then gradually became less.

In 1946, elections were held again in the frontier province. Khan first resisted taking part in the elections, a request to which Gandhi agreed at a meeting of the Congress Working Committee. Khan's reason was that he felt that even if he and his brother were able to form a ministry, it would not be able to do much good for the people because of constraints imposed by the British. He says that he, however, changed his mind when he saw that the Muslim League had recruited people from all over India to come and campaign. Khan alleges that even British women went around campaigning for the Muslim League, exchanging scarves with Pashtun women for the promise of votes. All this made Khan change his mind, and he decided to campaign only one month before the vote. The League made the vote revolve around the matter of religion, asking people if they would vote for the "mosque" or the "temple."[90]

Khan and the Khidmatgar won the elections in spite of opposition from the British. But they were adamant that they would not form a ministry unless the British government officers who misused their posts were punished. Through the intercession of Congress Party leader Maulana Azad, they got the viceroy to promise this and finally formed a government. The Congress ministry under Ghaffar Khan's brother Dr. Khan Saheb that had resigned in 1943 came back to power in 1946 and ordered the release of Ghaffar Khan and the other political prisoners.[91]

Khan was chosen to represent the region at the Indian Constituent Assembly. Later, he was one of three people representing the Congress at the Cabinet Mission meeting in Simla in 1946 to decide the fate of India. He alleges that it was Muslim League leader (and future founder of Pakistan) Muhammad Ali Jinnah's negative attitude that wrecked the negotiations. "We possess more weapons of violence than any other part of India and yet we adopted nonviolent methods," said Khan in a speech in Delhi in 1946 after being elected to the constituent assembly. "Why? I tell you that whether we are Hindus or Muslims, we can win the people only by being nonviolent, because violence breeds hatred and nonviolence generates love."[92]

Soon after this, Nehru visited the area in spite of opposition from the British. The British organized demonstrations against his visit throughout his trip, Khan says. While traveling in Malakand, the entourage was attacked by stones, and disaster was averted only when Ghaffar Khan's brother Dr. Khan picked up a revolver and pointed it at the crowd. At another place, Ghaffar Khan averted a stone meant for Nehru and got injured himself. A pot of filth was thrown at Dr. Khan, who got completely soaked in it. For the rest of Nehru's trip, Khan insisted on having the arrangements done with Khidmatgar members and other sympathetic Pashtuns, who, he says, "were not Red Shirts, and they said that if there was any violence, they would meet it with violence."[93]

Violence was unleashed in Calcutta in 1946 when the Muslim League observed Direct Action Day to press their demand for Pakistan, and this set off a chain of riots all across northern India. The frontier region was also affected with several waves of disturbances. The ministry, headed by Dr. Khan, was reluctant to use too much force because it feared that this would be a pretext for dismissal of the government. But it finally sent 10,000 Khidmatgar members to help restore the peace in Peshawar.[94]

Khan narrated in his autobiography the violence surrounding the partition and how he toured riot-stricken areas of Bihar with Gandhi to help speed up rehabilitation. Khan accused the Muslim League of fomenting violence in Bihar and Bengal and of colluding with the British in trying to destabilize the Khidmatgar ministry.[95] Because of his closeness with Gandhi and his commitment to Hindu–Muslim unity, Khan was firmly opposed to the creation of Pakistan, which was founded as a homeland for the Muslims of the Indian subcontinent. He also thought that the rights of the Pashtuns would be better respected in a large, decentralized united India rather than in a smaller, more centralized Pakistan.

"Mahatmaji, you will henceforth regard us as Pakistani aliens, will you not?" Khan asked Gandhi on the eve of the acceptance of the partition plan by the Congress. "A terrible fate awaits us. We do not know what to do." "Nonviolence knows no despair," Gandhi replied to Khan. "What fear can there be for those who are pledged to do or die? It is my intention to go to the frontier as soon as circumstances permit. I shall not take out a passport because I do not believe in division. And if as a result somebody kills me, I shall be glad to be so killed. If Pakistan comes into being, my place will be in Pakistan."[96]

On June 3, 1947, Lord Mountbatten, the last viceroy of India, unveiled his plan for the partition of India, which included a clause for a referendum in the frontier province. Soon after, the Congress Working Committee met and approved partition and the referendum, much to the astonishment of Khan. Only Gandhi and he were opposed to the plan. Khan never forgave those who went along with India's division.

"We Pashtuns stood by you and had undergone great sacrifices for attaining freedom, but you have now deserted us and thrown us to the wolves," Khan told the working committee. "We shall not agree to hold a referendum because we have decisively won the elections on the issue of Hindustan (India) versus Pakistan and proclaimed the Pashtun view on it to the world. Now as India has disowned us, why should we have a referendum on Hindustan and Pakistan? Let it be on Pashtunistan or Pakistan."[97]

The rest of the members also did not support his demand for a referendum on Pashtunistan. Khan's complaint that Congress had "thrown him to the wolves" became a constant refrain of his over the next many years. "When the Congress Working Committee agreed to the partition of the country and the referendum, I felt as if they had pronounced a death sentence on all the Pashtuns," he wrote in his autobiography.[98]

Khan was so stunned that he came out of the meeting room muttering, "*toba, toba*" (heaven have mercy). When he complained to Gandhi about the position he was in, Gandhi told him, very interestingly, that if the Khidmatgar were mistreated, the Indian government would regard it as a casus belli. (Later, Gandhi assured his son Ghani that even if he was committed to nonviolence, the Indian government was not.)[99]

"I must confess that it also hurt and grieved me deeply that even the Congress Working Committee did not lift a finger to help us, as we had hoped they would," Khan stated in his autobiography. "Tied hand and foot, they delivered us into the hands of our enemies."[100] He reverted to the notion of Pashtunistan from then on.

"Mahatmaji has shown us the true path," Khan remarked during his last meeting with Gandhi. "Long after we are no more, the coming generations of Hindus will remember him as an avatar like the Lord Krishna, Muslims as God's messenger, and Christians as another Prince of Peace. May God spare him for long to give us inspiration and strength to fight for truth and justice to the last." Gandhi, on his part, told him his duty was to make Pakistan *pak* (pure). This was to be their last meeting ever.

"Mahatmaji, I am your soldier," Khan told Gandhi at the railway station the following day when they parted. "I have full faith in you. I look for no other support."[101] "My life's work seems to be over," Gandhi despaired.[102]

The next stage was the holding of a referendum on joining India or Pakistan, which the Khan brothers were opposed to. Nehru wanted them to fight the referendum rather than boycott it. Khan appealed to Gandhi, and even though

Gandhi was in favor of a third Pashtunistan option, the Congress Working Committee overwhelmingly voted against it. Gandhi was caught in the middle because if he encouraged Pashtun independence, he opened a can of worms in the rest of India, and if he didn't, he betrayed his friend. He hence went back and forth and finally remained silent.[103]

Khan pleaded that, at the very least, the referendum should be postponed until conditions had settled down. The Congress high command was of a different opinion, thinking that the referendum was the best option and that the Congress could perhaps even win it. Gandhi suggested to Jinnah that as an alternative to the referendum, he should try to personally tour the region and persuade the people to join Pakistan. When Jinnah said that he was prepared to do this provided that the Congress completely stayed out of the area, Gandhi withdrew his offer. Khan and Jinnah held talks on providing the frontier province a large degree of autonomy within Pakistan, but the talks were inconclusive. The fate of Khan and the Khidmatgar kept Gandhi awake at nights. Khan and his allied organizations reiterated the demand for an autonomous Pashtun state and complained about intimidation and harassment by the Muslim League. They finally decided, much to the chagrin of Jinnah, that if a referendum did not include the option of an autonomous Pashtunistan, they would boycott it. Gandhi pleaded with Khan to keep the boycott peaceful, to which Khan replied that it was the Muslim League that was resorting to intimidation and coercion.[104]

Khan started preparing a boycott of the referendum. He announced the formation of Zalmai Pakhtun, an organization founded by his son Wali that did not disavow violence. He revealed an equivocal attitude toward the organization, maintaining that he was a firm believer in nonviolence but also stressing that circumstances had forced its formation. The Zalmai Pakhtun, like the Khidmatgar, wore deep-red uniforms but unlike Khidmatgar members carried firearms. On June 21, 1947, a joint meeting of the Congress, Khidmatgar, and the Zalmai Pakhtun passed a joint resolution asking for a free Pashtun state based on the "Islamic conception of democracy, equality and social justice."[105]

He considered retiring from politics, partly because of disgust at what he had seen in Bihar, but felt that the Pashtun community needed him at this time of crisis. He appealed in vain to the Muslim League to convene a *jirga* to work out their differences.[106]

The vote was held, and on July 18, 1947, the results were announced: fifty percent of the electorate had abstained, although of those voting a huge proportion had voted in favor of Pakistan. Khan alleged that large-scale rigging and collusion between the British and the Muslim League had taken place and that the League had instigated violence. He again charged the Congress with deserting him. Khan alleges that the British massively misused the machinery, including using the police and the army to canvas for votes and forging signatures. In spite of this, he says, there was no mandate for Pakistan since only 50 percent of people cast their votes.[107]

Khan was still bitter when he narrated in his autobiography many years later that in spite of the clear mandate that his movement received from the people of the region just a year before partition, the British imposed a referendum on choosing between India and Pakistan. He was also angry at the Congress Party's attitude toward the whole affair.[108]

IN PAKISTAN

After partition, Gandhi advised Khan in a letter to migrate to India to escape persecution by the Pakistani authorities. Khan declined, asking him for his blessings. On January 30, 1948, Khan heard of Gandhi's assassination while eating a meal with his son. He was in a daze for a while. He and the Khidmatgar passed a condolence resolution. "He was the only ray of light to help us through these darkest days," Khan lamented.[109]

Ghaffar Khan's travails did not end with the referendum. What made him at odds with the Pakistan government was that he left it deliberately ambiguous whether he wanted Pashtunistan within Pakistan or as a separate country. Khan was inconsistent. Initially, he was very vehement in his criticisms of Pakistan, saying that it was created on the basis of empty slogans and hate and that it would keep the Pakistani people in a perpetual state of fear and war. Afterward, for some years, he toned down his demand for Pashtunistan, claiming that he just wanted the frontier province renamed on a linguistic basis (a demand finally met by the Pakistani government in 2010), along the lines of Sindh or Punjab provinces, and granted genuine autonomy.[110]

The confrontation between Khan and the Pakistani government started almost as soon as the new state was created. Dr. Khan Saheb and his colleagues were invited to an oath-taking ceremony without themselves being asked to take the oath. For a flag-hoisting ceremony afterward, they were warned by the governor that he could not take responsibility for their safety, and they did not attend. A week later, on August 21, 1947, Dr. Khan Saheb and his ministry were dismissed. At a meeting in early September, Khan and his affiliated organizations again put forward a demand for an autonomous Pashtunistan. In the first week of September, there was a massive meeting organized at Sardaryab. The groups represented included the Khidmatgar, the Zalmai Pakhtun, provincial *jirgas*, and representatives of tribal areas. The gathering passed a resolution demanding the right of Pashtuns to manage their affairs internally. "This state will enter into agreement on defense, external affairs and communications with the Dominion of Pakistan," the resolution said.[111] "I have been working for the establishment of Pashtunistan all my life," Khan said. "My path is clear. I will not forsake it even if I stand alone in the world."[112]

All this gave the Pakistani authorities the opportunity to accuse him of antinational activities. They jailed and killed his followers. Khan was imprisoned for more than a decade. This, added to the years that he spent in jail under the British, meant that Khan spent almost three decades in prison. But he never gave up his commitment to his social project and to nonviolence until his death in 1988, even though the Pakistan government banned the Khidmatgar movement and razed its headquarters.

To dispel any misconceptions about Pashtunistan may mean, Khan decided to attend in February 1948 a meeting of the Pakistan Constituent Assembly. He gave a long speech in March at the new Pakistani Parliament defending the notion of Pashtunistan and denying it was inimical to Pakistan, although he complained about the way Pakistan was functioning, including the curtailment of civil liberties in the frontier and the harassment of the Khidmatgar. He met with Jinnah. Still, the fears of the Pakistani government were not allayed.[113]

An interesting incident reported in the press at the time was that 30 Khidmatgar members, at their own expense, formed Khan's bodyguard retinue, protecting him with arms all the time but also showing Khan's deviation from the path of nonviolence at certain times. In the following months, he formed the People's Party with the Sindhi ethnic leader G. M. Syed, spurning offers from the Muslim League. Jinnah did initially show some desire to work with Khan but, Khan charges, misled by League officials in the frontier region, became aloof and uncooperative. When he met Jinnah, he complained about rampant corruption among League officials, further alienating Jinnah. Jinnah advised him to merge his organization into the Muslim League. Khan refused, on which Jinnah turned bitterly against him, asking the Pashtuns to "totally disown such people who make a pretension of loyalty to the Pakistan state but are out really to weaken its edifice."[114]

In May 1948, Khan announced that he was going to make the Khidmatgar a nationwide organization and have that serve as the nucleus of the Pakistan People's Party. The party demanded that Pakistan be a union of socialist republics, with full provincial autonomy, and that there be good relations with neighbors, particularly India. The party also called for the end of repression and the release of the "Baluch Gandhi," Abdus Samad Khan Achakzai, from prison. On June 15, 1948, Khan was arrested, along with his son Wali and two others. He had criticized Jinnah as a British agent and alleged that power in Pakistan had been taken over by immigrants from India. The Khudai Khidmatgar was subsequently banned in July 1948. At his trial, he was charged with sedition. He refused to defend himself or to even provide bail. He was sentenced to three years of rigorous imprisonment and sent to jail in Punjab, not being allowed to take his belongings or meet his companions.[115]

For the next six years, Khan was almost continuously in prison or under house arrest by the Pakistani government. Soon after his arrest, on August 12, 1948, in a gruesome incident, Khidmatgar members—some of them women carrying the Qur'an—were fired on outside a mosque. At least 150 people died, perhaps many times more. Several others were stripped and humiliated. Provincial officials alleged that Khan was in cahoots with India. In response, Nehru issued a statement expressing concern about the treatment of Khan and the Khidmatgar but denying any contact whatsoever. The Afghan government also expressed concern. Meanwhile, the Pashtuns of the frontier mobilized and hoisted the flag of independence.[116]

The Pakistani government claimed that he was being kept under good conditions, but Khan suffered from bad teeth, loss of weight, and other ailments. Even when he was released, along with his brother Dr. Khan Saheb and Achakzai (the "Baluch Gandhi"), he was placed under house arrest. His newspaper was banned, and the Khidmatgar two-story training center was razed.[117]

After this, Khan's life had many twist and turns, but he never reconciled himself fully to the notion of Pakistan. In 1954, he gave a speech to the Pakistani Parliament, where he said that he was ready to have his loyalty examined by a judicial tribunal if a tribunal also examined the killing of his followers and the shabby treatment he received in jail. He also dismissed the allegation that the East Pakistan (afterward to become Bangladesh) movement was secessionist in nature. Later that year, a single unit, dissolving all the constituent states, was established in West Pakistan, and Khan's brother, Dr. Khan Saheb, was won over to the extent that he agreed to become the chief minister of this unit. Khan was, however, resolutely opposed to the notion and began an agitation against it. Khan complained of continued restrictions on him visiting the frontier and of being tailed around all the time. He addressed a number of public meetings— including a visit to the site where Khidmatgar members had been gunned down a few years earlier—and constantly campaigned against the one-unit scheme. He joined forces with the Baluch Gandhi and was arrested again when he tried to cross over into Baluchistan at his invitation.[118]

In June 1956, both of them were arrested, this time with the intention of keeping them behind bars for a longer period of time. Khan submitted a 19-page written statement to the court in his defense. It detailed his background and his work, denying that he had any dishonorable intentions toward Pakistan or any plan to secede from the country. He did say that he had worked with the Congress Party and against partition but said that this was because the Muslim League was unwilling to join him and because he felt that the Muslim masses would be better served by a united socialist republic rather than a Pakistan dominated by capitalists and landlords. He reiterated that his demand for a Pashtunistan was just for greater autonomy and that Jinnah had been poisoned by his underlings against him. The court wasn't impressed. It imposed a sentence and a fine on him, and the judge asked him to "desist from indulging in activities which have a tendency to malign the country of which he is a citizen."[119]

Khan kept up his campaigning. In 1957, he joined the Pakistan National Party and demanded a federated linguistic system. In July 1957, Khan got together with others dissatisfied with the ruling coterie of Pakistan and formed the National Awami Party. The crisis in Pakistan worsened, and a succession of governments fell. On May 9, 1958, Dr. Khan Saheb was assassinated. Khan urged a full investigation into the murder and worried that it would deepen tensions between the Punjabis and the Pashtuns. Khan alleged that his brother had been killed by those very same people for whom he had compromised his career and his integrity.[120]

Khan was arrested that September and October. After a number of months in jail, Khan was released on grounds of old age but was barred by the military ruler, Ayub Khan, to contest any elections until 1966. He was detained again in 1961, along with hundreds of his coworkers. Ayub Khan accused him of wanting the secession of the frontier region. Amnesty International adopted him in 1962 as the "Prisoner of the Year." His son Wali Khan asserted in 1963 that thousands of Khidmatgar members were rotting in jails and that their property, worth billions of rupees, had been confiscated. He charged that his father was imprisoned in harsh conditions, an allegation that the Pakistani government denied. Khan suffered a host of illnesses while in Pakistani prisons. He was kept in solitary confinement and experienced partial kidney failure while imprisoned in Hyderabad. From there, he was sent to Lahore, where he finally went on hunger strike in protest. Finally, when his health started deteriorating, Khan was released on January 30, 1964. Khan was thoroughly embittered by this time with the Pakistani government, calling martial law in Pakistan much worse than martial law under the British and asking the people to throw out the military regime in the same way that the British were ousted.[121]

He began to exhibit high blood pressure and was finally allowed to go to England after being shunted around from prison to prison. Nehru remained worried about Khan's well-being until the end, and Khan mourned his death on May 27, 1964. Khan, ailing, went to England in September 1964. There he met his old nemesis Sir Olaf Caroe, the former governor of the frontier province, and other Britishers and changed his opinion of his former rulers.[122]

Nehru's daughter (and future prime minister) Indira Gandhi came to visit him, there, too. From there, Khan's plan was to go to the United States once the weather got colder in England. But U.S. embassy officials summoned him a number of times (he was treated "like a schoolboy," he says), and he finally gave up in frustration. Apparently, the U.S. government did not want to antagonize the Pakistani government. To make matters more complicated, his expenses in the United States were being guaranteed by the founder of the Pashtunistan movement in the United States. He finally went to Afghanistan, overcoming Pakistani government maneuvers to keep him from going there. While there, he corresponded with Gandhian Vinoba Bhave, returning to his theme about how the Congress had betrayed him. When an Indian parliamentary delegation came to meet him on the way back from Finland, Khan received them warmly but repeated this complaint.[123]

Meanwhile, Pakistan's military dictator Ayub Khan instituted policies that helped open the Pakistan–Afghanistan border and improve the economic situation for Pashtuns. A critic of Khan, Pakistani writer M. S. Korejo alleges that Khan was planning a tribal invasion of Pakistan and that this was stopped only because of the 1965–66 India-Pakistan War (though this isn't backed up by other scholars). Ayub Khan was succeeded by Yahya Khan, who held general elections in 1970. The National Awami Party, formed by Ghaffar Khan, formed the government in the state of Baluchistan and, in coalition, in the frontier province. It also helped draft the first democratic constitution of Pakistan, but soon after its relations with the government of Zulfikar Ali Bhutto worsened because of allegations that it had a hand in violent secessionist unrest in Baluchistan. Wali Khan became more involved in the politics of Pakistan, to the disappointment of his father, who still wasn't fully reconciled to the concept of Pakistan. "My son Wali Khan does not represent me. All he wants is some job or some portion from the Punjabis and he will remain in Pakistan satisfied," Khan said.[124]

In an interesting critique, Korejo points out that while Gandhi undertook a number of fasts in the last months of his life, Khan, in spite of a number of grievances, almost never did, with the notable exception of Ahmedabad in 1969. (The Indian city was convulsed by Hindu–Muslim riots shortly before Khan visited it for Gandhi's centennial. In protest, Khan went on a hunger strike.) Was it because he felt he lacked the stature of a Gandhi? Certainly his espousal of Pashtun nationalism left him without a broader base to challenge the Pakistani state in spite of his playing a pivotal role in the formation of various parties like the Pakistan People's Party and the National Awami Party.[125]

Gandhi's secretary Pyarelal visited him in 1965 in Kabul, Afghanistan, and found him adhering to the same ideals and living a frugal existence in the autumn of his life. He told Pyarelal that his teaching of nonviolence spread through education by direct, personal touch. "We told the Khudai Khidmatgar that they could serve God only by serving His creatures," Khan said. He claimed that his present movement was garnering even more support since people were not enslaved and brainwashed, as they were in British times.[126]

Khan initially wasn't inimical to the Soviet invasion of Afghanistan since he was disgusted by the atrocities of the ousted President Hafizullah Amin. But before not too long, he became firmly opposed to the Soviet intervention and even prodded Indian Prime Minister Indira Gandhi to take a clearer stance.[127]

Khan refused to rest in spite of frequent jailing, detentions, and hospitalizations. He made two trips to India in his nineties, in 1985 to take part in the centenary of the Indian National Congress, with which both Gandhi and he were associated, and in 1987 to receive the country's highest civilian honor.[128]

Khan's bitterness with Pakistan comes through in his autobiography. "In the course of the first eighteen years of the existence of Pakistan, I spent fifteen years in prison," he says. "And during this imprisonment—and may God save you all from this experience, Amen!—thousands of Khudai Khidmatgars lost their lives. They were not only imprisoned, but treated very badly and cruelties that no man can endure were inflicted upon them." He accuses the Pakistani government of numerous atrocities and compares them on several occasions unfavorably to the British. "The British had never looted our homes, but the Islamic government of Pakistan did," he says. "The British had never treated the Pashtun women disrespectfully, but the Islamic government of Pakistan did. I could go on and on but what's the use?"[129]

It is fascinating to see what the autobiography focuses on and what it doesn't. Although it mentions Gandhi respectfully on a number of occasions, he is far from a central character in it. There is no mention of Khan acquiring the title "Frontier Gandhi," although, interestingly, there is mention of him being bestowed the title of "Fakhr-e-Afghan." This reflects the concerns of Khan at the time, who was casting himself as a leader of the Pashtuns when he narrated the book rather than as a Gandhian. The book's central themes reflect this preoccupation, dwelling on the lot of the Pashtuns and the injustices suffered by them first at the hands of the British and then the Pakistani government, which emerges as the chief villain in the book. Interestingly, even when I spoke with his family, they downplayed the importance of Gandhi in his life, saying only that he occasionally mentioned Gandhi.

Khan died in January 1988 at the age of 98 after a prolonged illness. His funeral, like his life, was full of ups and downs. The border was opened up for a day, with all the warring parties declaring a cease-fire, and Pashtuns and his well-wishers poured in from all over Pakistan and Afghanistan by the multitude. Both Indian Prime Minister Rajiv Gandhi and Pakistani military dictator Muhammad Zia ul-Haq (in spite of the fact that he had arrested Khan as a 93-year-old) came to pay their respects. Bombs planted in some of the vehicles killed a number of people, however, and marred the moment. He was buried in the city of Jalalabad in Afghanistan, as he had desired.[130]

A top Pakistani civil servant confided to a journalist after retirement that if the Pakistani government had shown Khan even a little bit of respect, he wouldn't have been antagonistic at all. At a conference in honor of Khan, Ajmal Khattak, a leader of the Awami National Party, pointed out that Khan had been known by many names, including *Baba-e-Pakhtun, Baba-I-Pakhtunkhwa,* father of peace and father of destiny. He insisted, however, that the best title for him was *Baba-I-Asar:* the father who molded minds and hence changed history. One of the speakers at the conference, Malik Qasim, did point out that in spite of Khan's impact, none of his followers in Afghanistan or Pakistan thought of even attempting to stop the fratricide in Afghanistan or providing humanitarian relief. The major legacy that he did leave behind was the Awami National Party run by his family heirs (which is, amazingly, back in power in the province, partly out of the cachet given to it by Ghaffar Khan, as attested to by his prominence on the party's Web site).[131]

Why is the existence of such a remarkable personality almost a secret in the West? (Secretary of State Hillary Clinton did cite him, though, in a recent speech.[132]) It's for a number of reasons. First, he has been given a raw deal in South Asia itself. Because of his differences with the Pakistani authorities, Khan has been completely written out of official Pakistani history. Hence, he is almost unknown in Pakistan outside the frontier area (where the party run by his family is back in power). Some of my Pakistani friends are barely aware of him. "There's been a complete erasure of the man and the movement from Pakistani historiography," Banerjee says. "The younger generation even in that region hasn't heard of him."[133]

There was little distinction between the Khidmatgar and the Congress in the years immediately preceding independence and partition. Khan's association with Gandhi hurt him terribly during the creation of Pakistan, when the Muslim League was able to brand him as an Indian in disguise. If he is known at all, it is a Pashtun nationalist rather than as a proponent of nonviolence and social reform. This is partly due to the fact that the Awami National Party prefers to play up this side of his legacy. Banerjee feels that this silence about him in Pakistan—in contrast to the amount of work done on Gandhi in India—is largely to blame for why he is so unknown. Khan's treatment by the Pakistani authorities, Banerjee says, left him disgusted and disillusioned with politics.[134]

Even in India, Ghaffar Khan has been handled with unfairness. Most often, he is portrayed as an adjunct of Gandhi (hence the term "Frontier Gandhi"). Far from being seen as an amazing movement in its own light, the Khidmatgar movement is often seen in India as a curious anomaly formed largely because of Gandhi's charismatic influence on Khan and the Pashtuns. Typical is Prime Minister Indira Gandhi's comment that Khan was the greatest disciple of the Mahatma.[135]

Indian writers often attribute Khan's attributes as completely derived from Gandhi, a distortion: "Born in a community for its fierce martial qualities, Khan Abdul Ghaffar Khan—popularly known as the Frontier Gandhi or Badshah Khan—became a staunch convert to Gandhi's ideal of nonviolence and never even once did stray from the straight and narrow path the Mahatma set for his followers. He considered Gandhi as his master and, like Gandhi, he fought the British without hating them."[136]

But Ghaffar Khan started forming his project of nonviolence and social re-form before he came into contact with Gandhi. And his nonviolence drew its inspiration from the Qur'an and the Prophet Muhammad, in contrast to Gandhi, whose ideals were based largely on the Hindu holy book (the Bhagavad Gita), the Bible, and the writings of Thoreau and Tolstoy. "Khan talked about the ab-sence of violence very early on, as he indicates in his autobiography," Banerjee says. "His contact with Gandhi after 1930 bolstered this, since Gandhi offered him a philosophical exposition."[137] "There is nothing surprising in a Muslim or a Pashtun like me subscribing to the creed of nonviolence," Khan said. "It is not a new creed. It was followed fourteen hundred years ago by the prophet all the time when he was in Mecca."[138] "We did not follow nonviolence because Gandhi told us," a Khidmatgar member told Banerjee. "We followed it because in Islam our prophet said that violence does not solve anything."[139]

There are other factors that contribute to Khan's obscurity. "Gandhi left be-hind an enormous amount of written work," Banerjee says. "With Khan, the whole thing dies with him, apart from his autobiography." Nonviolence propo-nent Mubarak Awad says that Khan is not well known in the West because of prejudices about Islam. "It's because he's a Muslim," Awad says. Awad agrees with Banerjee that Khan's lack of a body of work and his choice to spend his life in Pakistan and Afghanistan, rather than touring the West, have also contributed to his anonymity.[140] But this shouldn't keep us from recognizing the remarkable journey embarked on by Khan and his fellow Pashtuns—a community given a terrible name by the Taliban. For his people, Khan had a fourfold message: Pash-tun nationalism, personal and social reform, nonviolence, and Islam.[141]

Khan's "claim to a Muslim platform is certainly not weaker than that of Osama bin Laden or Mullah Omar," writes Rajmohan Gandhi, the Mahatma's grandson. "The open and accessible life of Badshah Khan, who was rooted in the Peshawar valley, with links to Jalalabad and Kabul, is a contrast to the concealed and mys-terious figure of Kandahar's Mullah Omar."[142]

Certainly, Khan was not perfect. He could be self-important and stubborn, qualities that he shared with Gandhi. His immersion in religion may discomfit some staunch secularists. His commitment to women's rights, although remarkably progressive for the time and place, would perhaps still fall short of today's notions of full equality. In addition, the devolution of his political beliefs into that of advocacy for Pashtun rights, instead of the construction of a broader platform, left him open to the charge of sectarian politics. Incidentally, he had very little impact in the tribal Pashtun regions (as opposed to the "settled" areas around cities like Peshawar) since the British strictly forbade him from establishing any contact with the people in those parts.

But his achievements were certainly many, and his neglect in the West is quite unfair. Not only is he virtually unknown in this country, but he's even largely ignored among U.S. scholars of nonviolence, as Professor Stephen Zunes, chair of Middle Eastern studies at the University of San Francisco, confirmed for me. There isn't a single full-length biography of his written by a Western author (though famed media theorist Marshall McLuhan's daughter, Teri, has made a recent documentary on him in very difficult circumstances).

"The naturalness of his Islam, his directness, his rejection of violence and revenge, and his readiness to cooperate with non-Muslims add up to a valuable legacy for our angry times," writes Rajmohan Gandhi. "The legacy may be of help to Muslims and non-Muslims today in the task of overcoming divides between Islam and the West (and modernity)."[143]

Nonviolence, religious tolerance, women's rights, and social justice—certainly Khan could have done a lot worse than try to spread these ideals. And he did it while deriving his inspiration from a religion vilified by some as being intrinsically intolerant and practiced it among people thought by many to be inherently violent and incapable of social reform. Khan deserves a better fate than to languish in obscurity. And we need to learn from Khan and the Khidmatgar movement how wrong it is to label entire cultures and religions. The "Frontier Gandhi" is a person whose achievements can truly be compared with the original.

CHAPTER 7

Following in the Mahatma's Footsteps: Muslim Gandhians

GANDHI AND ISLAM

A little-known fact in the West is the number of prominent Muslims who joined with Gandhi in the Indian freedom struggle against the British, adopting his values of nonviolence and religious harmony. The most amazing case, of course, is Ghaffar Khan, exemplary enough to claim a chapter of his own in this book. But there were several others who deserve to be brought into the limelight.

Gandhi himself followed a strand of Hinduism that with its emphasis on service and on poetry and songs bore similarities to Sufi Islam. "The devotional character of Hindu songs and the appeal which the language made to Sufis brought Hindus and Muslims closer together than any other influence," writes historian Muhammad Mujeeb. Gandhi's family was very open-minded, and Gandhi himself had an assortment of friends from various religious backgrounds since a young age. His mother, Putlibai, though a Hindu, belonged to the syncretic Pranami sect, which drew a lot from Islam.[1]

When Gandhi went to South Africa to work as a lawyer, he came to know well a number of Muslims, such as his employer, a Muslim-owned business firm. It was here he launched his first campaign, one against discrimination toward Asians in that country—a category that included both Hindus and Muslims. Gandhi attempted to bond both communities together and tried to come up with a Hindu equivalent of jihad defined in the most rightful way. The result was *satyagraha* (a term now globally famous), literally meaning "truth force" but having connotations of civil disobedience. Here, Gandhi showed his "extraordinary facility in using language to inspire and direct the religious awareness of his hearers," writes scholar Sheila McDonough. From then on, he was convinced of the need for unity between Hindus and Muslims.[2]

Once Gandhi came back to India, he joined in several movements with a number of Muslims, a number of whom are profiled in this book. Although some of these campaigns were more successful than others, he succeeded in forming lasting bonds. He was dogged throughout, however, by his chief adversary, Muhammad Ali Jinnah, whose vision of a separate state for the subcontinent's Muslims contrasted sharply with his. And when India's partition came about, the accompanying violence left him distraught. But he never gave up his idea of "heart unity" between Hindus and Muslims, and his last fast was impelled in good part as protest against the forced exodus of Muslims from Delhi. He was assassinated in January 1948 by a Hindu extremist for allegedly being too pro-Muslim.[3]

Gandhi studied the work of Muslim reformer Shibli Numani and through him the lives of early Muslim leaders to understand how to combine piety with creative action. For him, Muslim extremism was based on "a corrupt understanding of Islam." "Islam is not a false religion," he said. "Let Hindus study it reverently, and they will love it even as I do. . . . If Hindus set their house in order, I have not a shadow of doubt that Islam will respond in a manner worthy of its liberal traditions."[4]

Gandhi was adept at using Islamic imagery to inspire Muslims. He thought the Prophet Muhammad's struggles akin to the efforts of the Hindu God Ram to set up a new society. He compared Muhammad's exodus to Medina to India's independence campaign. And he cited the martyrdom of Hasan and Hussain, the grandsons of Muhammad, comparing them to the Hindu notions of self-sacrifice and renunciation.[5] (At a gathering in Baghdad in 2010, Iraqi Member of Parliament Ali al-Allaq proudly noted Gandhi's invocation of Hussain, proving for the umpteenth time the incredible resonance of a good example.)[6]

Muslims often reciprocated Gandhi's affection. "Our Hindu brothers . . . are our brothers in all truth, for the Holy Qur'an teaches that the friends of the faith are our brothers," two Muslim leaders, Hakim Ajmal Khan and Mukhtar Ansari, said in 1922. "Let us remain faithful to our cause, our country, and to the leader we have chosen—Mahatma Gandhi." Another prominent Muslim, Abid Husain, declared, "In Calcutta and Noakhali, the fire of hatred was put out by the love of by Mahatma Gandhi."[7] And then there are the various effusive praises that the Muslim personalities profiled in this book heaped on him. "We can suggest that Muslim trust of Gandhi was based on four things: his respect for religion and religious commitment; his regard for Muslims as full members of what he once called India's 'joint family'; his peace-loving nature; and his honest friendship," writes scholar Roland Miller.[8]

AN EARLY GANDHIAN

Muslims in India joined the independence movement even before Gandhi became a force. Wedded to an inclusive nationalism—filled with mutual religious tolerance and respect—and nonviolence as a means of achieving independence, such figures were true trailblazers. One such person was Badruddin Tyabji, a Muslim lawyer and judge at the turn of the century and president of Gandhi's Congress Party decades before Gandhi took control of the organization. "In the main, he was concerned to life the Muslims from the decadence of their recent past and guide them into the national mainstream so that they could be at one with the rest of their countrymen in India's march to her destiny, and yet remain true to themselves—ardent Indians and devout Muslims at the same time," writes biographer A.G. Noorani. His central project was the education and upliftment of Muslims and to preserve the secular and composite nature of Indian society. He had a huge impact on future Indian President Zakir Husain (profiled later in this chapter), who said, "The influence of great personalities, even at second hand, can be the most effective educative force. And this was the case with me with the late Badruddin Tyabji."[9]

Tyabji achieved greatness in two legal spheres. He became the first Indian barrister and the first Indian judge in Bombay. "In India's legal history, there have been great lawyers and great judges, but very few who have been both," writes Noorani.[10] Tyabji was one of the pivotal figures in the early Indian nationalist movement. "The staunch and unflinching support he so constantly extended to the Indian National Congress was a source of great strength to that organization in its infancy," Noorani writes. "Perhaps his greatest service lay in articulating his broad, tolerant outlook in delineating for the Muslims a course of action which would conduce both to national integration and to the preservation of Muslim culture and the values dear to Muslims." Gandhi recalled with admiration on a number of instances Tyabji's services to his party, saying that "Badruddin Tyabji was for years a decisive factor in the deliberations of the Congress."[11]

"His aim was Indian unity—a united India," the *Madras Standard* newspaper wrote in a eulogy when he passed away in 1906. "He had the sagacity to see and the energy, capacity and patriotism to work for a brighter and more prosperous future for India." Another tribute summarized his contribution both to the Muslim community and to India, saying that he excelled in both spheres since he "represented a principle, and not a class or a community. . . . Great as he was as a leader among Muslims, he was greater still as a leader of Indians."[12]

THE GANDHIAN THEOLOGIAN

Perhaps the foremost Indian Muslim Gandhian was a remarkable person named Abul Kalam Azad. (Ghaffar Khan was Pakistani for a good portion of his life.) Azad was a renowned theologian—no less—who was awarded the title of *maulana* for his religious achievements. Azad stood with Gandhi's movement through thick and thin and served as the president of the Congress Party and after India's independence as the country's education minister.

Azad "remains an icon of secular nationalism in India," writes scholar Rahil Khan for a UCLA Web site.[13] Ramin Jahanbegloo, an Iranian dissident intellectual in exile in Canada, considers Azad a role model for Muslims in his advocacy

of pluralism and peace. "Maulana Azad clearly accepted principles of nonvio-
lence and participated in Mahatma Gandhi's nonviolent movement," writes
Jahanbegloo. "The end result was Azad's unequivocal endorsement of Hindu-
Muslim peaceful coexistence in an independent India."[14]

A seminal speech by Azad deserves to be quoted at length since it exemplifies
his way of thinking:

> Eleven hundred years of common history have enriched India with our
> common achievements. Our languages, our poetry, our literature, our cul-
> ture, our art, our dress, our manners and customs, the innumerable hap-
> penings of our daily life, everything bears the stamp of our joint endeavor.
> There is indeed no aspect of our life which has escaped this stamp.[15]

Azad grew up in a conservative environment. Born in Mecca as the son of
a traditional Muslim scholar, Azad's background was not that of someone you
would think would be a symbol of a progressive, inclusionary Islam. But from
the start he proved to be of a different mettle. Once he completed the standard
curriculum at the age of 16, he opted for the Islamic tradition of reinterpretation
of the scriptures rather than conformity. He then taught himself English and
learned a variety of subjects, including Western philosophy and politics.[16]

"He was fifty years old the day he was born," said fellow freedom fighter Sa-
rojini Naidu in admiration of all that Azad accomplished as a young man. Azad
was impressed by the ideas of other modern Muslim thinkers such as Sir Syed
Ahmed Khan, the founder of Aligarh Muslim University, one of India's most
prestigious institutions of higher learning.[17]

In 1912, he launched his major intellectual project, *Al Hilal,* a newspaper that
preached Islamic concepts in a progressive-minded way—Hindu–Muslim unity, religious tolerance, and adherence to nonviolence. He spent a good amount of space
in the paper refuting the arguments of those who asserted otherwise. The paper's
mix of journalism, opinion, and literature proved to be a hit with Indian readers
but not so much with the British, who fined and banned the publication repeatedly and put its founder in jail. All the time, Azad preached religious harmony.[18]

"Islam does not commend narrow-mindedness and racial and religious prejudice," Azad wrote in 1913. "It does not make the recognition of merit and virtue
of human benevolence, mercy and love dependent upon and subject to distinctions of race and religion. Rather, Islam actually teaches us to respect every man
who is good, whatever his religion, and to be drawn towards merits and virtues,
whatever be the religion or race of the person who possesses them."[19]

Azad attempted to establish a seminary with donated money to preach his
version of Islam, but the institution died an early death because of his stints in
jail. He then embarked on a translation of the Qur'an, but the British confiscated
his work.[20]

Azad was especially troubled by the sectarianism within the Muslim community
and the intolerance each sect showed toward adherents of different beliefs. "If religion expresses a universal truth, why should there be such differences and conflicts

among men professing different religions?" Azad asked. "Why should each religion claim to be the sole repository of truth and condemn all others as false?"[21]

Such questions led to deep anguish as he searched within himself. This period lasted as long as two-three years. At the end, Azad had a catharsis. "I passed from one phase to another and a stage came when all the old bonds imposed on my mind by family and upbringing were completely shattered," writes Azad in his memoir. "I felt free of all conventional ties and decided that I would chalk out my own path. It was about this time that I decided to adopt the pen name 'Azad' or "free' to indicate that I was no longer tied to my inherited beliefs."[22]

At the same time, he became more and more of a nationalist. He was first attracted to pan-Islamic doctrines but then became drawn to revolutionary doctrines in Bengal province. Azad's politics careened so much leftward for a time that he became a member of underground revolutionary movements in that state (where they were prevalent), becoming one of the very few Muslim members. The other members were initially suspicious of him but realized soon that he was trustworthy and dependable. He, in fact, suggested expanding such activities to other major cities in India.[23]

He was first imprisoned in 1920. In that year itself, Azad met Gandhi and, "without a moment's hesitation . . . fully accepted the program." He grew closer and closer to Gandhi and along with other nationalist Muslims helped found in Delhi the Jamia Milia University, to date one of the most important Indian institutions of higher learning. He became increasingly wedded to Gandhi's ideals, such as nonviolence and simple living.

"As soon as Gandhiji described his proposal, I remembered that this was the program which Tolstoy had outlined many years ago," states Azad. "To indulge in political murder was to sow the dragon's teeth. . . . The proper method to paralyze an oppressive government was to refuse taxes, resign from all services and boycott institutions supporting the government. . . . Such a program would compel any government to come to terms. I also remembered that I had myself suggested a similar program in some articles in *Al Hilal*."[24]

Rajmohan Gandhi, the Mahatma's grandson, points out that, actually, Azad had not talked much about nonviolence until this point. But that did not stop him from embracing Gandhi's message instantly.[25] In 1922, he offered a statement in court in defense that Gandhi termed "the most forceful and truthful statement offered by a *satyagrahi* (nonviolent protester)": "When I ponder on the great and significant history of the convicts' dock and find that the honor of standing in that place belongs to me today, my soul becomes steeped in thankfulness and praise of God."[26]

He did disagree in the same year with Gandhi when Gandhi called off the independence movement after a mob had burned a police station with policemen inside. Azad thought this to be impractical; it also created fissures between Hindus and Muslims since Muslims thought this to be an example of Gandhi's lack of consultation with Muslim leaders.[27]

Interestingly, Azad makes it clear at several junctures in his memoir that for him, unlike for Gandhi, nonviolence was much more of a political tactic. In this, he wasn't too different from many other associates of Gandhi, including the most famous of them all, Jawaharlal Nehru. (The significant exception here was Abdul Ghaffar Khan, whose devotion to nonviolence rivaled Gandhi's.)

"For me, nonviolence was a matter of policy, not of creed," he writes. "In the circumstances which obtained in the country, Gandhiji's method was right. Our decision to fight nonviolently was therefore compelled by circumstances."[28]

Because of his perspective, Azad sometimes even came into conflict with Gandhi. "Gandhiji stood firm in his view that nonviolence was a creed and must not be given up in any circumstances," Azad writes. "I repeated my earlier view that Congress must place greater emphasis on the freedom of India than on nonviolence as a creed."[29]

Azad was unequivocal, however, in his condemnation of violence as a tactic to win India's independence. When there was vacillation among his colleagues about violence by a mob, he made his position clear. "In all national movements, a stage is reached when the leaders have to decide whether they should lead or follow the masses," Azad writes. "It seemed that in India we had reached that stage. If the Congress Party believed that the Indian problem could be solved only through peaceful methods, Congressmen must be prepared to carry that message to the people and act according to it."[30]

In 1923, he was awarded the honor of becoming the youngest man to be elected the president of the Congress Party. He spent much of the following years traveling around and spreading the message of the party and the Gandhian vision. He was unswerving in his commitment to a secular state, calling repeatedly for a nondenominational independent India and an end to the British-imposed system of separate electorates based on religion.[31]

Azad's commitment to religious pluralism was paramount:

> If an angel descends from the heavens today and proclaims from the Qutb Minar [a famous Indian monument] that India can attain *swaraj* [independence] provided I relinquish my demand for Hindu-Muslim unity, I shall retort to it: "No my friend, I shall give up *swaraj,* but not Hindu-Muslim unity, for if *swaraj* is delayed, it will be a loss for India, but if Hindu-Muslim unity is lost, it will be a loss for the whole of mankind."[32]

Muslim scholar Mujeeb says of Azad that "the Qur'an inspired all his thinking" and that he avoided the pitfalls of "accepting traditional interpretations by deriving his opinions from other sources." Azad's writings did have a tension in that they championed an Islam of the past, but this was accompanied by a pluralistic and tolerant outlook. His commentaries are "perhaps the finest example of the constructive thinking enjoined on the Muslim," says Mujeeb. Western scholar Wilfred Cantwell Smith said, "Azad is a thoroughly profound scholar of Islam, his scholarship being liberal in the very best sense. . . . His Islam is humanitarian."[33]

In conjunction with Gandhi's famous salt march in 1930, Azad organized a nonviolent raid on a saltworks in Dharasana to protest the British tax on salt. He went to jail as a consequence along with numerous others. He was frequently jailed in subsequent years. He campaigned vigorously in the mid-1930s for the Congress Party in elections, though he didn't contest himself. He also came into increasing tensions with the right wing of the Congress Party over his commitment to socialism and his advocacy of a dialogue with Jinnah's Muslim League. His adherence to Gandhi and his criticism of Jinnah increased as time went on and as the Muslim League became more and more adamant about a separate nation for the subcontinent's Muslims. His stature in Gandhi's Congress Party grew, with his being elected a second time as party president in 1939.

On the occasion, he gave a famous speech in which he argued for the composite culture of India: "If Hinduism has been the religion of the people here for several thousands of years, Islam also has been their religion for a thousand years. Just as a Hindu can say with pride that he is an Indian and follows Hinduism, so also we can say with equal pride that we are Indians and follow Islam."[34]

All the while, the interreligious atmosphere was degenerating. Azad dedicated himself to religious harmony, on occasion even rescuing members of beleaguered communities trapped as a result of religious riots. The demand for Pakistan divided the Indian Muslim community, with Azad firmly coming down on the side of a united India. He was the target of increasing criticism by Jinnah, who called him "a Muslim showboy Congress president." Azad nevertheless held his ground, again and again emphasizing Hindu–Muslim unity: "Providence brought us [Hindus and Muslims] together over a thousand years ago. We have fought but so do blood brothers fight. . . . It is no use trying to emphasize the differences. For that matter, no two human beings are alike. Every lover of peace must emphasize similarities."[35]

"The clarity of Maulana's view on the idea of unity of diverse cultures and faiths was an example for many of his contemporaries," Jahanbegloo states. "His distinctive contribution to Indian democracy was that he combined his spirited advocacy of secularism and India's national unity with his devout faith in Islam. . . . Maulana Azad spoke of an Islamic vision that could be in a confident partnership with other cultural and religious entities."[36]

In the mid-1940s, Azad threw himself into the Quit India movement and was imprisoned for a spell that lasted almost four years. He used that time to work on a book and to teach his companions the Urdu and Persian languages. With the war coming to an end and independence imminent, the British released him and other prisoners. He became an ardent advocate of a British-proposed Cabinet Mission Plan to keep India united as a loose federation of states grouped according to religion. Azad felt that this would be the best counter against Pakistan. A Direct Action Day campaign launched by Jinnah that led to thousands being killed in Calcutta made the whole thing moot. Jinnah became increasingly critical of Azad, and Azad lost some of his influence when he gave way to Nehru as the Congress Party president.[37]

Azad went to jail for yet more stints during World War II, leaving the Pakistan platform of Jinnah uncontested since Jinnah was handled with kid gloves by the British. At the same time, he suffered personal tragedies, with his wife constantly ill and his child dying a few years before. Finally, his wife expired in 1944, far away from her husband in prison. A few months later, his sister passed away, too. Gandhi was increasingly accepting the leadership of Jinnah and reaching out to him in an effort to compromise, a fact that pained Azad. With the war ended and the creation of Pakistan seeming inexorable, Azad felt increasingly anguished, feeling (as he later wrote in his memoir) that a willingness to compromise by the Congress leadership could have staved that off. He was even initially unwilling to join the interim government. And he continued to fight a lonely battle against the creation of Pakistan, acquiescing in the end when almost the entire leadership of the Congress was pitted against him.[38]

With the partition of India and the accompanying violence, Azad's values were tried and tested, but he did not completely lose hope. He gave his level best to protect the Muslim minority in Delhi (clashing with party bigwigs such as the right-leaning Home Minister Vallabhbhai Patel in the process) while at the same time not being afraid to admonish his fellow religionists for letting a section advocate for partition. He spent Gandhi's last afternoon with him. Retracing his way to Gandhi's place to discuss some things he had forgotten to do so earlier, he saw that "thousands were standing on he lawn and the crowd had overflowed into the street. Someone said, 'Gandhiji has been shot.' I had a dazed feeling and heard, as if in a dream, 'Gandhiji is dead.'"[39]

He then served as India's first education minister, continuing his strong advocacy of Gandhian values, such as secularism and nonviolence. He pushed for Nehru's policies for the underprivileged and for expanding education for all, fostering modern education and setting up a number of higher institutions of learning in his decade-long tenure. He left behind an autobiography that was controversial in its castigation of the Congress leadership, especially Patel, for letting partition happen. (Thirty pages were so sensitive that they were released by Azad's instruction only three decades after his death.) He wrote his memoir but little else, a loss to scholarship.[40]

Azad mocked the attitudes of his colleagues when he wrote his memoir in 1957, asking that if nonviolence was a belief for them, how could they reconcile themselves with India's standing army. He went on to underline that all these previous votaries of nonviolence wanted the army immediately divided up at independence into Indian and Pakistani components and didn't mind after that spending tons of money on defense expenditure. Azad attributes this inconsistency to the fact that they were blind followers of Gandhi, unlike him and Nehru, and that Gandhi's assassination left them floundering.[41]

Azad was quite disgusted, however, with Hiroshima and Nagasaki and came out quite strongly against the dropping of the atomic bombs. This utterly offended his moral sensibilities. "I am still convinced that there was no justification for the use of atom bombs on Japan," he writes. "I felt that the use of the atom bombs exceeded the limits of permissible destruction and did not redound to the prestige or heroism of the Allies. I also noted with regret that the Allies hailed this event as a magnificent victory and there was hardly one word of protest."[42]

All in all, Azad was a remarkable man who never gave up his adherence to Gandhian values and was an Islamic scholar in the best, most wonderful way. He died in 1958 but is still remembered today as an amazing amalgam of the traditional and the modern—committed to Islam but also to secularism, pluralism, and nonviolence.

THE GANDHIAN EDUCATIONIST AND PRESIDENT

Zakir Husain was another proud Indian Gandhian Muslim just like Azad, except he didn't even need an epiphany to realize that his life should be dedicated to pluralism and nonviolence, finally culminating in his holding the highest post that India had to offer. Husain came from a family of Pashtuns that migrated from the then India–Afghanistan border region first to North India and then to southern India, where Husain was born. Like Azad, he also underwent a traditional education, with a strong emphasis on learning Islam and Arabic. He also became an activist at an early stage, galvanizing around the treatment of the Ottoman Empire by the Allies at the end of World War I.[43]

Husain excelled at college, even though it was initially a big change of environment for him. He also became friendly with Hasan Shah, a Sufi mystic who was a distant relative. Shah instilled in him the values of religious pluralism and tolerance. (Shah himself was a fascinating personality. When he was once admonished for showing prejudice against Hindus, he walked thousands of miles from north-central India to Peshawar on the Afghanistan border and back.) Initially, Husain studied science but after a year's illness switched to English, economics, and philosophy.[44]

Then Husain made the most momentous decision he had ever made—"the first conscious decision of my life, perhaps the only one I have ever taken, for the rest of my life has but flowed from it." He decided to drop out of college in response to Gandhi's call to boycott British-aided institutions. Husain had already been stirred by the massacre at Jalianwala Bagh (where security forces had gunned down hundreds of unarmed protesters) and by the writings of Gandhi and Azad. Ironically, the day that Gandhi and Muhammad Ali (a Muslim leader) came to his college town, he was getting a medical checkup in some other place by yet another prominent Gandhian Muslim, Dr. M. A. Ansari. When he returned to the railway station, he heard disparaging remarks about Gandhi that some of his friends seemed to agree with. Husain was filled "with the deepest shame" and immediately wanted to repent.[45]

When the Ali brothers appeared the next day at the campus student union, they were so despondent that many students, including Husain, started crying. Then Husain got up unplanned and announced that he was resigning his teaching assignment and forgoing his scholarship at the Aligarh Muslim University. Other joined in. Husain went to Delhi and met other Muslim leaders, pledging to them that if a truly Indian institution were born, there would be a large number of Muslims willing to support it. From this, later that year the Jamia Milia University was formed—one of India's premier institutions even today.[46]

Husain and his band of rebels stayed on their old campus while plotting their moves. When finally in exasperation, after trying other machinations, the

British government tried to remove them, the news made headlines. People from all over India joined them in their efforts to set up a homegrown Muslim institution, including a good number of Hindus. The top staff consisted of Muslim Gandhians—the students much more interested in politics than their courses. Husain taught there for a while, translating into the Urdu language Plato's *Republic* and Cannan's *Political Economy*. But then, at the urging of a mentor, he left for Germany.[47]

In Germany in the 1920s, he did his PhD on British agrarian policy in India. He also dabbled in the philosophy of Arabic, made lasting friends with both men and women, and ardently defended Gandhian nonviolence in conversations. He even wrote a short book in German on Gandhian economic thought and had that published, along with a book of poetry by the famous Urdu poet Iqbal. He hoped that India could emulate some of the good qualities of Europe and tap its creativity. Significantly, Husain in a speech warned Germans not to be taken unduly with the new.[48]

Jamia Milia University was facing bankruptcy because of changing circumstances. It was moved to Delhi and carried on at Gandhi's insistence. While in Germany, Husain repeatedly confirmed his commitment to the university. After one such conversation, he and two other friends sent a telegram to the principal stating that they would like to serve Jamia and requesting that any decision be held off until they came back. A year later, they sailed to Sri Lanka and made their way to Jamia via South India. They found that Jamia Milia occupied a sum total of five buildings in Delhi: the staff of 80 lived on the first floor of one, three hosted classes, and one was an office. It was the last one that Husain occupied when he was appointed as the vice-chancellor (the Indian equivalent of university president) at the age of 29. For a year, he slept in a room adjacent to the office.[49]

Husain juggled multiple roles: fund-raiser, counselor, accountant, secretary, and editor of the campus journal. His salary started at 100 rupees a month but was later self-reduced to 80. Of this, he got half in cash and the other half on credit; it wasn't until 1944 that the arrears were cleared. Times were hence tough for the Husains and involved a lot of borrowing and buying on credit. But Husain's background and bearing instilled in him a notion of noblesse oblige. This meant that he gave his money and possessions to anyone who asked, often at personal loss to himself and family. Fund-raising was always a dilemma; someone of importance was of help—but discreetly since Mahatma Gandhi didn't want to interfere too directly in what was perceived to be an Indian Muslim institution.[50]

"The two met for the first time at Gandhi's Ahmedabad ashram in June 1926 and took to each other instinctively," writes Rajmohan Gandhi. "That a Muslim convinced about Hindu-Muslim unity was in charge of Jamia pleased Gandhi; and Zakir Husain was glad to find that the Mahatma trusted him and offered no advice on how the Jamia should be run."[51]

Even Gandhi's use of Hindu imagery, which perturbed many other Muslims, did not faze Husain. He reinterpreted Gandhi's notion of *Ram Raj*, Gandhi's vision of an ideal society (such as that ruled by Hindu God Ram). "I shall do my utmost to take our people toward what Gandhiji strove to achieve . . . an active and sustained sympathy for the weak and downtrodden, and a fervent desire to forge unity among the diverse sections of the Indian people as the first condition for helping to establish peace and human brotherhood in the world based on truth and nonviolence," Husain said. "This is what he called *Ram Raj*."[52]

Not that their paths didn't diverge sometimes. When Gandhi embarked on his civil disobedience campaign in 1930, Husain's Jamia Milia had to decide what to do as an institution. Husain decided that the work the university was doing was too important, and he left it to individual teachers if they wanted to answer Gandhi's call. Some did, including Gandhi's youngest son, Devdas, who was teaching at Jamia Milia. Gandhi understood Husain's decision; some others with him didn't.[53]

Things seemed to be going well at Jamia Milia. Books and a magazine targeted toward children were brought out regularly, and even an elementary school was established. But then personal tragedy struck. One morning, while Husain was handing out treats to the primary school children, a school worker came and whispered in his ear that his three-year-old daughter, Rehana, was very ill. Husain did not interrupt what he was doing. A little afterward, the person came and whispered to him again that Rehana had died. Husain became ashen but still did not cut short handing out sweets to the children. It was only a little later that a bell was rung and all the students were informed that Rehana had passed away. Husain later explained that he didn't want to disrupt the happiness of the children. His wife told a biographer that for many mornings after, his pillow was wet every morning.[54]

Jamia Milia had the unique situation of all three streams of Muslim thought converging on campus: the traditionalist, Muslim, and modernist. But it was difficult for Husain to walk the tightrope: while some Muslims found him too secular, some Hindus thought him too assertive on behalf of the Muslim community. But Husain was clear about one thing: though Jamia was a "Muslim institution with Islamic ideals," it was absolutely certain that "no narrow or false interpretations of these ideals will be allowed to convert Jamia into a breeding ground of communalism [sectarianism]."[55]

Husain's main project was to have a modern and expansive version of Islam. "Releasing woman from the four walls of an unhygienic house" was essential, he argued. And the Islam he believed in was "the religion that made believers out of unbelievers, civilized men out of barbarians, that gave woman a status and a place in society in which she had none before, which recognizes only an aristocracy of character amidst a brotherhood of man."[56]

While with the deepening of the Hindu–Muslim divide many of India's Muslim intellectuals turned either reactionary or radical, Jamia Milia insisted on combining religiosity and progressivism. The university introduced subjects like painting and theater over the objections of orthodox scholars and had girls and boys sit together in the primary school. "[Husain] did not enforce orthodoxy in any form," writes friend and biographer Mujeeb. "His practicing the tolerance envisaged in the Qur'anic verse, 'There is no compulsion in belief,' created an atmosphere in which views could be freely expressed and differences of opinion and belief respected."[57]

Zakir Husain joined Gandhi at doing what he did best—refining education. Gandhi had a model called new or basic education, where kids were taught practical education instead of rote learning. Husain disagreed with certain aspects of Gandhi's perspective, saying that this overemphasized hands-on learning and potentially set the stage for teachers exploiting the labor of their students. While others were shocked at Husain's audacity, Gandhi was not fazed. He invited Husain to head a committee to modify the tenets of basic education. The results were so impressive that even agencies of the British government paid heed. Some schools actually implemented the recommendations. Husain got national fame. But Husain's close association with Gandhi and the Congress Party increasingly hurt his institution, as the battle lines were drawn in the Muslim community over the demand for Pakistan.[58]

Still, the institution flourished. Land was bought for a new campus. Some bigwigs donated huge sums. Jamia Milia's degree was recognized. Technical education was introduced. All the while, his biographer faults him on two counts. First, he was unable to say no to anyone who barged in, taking a toll on his time and energy. Second, he did not know how to efficiently allocate his time, volunteering to be involved with a number of institutions instead of just confining himself to Jamia Milia. Even then, a British author writing in 1946 called Jamia's education system "one of the most progressive and one of the best in India."[59]

Husain was deeply influenced by the Sufis and loved to quote stalwarts like Rumi. He also was a collector of things big and small and a lover of good food, which contributed to his diabetes and glaucoma. Husain's stature was so immense that when the Congress Party wanted to name a Muslim to the interim government, he was considered as a replacement candidate to Azad since it was thought that he would be more acceptable to Jinnah. Jinnah squelched any such notion by referring to him as a "quisling." In the midst of all this, Jamia celebrated its silver jubilee in 1946. Husain managed to pull off the astonishing feat of having Nehru, Jinnah, Azad, and future Pakistani Prime Minister Liaqat Ali Khan come to the main function, with all the four sitting beside him while he gave, according to his biographer, "the most eloquent and moving speech of his life."[60]

"The fire of mutual hatred which is ablaze in this country makes our work of laying out and tending gardens appear as sheer madness," he said. "For God's sake, put your heads together and extinguish this fire. This is not the time to investigate and determine who lighted this fire. The fire is blazing; it has to be put out."[61]

He himself was nearly consumed by the fire. While traveling on a train in the strife-torn province of Punjab, Husain, a future president of India, was almost killed. Two men pointed their guns at him, but the intervention of his traveling companion and a stationmaster saved his life. Even then, a crowd gathered around and demanded that the Sikh army officer who was protecting him hand him over. Only when the officer threatened to open fire did the crowd retreat. Husain's troubles were not over.[62] He wrote a friend on his perilous and life-changing journey,

What I saw in Delhi after I returned made insignificant what I had witnessed at Jalandhar. Such wretched scenes of meanness, barbarism, and ruthlessness that they left you stunned. But, with the passage of time, all those experiences have faded. Now I only remember this: Kapur Sahib [a respectful appellation], a Hindu unknown to me, learned somehow who I was; he then spoke to a Sikh army officer, another stranger to me, who put his own life at risk to save mine; Bedi Sahib, who looked after me like a brother; and then that young student and his friends who escorted me back to Delhi.

He concluded, "I escaped death, but I can't decide whether I'm happy about it or ashamed."[63]

His troubles were not over. Employees of the Jamia were attacked as part of the religious frenzy sweeping Delhi at the time. Nehru had to visit the campus in the middle of the night, and General K. M. Cariappa, army chief of staff, came in and left a platoon behind. When Gandhi arrived from Calcutta, his first question at the Delhi station was "Is Zakir Husain safe, is the Jamia safe?"[64]

Gandhi visited the campus the very next day. Husain's recollection of the visit is worth recounting in detail: "His fingers had got crushed in the door of the car and he was suffering great pain. In spite of this, he laughed and provoked others to laugh, he infused courage into us, and advised us to stay where we were. He talked to the Muslim refugees on the terrace of the secondary school, took an orphaned girl in his arms and hugged and kissed her. Then he left, saying that he would do all that was necessary for our safety or perish in the attempt."[65]

Husain did have some divergence of opinion with Gandhi on occasion, and that's why he preferred to call him a "powerful influence" (though he did sometimes refer to him as a guru or teacher) in whom he admired most greatly "his capacity to laugh at himself." Husain took his cue from Gandhi's visit and organized Hindu and Sikh refugees from Pakistan to come to Jamia and meet Muslims. A few days later, when Gandhi undertook a fast to protest Hindu–Muslim violence, Husain approved, unlike some others of Gandhi's colleagues, saying that he had "chosen the right moment to urge . . . people to purify their hearts." Husain added, "We are overwhelmed with shame that free India should have nothing to offer you but bitterness and distress." A couple of weeks later, Gandhi was assassinated.[66]

Independent India was a mixed blessing for Husain. He hated having to go hat in hand to Nehru and Azad (the education minister) for funds for the Jamia. Added to this was the complicated relationship that he had on a personal level with Azad. Fortunately, however, when the time came to fill the post of chancellor of Aligarh Muslim University (his alma mater), Azad put forward Husain's name. Husain accepted on the condition that the university board approve of him unanimously. And so he returned to a campus from which he had been expelled in 1920 to a city that he considered "my home, my garden, my native land." He also took charge of a campus that, unlike Jamia, had pro-Pakistani leanings in the past. The status of Muslims in India would be "largely determined" by "the way Aligarh works, the way Aligarh thinks," and by "the way India deals with Aligarh," he remarked.[67]

Aligarh Muslim University was in need of a fix. Some of the staff had migrated to Pakistan, some of the others indeed were pro-Pakistan, and many of the students and faculty resented Husain since they thought he was a stooge of the government. Indeed, the welcome speech by the secretary of the students' union turned into a "sarcasmfest." But Husain took it all calmly. He brought a spirit of equanimity and calmness to campus. He recruited professors from all over the country. And he got a German-designed engineering college built. When he admonished students, it was in a gracious, roundabout way. Health problems plagued him; a heart attack would have killed him if a doctor hadn't arrived promptly. A government act to modernize the university alienated some students, and Husain became unhappy, saying that it was hard to get anything of usefulness done at Aligarh Muslim University. A year before his term was to end, he resigned in 1956.[68]

Husain was conflicted about leading an active life, but when he was nominated to the upper house of the Indian Parliament, he grabbed the opportunity. Another, bigger opportunity soon came, but no one knew where he was to offer it to him. While he was recuperating from eye surgery in Germany in 1957, the position of the governorship (largely ceremonial) of the state of Bihar opened up. On returning to India, he said yes. He took his duties seriously, meticulously preparing for and writing out speeches for every ceremonial occasion. His utterances contained an equal number of Sanskrit and Urdu words, to the consternation of some Muslims. As a titular head, he signed all the bills he was presented, except when one would have curtailed the autonomy of the state's universities. In this instance, he firmly put his foot down until the bill was amended.[69]

The next big opportunity in the limelight came when Nehru in 1962 chose Husain to be the vice president of India. Although in India the main functions of the vice president are to preside over the upper house of the Indian Parliament and to be available for ceremonial functions, Husain's being chosen for the position was a reflection of the high esteem he was held in. He performed both his roles with relish: he learned to raise his voice to silence unruly parliamentarians, and he rewrote speeches when he visited foreign lands to be more gracious to his host countries. A war with Pakistan in 1965 raised uncomfortable questions in Husain's mind about his loyalty being questioned and about the impact on Hindu–Muslim relations.[70]

After the death of Nehru and his successor, Lal Bahadur Shastri, Nehru's daughter Indira Gandhi assumed the office of the prime minister. She backed Husain for the post of president of India in 1967 when the previous president's term expired, but because of an internal conflict within the ruling party, some other leaders wanted a person who was seen as less pliable by Indira. Because of this rift and the way that Indira was thought to impose him on the public, Husain faced some opposition. He won by a four-to-three margin in the electoral college (national plus state legislatures) that chooses the president. On the morning after winning, he went to Gandhi's memorial and "pledged to rededicate myself at the memorial of the man who first showed him the way to devote myself to the service of my countrymen," stating that he would be committing himself "to the totality of my country's culture." He even went to seek the blessings of a Hindu and a Jain religious leader, causing some consternation among a few Muslims. But Husain saw this as a way of atoning for the lack of respect for Hindu traditions among some of his coreligionists.[71]

He worked tirelessly for religious harmony as president and traveled abroad on a number of occasions as a symbol of India. He tried to introduce a note of cordiality into India's increasingly rancorous politics. And he never forgot his beloved institution. Once when told that the Jamia Milia University had a stall at a book fair that he was attending, tears welled up in his eyes. On the morning of May 3, 1969, he was due for a medical checkup. He went to the bathroom, where he was found dead from a heart attack some minutes later, after barely two years in office. Once he had semijokingly told his friend and biographer after a funeral they attended that he would get up and start shouting if things were done as shabbily for him. He needn't have worried. As bearer of the highest office of his country, he was accorded full honors, with world leaders in attendance. He was buried at his beloved Jamia, surrounded in three directions by a school, a mosque, and a library, a very fitting resting place for an amazingly incredible Muslim Gandhian educationist and social reformer.[72]

CONCLUSION

The profiles presented here are only of some of the Indian Muslims who joined with Gandhi in his campaign, sharing with him his values of nonviolence and religious tolerance. (Some of the other prominent ones are also referenced in this chapter.) They ranged from social workers and politicians to educationists and administrators. And after India's independence, many of them went on to serve the new country in various capacities. (Fakhruddin Ali Ahmed, an active participant in the Gandhian struggle, also became president of India in the 1970s.) The commitment of Indian Muslim Gandhians to Gandhi's program and their determination that nonviolence and pluralism were the best values to adhere to went a long way toward ensuring that India became a secular republic, committed to the full protection of people of all religions. While these figures are well known and highly regarded in India, they're unheard of in the West. The fact that numerous Muslims joined with the best-known proponent of nonviolence gives the lie to the perception that peacefulness is anathema to Muslims.

CHAPTER 8

A Refusal to Cooperate: The Struggle of the Kosovar Albanians

GANDHI OF THE BALKANS

The Balkans were globally known in the 1990s for multiple wars, bloody massacres, and ethnic cleansing, most notably for the horrific violence unleashed by Serb leader Slobodan Milosevic. In this violence-prone setting, a leader emerged in an overwhelmingly Muslim society in the area who became known as the "Albanian Gandhi" or the "Gandhi of the Balkans" as a respectful acknowledgment of his pacifist tactics. The movement he led adopted Gandhian tactics and established a parallel social setup in protest against Serb repression in a decade-long mass experiment. Although Ibrahim Rugova yielded mixed results for his community, he died as the head of state of Kosovo and the most prominent public figure in the nation. And the effort he directed did eventually lead to de facto independence of Kosovo and its recognition by dozens of countries (including the United States, Canada, and most of Europe), albeit accompanied by many twists and turns.

Kosovo is a region in the former Yugoslavia with a population of roughly 2 million that is predominantly ethnic Albanian and Muslim, though there is a notable Serb Christian minority. During the communist rule of Marshall Tito, Kosovo was governed as an autonomous province, and this was mostly honored in practice in spite of ethnic tensions between various groups in the province and Kosovar resentment against Yugoslav authoritarianism.[1]

Starting with Tito's death in 1980, the Kosovar Albanians suffered intense repression at the hands of the Serbs in Yugoslavia. Milosevic made this policy the centerpiece of his rule. He took away Kosovo's autonomy in 1989 in a series of swift steps. He sacked the provincial chief, made hundreds of political arrests, and imposed top-heavy strictures on the educational curriculum, including a

decree that everything be taught in the Serb language and an order that instituted de facto segregation of Serb and Kosovar Albanian pupils, with discrimina-
tory funding. Tanks often surrounded schools to prevent Albanian students from
attending. These measures extended all the way up to the University of Pristina
in the province's capital.

The Serb authorities also set about renaming the streets and government departments and extending tight control to virtually all media organizations, both
print and broadcast. Those independent outlets that were allowed to function
were severely harassed. To top this, the government introduced several other
measures, such as economic incentives to encourage Serbs to relocate in Kosovo.
When few Serbs took advantage of this, Serb refugees from Croatia were forcibly
transferred. At the same time, life was made difficult for the Kosovar Albanians
by a forced national service draft, penalties for large families, and barriers for
families wanting to return from abroad. To make matters worse, there were large-
scale firings of Kosovar Albanians from state enterprises. The health care system
was rife with discrimination down to the minutest level, with prescriptions, for
instance, being written only in the Cyrillic script. To add to all to this was the
systematic violence directed at the Kosovar Albanians. "When an Albanian is
accused of violating the territorial integrity of Yugoslavia, we can beat them and
even kill them," the head of the highest court stated in 1994. Not surprisingly,
more than 300,000 Albanians left Kosovo between 1991 and 1995.[2]

Commentator Stephen Schwartz contends that the Serb leadership made a
number of errors that eventually led to the de facto separation of Kosovo from
the rest of the country. Among them was creating a large Kosovar Diaspora by
forcing people to emigrate, a segment that helped sustain civil society back home
by sending to the mother country sizable remittances. As part of his crackdown,
Milosevic also cut off the Albanians from state subsidies, fostering self-reliance
and entrepreneurship. Another central mistake he made was dismissing a whole
Albanian intellectual class from state employment, thus providing the Kosovars
able leadership. Among these intellectuals, much to Milosevic's detriment, was
Rugova.[3]

THE NONVIOLENT PROJECT STARTS

Kosovo seemed on the verge of violence by 1990. Here is where Rugova and the
civil resistance came in, with Rugova saying that the Kosovars would embark
on the path of nonviolence to attract international backing and "because to do
otherwise would have disastrous consequences for our people."[4]

Two events marked the advent of the nonviolent path for Kosovar Albanians
in the early 1990s. First, some of them embarked on a peaceful 55-kilometer-
long march. Then miners launched a hunger strike to ask for Kosovo's autonomy.
These two actions initiated the project of nonviolence in Kosovo in the decade
to come.[5]

In 1990, village soccer teams suddenly started springing up with names like
Endurance and Standing Firm. Added to this were the successful examples of

nonviolent resistance across much of Eastern Europe in 1989 that the Koso-vars took inspiration from, underscoring yet again the importance of global role models.[6]

The starting point for the campaign may have been even slightly further back, a demonstration of 300,000 miners and 100,000 other participants in November 1988 to protest the annulment of Kosovo's autonomy. It was a large but entirely peaceful gathering that attempted to signal to the Serb regime that the Kosovars would resist resolutely though nonviolently. The protesters even tried to differen-tiate between the Serb people and the regime, raising the slogan "Long live the brave Serbian people." The demonstration set the stage for the nonviolent tactics that were embraced in the province in the years to come.[7]

Three months later, 7,000 miners followed up by shutting themselves, some on a hunger strike, in a mine complex in the city of Trepca. The miners proved resilient, and soon a general strike spread throughout Kosovo. On February 26, their immediate supervisors resigned, and the miners emerged into the open. The Serbian government immediately reversed the resignations, imposed a state of emergency, and started arresting the miners. The strike this time received cover-age outside Kosovo, especially in Croatia and Slovenia. Half the Slovene popu-lation signed a petition protesting the state of emergency, but the Slovenians soon decided that they would have to start moving toward independence without getting themselves embroiled in Kosovo's troubles. Milosevic's reputation as a de-fender of Serb honor was solidified by a vitriolic speech he gave in Belgrade. The Kosovars engaged in yet another follow-up strike in March but were forced to go back to work after the Serb regime warned them that they would all be fired if they didn't. The annulment of the autonomy of the Kosovar legislature followed, which was met by protests but unfortunately of the violent kind. Serb repression resulted in as many as 140 deaths and hundreds injured and jailed. Further dem-onstrations and repression followed.[8]

Around this time, the Albanians took lessons from the rest of Eastern Europe and formed groups that called for the democratization of Yugoslavia, like the As-sociation for a Yugoslav Democratic Initiative and the Kosovo Writers Associa-tion. The president of the writers' association was Ibrahim Rugova. Rugova was a French-trained expert on Pjeter Bogdani, a 17th-century Albanian Catholic author, and was the son of a peasant killed by Titoites in the mid-1940s. Rugova was already well established as a scholar, being in his mid-forties when he got involved with politics. Rugova's tastes were quite different from that of his coun-trymen. He exhibited a fondness for poetry, rocks, and Sar mountain dogs. He always dressed in a silk scarf. All this did not stop the Albanian people from choosing him as their leader. (Serb writers had resigned from the organization in 1988.) Rugova soon became more and more prominent, especially since he was one of the first persons to ask for the independence of Kosovo.[9]

On December 23, 1989, a group was founded that would dominate Kosovar politics for the next decade. Its name was the Democratic League of Kosovo. For the president, the group turned to outside its organization and asked Rugova, al-ready well known for his work with International PEN, the writers' organization.

The Democratic League's membership swelled within the first few months, if not to the claimed 700,000, then at least to 200,000. Its initial lack of influence was shown, however, by its inability to stop the out-of-control demonstrations in early 1990. Soon, though, it established a network of branches both in Kosovo and among emigrant Kosovars.[10]

So, the Albanian response in the face of repression was remarkable. "Without resort to violence—which all among them then viewed as a suicidal option—they had organized and maintained a free or liberated zone such as revolutionaries and reformers of the past, worldwide, had long dreamed," Schwartz writes. "Unfortunately, these fine points of political science were largely ignored by the rest of the globe."[11]

Intellectuals such as Rugova but many others lesser known in the West, among them poets, played a major role in this project. The very peacefulness of the Kosovars ensured that they wouldn't get as much media coverage as compared to what they would have received if they had taken to more violent, dramatic forms of resistance. When Rugova came to Washington and attended a Carnegie Endowment for International Peace seminar, the event didn't create half as much of a media buzz as the visit to town of an armed insurrection's leader would have.[12]

The Democratic League of Kosovo, in conjunction with other groups, quickly developed a series of protest methods. These ranged from the sounding of factory hooters and car horns on a day of sorrow to the putting of candles on balconies and windows and the rattling of keys in a tin at the start of curfew to indicate that the Albanians still held the keys to their future. The League kept regular tabs on Serb repression, visiting villages often, even if Rugova didn't himself because of a fear of inciting violence.[13]

MOTIVATIONS FOR NONVIOLENCE

As with every society, there were strands in Kosovar Albanian culture that worked for and against a nonviolent mode. The widespread possession of weapons and the tradition of blood feuds were major obstacles. One major factor that did work in the favor of a nonviolent approach was the desire to integrate more closely with Europe. This desire was so strong that in 1990 some Kosovar Albanians even discussed mass conversion from Islam to Catholicism, which they rejected because it would seem too artificial. This did not prevent them from repeatedly rallying around Catholic symbols like Mother Teresa, observing Catholic holy days and ceremonies, and forming a Christian Democratic Party with a majority Muslim membership—all this to disprove the charge of Islamic fundamentalism often leveled at them by the Serbs. "We have learned that nonviolence is the modern European preference," Rugova said.[14]

Another motivating factor was the success of such movements all over Eastern Europe in 1989, although this underestimated the years of work it took in bringing conditions in these countries to such a pass. So certain basic themes became clear—the use of nonviolence to avoid the pretext of Serb retaliation, the importance of appearing European, and getting international support.

The Albanian strategy became fourfold: to contest the legitimacy of Serb institutions, to refuse to be provoked, to mobilize international support, and to maintain Albanian civil society. The Serb retaliatory strategy took the form of denying the Kosovars any cultural autonomy, such as the use of their language, and punitive measures of various sorts. Between 1990 and 1992, one Kosovar lawyer calculates that as many as 32 laws and 470 decrees were passed in addition to two detailed government plans. These tightened control at various levels, such as the police, the media, the municipalities, the judicial system, and the economy.[15]

All this did not intimidate the Kosovar Albanians, whose parliament met in July 1990 to affirm a declaration of independence. Albanian workers formed the Union of Independent Trade Unions of Kosovo, to which the Serb authorities responded by wholesale dismissals, affecting as much as 45 percent of the workforce in the first year and 90 percent eventually. The police and medical personnel were particular targets. Some Serb leaders contended that an Albanian boycott was what was going on, but the evidence belies this. Intense police repression followed, including arbitrary harassment and torturing to death in custody. Leaders like Rugova were left alone, however. Each Friday, he or one of his colleagues held a press conference in the party headquarters, which was left unraided, unlike party offices at the lower level. Rugova's followers built him a nice house with donated materials and labor. During all this time, the Albanians attracted international support by taking the repression stoically.[16]

To coordinate resistance, the Albanians formed the Coordinating Council of Political Parties, which, apart from Rugova's group, contained a number of other political groups. The Kosovars stepped up their nonviolent resistance. A number of successful peaceful demonstrations were organized, such as a "Quiet Burial of Violence," a mock funeral attended by perhaps 100,000 people, and a one-day general strike with the slogan "We are for dialogue. And you?"[17]

In response to the firings of Kosovar workers and the deliberate Serb mismanagement of the economy, the people developed a multipronged strategy to cope. People engaged in social solidarity, organized by groups such as Rugova's party, trade unions, and the Mother Teresa Association. Members of family abroad sent money home; this number eventually rose above 350,000. People cut back on expenditures ranging from daily needs to wedding extravaganzas. And lots of new small businesses started up. The result was that the Kosovo economy was doing better than the mismanaged Serb one in spite of bearing the brunt of sanctions twice over—the first one imposed by the international community on the larger Yugoslav entity and the second one by the Serbs on Kosovo. The absence of any planned economic strategy did hurt, however. There was unnecessary duplication of certain business types and wasteful importation of goods from Serbia. Police harassment added to the troubles. The lack of any economic strategy stood out in contrast to Gandhi's carefully thought-out program of *swadeshi* (indigenous) economy.[18]

"Oppressed, but organized," said Rugova. "This is the first time that [Kosovars] feel that they have a power . . . that they feel like citizens, despite the occupation. . . . With our organization, we are active, not for war but for something else. We have this internal, psychological freedom, and these are the first steps toward physical freedom and, one day, collective freedom." In reality, the patience of the people and the efficacy of his strategy was in question. Rugova was heavily infused in symbolism, not surprising for someone who studied semiotics and literary history with famed intellectual Roland Barthes in France. He believed that the whole parallel enterprise was symbolically and actually undermining Serb power. But his analysis was overly optimistic. People invested a lot of hopes in him and his ability to get countries like the United States to take notice. The problem was that his strategy was not well thought out. The Kosovo Parliament did not function after being elected. And the parallel school system became more decrepit over time.[19]

One of the main struggles between the Serb authorities and the Kosovars was over control of the media. Journalists transformed previously specialized outlets, covering topics like agriculture, into general newspapers. Many of them were imprisoned for various lengths. A couple of journalists in 1993 conducted a hunger strike against the forced assimilation of some publications and were successful in getting it rescinded. Until the spread of satellite television, Kosovars had to rely on broadcasts from neighboring countries or from Western services, such as BBC and Voice of America, to get a non-Serb perspective. But with the sprouting up of satellite dishes, Rugova's party got a tremendous platform for its views since it controlled the broadcast from Albania. This meant that often the success and international support for Rugova's experiment was exaggerated. Rugova's supporters also controlled the Kosovo Information Center, which disseminated abroad news about conditions in Kosovo. An organization called AIM, a network of independent journalists, was founded by Kosovars and Serb journalists, one of the few successful examples of such collaboration.[20]

A series of elections were held during this period. The Kosovar Albanians held a referendum and an election in 1991. With a 75 percent turnout, 95 percent opted for independence and elected Rugova as their first president. Rugova reiterated his commitment to the nonviolent path and to get international recognition. "We would have no chance of successfully resisting the army," he said. "In fact, the Serbs only wait for a pretext to attack the Albanian population and wipe it out. We believe it is better to do nothing than to be massacred."[21]

In May 1992, elections for parliament and president were held. Rugova's party overwhelmingly triumphed in the parliamentary elections, while in the presidential one Rugova won as the sole candidate. Surprisingly, the Serb authorities did not heavily interfere with the vote but threatened reprisals if the parliament tried to convene. Although journalists and observers from Albania and Croatia were ejected, eight teams from the West and 82 international news agencies managed to observe the elections, thus lending them international legitimacy. Rugova's party also dominated local councils, hence raising concern about the predominance and governing style of Rugova and his colleagues.[22]

A question that arose on a number of occasions during this period was whether the Albanians should participate in the official Serbian electoral system to try and reform it or whether to boycott it with the notion that such attempts were futile. Repeatedly, in spite of some dissenting voices, the Albanians opted for the latter (much to the disappointment of some Serb democrats) since they felt that there wasn't scope for maneuver within the system. Nonviolence scholar Howard Clark suggests that this was probably the right move since participation would have muddied the waters about the legitimacy of the Serb-imposed system. Rugova's party contained both views, but the boycott approach was very dominant, and some of Rugova's colleagues left the movement because they favored more contact with the Serbs. As time went on, the boycott became an immutable principle.

PARALLEL SOCIETIES

The Democratic League of Kosovo became the most formidable political entity in Kosovo, with Rugova selected as the head of the government. It declared independence for Kosovo, a move that was recognized only by Albania, although the Kosovars saw this step as legitimate as the independence declarations made by Croatia, Bosnia, and Slovenia.

This heralded the setup of a parallel civil society. This was the most remarkable thing about Kosovo in these years: the setting up of parallel systems in various spheres, such as education and health care. "All of Kosovo was doing some work in the parallel society, volunteering," said one person. "The Serbs tried to kill our society, but we woke up instead." Rugova proudly remarked, "In Kosovo, only our system functions." This parallel structure lent some stability to Kosovar society.[23]

Two separate and parallel societies were thus established. This endeavor extended to the sports and the cultural realm. Houses, cafés, and restaurants became the venue for schools, art exhibitions, and sporting events. Albanians moved out of the public sector into private businesses.[24]

The efforts in education will be described in detail later. But even in health, the Albanians set up a new network. Kosovo had the worst health indicators in the whole of Yugoslavia, a situation compounded by frequent epidemics. Still, Kosovars were reluctant to visit Serb-run facilities, preferring to go abroad. When the crisis hit, Serb authorities dismissed a number of Kosovar doctors. The majority stayed within the system, however, offering voluntary services. As a supplement to this, the Mother Teresa Association was formed (it was just named after her) to offer medical services, including maternity facilities. This was quite a remarkable example of self-organization since local businesses donated the equipment, while the staff volunteered its services. The group got critical support from organizations such as Doctors Without Borders and Catholic Relief Services, which helped it greatly expand its services.[25]

The Kosovars also established a system of dispensaries run on private premises. Many Albanian babies were delivered at home. All these activities were financed by the Rugova government mainly through taxes collected from emigrants. Interestingly, Catholic priests and Muslim imams worked together to coordinate these activities. And a Christian Democratic Party, comprising Christian and Muslim personalities, worked alongside Rugova's organization.

The health care sector was just one example of a Gandhian agenda that Rugova and his colleagues tried to adopt. The Gandhi- and King-like approach of Rugova attracted some attention abroad, including that of Senator and Republican presidential candidate Bob Dole. He worked together with colleagues in the U.S. Congress to pass a number of resolutions warning Milosevic of the consequences of responding with violence. Slovenian youth also came to the defense of the Albanians, ignoring Milosevic's threats and demanding the implementation of the 1974 constitution promising autonomy.[26]

As time passed, Serb repression intensified. Albanians were banned from purchasing or selling land without official permission. The cultural autonomy of the area was stripped. Albanian-language books were taken from the University of Pristina and pulped. Theaters, galleries, cultural associations, and even sporting events were shut down.

That the Serb repression was widespread and systematic was well documented in many reports, such as one issued in the early 1990s by Human Rights Watch. "Kosovo is a police state," the report stated. "Stripped of the relative autonomy it enjoyed in Tito's time, Kosovo is now under the direct and immediate control of Serb authorities who rule with an iron fist." The report pointed out the existence of the parallel Albanian society, which it said was (barely) tolerated by the Serbs. But even these attempts faced reprisals by the Serbs. There was frequent detention of targeted Albanians, such as intellectuals and those with military experience. Albanian civilians were frequently harassed by Serb security forces, and, even as early as 1993, there were signs of the beginnings of ethnic cleansing in the province by Serb authorities. Because of the subservience of the Serb judicial system to the authorities, recourse was almost nonexistent.[27]

The Human Rights Watch report documented 5,700 cases of maltreatment and 1,400 arrests just in the first eight months of 1993. At least 15 Kosovar Albanians died because of human rights abuses by the police in 1993. Rugova's party members were frequent targets of repression. Although Rugova himself was subjected just to constant surveillance, his deputies were routinely picked up for detention and often subjected to beatings.[28]

There were massive purges of Kosovar Albanian workers from all state sectors after they refused to sign loyalty oaths. By 1993, only 20 percent of Albanian workers were employed, almost all of them in the private sector. Immense hardships were brought on by the layoffs, including malnutrition and forced large-scale emigration. There were also mass firings of Albanian teachers after they refused to teach a new Serb-centered curriculum and sign a loyalty oath. Serb officials denied the firings or even the existence of a parallel system. There was also a complete exclusion of Kosovar Albanians from the University of Pristina and the constant harassment of Albanian teachers participating in the parallel system, including beatings. A similar situation existed in the health care sector, with the same massive dismissals of Kosovar Albanians for political reasons and the constant harassment, including the arbitrary denial of licenses, of the parallel private medical facilities. Not surprisingly, there was a significant deterioration both in the general quality of health care and in the level of health indicators among the Kosovar Albanians.[29]

During all these years, the option of military resistance was actively considered, especially among impatient strands of the Diaspora. Croatia's leader Franco Tudjman also offered military help if the Kosovars opened up a second military front during the Croatia–Serbia conflict. Rugova and his colleagues did consider bolstering Kosovo's military defenses, at the least, as a fallback option but gave up the idea as being too risky. The Serbs nevertheless found out and conducted a series of show trials. In the end, Rugova said, nonviolence was "a necessity and a choice." "The practice of nonviolence in this situation corresponds to an aspect of our character, to a tradition of patience and prudence in the face of all domination," he stated. "By means of this active resistance based on nonviolence and solidarity, we 'found' ourselves. Today, we have succeeded in touching this point of the spirit of the Albanian people." Interestingly, in the first 18 months of separation, a total of 136 "violent" attacks took place in the province, even according to exaggerated Serb figures.[30]

As part of the civil resistance campaign, the Albanians set about reforming deleterious social practices. Among the chief ones was the practice of blood feuds, some of which went back generations. The campaign was led by Anton Cetta, a legendary folklorist who went from village to village organizing public campaigns of forgiveness. Some 1,000 feuds were settled between 1990 and 1992 in the course of the campaign. Soon the Serbs caught on and started banning large gatherings associated with the campaign, which responded by proceeding more clandestinely.[31]

SETTING UP AN EDUCATION SYSTEM

"The situation in Kosovo is stable and explosive," said a 1993 Council for Security and Cooperation in Europe report. Nowhere was this truer than in education. In September 1989, the Serbs introduced ethnic segregation in schools and in August 1990 imposed a uniform curriculum on the region. The Kosovars started their system immediately, with the principal of the first school of this type sentenced to 31 days in prison for his impertinence. The Serbs had ceased to pay schoolteachers by 1991 and had dismissed thousands of them as well as scores of principals and deputies. By 1991–92, students were being barred from entering the premises of schools unless they accepted the Serb curriculum. The Kosovars began meeting wherever they could—in houses, garages, basements, warehouses, and mosques. In 1992–93, Kosovars tried to reenter the schools but encountered repression. In October 1992, there were massive demonstrations throughout Kosovo, only to be met with a huge crackdown.[32]

The new system was simultaneously a prison and a symbol for freedom. The seizure of control of the schools by the Albanians repeated episodes during World Wars I and II. During the communist era, education had been provided to each community in its language. In 1981, Albanian students protested the heavily censored curriculum. Instead of giving in, the government only intensified control of the material throughout the decade. Ironically, the Serbs initiated segregation by demanding separate classes because of what they said was the marginalizing of Serbians in the system, both in numbers and otherwise. (An alleged poisoning episode of Albanian students considerably increased the distrust between the two communities.) One of the main targets of this move was the educational system. This had the result of effectively abolishing the presence of Albanians in the conventional educational apparatus.[33]

Albanians responded in massive numbers. Some gave up their houses to be used as schools. A tax system was created to finance education. The associated effect was that social segregation in Kosovo was now almost total. Before, for example, an Albanian rock band had a Serb member. Now such examples became much rarer, and animosity grew. On the way to their new, makeshift schools, Albanians saw their old buildings housing a sparse Serb student population. Some of these schools were turned into Serb refugee camps after the fall of Krajina to the Croats. The separation was almost complete. Serb and Albanian neighbors didn't even engage in basic courtesies toward each other. "We used to dip bread in the same goulash, and now we don't know each other," said an Albanian of a former Serb colleague. Even shared spaces became contested domains. Marshall Tito Street, a major thoroughfare in Pristina, became St. Vitus Day Street for the Serbs, referring to a famous 1389 Kosovo battle, and Mother Teresa Street for the Albanians.[34]

The Kosovar schools suffered from a severe lack of equipment of various sorts. With the production of Albanian-language textbooks banned, they had to initially be smuggled in by mule from Albania, and then, later, new ones were printed elsewhere and smuggled in, too. There was also a big dropout rate, disproportionately affecting girls. Still, by 1996, approximately 325,000 students (down from roughly 375,000 seven years before) participated in the system. Police brutality was rampant, especially at the start of the school year. Students and teachers were imprisoned, tortured, and, in extreme cases, even killed. At the same time, the Serbs tried to lure students into attending their school system, an offer very few took up.[35]

The University of Pristina felt the brunt since it was seen, in Rugova's words, as having "contributed immensely to the cultivation . . . and consolidation of national consciousness, as well as to the intellectual and civilized development of Albanian people." The purge began in the medical department and spread to the other faculties. The departments had to reopen in private buildings. Students often had to go abroad to get practical training. Not surprisingly, this affected the standards of the university, although the teaching faculty worked very hard at maintaining them. The funding of the education system was done by a voluntary tax on Kosovars both inside and outside Kosovo. Families and businesses were assessed according to their capabilities. International agencies such as George Soros's Open Society gave some aid, too. Serb authorities sometimes confiscated the money and beat the collectors, pounding one person to death in 1995. Nevertheless, in spite of the hardships, the money collected ensured that teachers got paid an amount that compared favorably with what the Serb authorities were paying their teachers in the rest of Serbia.[36]

Under this arrangement, the Albanians gained more independence than they ever had, even while they were bearing the brunt of Serb repression. Their ability to decide for themselves on socioeconomic and political issues instilled in them a sense of self-confidence and maturity. It also convinced them that the time had arrived for them to declare their independence. The textbooks in their schools talked about the joys and pride of an independent Kosovo. Surprisingly, the Serb authorities tolerated all this, perhaps because it took away from them the burden of caring for and teaching Albanian kids. With rare exceptions, even high school and university students were taught in private homes. Albanian students were, however, constantly harassed by the Serb police, particularly when their documents had the stamp of "Kosovo Republic." As an observer contends, the effect was to transform the educational system into a "life school of resistance." The flip side, however, was that there was a sharp fall in school enrollment at the primary, secondary, and university levels.[37]

There was a debate about the quality of the curriculum and whether it was inculcating hatred of the Serbs. Clark gives examples of people complaining that there was too much emphasis on rote and conflict but says that the alternative could have been far worse, with the syllabus at least giving the Kosovars a sense of purpose and self-worth.

The effect of Rugova's move toward a separate educational system was captured by a critic who said: "At first it gave them dignity, and in the end it became a cause of self-destruction." Initially, it provided the Albanians a huge psychological boost, but later it became emblematic of a "national movement that made no move."[38] There were all sorts of arrangements for these schools: private homes, schools completely used by Albanians in all-Albanian areas, and an exchange of schools whereby two mixed schools each became a segregated bastion. What was illustrative of the new system, however, was the situation where Serbs and Albanians had separate entrances or shifts for the same buildings. In these instances, the Serbs got the better end of the deal because of the much larger Albanian population that resulted in overcrowding. These arrangements held true only for primary and, to a much lesser extent, for secondary students. University students had to settle for private homes all the time.[39]

Although education was the most important segment where the Albanians set up their parallel system, this extended to other spheres, too. But the schools were the most emblematic—so much so that one Albanian analyst sardonically commented that Rugova should have been titled the "president of the parallel schools of Kosovo" rather than "President of the Kosovo Republic."[40]

Interestingly, the schools were the only pivotal centrally administered institution that the Serbs tolerated for the Albanians to run since Kosovar attempts to initiate a parliament or a police force were constantly stymied. But, ironically, the very same system became like a prison, too, accentuated by the prisonlike conditions of many of the schools, such as single, long benches. Even in proper schools,

classes were often held in cellars with security rails and a single, bare lightbulb.
Albanians started referring to the system as a megaburg (megaprison).[41]

Under Rugova, the situation in Kosovo was thus generally described as being
"neither of war nor peace." The one agreement that Rugova and Milosevic were
able to reach was on education in 1996. It was secretly brokered by the Vatican
and allowed for the return of Albanian students and teachers to the educational
system. The agreement, which held out hope in the beginning as a possible model
of conflict resolution, was never truly implemented. Both sides were not sincere
since the Serbs just wanted to show their "cooperation" with the international
community, while the Albanians were looking for something approaching independence, not just cultural autonomy. In 1998, the agreement was finally put in
place under pressure from Western diplomats. Strangely, it created the arrangement of Serbs and Albanians using the schools and colleges in shifts, thus continuing with de facto segregation. The Serbs claimed a victory of sorts by pointing
out that the Albanians had "reentered" the system.[42]

THE INTERNATIONAL ARENA

The Albanians had some luck garnering support for their campaign at the international level. The Albanian American community in the United States proved
particularly effective. Both President George H. W. Bush and President Clinton
threatened to bomb Serbia if it let loose repression in Kosovo. Congress invited
Rugova and other leaders to testify, while delegations led by prominent figures
such as Bob Dole visited Kosovo. The government in exile set up offices throughout Europe. Both the European Parliament and the United Nations addressed the
issue, as did the Conference on Security and Cooperation in Europe and the 1992
London Conference on Former Yugoslavia. Rugova began to visit and receive
foreign dignitaries. What his party's public relations machine did not reveal to
the Kosovar people, however, was that in spite of pious acknowledgment of the
nonviolent method, none of these foreign governments recognized the independence of Kosovo. So, while all this time, the Kosovars held out hope for their
"maximalist" goal of independence, they failed to persuade foreign governments
that if Serb abuses continued, they (like several other parts of Yugoslavia) should
have the option of delinking from the existing setup and becoming a sovereign
nation.[43]

In some ways, Rugova's approach hindered international recognition because, in spite of increasing American and European awareness of the deteriorating human rights situation in the province, their attention became focused
on the much more violent dissolution in republics such as Croatia and Bosnia. The international community also feared that recognizing Kosovo's independence would encourage Serbs in Croatia and Bosnia to secede and argued
that the Kosovar Albanians did not control their own territory. In spite of the
October 1991 referendum in which almost all the Kosovars voted in favor of
independence, Lord Carrington, who presided over negotiations on the future
of Yugoslavia, did not respond to Rugova's request to consider independence,

nor did an arbitration commission. Carrington also refused to permit a Kosovar delegation to attend talks in London in 1992. A delegation did arrive and present its case but was disallowed participation in the actual proceedings. The only positive by-product was an agreement between Yugoslav prime minister Milan Panic and Rugova to bring back Kosovo's autonomy and permit freedom of the press as well as to readmit Kosovar Albanian students into the university at Pristina. Unfortunately, this agreement was honored in the breach. The minimal allowance that Milosevic made was to let Kosovo be part of the agenda of a working group that was formed to work on the issue of "national minorities." Rugova hoped that the Kosovo issue would eventually be upgraded to that of independence for a distinct republic, but this was not to be the case. British statesman and diplomat Lord Owen unsuccessfully tried to persuade Rugova and the Albanians to take part in the December 1992 Serb presidential elections and vote for Panic against Milosevic. The attempt was not persuasive because it wasn't backed up by promises of international help if Panic won. The Kosovar Albanians boycotted the elections, and Milosevic won by a big margin, with the boycott being a contributing factor.[44]

Even within adherents of the pacifist approach, there was a divergence of viewpoints. Rugova argued for dialogue with the Serbs, while a group around journalist Adem Demaci said that such an approach only legitimized Serb rule and that all the focus should be on creating a functioning parallel system that proved itself worthy. Rugova thought his approach to be the best way for getting international sympathy for his side. An European observer mission deployed in the province seemed to legitimize his approach. However, it did not lead to a lessening of human rights abuses, although it did initiate the coming into the region of a host of nongovernmental organizations, such as the Soros Foundation, Oxfam, and Save the Children, that helped out in the passive resistance strategy. Oxfam, for instance, assisted with water and sanitation facilities after the Serb authorities stopped supplying such services in some regions. The European mission was expelled in 1993, with the aftermath being marked by an increase of human rights abuses. "Since the [mission] left, villages have been surrounded and searched with brutality," Rugova told reporters. A working group set up to look into the "national minority" question also ran into a dead end. The Serbs objected to internationalization of the issue, while the Kosovar Albanians said that since they were 90 percent of the province's population, the rubric was a misnomer. The group tried to narrow its focus to deal with the education situation in the province but hit a dead end when the Kosovar delegation, led by the vice president of Rugova's party, Fehmi Agani, insisted that the mandate be broadened and that Serb repression be immediately stopped. Soon, Lord Owen removed Kosovo from the working group's mandate. The international community then began a slow process of disengagement from the province, starting with Clinton's inauguration, and only the UN special rapporteur on human rights for Yugoslavia, Tadeusz Mazowiecki, continued to scrutinize the human rights situation in the province. A Kosovar delegation traveled to Belgrade in June 1994 for negotiations, a triumph for Milosevic, but nothing came out of it. Just the fact that the delegation was formed, however, represented a victory for Rugova's viewpoint, which argued that since there was no international help forthcoming, the best approach was to negotiate with Belgrade for an improvement in living conditions in the province.[45]

AN IMPASSE

Rugova's experiment in civil resistance hence had only some success. The West had ample advance warning and information to act before violence took place. However, it chose to do so only after the Kosovo Liberation Army was formed and attacks and reprisals became a pattern. The West was interested only in "stability" and maintaining the status quo in Serbia, at least partly so that it could send back refugees from the area. Howard Clark, the author of a book-length study of the nonviolent movement in Kosovo, blames the West for a failure of imagination and for not urging the start of a process in Kosovo that could have brought about meaningful self-determination without necessarily complete secession. So Rugova's proposal for a three-year UN protectorate (albeit as a transitional step toward full independence) was never considered. There were minor triumphs for the Kosovars on the international front, however. There was an increasing international presence, including a UN High Commission for Refugees office and a U.S. Information Office. The United States refused to lift sanctions completely until the Kosovo situation had been resolved. The European Union offered the incentive of aid to the region.[46]

The returns to the Rugova government were minimal, though. Instead of being up front with the Kosovar people about this and trying to remedy the situation, the Rugova administration overplayed its international status, such as his April 1990 visit to Washington, where he was reported to have been treated like a head of state. Clark faults the Rugova leadership for failing to engage in goodwill gestures such as postponing the drive for full independence and promising fair treatment for ethnic minorities and for not reaching out to countries in the Non-Aligned Movement and Serb allies such as Russia. He also reproaches international solidarity groups for not focusing more external attention to the Kosovo experiment and international aid groups for not doing more to help inside Kosovo. There were a few successful initiatives, such as a polio immunization drive organized by the World Health Organization, UNICEF, some charities, and, interestingly, the government, but these were isolated examples, at least partly because of the inertia of the Rugova regime.[47]

Over time, the leadership of the resistance came for increasing criticism for hogging all the power and Rugova for his remote hands-off style. Paradoxically, however, this approach of his increased his popularity among the people, who saw this as a sign that he was above the fray. Some people called Rugova's party a dinosaur with a large body and a small brain. One critic dismissed it as a "movement of stagnation," while another said that "its political organism is petrified and based on clichés, so that all criticism is regarded as destructive." Such criticism, however, had little impact on political opinion, and these critics were soon sidelined. A chasm also opened between Rugova's circle and the government in exile, with each appointing a different ambassador to Albania. Bujar Bukoshi, prime minister in exile, complained during a 1994 visit to the United States that the Rugova government's pacifist approach was losing credibility among the people. "Meanwhile, this nonviolent attitude is viewed by Belgrade as an invitation to increase oppression, and seen by the international community as an excuse to ignore the situation," he said. Rugova redoubled his commitment to independence to dispel doubts that he was willing to settle for less.[48]

Meanwhile, Rugova insulated himself even more, personally appointing three board members of the party. In a sign of dissatisfaction, two of his vice presidents resigned, though Rugova managed to urge them to rescind their resignations. At this stage, although there was a widespread agreement among the people of Kosovo that the nonviolent approach was needed, a lot of people thought that some reappraisal of tactics and strategy was warranted to perhaps accelerate the program. Rugova and his colleagues, however, seemed not very much up for the challenge. By this time, in 1994, the situation had reached a level of stagnant equilibrium. Few Serbs were willing to speak out on behalf of the Kosovars. The international community had made it clear that it was unwilling to countenance an independent Kosovo. The education and health care system were in the doldrums, though the economy was in decent shape. The leadership was increasingly concentrated, with women and youth especially excluded. The last public demonstrations had been held in 1992. People's enthusiasm was waning. The movement needed fresh steam.[49]

Rugova, who was talked about this time as the Albanian Gandhi or the Gandhi of the Balkans, was not keen on comparisons to the original. Misinterpreting Gandhi, he said, "I'm not too keen about talking about passive or Gandhian resistance. I say it's about a political resistance, not passive and so not Gandhian." One of the major drawbacks of the Kosovar application of the nonviolence was that it still engaged in the demonization of the Other, in this case of the Serbs, and refused to reach out to them. The whole Gandhian concept of dialogue with the adversary was absent here, as was to a large extent the notion of empowering the population to make it fit for self-rule.[50]

A turning point was the signing of the 1995 Dayton Peace Accords between the Yugoslav government and the West. The accords made scant reference to Kosovo in spite of rumors among the Kosovar population of a secret addendum. There was restlessness at Rugova's leadership after this. He was accused of being undemocratic and too nonconfrontational even by standards of nonviolent tactics, not having a good negotiating position, and being indifferent toward democratizing forces in Yugoslavia. The Dayton agreements in 1995 were a real landmark for Rugova and his leadership on the road to failure. Not only did the accords solidify Milosevic's position internationally, but they completely ignored the situation in Kosovo.

Dayton thus had two big negative results for Rugova and his approach. First, it gave a huge boost to the self-importance of the Serbs, who felt that they were being taken seriously on the world stage instead of being treated as international outlaws. This emboldened the authorities to intensify their repression in Kosovo. Police brutality, torture, and mistreatment of the Kosovar Albanians intensified, as did censorship of independent print outlets and publishing houses. Second, the fact that Kosovo was not included in the negotiations resulted in a loss of confidence among many, including some of Rugova's colleagues, in his nonviolent stance. Although Albanians did continue to support him, there was an accompanying disillusionment with his tactics.[51]

THE RISE OF THE GUERRILLA MOVEMENT AND NATO INTERVENTION

The space opened up for a more violent alternative, which finally emerged in the form of the Kosovo Liberation Army, which proclaimed its existence with a series of attacks in mid-February 1996. Almost as a response to the prolonged stalemate in the province, the Kosovo Liberation Army sprung up to challenge Rugova's approach. In April 1996, after the shooting death of a student, the Kosovo Liberation Army announced its arrival on the scene with the ambush killing of three Serb civilians and two Serb policemen. Instead of taking the counterinitiative, Rugova's party issued a decree the following month extending parliament's life by a year. Over the next two years, at least 50 people were killed on both the Albanian and the Serb side, To make matters worse, the international community, in the form of European countries, sent many signals that it was not willing to accept the separation of Kosovo.[52]

Milosevic responded in a number of ways to the rise of a guerrilla movement. He strengthened the security forces to combat the Kosovo Liberation Army. He also tried to appear reasonable. So he allowed the setting up of a U.S. Information Center in Pristina, which actually provided a boost to Rugova's claim that the international community was paying attention. He also signed an agreement with Rugova (although the two didn't actually meet) to reopen the education system to Kosovar Albanians. The agreement ran into problems on several fronts, dashing Rugova's hope that it would bolster his standing. The two sides had differing interpretations because of disparities in the different language versions, with the Serbs insisting that it applied only at the school, not the university, level. In addition, the agreement also contained language that stated that it was "above political debate." This made Rugova seem like a sellout. Rugova received a further blow when his education adviser was killed in a car accident while traveling to attend a commission meeting on execution of the agreement. The Serbs stalled implementation of the accord and finally prevented it altogether. Observer Miranda Vickers wrote at the end of 1996, "Mr. Rugova, now a tired and withdrawn man, is fast losing credibility amongst his increasingly frustrated followers. Realizing that their passive stance has been ignored by the international community, many Albanians are now demanding more aggressive action to achieve their goal of an independent Kosovo."[53]

Although UN representative Elisabeth Rehn did respond favorably during a visit to a suggestion by Rugova that the province be placed under international cooperation, this did little to stop his marginalization. The Kosovo Liberation Army started occupying center stage. Even though President Clinton dispatched a special representative to meet with him and the Serbs, he was becoming irrelevant.[54]

The population was increasingly restive about the state of the education system and the forced unemployment. Instead, the Rugova leadership was negotiating in secret under the auspices of an Italian Catholic body for the return of students and teachers to the schools. A mixed group was set up to oversee the process. Groups such as students and fellow dissidents became increasingly restless with Rugova's approach, but he urged patience. Fellow Kosovar dissident Adem Demaci called for an "active Gandhism" and urged more contact with oppositionists in Belgrade. In December 1996, something unprecedented happened in Belgrade when demonstrators observed one minute of silence in sympathy for a Kosovar teacher killed in police custody. Unfortunately, this gesture wasn't built on, and ties between Kosovars and Yugoslav activists weren't strengthened. In the same month, Pristina students submitted a petition to Rugova calling for, among other things, the reopening of the school buildings, the convening of the parliament, and a change in the functioning style of the relationship. However, instead of a crisis erupting for Rugova in the coming months, the Albanian government of Sali Berisha fell, giving Rugova the opportunity to cast himself as a stabilizer and to extend parliament's mandate yet again. An attempt to oppose this failed resoundingly.[55]

Women were among the first groups to challenge Rugova's passive approach. In April 1996, 10,000 women gathered with candles and flowers at the spot where an unarmed student was shot dead in spite of discouragement by Rugova's party. Another group to defy him were the students. An organization of students, the UPSUP, organized a series of demonstrations in the fall of 1997 using a variety of nonviolent techniques over Rugova's objections. These demonstrations were successful in capturing the attention not only of Serbs but also of international observers who marveled at the finesse of these students. This was the first challenge to the segregated school system and was made by Albanian university students in the fall of 1997 as they peacefully occupied university buildings. In that fall, Albanian students held a series of demonstrations in Pristina with the intention of "liberating" "occupied" university buildings. Implicit in this was also a criticism of Rugova's leadership in that Rugova centered on education as a centerpiece success of his strategy, but critics like the students pointed out that the only success was in keeping Albanian students off the streets. The initiative was slipping out of Rugova's hands in more ways than one.[56]

Unfortunately for Rugova, the focus of the international community on the Kosovo question seemed to proportionately increase with the amount of violence in the region. In this sense, the Kosovo Liberation Army's strategy seemed to be vindicated. Rugova and Milosevic concluded another (unimplemented) education agreement, but this did not stop his haplessness. International mediators persuaded Rugova to have regular weekly meetings with Milosevic, but this pointless exercise soon ended, too. Meanwhile, both the violence in the province and the number of refugees intensified. Attempts by diplomat Christopher Hill to negotiate a settlement foundered on concerns by Rugova's party that the terms were too favorable to the Serbs. Rugova's approach proved ineffective in the end because he failed to convince the West and the international community. In fact, paradoxically it served only to delay the Western nations' desire to tackle the issue. This discredited Rugova's approach in the eyes of his countrymen and led to the rise of the Kosovar Liberation Army, which, in turn, forced the West to pay attention to the problem.[57]

In March 1998, parallel "elections" were held as scheduled, which Rugova won resoundingly, indicating his continued relevance in spite of his inaction on other fronts. In May, Rugova, prodded by the United States, met Milosevic without even consulting his colleagues.[58]

Throughout 1998, the ambushes and the reprisals continued, with nearly 2,000 civilians being killed that year. The space and popular support for Rugova's nonviolent approach shrank rapidly. The 1998 funerals of two people killed—a Serb official and an Albanian factory worker—attended by thousands on either side marked the end of the nonviolent era in the province. From here on, Kosovo Liberation Army attacks and Serb reprisals intensified. Both the number and the severity of the incidents multiplied. Finally, a Serb massacre in Racak that killed 45 people caused the world to take notice.[59]

An unarmed observer mission sent by the Organization for Security and Cooperation in Europe proved increasingly ineffective, and peace moves by international mediators stalled in spite of Rugova's efforts to cooperate. Even though Rugova was present at the 1999 Rambouillet conference in France to decide the future of Kosovo and accepted the terms of the accords, the course of future events already seemed clear. NATO military action was in the offing.

When attempts at international mediation and negotiations broke down in Rambouillet, NATO commenced a campaign of bombing. Serb reprisals against Kosovo civilians increased. One of the most embarrassing episodes for Rugova took place shortly after the start of the war. He was placed under house arrest and was shown on television having tea with Milosevic and discussing "peace." After some negotiation, Rugova was released to the Italians.[60]

Rugova seemed increasingly irrelevant as the conflict went on. Milosevic eventually backed down, placing Kosovo under the United Nations, as an international protectorate, a limbo status that continues to this date, with dozens of countries recognizing it as sovereign and the rest of the world not willing to take that step.[61] The rise of the Kosovo Liberation Army and the NATO bombing that followed in 1999 thus soon made the entire project of nonviolent resistance moot. A unique chapter in the history of nonviolent resistance was soon sidelined.[62]

Clark says that the real tragedy of Rugova and his colleagues was that the leadership failed to (with the exception of some students and other small groups) build on its achievements after offering parallel structures of resistance. This tragedy was compounded by the frustration of the population that led them to turn first to the Kosovo Liberation Army and then ultimately to NATO for salvation. The orgy of revenge let loose afterward on the Serbs sounded the death knell of the nonviolent strategy.[63]

Clark points out the strategy of the Rugova leadership had some successes but great limitations, too. People did attain great satisfaction from the persistence of nonviolence and their parallel structures of governance, but the situation had reached an impasse by 1996. Although there was international attention to the problem, there was little enthusiasm for accepting full independence for Kosovo. The other goal was to change Serbian policy by wearing them down. Although there were glimpses that this was working, the strategy was too long drawn to be of immediate use. Calls came for a more active strategy from other figures, but there was no clear long-term vision. But Albanians were understandably wary of the attitudes of Serbs toward them in a situation where polls showed that a majority of the Serbs harbored negative feelings toward them. In addition, a lot of Albanians wanted ethnic separation rather than coexistence. Hence, no attempts were made to arrive at a working solution, such as cantons and dual sovereignty, that would implement the notion of self-rule. The Gandhian notion of reaching out to the adversary fell by the wayside.[64]

Clark admonishes Rugova for not taking lessons from Gandhi and engaging in a program of constructive work involving the population at large. This not only would have given the movement impetus and lessons on the right opportunities to usher in specific initiatives but also would have been a good way to bring about social reform. The one positive example was the campaign to end blood feuds, but this was almost never repeated later. Clark compares Rugova's party to the Congress Party in India before Gandhi, unwilling and unable to bring about mass change. Unlike Gandhi, who "tested" various tactics, such as demonstrations and closings, the too-cautious Rugova let things slide. Instead of seizing the moment and engaging in various projects, the Kosovars adopted an attitude of blaming everything on the Serbs. Gandhi's maxim that "if we impute all of our weaknesses to the present government, we shall never shed them" was forgotten. Gandhi's concept of *swadeshi* was also forgotten, and no attempt was made for the boycott of Serbian goods, either generally or specific items. Instead, Gandhism in Kosovo became interpreted as "waiting."[65]

The commitment to nonviolence among the Kosovar population was a strategic and pragmatic commitment rather than a philosophical one, like with most mass movements, and there was nothing wrong with that. Where it fell short was not having a more dynamic approach, such as opening up communication with the Serbs. Certainly, Rugova and his colleagues tried to soften the demand for independence by envisioning Kosovo as a demilitarized and neutral state and even conceptualizing a long transitional period as an international protectorate (the current status of the area). But they did not work harder to lay out interim steps to mobilize the masses, such as reopening the schools, reinstating dismissed workers, and having an international observer presence. In addition, they were oblivious to the most Gandhian and most demanding of the components of a nonviolent strategy: recognizing the needs of the opponent, an essential part of the technique of *satyagraha* being the attempt to find the Truth in the Other. These confidence-building measures to reach out to the opposition—admittedly a tricky task when the adversary is Milosevic—were not attempted by Rugova and his colleagues.[66]

So how can the success of the Rugova experiment in Kosovo be assessed? Analyst Tim Judah wrote in 1997, "Of all the leaders of former Yugoslavia, Rugova has perhaps played the shrewdest game. . . . Despite discontent aroused by the belief that so far it has achieved nothing, in fact it has achieved much. It has saved lives and, unlike the Krajina Serbs, for example, kept Kosovo's Albanian population . . . in their homes." When two top Kosovar leaders, Veton Surroi and Fehmi Agani, were interviewed and asked whether Rugova's approach was a mistake, both replied no. Both saw it as a necessary phase needed to stave off violence and to let the world deal with the issue. Agani also pointed out the high price that civilians had paid for the Kosovo Liberation Army's violent approach.[67]

Clark says that a more active constructive program instead of a passive approach could have yielded even more results. Where it failed, he says, is bringing about a sea change of consciousness among Kosovars, evident in the mass reprisals against Serbs after the NATO intervention. Clark also compares the leadership of Rugova with that of Gandhi and King and finds it wanting. Unlike both of them, Rugova did not attempt to build any social movements, nor was he in the heroic mold. Instead, his was a remote and aloof style. Interestingly, he had not founded the Kosovo Democratic League, nor was he the first person offered the leadership. Instead, he got it on his track record of integrity as the president of the Kosovar Writers' Association. Oddly, his style suited the moment. "He precisely is the man who was best suited for this situation of neither war nor peace, the politics of non-doing," said a fellow Albanian leader in 1996 in a remark that wasn't meant as criticism. After some time, almost the only public appearances he made were at his Friday press conferences, but this did not seem to dent his popularity with the people. Both Western journalists and young critics found that any criticism of him rebounded on them. The whole attitude in Rugova's circle became one of passivity, of waiting for something to happen on the international stage. Crucial elements, such as building up a development program and opening a Belgrade office, were ignored.[68]

Yet, in spite of all these problems, Rugova continues to command allegiance among the population. He was repeatedly written off in 1998 and 1999, especially after his television tea appearance with Milosevic, but bounced back, even when he halfheartedly came back from Italy in a style more suited to a monarch than a movement leader. He returned after the war with his popularity retained. Kosovars preferred his naïveté to the crookedness of others.[69]

AFTERMATH OF THE NONVIOLENT MOVEMENT

In 2002, the Kosovar Parliament again elected Rugova the president of Kosovo. The BBC writes that in spite of all his missteps, two things stood him in good stead. First, he was seen as someone who had been dedicated to the independence struggle for a long time. Second, the Kosovar people perceived him to be cut from a different cloth than his opponents.[70]

A burst of violence that was let loose in March 2004 against the Serbs for their alleged killing of two Albanian youths did much to damage Kosovo's reputation and brought back memories of the massive anti-Serb campaign immediately after the end of the NATO bombardment. At least 28 people died, and an estimated 4,000 Serbs and Gypsies were driven away, with 41 Serb Orthodox churches and monasteries being attacked in the frenzy. Although the Kosovo prime minister termed the violence a "disaster," the government, including Rugova, seemed unwilling or unable to stop the pogrom.[71]

Elections in October 2004 were marked by a massive boycott by the Serbs, weakening Rugova's legitimacy. Besides, real power rested in the hands of the UN administrators and the 20,000 NATO troops in the province. A strong animosity continued between the two ethnic groups, exacerbated by the weak economy. Rugova's party won almost half the vote, not enough for it to form the government on its own.[72]

By this time, Rugova's stature had diminished to the point that Julie Mertus, professor at American University, wrote a biting commentary in the *Chicago Tribune* saying that both George W. Bush and Ibrahim Rugova were quite similar in that both were convinced that they possessed the truth but were out of touch with reality. "Instead of being guided by the facts, Presidents Bush and Rugova consistently base their behavior on the mythologies they have created for themselves," she wrote. "For Rugova, this means ignoring the issue of revenge killings, and overlooking the complicated nature of his demands for Kosovar independence. For Bush, this means ignoring how things are really going in Iraq and reimagining the economy at home to somehow account for rising prices and lost jobs."[73]

Rugova died in office in January 2006 of lung cancer, almost certainly caused by his chain smoking. Hundreds of thousands of Kosovar Albanians turned out to pay their final respects to a man who until the end was regarded by many as the "father of the nation."

The saga of Rugova and his nonviolence project was a mixed one. Because of several slipups, he was not able to realize the full potential of his nonviolent strategy, nor was he able to reach out to his adversaries in a Gandhi-like manner. The fact, however, that he managed to sustain a nonviolent campaign for years in extremely difficult circumstances is by itself no mean achievement. Even with all his flaws of personality and tactics, the Rugova path was surely preferable to that of most other leaders in the Balkans, past and present. And in the end, after many detours, eventually Kosovo did attain de facto separation from the rest of Yugoslavia and actual recognition as an independent entity by dozens of countries around the world (with the International Court of Justice recognizing in July 2010 the legality of its secession). For this, Rugova's embrace, no matter how imperfect, of the Gandhian approach should be given some credit.

CHAPTER 9

Not Just a Land of Conflict: Nonviolence in the Middle East

NONVIOLENCE IN THE MIDDLE EAST

There are multiple arguments some people give for why nonviolence cannot work in the Middle East. They contend that nonviolence doesn't have any resonance in Middle East history or in Islam (wrong notions, as this book proves). They also maintain that a bit of violence in any struggle is necessary to give people a sense of dignity and self-worth. In addition, they say that violence is very often more efficient (such as in coups) in getting rid of oppression and garners more attention.[1]

To this, proponents of nonviolence reply that nonviolent action is not passive but a dynamic response to repression and social injustice and is not to be confused with appeasement. Besides, they point out that it has had success in the Middle East, such as in Iran, Egypt, Iraq, and Palestine (detailed in this book). And, very importantly, use of violence for political purposes ensures that a culture of brutality permeates and pollutes the entire society. In the Middle East, this can be seen in the long descent into chaos in Lebanon in the 1970s and the 1980s. Adherents of nonviolence are always willing to reach out to the other side and admit that they don't have a monopoly on truth. This changes the rules of politics and fosters consensus building. Besides, the utilization of violence tarnishes both the people who exercise it and their cause. The use of terrorism in the Palestinian struggle has alienated a significant part of the global public and made it that much harder for the Palestinians to achieve their aims. Conversely, nonviolent protests (be it Gandhi's movement in India or the U.S. civil rights struggle) have often resulted in a massive swing in opinion toward the practitioners. Additionally, the use of nonviolence has a salutary effect on the people exercising it—since it gives them courage and self-confidence.[2] And, to top it all, nonviolence is twice as more effective, as has been demonstrated by the comprehensive study cited in the introductory chapter.

IRAN'S GREEN MOVEMENT

The Middle East has been home to a number of nonviolent campaigns over the years, but without a doubt, the one that has most captured the imagination of the world in recent times has been the Green Movement in Iran. It began in June 2009 in protest against the dubious reelection of President Mahmoud Ahmadinejad. A year after the movement started, its future looks uncertain, though its supporters contend that it's too soon to cast a verdict. Regardless of how things ultimately pan out, the campaign has provided us yet another example of the use of nonviolent tactics in a Muslim society.

Indeed, defeated presidential candidate Mir-Hossein Mousavi invoked the name of the ultimate icon of modern pacifism—Mahatma Gandhi—in urging his followers to fight on. He asked his supporters to "adopt the tactics of Gandhi, the tactics of nonviolent protest and civil disobedience," said his spokesperson Mohsen Makhmalbaf, a globally acclaimed film director.[3] Renowned scholar Fred Halliday notes that the uprising happened due to a confluence of factors:

- A long-term growth of dissatisfaction with the social, economic, and political actions of the Islamic Republic
- A particular revulsion with the political direction and economic failures of Iran since Ahmadinejad came to power in 2005
- A set of short-term events and processes in the days leading up to the election (including disgust at the vulgarity of Ahmadinejad in his television debate with Mousavi and the creative use by the opposition of SMS, Facebook, and other technology)

Halliday says that the events of the summer of 2009 can be seen as a corrective to the hijacking of the 1979 Iranian Revolution by Ayatollah Khomeini's clique. "Khomeini and his associates set out to monopolize the post-revolutionary state and extinguish both their political rivals and the very memory of their contribution to a history that belongs to all Iranians," Halliday writes. "It is the great contribution of the brave citizens of Iran who took to the streets in June 2009, and affirmed their rights in peaceful and dignified fashion, to have reclaimed this truth."[4]

The movement was basically nonviolent in spite of some rock throwing and a mysterious bombing at the tomb of Khomeini (and rage many months afterward at a brutal government crackdown). So measured was the protesters' response to the violence the government unleashed on them that when people caught the suspected killer of Neda Agha-Soltan, whose murder became a global symbol of the repression, they let him go after confiscating his weapon and ID.[5]

"What we are witnessing since the first demonstrations against the results of the presidential elections might very well be considered as a major nonviolent movement in a Gandhian style," wrote Ramin Jahanbegloo, an Iranian dissident in exile in Canada. "Today, Mousavi has become the symbol of nonviolent protest in Iran, but the true hero of the Iranian civic movement is the emerging republican model of nonviolent resistance."[6]

Protesters depicted themselves as on the side of Islam, defined by them as being for righteousness and justice. "In the battle to control Iran's streets, both the government and the opposition are deploying religious symbols and parables to portray themselves as pursing the ideal of a just Islamic state," reported the New York Times.[7]

The opposition often draped itself in green colors, identified with Islam, and invoked the cry of "Allahu Akbar, or "God is great." Their struggle was helped by the fact that Shiite Islam, the predominant form in Iran, has a reverence for the underdog and for social justice. "What is really smart about Mousavi and his group is that they say they are part of the Islamic Revolution and they want to say 'God is great' and overthrow tyranny," Professor Said Arjomand told the New York Times. "It is a struggle over the appropriation of the old symbols. If the public says we want Hussain [the grandson of the Prophet Muhammad] and 'God is great,' and then the militias are told to go kill them, that will be a little hard."[8] "The demonstrations show that Islam has a genuine liberating potential to find a 'good' Islam," philosopher Slavoj Zizek wrote. "One doesn't have to go back to the caliphs of the tenth century—we have it right here."[9]

The nonviolent tactics of the protesters were very compatible with Islam, as Jahanbegloo told me. "Iranians can be inspired by tolerant Islam as much as by other spiritualities," said Jahanbegloo, a professor at the University of Toronto who was imprisoned by the Iranian regime for four months. "Nonviolent resistance against injustice, which has come to be closely associated with a 'Gandhian ethos,' has strong resonance within Iranian Islam."[10]

The Green Movement has been more promising than its putative leader. Some of Mousavi's past gave one hope for what sort of head of state he might be. He has a background as an architect and painter (his wife is also an artist) and has reportedly created some impressive abstract expressionist works. But other parts of his résumé are more dubious since he held the (ineffectual) post of prime minister in the 1980s, when the regime was at the height of its repression.[11]

In spite of his checkered history, Mousavi garnered a broad base of support. A significant part of his backing was from artists who hoped for a cultural thaw after the repressive freeze of Ahmadinejad, during whose tenure everything from reformist movies to a translation of Gabriel Garcia Marquez's latest novel was curbed. Among Mousavi's supporters are a who's who of the luminaries of Iranian cinema (perhaps the best in the world), with names like Makhmalbaf, Majid Majidi, and Dariush Mehrjui.[12]

Artists were just a small part of the protesters, however. It has been an inclusive movement that encompassed many segments of Iranian society, from students to unionists, posing the Islamic Republic a threat like no other since the Iranian Revolution 30 years ago. "Grandparents walk alongside their children and grandchildren," reported the Inter Press Service. "University professors, artists, and intellectuals have joined. Even some members of the Iranian national soccer team wore the color of protest—green—on their wrists while playing South Korea to a 1–1 draw earlier in the week."[13]

"Contrary to the caricature, the demonstrators around me represented an impressive cross-section of Iranian society," a reporter for the New Yorker observed. "The crowd in Azadi Street was dominated by young people, and many of the girls wore the regulation black maghna'eh, or hooded cloak, that they wear in class. There were also elderly men and women, and families whose dress and appearance suggested that they had come from modest precincts of Tehran or the provinces."[14]

The breadth of the movement led to an initial vagueness of agenda beyond the call to redo the elections. The people on the side of Mousavi formed an amorphous mass. While some were for the abolition of the clerical domination of the Iranian political system, others were just hoping for a moderate, less repressive theocracy. Mousavi's promise to reduce patrolling by the morality police resonated well, for instance. The hard line taken by the top religious leadership, however, soured more and more Iranians on the basic system itself. "The students in Tiananmen wanted real democracy, the Poles wanted regime change, but the Iranians might be looking for something in between," an adviser to President Obama told the New York Times. "But the more the supreme leader cracks down, the more radicalized the opposition may become."[15]

A wonderful aspect of the mass mobilization was the prominent role played by women. They were in the forefront of many of the protest events, often jostling with the security forces. Underlying this activism was a paradox: while the Iranian social setup discriminates against women on several fronts, women have taken full advantage of the limited opportunities offered them and now comprise, for instance, more than 60 percent of university graduates. The result: they increasingly chafe at the restrictions placed on them. "The root of the current unrest is the people's dissatisfaction and frustration at their plight going back before the election," said Iranian Nobel Peace Prize winner Shirin Ebadi (whom I've interviewed for The Progressive). "Because women are the most dissatisfied people in society, that is why their presence is more prominent."[16]

Ebadi has particularly praised the courage of the Mourning Mothers, a group of women whose loved ones have been imprisoned or killed or are missing at the hands of the Iranian government. To honor their family members, they meet each week at a park in Tehran. "Every Saturday they gather peacefully and every Saturday the police attack, beat, and arrest them," Ebadi wrote for The Progressive. "This excessive violence and repression by the government has sadly become routine in Iran—but has not deterred the Mourning Mothers. Courageously, they are defending their human rights and, ultimately, those of women everywhere."[17]

An additional factor in the mobilization of women was Mousavi's wife, Zahra Rahnavard, a former university chancellor who campaigned prominently alongside her husband. Even as timid a public display of affection as the couple walking into public meetings while holding hands galvanized young women. "Many compared the role of Rahnavard with Michelle Obama," Kianoosh Sanjari, an

Iranian blogger, told reporter Benjamin Joffe-Walt. "She has become a symbol for the women's rights movement."[18]

Ebadi mentioned other women's rights organizations active in Iran, such as the One Million Signatures Campaign, which aims to collect that many Iranian signatures to press for an end to official gender discrimination in Iran. For Ebadi, all these groups working together will usher in true democracy in Iran. "Women were at the forefront of this year's election anniversary protests, as they were yesterday and will be tomorrow," she writes. "And, mark my words, it will be women who will bring democracy to Iran."[19]

The anti-Ahmadinejad demonstrations in Iran inspired a mix of awe and disbelief in Iran's Arab neighbors, such as Egypt, with activists in these countries wondering why they couldn't emulate their Iranian brethren. The prominent role of women especially engendered a debate on their role in Arab societies. "For the first time, [Arab women] are seeing that the Muslim woman is also a leader and a partner," Sawsan Zakzak, head of the League of Syrian Women, told the *Washington Post*.[20]

The Green Movement crowds were very creative in their slogans. As they passed the Employment Ministry, the marchers improvised a chant: "Ministry of Employment, why so much unemployment?" Another one referred to Ahmadinejad's claim that there was a "celestial halo" surrounding him while he was addressing the UN General Assembly in 2005: "He saw the celestial halo, but he didn't see our votes."[21]

A *New Yorker* reporter witnessed an inspiring moment when there was a to-and-fro chanting in a Tehran neighborhood of Allahu Akbar that went on for half an hour. "These may be only words, but I can assure you it was 'Allahu Akbar' as much as the strikes and the demonstrations that did in the Shah in '79," his host told him.[22]

Interestingly, the Iranian government blamed (credited?) American nonviolence strategist Gene Sharp (someone I've also interviewed for *The Progressive*) as being the intellectual mastermind behind the uprising. "After massive protests shook Iran this past summer, Iran singled out an obscure American political scientist in his eighties as a key figure behind the unrest," the *Christian Science Monitor* reported. "In a mass trial of some 100 key reformist figures this past August, Iranian prosecutors charged that postelection protests were 'completely planned in advance and proceeded according to a timetable and the stages of a velvet coup [such] that more than 100 of the 198 events were executed in accordance with the instructions of Gene Sharp.'"[23] A cartoon video created by Iranian intelligence a few years prior went so far as to depict Sharp as "the theoretician of civil disobedience and velvet revolutions" and "one of the CIA agents in charge of America's infiltration into other countries."

Sharp was modest enough to point out that the Iranians had ample homegrown sources of inspiration, such as the 1979 Iranian Revolution. Still, the protests sparked a huge increase in the copies downloaded in Farsi of his most popular manual, *From Dictatorship to Democracy*. A former member of the Iranian Revolutionary Guard, Mohsen Sazegara, eagerly helped in disseminating Sharp's ideas in Iran through downloadable videos on the Internet. And there were traces of Sharp's influence visible in the adherence to nonviolence and a resolve to stand firm. "These regimes always present themselves as all-powerful—absolutely omnipotent, so that resistance becomes futile," said Sharp. "But if you learn this regime has these five . . . or twenty weaknesses—and you can deliberately aggravate those weaknesses—it weakens the regime. It helps it fall apart."[24]

Sharp was remarkably prescient when I met him in 2006. "Our work is available in Iran and has been since 2004," he told me. "That kind of struggle broadly has important precedence in Iranian/Persian history, both in the 1906 democratic revolution and in the 1979 struggle against the Shah—all predominantly nonviolent forms of struggle. If somebody doesn't decide to use military means, then it is very likely that there will be a peaceful national struggle there."[25]

A couple of months after the elections, the crackdown continued. "The office of the Association for the Defence of Prisoners' Rights was also ransacked, and evidence of the torture, rape and killing of detainees confiscated," reported Nazenin Ansari for the openDemocracy Web site. "A number of top advisers to the opposition are among the thousands of people arrested in the post-election crackdown."[26]

Ansari contended that the detention of a number of high-profile figures with connections to the regime revealed fissures within the regime, most prominently between the clerical authorities and the Revolutionary Guard militia. Even with the odds stacked against it (because of a harsh and byzantine security apparatus and the lack of a charismatic leader), the opposition movement continued its endeavors. Ahmadenijad's government has proven to be so unpopular over the past year that Iran premier-league soccer matches have had to be held without any spectators in the stadiums in order to prevent people from being seen and heard publicly criticizing him and Iran's supreme religious figure Ayatollah Khamenei. Public gatherings of any type are routinely broken up.[27]

The deadliest single episode over the course of the year occurred in December 2009, when, during protests marking Ashura, the Shiite commemoration of Hussain's martyrdom, firing by the police killed at least 10 people. The willingness to use force on such a holy occasion marked a notable departure from the past, when Iranian authorities had shown respect for the occasion by backing away. Added to these deaths was the targeted assassination of Ali Mousavi, nephew of the defeated presidential candidate, who was run over and then shot in a gesture apparently aimed at his uncle. In response to the repression, protesters engaged in violence of their own, burning things and attacking security forces.[28]

"It was very, very disturbing to see that on the holiest day of the Shiite calendar the government felt free to use violence," Hadi Ghaemi of the International Campaign for Human Rights in Iran told Amy Goodman of Democracy Now! "Even thirty years ago when protests were taking place against the Shah, the Shah's military did not open fire on that day. And now we see a government that has claims to religious authority basically overlooking all that and killing its own people on that day."[29]

After months of repression, the opposition Green Movement in Iran was at a crossroads. Large-scale protests called by the movement in February 2010 on the occasion of the 31st anniversary of Iran's Islamic Revolution fizzled out. This was at least partly due to repression and arrests by the government but also due to the opposition's being so reliant on "virtual" technologies that it was unable to mobilize real people. "Many in the opposition have concluded that their lack of clear leadership, and their reliance on exiles who work through the Internet—factors that provided crucial resilience in the waves of brutal government crackdowns last summer and fall—may now be holding them back," the *New York Times* reported.[30] Part of the problem was the disconnect between the leaders and the followers. Some drew solace from the fact that the government was able to bring out many fewer people than last year. But the question on everyone's mind was, as Professor Mehrzad Boroujerdi of Syracuse University put it, "What next?"[31]

For a long time, the Green Movement was hobbled by the lack of a specific program. It took until New Year's Day 2010 for Mousavi to come out with a five-point agenda, including "an indirect call for the impeachment of Ahmadinejad by *Majlis* (the Iranian Parliament) and a reference to free elections with preconditions such as freeing of political prisoners and freedom of political parties, assembly, and the press," Georgetown Professor Mehrdad Mashayekhi writes. Even then, Mashayekhi asserts, Mousavi didn't dispel many of concerns he has engendered by hearkening to the millenarian notions of Khomeini. Instead, Mashayekhi contends, he needs to reach out to different sectors of Iranian society, such as women, secular Iranians, and others (some of whom he later did extend a hand to).[32]

Around the same time as Mousavi, two other groups issued manifestos of their own. The boldest was by a group of exiled intellectuals who called for a radical overhaul of the Iranian sociopolitical system, including Ahmadinejad's resignation, an independent judiciary, a truly free electoral process, and the release of all political prisoners. "Some people expected the Green Movement to do miracles, to do the impossible. We wanted to make it clear that it's a democratic movement, and if it has a godfather, it is Gandhi," Professor Abdolkarim Soroush, one of the authors of the manifesto, said. "We are insisting adamantly that democratic, nonviolent change is at the heart of this movement. That will minimize the violence from the other side, which is ready to engage in any kind of violence."[33] In an even bolder move, since it came from within the country, 88 professors at Teheran University called for an end to the repression and prosecution for those responsible for the crackdown.[34]

In March 2010, Mousavi tried to broaden and revitalize the opposition by calling on the working class and education sector to join in the reform movement. Oddly, even though both of these groups have protested in the recent past, they haven't become part of the prodemocracy movement. Khamenei issued a stern warning around the same time about the threat of subversive activity. "Ever since a planned major protest evaporated in February, the movement has seemed disoriented and leaderless, and uncertain how to move forward," the *New York Times* reported. "[At the same time] for all its crowing about having crushed the opposition, the hard-line clerical elite has sounded some unusually anxious notes lately, suggesting a deep concern over the possibility of renewed protests."[35]

A year after the protests, the stalemate continued. The government intensified the crackdown as the anniversary approached. "Just a few weeks ago, on May 9 [2010], the lengths to which the regime will go to crush its opponents came to light," Nobel laureate Ebadi wrote in a column distributed through the Progressive Media Project (the outfit I'm the coeditor of). "Five political prisoners were executed in secret. Not even their families or their lawyers were notified." She added, "At least twenty-five other men and women await the same fate."[36]

Ebadi herself was the target of repression. Her Nobel medal was reportedly confiscated, and her accounts were sealed. Even more egregiously, in order to get at Ebadi, who was self-exiled, the regime allegedly assaulted her husband and imprisoned her sister. "In an attempt to stop me from doing my work from abroad, the government arrested my sister, Dr. Noushin Ebadi," Ebadi wrote in her column. "My sister has never been politically active or participated in any rallies or demonstrations. She was arrested and detained for three weeks solely because of my work fighting for human rights."[37]

The paradox is that both the government and the opposition seem fearful, almost paranoid of each other. The first anniversary of the protests, in June 2010, was marked by arrests and sporadic demonstrations. Perhaps as many as 200 people were detained, the *New York Times* reported. "After dark, rooftop chants of 'God is great' echoed across the city, mimicking what had been a symbol of defiance to the shah," the paper reported. "On Saturday, it was a direct, yet safely anonymous challenge to Iran's current leadership."[38]

And the repression was stepped up. "Amnesty International has documented a widening crackdown on dissent that has left journalists, students, political and rights activists as well as clerics languishing in prisons," the human rights organization stated. "Lawyers, academics, former political prisoners and members of Iran's ethnic and religious minorities have also been caught up in an expanding wave of repression that has led to widespread incidents of torture and other ill-treatment along with politically motivated execution of prisoners."[39]

The organization documented hundreds of Iranians jailed for connections to the protests, and politically inspired death sentences were used as a tool of intimidation. "The Iranian authorities must end this campaign of fear that aims to crush even the slightest opposition to the government," Amnesty's Claudio Cordone said. "They are continuing to use the death penalty as a tool of repression. . . . The Iranian authorities blame everyone but themselves for the unrest but they are failing to show any respect for their own laws which prohibit the torture and other ill-treatment of all detainees."[40]

The efforts of the past year hadn't been in vain, however. "People have absolutely gained something, a certain degree of individual independence," a 20-year-old medical student told the *New York Times*. "They began to decide for themselves that they would go out to protest, to follow the news. This is something that has happened for everybody. In different areas of their lives they are losing patience and are not likely to say anymore that they will put up with things."[41]

Mousavi issued a charter on the first anniversary of the protests calling for sweeping reform while at the same time professing fealty to the basic principles of the Iranian Revolution. Curiously, there were two versions. "[The statement] went on to lay out the principles and objectives of the movement, which, taken together, present a vision for a nationalist, reformist Islamic Iran with free elections, and an independent judiciary and press," the *Los Angeles Times* reported. "However, the PDF version of the statement includes a vital paragraph not published in the version that went up on Mousavi's website in which the former pillar of the regime calls for the separation of religion and state."[42]

Commentator Danny Postel argues that whether you characterize the Green Movement as reform, revolution or "refolution," it is here to stay. "Whatever concrete outcome emerges, or fails to emerge, from the events unfolding, something very important has already happened," Postel says. "As [Professor] Nader Hashemi has argued, 'The Green Movement has already won an overwhelming ideological victory against the regime. In the realm of political ideas, the battle is over and Iran's clerical oligarchs know it—liberal democratic ideas have triumphed.' "[43]

An American scholar working inside Iran, Shane M. (who withheld his full name so as not to reveal his identity), in an insightful commentary on the Iranian Green Movement, said that the Western media oversimplified things. He claimed that in actuality, the opposition in Iran was far from certain that it would want to completely abolish the role of Islam in the political sphere. "It was not by accident that we heard 'Allah Akbar' from the rooftops throughout the summer and during the November 4 protests, or that protestors carry signs such as 'Islam = Honesty,'" wrote Shane. "This type of godly language and repertoire is being used by protestors because it resonates, because it makes sense. No matter what happens, long after the Islamic Republic of Iran comes and goes, Islam will remain in Iran."[44]

Besides, Shane said, quoting political scientist Farideh Farhi, a lot of people in Iran are concerned not with high abstractions but with the most practical of things—how to get life to be more normal and less arbitrarily dependent on a whimsical state. "As a candidate, Mousavi represented the possibility that daily life might just be improved, if only slightly," Shane wrote. "Some thirty years after the ideological struggles of the late 1970s and early 1980s, large numbers of weary Iranians are more concerned with bringing to power a government that can get things done and improve their daily lives."[45]

Shane encountered a group of war veterans who while deeply devout, were highly critical of Ayatollah Khamenei for endorsing the election results, and were profoundly ambivalent when they heard people (such as one person's son) denounce the Islamic Republic. "Conflicts such as these had led a good number of my interview subjects to reassess whether the Islamic Republic itself were viable any more," writes Shane. "Above all, they stressed that Islam had to be preserved. If it took changing the political system, so be it."[46]

THE IRANIAN REVOLUTION

Iran's history carries a hugely positive example for the Green Movement protesters. The 1979 Iranian Revolution itself was essentially a broad-based nonviolent
uprising against the shah, with nearly all the violence being inflicted on the
protesters by the monarch's security apparatus. (The movement against the shah,
in turn, derived inspiration from the 1906 Constitutional Revolution, when a
popular movement forced the then ruler to create a constitution that introduced
popular participation and limited his powers.) The anti-shah forces represented
a broad spectrum of society, ranging from workers and students to intellectuals
and clerics. They engaged in a vast array of devices to topple the king, including
strikes, civil disobedience, and massive rallies. (There was a parallel, independent
guerrilla movement operating at the same time, too.)[47]

Protests against the shah's rule had their genesis in the 1960s. The first such
attempt, in the holy city of Qom, led to a merciless crackdown by the shah's
forces that killed numerous Iranians. The Ayatollah Khomeini was exiled after
this episode. Finding no outlet within the country, Iranian expatriates took up
the mantle. For instance, six students chained themselves inside the Statue of
Liberty in 1977 in protest.[48]

Starting the same year, Khomeini sent communiqués to Iran urging nonviolent strikes, boycotts, and noncooperation. Just a couple of days after a newspaper
was directed to publish an anti-Khomeini article in January 1978, massive demonstrations in Qom again resulted in a police crackdown that led to the deaths
of many. In Islam, mourning is done for 40 days. This set up a vicious cycle for
the shah since every 40 days there was a fresh demonstration, and if there were
protesters killed, then the cycle continued. So, there was a continuous chain of
protests, deaths, and further demonstrations.[49]

Two events proved pivotal in the shah's downfall. In the first, on August 28,
1978, a cinema hall in the city of Abadan was set on fire, claiming more than
400 victims. The Iranian people blamed the government for it (though it is still
unclear who was actually responsible). And on September 8, there was a huge,
mainly peaceful demonstration in Tehran in response to the declaration of martial law a day earlier. The shah's forces opened fire and killed a large number of
people. Both these events strengthened the determination of the Iranian opposition.[50] "At the end of the fasting month of Ramadan, 100,000 people poured
into the streets, the first of the grand marches against the Shah," writes Nobel
laureate Ebadi in her memoir, *Iran Awakening*. "An ocean of Iranians as far as the
eye could see filled the wide boulevards of Tehran and raised their voices against
the Shah."[51]

Anti-shah forces went into noncooperation mode, with state hospital employees going on strike in early October. Two prominent newspapers stopped publishing shortly after. In late October, oil workers struck with demands for release of
all political prisoners, paralyzing a crucial industry. (They were forced to return
in mid-November after the arrest of strike leaders.) On November 6, there was
a nationwide general strike. There was such widespread dissatisfaction with the

shah that radio workers would sabotage from within his broadcasts to the nation, pretending that there were glitches until the speech was finished. By December 1978, things had spun out of the shah's control, with repeated strikes and demonstrations. The shah appointed an interim prime minister and left the country, never to return.[52]

Nonviolence scholar Professor Stephen Zunes points out that the Iranian Revolution protesters took pains to keep their movement nonviolent. They were explicitly given instructions to try to win over the troops to their side, and thousands of troops did cross over. The main means of propagation of revolution literature was the cassette tape, through which there was mass dissemination of Khomeini's speeches. A Shah official remarked, "Tape cassettes are stronger than fighter planes." There were very few incidents of violence to life or property, with even these few occurring without the sanction of the leadership. On the contrary, there was a very strong notion of martyrdom, derived from Shiite tradition, which led people to be willing to defy repression nonviolently. Zunes tallies as many as 20,000 killed by the shah's security forces.[53]

"During the resistance, thousands of Iranians—most of them nonviolent demonstrators—lost their lives at the hands of Savak [the Shah's security apparatus] and the army," writes nonviolence scholar Brad Bennett. "Martyrdom was a vital component of the revolt, fueling the spirit to resist. . . . Strikes, tax resistance, solidarity, civil disobedience, demonstrations, and rallies were the major methods of the resistance."[54]

IRAQ'S BELEAGUERED NONVIOLENT RESISTANCE

Iran has not been the only nation in the Middle East to witness peaceful protest campaigns. A small, beleaguered nonviolent resistance movement sprung up in Iraq in response to the U.S. invasion, overshadowed both by the violent insurgency and the American troops. It was comprised of segments of the population such as oil workers and women's rights defenders. Members faced violence by both sides. For instance, Abdel-Hussein Saddam, a member of the Iraq Freedom Congress, a civil resistance group, was taken into custody on July 4, 2007, through a joint raid of U.S. special forces and Iraqi troops. His body was found two days later at a local morgue.[55]

The Iraq Freedom Congress was founded in 2005 as a loose coalition of unions, women's groups, student organizations, and other associations to achieve a secular Iraqi state and an end to the U.S. occupation. Other leaders of the group were killed—often by shadowy militias—and the offices were raided twice by U.S. troops. It professed to have a broad, multisect membership and a presence in 20 Iraqi cities. It claimed to have set up a self-governing zone in Baghdad where Iraq's different communities live together. It also joined hands with the Iraqi Federation of Oil Unions in opposing the privatization of Iraq's oil industry.[56]

The union federation, for its part, went on a four-day strike in mid-2007 to protest a new oil law allowing the entry of multinationals and the curtailment of benefits to oil workers. Four union leaders were arrested for "sabotaging the Iraqi economy." A number of union activists were killed, mostly by death squads of shady provenance. But the unions persevered in their work. A rally in September 2007 to protest the oil law in Baghdad drew hundreds of participants.[57]

Women's groups have also been in the forefront of Iraqi civil society, leading protests against regressive laws in the new constitution. The Organization of Women's Freedom in Iraq also organizes women's shelters for women escaping honor killings.[58]

Another beleaguered organization operating in Iraq has been La'Onf, which means "no violence" in Arabic. "Please, spread the message: There is not only violence in Iraq, there is something more; people are building peace and seeking real change," said Ismaeel Dawood, a founding member of the group. "La'Onf seeks to create a third way with its message that nonviolence is a tool to resist occupation, terrorism, and corruption."[59] In a 2008 article for the War Resisters League's publication, the group's genesis was traced to the question "Can nonviolence be a tool for change in the midst of occupation, violence and suffering?" From a handful of trainers teaching Iraqis methods of nonviolent resistance, the organization grew in two years to a network of more than 100 organizations in 18 Iraqi directorates. "Members include a diversity of men, women, and youth from Iraq's many ethnic and religious groups," wrote the authors, members of September Eleventh Families for Peaceful Tomorrows, an organization founded by kin of September 11 victims. "They are united by their commitment to nonviolence and reconciliation as the best path for building a peaceful Iraq free from foreign occupation."[60]

There were several inspirational stories. So, Azam, a former major in Saddam Hussein's army, worked to spread nonviolence among the Iraqi army and police. Thawar, a high school teacher, defended women's rights. And the organization held in October an annual week of nonviolence, distributing pacifist works, including literature on Gandhi and King, throughout Iraq. Doves and balloons were released in the skies (the organization's symbol is a dove clutching a ballot box), and children were particularly involved in the celebrations. The organization successfully got toy guns banned in the Muthanna directorate. And it coordinated with women's groups to focus on violence against women in particular.[61] "Many new members have joined La'Onf as a result of the activities," wrote the authors. "Through personal interaction, cultural displays, political organizing, and discussion, nonviolence is bringing hope to the people of Iraq."[62]

MIDDLE EAST NONVIOLENT PROTEST IN EARLIER TIMES

Egypt won its independence from Britain early in the 20th century through a nonviolent campaign, using demonstrations, strikes, and boycotts. After the British occupied the country in the late 19th century, they engaged in a hands-off governance mode and gave the country a protectorate status. But the charade of this arrangement was exposed during World War I, when more than 1 million Egyptians were conscripted and essential goods seized from the population.[63]

The protests sprang out of a chain of events that began in late 1918. A couple of nationalist leaders made a request to go to London and negotiate Egypt's future. When the British stonewalled, the leaders collected 2 million signatures in support. The British authorities swiftly exiled them to Malta. This galvanized the Egyptian population across the country, with strikes by a cross section of society, including students and the legal community. There was unfortunately some violence, as a part of these protests fatally targeted some Britishers; the vast majority killed, however, were by the occupying authorities.[64]

The British played it both ways, recognizing a new Egyptian government but reaffirming Egypt's protectorate status at a Paris peace conference. The strikes continued, this time joined by workers in crucial segments of the economy, such as post and telegraph and railways and trams. Egyptian government officials joined in, asking for far-reaching political reform. The British general in charge threatened a mass sacking of all the striking civil servants; the threat briefly worked.[65]

But a short one month after, the British sent a commission of inquiry to the country. During its stay in the country from December 1919 to April 1920, the mission was pretty much unanimously boycotted by the Egyptians. For instance, when a member of the commission went to look at a typical court proceeding, everyone in the court walked out.[66] The pressure had its effect. When the commission came out with its report, it urged an abandonment of the protectorate system. In response, the British authorities announced conditional independence for Egypt, provided that certain British interests were maintained in Egypt. The Egyptian nonviolent campaign—involving noncooperation, strikes, and boycotts—bore fruit.[67] As an interesting footnote, Gandhi stopped by in Egypt on the way to India after two decades in South Africa. He was so impressed by the Egyptian effort that he incorporated a lot of the techniques into the *satyagraha* campaign he launched for Indian independence.[68]

Iraq has also witnessed episodes of nonviolent activism earlier. In 1948, the British tried to continue the mandate status of the country by forcing an agreement on the Iraqi government of Salih Jabr. The news led to massive demonstrations in Baghdad, led by students but joined by workers and other segments of society. Jabr had to smuggle himself back in the country in disguise and then ordered a severe crackdown in which more than 100 Iraqis were killed in machine gun firing in Baghdad. Finally, the security forces gave up, and the government resigned.[69]

Demonstrators kept up the pressure by protesting for 10 days until the treaty was completely repudiated. There was some scattered violence (one police officer was killed, and the American information center was burned), but, by and large, the movement was nonviolent. The demonstrators were inspired by the poetry of two poets, al-Jawahiri, whose brother was killed in the Baghdad police firing, and Bahr al-Ulum. The protestors were successful in their aims in getting an unpopular government to resign and forcing an iniquitous treaty to be rejected.[70]

Another lesser-known nonviolent uprising in the Muslim world that occurred against a malicious dictatorship was in Sudan in 1985. The protests against Jaafar

Nimiery, who had been in power since 1969, started as small demonstrations in late March against food inflation after Nimiery announced price increases in several essential items. In response, students in the capital of Khartoum demonstrated. Coincidentally, Nimiery left the next day for talks with President Reagan. The protests worsened, with attendant rioting. The crackdown was harsh. Thousands were arrested and hundreds sentenced to flogging, prison, or fines. A number of protesters were killed, some at point-blank range.[71]

At this juncture, the movement embraced nonviolent methods. The doctors at the main teaching hospital went on a strike, renewing their strike pledge daily. They were soon joined by a wide array of society, with leaders of various sectors pledging in a secret meeting a nationwide strike on April 1. Other segments joined in, with a section of the police force refusing to use force and many judges affirming their support of the revolt, too. A general strike on April 3 had a near-total impact. The strike kept on gaining momentum, and on April 6 the leader of the army, General Siwar al-Dhahab, announced the overthrow of Nimiery. The protesters kept up the momentum, forcing a release of political prisoners and a pledge for immediate civilian democratic rule. The military kept its pledge, and a vicious dictatorship came to an end after more than a decade of rule. "The nonviolent civil disobedience campaign and general strike, led primarily by doctors and other professionals, had successfully toppled an unpopular, repressive regime," writes Bennett.[72]

CONCLUSION

As the examples in this chapter show, the Middle East has had a vibrant history of nonviolent protest. But the image of the region is so associated with violence that an average American would be fairly astonished to find such a rich vein of nonviolence in the area. And the cases narrated here are far from exhaustive. Egypt, for instance, has an active prodemocracy campaign named Kefaya (Enough!) aimed at the long-standing Hosni Mubarak dictatorship. It hasn't been able to strike the same chord or get similar-sized crowds out in the street as Iran's Green Movement, but it courageously persists in the face of intense government repression, including sexual assaults on female participants.[73]

Another recent acclaimed mass movement in the Middle East, in Lebanon, has been the Cedar Revolution, which erupted in 2005 to demand an end to the Syrian domination of its neighbor. The movement was successful on some level in that Syrian troops were compelled to leave the country, but Syrian influence in Lebanon is far from over, both direct and through proxy political groups. What makes analysis of this movement really complicated for the purposes of this book, which focuses on Muslim nonviolence, is the large Christian population in the country (between 30 and 40 percent). The Cedar Revolution was backed by a large number of the country's Christians (though it was a multiethnic alliance, and on the flip side there were pro-Syrian Christian political formations, too). So, classification of the protests as occurring in a Muslim society becomes difficult. Still, here is yet another wonderful instance of nonviolent mass dissent in the Middle East.[74]

As all these examples show, the Middle East has had a rich tradition of nonviolence. To assume that the region is replete with only violence and mayhem is to engage in a huge libel. This book dedicates a separate chapter to the most sustained example of nonviolent protest in the area.

CHAPTER 10

Struggling against Heavy Odds: Palestinians and Nonviolence

BACKGROUND AND START OF THE FIRST INTIFADA

The Israel–Palestine issue has been one of the central disputes of the 20th century, occupying the spotlight for the past 60 years like perhaps no other. What has been covered extensively has been mostly the violent side. There has been much less of a focus on the nonviolent aspect, best represented in the First Intifada and, to a lesser extent, ongoing protests against the Israeli separation wall.

The First Intifada started in the late 1980s primarily out of a realization on the part of the Palestinians that their situation had reached a dead end because no one was paying attention. They concluded that they would have to become proactive and seize control of the situation.[1] Although the uprising was facilitated by a decision in 1987 in Algeria to have all the Palestinian groups to work together, the roots went further back to the 1970s, when a number of organizations formed in the Occupied Territories to deal with health, women and other issues. These institutions formed the underpinning of the resistance. During the Intifada, they grew in both number and size, playing a key role. The work they did on a number of levels helped immeasurably in sustaining the resistance. Among these were women's organizations since women's wings had been formed by virtually all the political players in Palestine in the 1970s.[2]

"The Palestinian uprising should not have been a surprise to anyone," writes analyst Joost Hiltermann. "A particular conjunction of forces is required for mass mobilization to occur in any social situation, and for mobilization successfully to culminate in collective action. This conjunction of forces was present in the West Bank and Gaza in 1987."[3] These forces included a widespread dissatisfaction with Israeli rule and the desire for change since the occupation had a negative impact on virtually the entire Palestinian population. The external impetus was the encouragement by the Palestine Liberation Organization (PLO) of activism in the territories. The provision of services by the Israeli authorities was so woeful that the activists earned a lot of appreciation by filling in the gaps. A number of events provided the spark: several leaders were deported by the Israelis. There were clear signals that other Arab nations were ignoring the plight of the Palestinians. And a road accident in which Palestinian workers were killed brought to the surface all the pent-up anger.[4]

Before the Intifada, the Israelis ruled the territories effectively with an iron hand (though the application of harsh laws was somewhat uneven). There were some small success stories of nonviolent protest. Most notably, Palestinians had organized to defend the Dome of the Rock and the Al-Aqsa mosque from Jewish fundamentalist groups. Soon after the occupation began in 1967, parents and teachers went on strike to protest changes in the curriculum. The Israelis relented. A 1979 general uprising led the Israelis to cancel a deportation order against the mayor of Nablus. A 1983 directive asking foreign faculty at West Bank universities to sign a loyalty oath was rescinded following mass actions by faculty and their supporters. And a 34-day hunger strike in 1985 organized by the Committee Confronting the Iron Fist led to the dropping of charges against a prisoner, Jabril Rajoub. But these were the exceptions. In general, as an Israeli military officer described it, the Israeli occupation was a "success story," with "the burden resulting from it minimal, neither an unbearable security burden, nor an economic burden, nor even—as far as the local Arab population is concerned—a political burden."[5]

The Intifada carried echoes of a distant past since there had been nonviolent protest episodes in previous times, too, such as in the 1930s. The groundwork for the tactics employed in the Intifada was laid a few years earlier through the work done by groups such as the Center for the Study of Nonviolence, founded by Mubarak Awad (someone I've interviewed), who traveled around the West Bank on a scooter for years propagating his message. His work included the creation of a booklet in Arabic on Ghaffar Khan and the translation of materials by Gene Sharp, Gandhi, and King. The Intifada was thus far from a spontaneous uprising.[6] Even before the Intifada, in the early 1980s, fliers were appearing in public places asserting the right to resist the Israelis using nonviolent methods. Three individuals—Mubarak Awad, Jonathan Kuttab, and Gene Sharp—were the masterminds behind these leaflets.[7]

The year 1987 was a harsh one for the Israeli–Palestinian conflict, with widespread unrest and confrontation. The Intifada was triggered at the end of the year when a collision between an Israeli truck and two vehicles carrying Palestinian laborers blew the lid off simmering discontent. Protests started occurring the next day, and by New Year's Day 1988, large groups of Palestinians were regularly coming out to protest. The backdrop was the neglect of a recent Arab summit to highlight the Palestinians and of Reagan and Gorbachev to even discuss the issue during a summit.

The implications of the term "Intifada" were well thought out by the intellectuals who came up with the word to encapsulate the whole movement. The Arabic root verb is *nafada,* which is derived from the notion of recovery or recuperation. The expression itself implies a shrugging off, such as of the Israeli occupation. It "connotes the removal of unnecessary elements; shaking off preexisting weaknesses, . . . updating and revitalizing the system," says Palestinian cultural anthropologist Hussein Qleibo. Author Mary King says that the closest equivalent in English would be "take back America." By the end of the 1980s, the word had entered into English dictionaries, one of the few Arabic words to do so.[8]

The opening of the Intifada was quite violent. Rocks and Molotov cocktails were thrown, and a spirit of disorder reigned. But as soon as this started, some ground rules were laid down because of existing realities. The use of violence was quite limited because of the desire of the Palestinians to be seen as David to Israel's Goliath and because of the recognition that it would be met with extremely heavy retaliation. People like nonviolent strategist Sharp warned against the use of even limited violence, warning that it would be counterproductive, even as he acknowledged that "given the severity of Israeli repression," it was very hard for the Palestinians to prepare for and exercise nonviolence.[9]

The leadership soon coalesced, announcing itself through a series of leaflets—the Unified National Command. The PLO climbed abroad, reluctantly at first since it had so much invested in the notion of guerrilla warfare. But popular opinion forced its hand. "One Israeli journalist commented that in just a few weeks' time, youth protests had accomplished more for the Palestinian cause than the PLO had accomplished in three decades," write nonviolence chroniclers Peter Ackerman and Jack Duvall.[10]

Soon the leaflets started appearing. The internal contradictions in the directives were apparent. Exhortations to nonviolence coexisted with a call to use knives and Molotov cocktails. The leaflets were drafted sometimes by a surprisingly democratic process, with subsequent drafts amended according to feedback received from the street. The language was sent to the PLO headquarters for approval, however. One fascinating aspect of the leaflets was how much they reflected Awad's writings, such as the call for sit-down strikes and local production of food. "If they use my writing, I'm proud of it," said Awad. The PLO saw the leaflets as a stopgap measure before violence was reintroduced, but the resident population of the territories disagreed profoundly with this perspective.[11]

A group of 20 Palestinian intellectuals formed a bulwark of nonviolence, an informal think tank that encouraged the adoption of a variety of nonviolent tactics. The coterie fed ideas to the Command and helped mold strategy. In addition, it also presented the public face globally, getting members into seminars and conferences and in the international media and reaching out to Israeli groups.[12]

The PLO got involved, and divisions arose between the local residents and the Tunis leadership. The PLO feared that the divisions in the ranks would be exploited by the Israelis and were intent on keeping control. The indigenous leadership and allied organizations insisted, on their part, that the uprising be kept completely nonviolent, calling for a two-state solution, through "entirely civilian struggle," as prominent intellectual Sari Nusseibeh put it. So not a single leaflet called for the destruction of Israel or the killing of Jewish people. The few acts of violence directed at the Israelis were regretted. "Villagers would disarm Israeli soldiers, strip them, and then return their clothes and guns to Israeli military authorities," reports King. "Our uprising is not aimed at the destruction of Israel," said Nusseibeh. "It is aimed at establishing freedom for ourselves in our own state." The leader in the PLO most sympathetic to the goals of the Intifada, interestingly named Abu Jihad, was assassinated by the Israelis in 1988, and the proponents of nonviolence lost a crucial link.[13]

At the grassroots, the new leadership was comprised of youth who had lost faith in the PLO. They were across the spectrum in their views—from Marxist to nationalist to religious. But the focus was self-determination and not social change. Cultural signs, such as flags, clothing, theater, and poetry, played a huge part. The activists had a number of tasks: to organize mass actions, to ease Palestinian hardships, to inform the global media about what was happening, and to counter the Israelis. The leaflets served the purpose of mobilizing the masses. Printed in East Jerusalem opposite a Jewish neighborhood, they were smuggled into the territories in a roundabout way. The leaflets called in total for 27 different types of actions, of which 26 were nonviolent. A detailed study found that a mere 5 to 10 percent of the leaflets called for violence. But even the calls for "limited violence" were counterproductive since they threatened Israeli soldiers, especially because those who were throwing stones and other things most often ran away. The violence took away energy and focus from building alternative institutions.[14]

Awad, with the help of a Palestinian leader named Hanna Siniora, tried to present a completely nonviolent plan of resistance. He proposed 120 different types of nonviolent action. This involved a boycott of Israeli goods, withholding of tax payments, and a boycott of workplaces. "The point is power, the point is that we are challenging the power of the Israelis," explained Awad. The Palestinians hoped to do what the "Gandhi movement did in India and the black civil rights movement did in the U.S." The Intifada leadership met with Awad and Siniora. Their recommendations included a refusal to produce identity cards at checkpoints and the mass resignation of Palestinian policemen. Soon Palestinians took up both these measures.[15]

INTELLECTUAL INSPIRATIONS FOR THE INTIFADA

Mubarak Awad has been the foremost Palestinian exponent of nonviolence, though he is too modest to claim credit for being a pioneer. Awad told an interviewer, "I don't think it's easy for the Palestinians to be nonviolent, and I don't want to take the credit to say that I introduced nonviolence there at all. What I did, really, was bring the ideas together and say to the Palestinians, 'Look, fellows, your grandfather, your father, your mother, everybody has been using nonviolent methods all along.' These were already there. . . . Believe me, a lot of these villagers are nonviolent people. Their entire life has been nonviolent. I mean, what else do you expect from a farmer?"[16]

Awad was born in Palestine in 1943. When he was just five years old, his father was slain while trying to carry a wounded friend to safety. Awad's mother did not have the means to support her seven children. Afraid of their fate and threatened that they all would be killed, she gave all but two of them to orphanages. Even though she never had legal custody again of her children, she visited them regularly and instilled in them values of forgiveness and compassion. Awad got to study at St. George's in Jerusalem, one of the most prestigious schools in the country, courtesy of an American friend of his foster family. He first got arrested at the age of 12 for protesting Jordanian rule and subsequently got into trouble for questioning the finances of the Greek Orthodox Church and for refusing to carry a gun during the school's military training.[17]

He got a scholarship to Lee College in Tennessee in 1959 but was disillusioned with the way African Americans were treated and went back to Palestine. He taught at a Mennonite school there for the next 10 years before returning to the United States to study at Bluffton College in Ohio. The country was then divided over Vietnam, and Awad became increasingly influenced by antimilitaristic and pacifist principles, from Gandhi and King and also from Elmer Neufield at Bluffton, who impressed on him the notion of the divine in every man. Awad eventually did a master's in social work from Indiana University and a PhD in clinical psychology from the International Graduate School in St. Louis. He established the Ohio Youth Advocate Program in 1978. His effort to obtain a U.S. citizenship hit a snag when he refused to pledge allegiance to the U.S. flag. A judge eventually waived that requirement in 1983, clearing the path for him.[18]

In 1983, Awad took the key step of establishing the Palestinian Counseling Center. He also started writing a series of newsletters arguing for the Palestinians to use to nonviolence to resist occupation. In this, he was helped by his cousin Jonathan Kuttab, who had opted to return to his homeland after receiving a U.S. law degree and working for a Wall Street firm. Kuttab had subsequently learned Hebrew and passed the West Bank bar and founded a human rights organization. Awad's workshops became in demand, although resistance was strong, too. He was constantly peppered with hostile questions about the efficacy of nonviolence and the suitability of such a strategy for the Palestinians. "A Westernized exile come home, influenced by Christian pacifists, [Awad] bore a passing resemblance to the man who led India to independence," writes journalist Gershom Gorenberg. "In Awad's description, though, his ideas at the time were shaped more by humanist psychologist Carl Rogers than by Gandhi."[19]

The Israelis tried to disrupt the first big workshop, but it went on despite having to change the venue. Awad encountered a lot of hostility by supporters of the PLO who thought that he had come to challenge the organization's dominance. Nafez Assaily, a Jerusalem schoolteacher and ally of Awad, said that since Awad used the word "organization," "people thought he wanted to replace the PLO" because for residents of the Occupied Territories, "organization" meant the PLO.[20] Awad and Kuttab distributed handouts detailing the problem and their nonviolent solutions. Many of the ideas were derived from Gandhi and King.[21] "Awad drove through the West Bank countryside, parking at the center of villages, sleeping in his van, setting up placards describing Gandhi, talking to whoever walked by," writes Gorenberg.[22]

In 1984, a preparatory meeting was held for the opening of a nonviolence center in the West Bank, attended by Awad, Kuttab, Sharp, and a host of other dignitaries. Kuttab raised money in the United States and delivered a check for $30,000 a few months later. In April 1984, Awad married, and the following year, he and his wife went to India to find out about Muslims who had participated in the Indian freedom struggle with Gandhi. Again and again, they were told about Abdul Ghaffar Khan. Awad and his center translated into Arabic spiritual teacher Eknath Easwaran's biography of Khan. The story of Khan and the Khudai Khidmatgar movement (recounted elsewhere in this book) gave Awad and his group a wonderful example of a group of Muslims who were considered to be traditionally violent but who were united together in a nonviolent movement. Regular seminars were held at the center's library, which contained books about and by Gandhi, Nehru, Khan, King, and many others. Awad was bothered by how little literature there was on Islam and nonviolence and highlighted Khan as an exemplar of how Islam was compatible with pacifism.[23]

He wrote a long article recommending 120 nonviolent ways to resist the Israelis. He organized a three-day seminar to discuss his ideas, which generated a much more favorable response than he expected. He returned to Ohio determined to put his ideas into action in Palestine but lacking the funds for it. Once again, someone came to his rescue. This time it was a Palestinian American professor, Hisham Sharabi of Georgetown University, who read of Awad's endeavors and offered to fund him.

Hence, the Palestinian Center for the Study of Nonviolence was founded in 1985. One of the main notions of the center was to produce literature with examples of nonviolence in Islamic and Arab tradition and history to prove to Palestinians that nonviolence was inherent to their culture. The Israelis tried to make Awad's life as difficult as possible. They picked him up for minor infractions and, Awad claims, tortured him. "I think you have to experience what you talk about," Awad said. "I got beaten, I got electric-shocked, I got harassed with tear gas thrown at me, so I know what it is to have those difficulties."[24] Shortly afterward, Awad met Jimmy Carter and handed him his booklet for critique. Carter insisted that the approach taken be a thoroughly nonviolent one. Awad, even though he was fearful that word may leak out of the Carter meeting, took the advice to heart.[25]

The Intifada that started in 1987 incorporated many of Awad's ideas, such as a refusal to pay taxes and obtain business permits. A parallel education system was organized with underground schools and teachers in spite of harsh penalties imposed by the Israelis on people who engaged in such activities. Other methods of nonviolent protest included the raising of the Palestinian flag and the boycotting of Israeli goods. Like other practitioners of nonviolence, Awad hoped that his particular struggle could serve as a global role model. "Now if there have been any victories in this, and in the Palestinian struggle I think there have been, it

will help nonviolent struggle around the world," he said. "If you don't want to
be killed, you also have to make it clear that you don't want to kill. This is the
beauty of nonviolence."[26]

Awad has been honored for his work by being called the "Gandhi of Palestine"
but shies away from the phrase. "I am not Gandhi, I am Mubarak," he says. "Gandhi was a different man; his spirituality was different. He was a greater man than
me, and I am not in his league. . . . I am in his footsteps, but not in his league."[27]

He and Gandhi had other dissimilarities in that Gandhi looked at things from
a lawyerly perspective and analyzed carefully rules and regulations, while Awad
does not care for that approach. Awad says that this difference stemmed from
the fact that while Gandhi showed some deference toward British rule, Awad
has no respect at all for the Israeli occupation. Instead, Awad says, he has opted
for the psychological route, whereby he counsels people and tries to give them
nonviolent alternatives. Like Gandhi, however, he spent a good part of an interview emphasizing the humanity of the Israelis and the need for Palestinians and
Israelis to understand each other. In a similar manner to Gandhi and Ghaffar
Khan, he has tried to interpret religion as being essentially peaceful, in his case
Islam. "I think the aim of Islam, like Christianity or Judaism or other religions, is
to help people live together in peace," Awad has said. "Islam has enlightenment
in it. Muhammad's message from God was for people to love each other and to
understand each other. When Islam came along, in that time in the Arab world
they were burying girl babies alive because they didn't want girls. Islam stopped
the practice."[28]

One person whose scholarship Awad and Kuttab have relied on is Gene Sharp
(someone I've had the privilege of meeting and interviewing, as I've mentioned
in a previous chapter). They compiled their list of 120 methods of nonviolent
civil disobedience from Sharp's original 198 in a three-volume work, *The Politics
of Nonviolent Action,* which is considered to be a classic on the subject. Awad
and Kuttab also made use of a Sharp treatise on civilian defense that offered a
program of defending civilian society in a nonviolent way using direct action and
noncooperation to make society ungovernable. Thousands of copies of Arabic
translations of Sharp's work were produced. Awad and Sharp's handouts were
put in public places, and Palestinians devoured them clandestinely, giving them
a status comparable to the underground literature in Eastern Europe in the 1970s
and 1980s.[29]

"I was there in the mid-1980s on at least three trips, and met with people in
the West Bank and Jerusalem," Sharp told me. "I also met with Israelis. I spoke
at the Hebrew University in Jerusalem and even spoke at the Israeli Institute of
Military Studies. Most of the methods—90 percent of the methods—used in the
First Intifada were that of nonviolent struggle."[30]

Awad was hit by skepticism from all sides. The Palestinians wanted him to
more clearly endorse the PLO, while the Israelis wanted him to more explicitly
condemn violence. Adding to the ambiguity was his position on the final setup in
Israel/Palestine. He eventually came out for a single secular binational state. On
the subject of violence, he stopped short of a blanket condemnation in a desire

not to burn bridges with the PLO and even in his literature left a window open. This exposed him to charges of hypocrisy and lessened his acceptance within Israel and abroad.[31]

One campaign that Awad took up in earnest was that Palestinians should visit their ancestral homes to contradict the official Israeli line that virtually everything in the country was Jewish derived. He said that the Palestinians should carry a rosebush, explain to the current residents that their families were staying there previously, and ask that the bush be planted in the garden in memory. The object should not be to "cause hatred to those who are living in our houses, but sorrow for the lost humanity," explained Awad. "We don't want them to be our enemies. We want to explain to them that these are our houses." Another campaign that Awad tried in the summer of 1985 was for the first Monday to be a Local Products Day to buy indigenously made Palestinian products. This soon fizzled out, however.[32]

Awad ran into several obstacles. Many Palestinians saw nonviolence as inaction, forgetting their own history of nonviolent action. They also saw it as cowardly and unmanly. Gandhi and King evoked mixed feelings, too, since Gandhi had opposed the creation of Pakistan and King was silent about Palestinian rights. Awad even struggled to come up with an Arabic word equivalent to nonviolence. Many people felt that he was overreliant on the media as a strategic tool to carry his message. But Awad persisted. The center's newsletter carried articles by progressive Israelis. He started a program of village outreach, modeled on Gandhi's efforts that had involved everything from the empowerment of women to cottage industries. Awad's efforts included a library and efforts at cleaning up rural areas. He never aligned himself with any particular PLO faction but benefited from the patronage of Feisal Husseini, who belonged to one of the most prominent families in Palestine. They developed a "symbiotic relationship," according to King.[33]

Awad was prodded into direct action when an elderly man visited the center and, refusing to look at the literature, insisted that Awad launch demonstrations in his neighborhood to protest land seizures by Israeli settlers. Awad elicited a guarantee from the elder that his fellow villagers would promise to carry no guns, engage in sacrifices, and not run away. Three days later, a crowd was ready. When Awad took the crowd to dismantle a fence set up to seize the land, settlers first fired around the crowd and then into it. Local officials came and insisted that the villagers take the matter to court. They then set up a meeting in two days' time. Within those two days, the settlers removed the fence. This was the first time on record that a West Bank village had gotten back confiscated land. Soon, Awad and his center started receiving similar requests from other villages.[34]

Other actions followed. Villagers in a certain section of the West Bank complained of the mass destruction of olive trees as a prelude to confiscation of their land by the Israeli authorities. Awad led a tree-planting session. The settlers uprooted the saplings and trampled them as soon as they were planted. Awad's people were not deterred and kept on working, shielding the saplings with their bodies. Soon, a major arrived and pledged that the saplings would not be touched.

The campaign was a success for the moment; there was no violence. But an hour after they had left, the trees were uprooted. "We lost those seedlings . . . but the villagers proved that, in a nonviolent way, they could confront the authorities and their guns," Awad said. Ironically, some of them were transferred to a memorial dedicated to Martin Luther King. Awad's group organized a demonstration outside the memorial.[35]

On a small scale, the center continued offering the Palestinians ways to resist the occupation, such as civil disobedience and refusing the pay taxes. It also included an effort to stop the blockade of Arab stores by Israeli security forces and to focus attention on families split apart by strict Israeli residency and permit rules. Palestinians "don't want to throw bombs, but they want to do something. I am trying to offer them a revolution by nonviolence," said Awad.[36] "We are not militaristic—even Saladin was a Kurd. The Arab civilization . . . never pioneered a single weapon, tactic or campaign. The prophet had an Ethiopian convert, who taught him how to build moats and trenches."[37]

Not surprisingly, his activities did not endear Awad to the Israelis. Israel deported him in 1988 by using archaic residency laws. President Reagan and Secretary of State George Shultz sent messages to the Israeli government urging that he be released. (The U.S. ambassador sent a message saying, "You need more Awads in Israel, not fewer.") In response to appeals by Coretta Scott King and Senator Claiborne Pell, Israeli Prime Minister Yitzhak Shamir said, "His description of himself as a disciple of Mahatma Gandhi and Martin Luther King is not only an Orwellian inversion of language but a gross insult to the memory of those great leaders." It was the very effectiveness of his tactics that forced the Israeli hand. He went on a hunger strike in jail, causing the Israelis to remove his mattress. The court ruled against him while acknowledging his message of "reconciliation . . . and the opening of a new chapter in the relations between the Jewish and the Palestinian peoples."[38]

The "Gandhi of Palestine" had become an international embarrassment for Israel. By this time, had become a global cause célèbre. Since then, he has set up base in the United States. He returned to Maryland, where he now resides. In addition to the Palestinian Center for the Study of Nonviolence, he has set up Nonviolence International, which has offices in several countries and endeavors to train governments and institutions in nonviolence.[39] The Israeli deportation only raised Awad's stature and helped make him a hero to many Palestinians. His ideas spread and helped catalyze the Intifada, especially his "interpretations of Sharp's emphasis on self-reliance."[40]

Awad was able to foresee the dire consequences of the nonsuccess of his approach. "If we fail now with this uprising as a nonviolent struggle, then the individual whose brother or sister or somebody died will say, 'Look, I tried to contain myself with all my discipline; now I am fed up,'" Awad told an interviewer in 1989. "'I'll go and get my gun or I'll get ten or twenty bombs around me, and I'll go to a movie and let it go, and I'm willing to take two, three, or four Israelis with me.'"[41]

NONVIOLENCE IN THE INTIFADA

There have been a number of objections raised to the adoption of a strategy of nonviolence by Palestinians. There is said to be a lack of common bonds between the Palestinians and Israelis that would make empathy and identification possible with the victims. Moreover, it is argued, the Palestinians lack a culture of consensus and popular participation in decision making, key in any nonviolent struggle. This lacuna extends all the way to the top, with different Palestinian factions using the gun to settle any differences. More to the relevance of this book, it is also said that Islam accords an important place to jihad and lacks a notion of nonviolent struggle that would give legitimacy to any such campaign.[42]

To this, proponents of Palestinian nonviolence counter that Israel's occupation rests on a social order that can be completely shaken by a comprehensive nonviolent campaign consisting of boycotts and strikes. It is also claimed that nonviolence has a universality that can help bridge the cultural chasm between the Israelis and the Palestinians and can transform and educate Israeli society. And, as discussed elsewhere in this book, jihad can be very legitimately interpreted in a much more benign fashion to indicate an inner, personal struggle rather than literally war. A nonviolence campaign also would entail the building up of autonomous political and economic institution, something that would be enormously beneficial for Palestinian society.[43]

Was the First Intifada nonviolent? "The bulk of the resistance was nonviolent, consisting primarily of peaceful demonstrations, strikes, boycotts, tax refusal, occupations, blockades and the creation of alternative institutions," Professor Stephen Zunes writes. "A combination of Israeli repression and factionalism within the resistance led to increased violence in the latter part of the six-year uprising, yet virtually no firearms were used by the Palestinian resistance and it remained a primarily nonviolent movement."[44]

Scholar Philip Grant contends that even though most of the methods used were nonviolent, the movement cannot really be labeled a nonviolent one since these methods were applied more out of common sense rather than deep-seated belief, with the exception of small groups like Awad's. There was also little attempt to formulate a comprehensive blueprint of nonviolent action. But "even the occasional use of nonviolent means by those seeking to oppose the occupation from within the territories prompted a familiarity with some of the weapons of nonviolent combat that later significantly affected the policy and practice of the Intifada," writes Grant.[45]

King asserts in her book that a defining feature of the First Intifada was the predominance of restraint. With 70,000 Israeli soldiers deployed in the West Bank and Gaza, very few were fatally injured. Journalist Daoud Kuttab says that incidents arising out of Palestinian weapons were "very small" and that at the end of the first year, Palestinians had implemented a nonviolent approach "almost perfectly." "Not a single Israeli soldier . . . [was] killed in the first year of the uprising," stated a Palestinian human rights monitoring group. In the first four years of the uprising, Israeli authorities themselves estimated that 12 soldiers were killed, as opposed to 706 Palestinian civilians. (By comparison, Israeli sources had nine Israeli civilians killed in the first year of the uprising.) Two years after the Intifada started, an Israeli journalist wrote, "The decision not to use [weapons] against the occupation soldiers has been generally obeyed. This is all the more remarkable, and perhaps even unique, if one considers that thousands of close relatives of people killed, maimed and imprisoned are seething with rage."[46]

An analysis of the first 39 leaflets issued found that of the first half, chronologically, more than 90 percent of the actions called for were nonviolent, such as withholding taxes, boycotts, marches and strikes, and included symbolic funerals, ringing of church bells, and renaming schools and streets. The second half of the leaflets focused more on economic matters and were yet again predominantly (90.6 percent) nonviolent. In fact, King says that of the 15 major types of methods attributed to Gandhi, the Palestinians employed 14. (Ironically, the exception was migration—the hallowed tradition of *hijrah* being very much Islamic, but this option not being practically available to the Palestinians.) Gene Sharp observed, "Given the severity of Israeli repression . . . the Palestinians during the Intifada have shown impressive restraint." An instance that King cites is when Palestinian youth blocked the Jerusalem–Ramallah road in 1988 and there was no attendant violence. When an outdoor light was switched on at a nearby house, the occupants were asked very politely to switch it off.[47]

"When one leaflet called for the death of one Israeli for each Palestinian killed during the Intifada, there was little response from the grassroots and no increase in potentially lethal attacks on Israelis," writes Grant. "Intifada participants later told interviewers that they considered their greatest successes to have come through nonviolent means, and they expressed unwillingness to abandon this tactic on such a wide scale as the directive recommended."[48]

But there was some ongoing violence against collaborators (claimed as a last resort) and Israeli settlers (claimed in self-defense). The chronology of the protests and the response usually ran thus: There were protests in response to calls for action. When Israeli soldiers responded, Palestinians often threw stones, and then Israeli soldiers retaliated with force, often lethal. The Israeli response grew harsher and harsher; the parameters of force allowed became more expansive. Thousands of Palestinians were arrested, hundreds deported, and heavy fines imposed, sometimes collective. The Israelis even attempted to stop the Intifada by bombing camps in Lebanon and assassinating the PLO official said to be in charge of coordinating the Intifada, but to no avail.[49]

There were two major factors that prevented the First Intifada from being completely nonviolent. First, there was a lack of systematic education in the tactics and principles of nonviolence that prevented the protesters from having a lack of complete faith in the efficacy of nonviolence. (Here is where the efforts of people like Awad were not totally effective.) Second, the hostility toward the Israelis was so deep that it inevitably bubbled to the surface in demonstrations and protests. Adults were unable or reluctant to impose discipline on Palestinian youth who were inclined toward losing control. Added to these two factors, Grant says, was a lack of strategic thinking caused by a number of reasons—the different factions of the leadership were unable to arrive at a consensus; there were unrealistic hopes of outside, perhaps Arab, intervention.[50]

What the protesters also lacked understanding of was, Grant argues, the way that their struggle could influence Israeli public opinion if done in the right manner. "The current treatment of Palestinians in the territories violates many of the ideals of justice and freedom espoused by Israel's wisest citizens," writes Grant. "Through a strong nonviolent campaign by Palestinians, this Israeli population could be mobilized to change its government's official policy."[51]

Nonviolence exponent Muhammad Abu-Nimer says that while the Intifada was largely nonviolent, a number of things made this ambiguous. (In fact, even the Palestinians were hesitant to embrace the description "nonviolence," preferring the term "civil disobedience.") Still, he says that the most massive use of force was by the Israelis and that the Intifada was largely peaceful. And he blames the media for oversimplifying and distorting the phenomenon by foregrounding the violent acts and by implying that both sides were equally responsible for the violence.[52] "The willingness to bear more suffering than your opponent without retaliating in kind was a central feature of the Intifada," he writes.[53]

Abu-Nimer insists that in his multiple interviews with Palestinians involved in the uprising, very few expressed a personal hatred of the Israelis. In fact, he says that the resisters were on the Gandhian path in that they were intent on arriving at a solution that would be mutually beneficial for both sides. (This also explained the willingness to work in solidarity with Israeli peace activists.) Alas, that quest proved elusive.

The nonviolence of the Intifada took part in a number of innovative ways far out of the media gaze. For instance, the Israeli authorities forbade the gathering of z'atar, a key herb in Palestinian cooking because the congregation of Palestinians in the hills to collect the herb was considered a potential security risk. So, Palestinians went surreptitiously to do the gathering. Similarly, when the Israelis shut down schools as a potential threat, Palestinians organized a parallel education system.[54]

The primary dilemma that complicated the nonviolence of the Intifada was the rampant stone throwing by crowds of youth confronting the Israeli soldiers. Palestinians themselves did not consider the throwing of stones as violence when they faced machine guns and contended that if they did want to cause death and injury, they would have used far more lethal weapons. Rather, the use of stones was to provoke the Israeli army to use excessive force. In this, the tactic succeeded, both in the change of rules and in day-to-day application, and consequently lowered the morale of the army. Additionally, the stones also served to bolster the courage of the Palestinians.

But this tactic partly undercut the nonviolent message of the Palestinians. Ideally, the use of purely Gandhian tactics, such as filling Israeli jails, would have been more effective on this front. But the ground realities were quite different than in British India: the British were far away and had a proportionately much smaller occupying force. In a perverse way, stones "created a breathing space for the Palestinians that permitted the growth of political and economic infrastructure," writes Abu-Nimer. But at the same time, the use of stones did complicate matters.[55] "To refer to stone throwing as limited or restrained violence links it clearly with violence, which does an injustice to its intention and effect and some of the attitudes that accompany it," writes Abu-Nimer. "Perhaps we should refer to it as using nonlethal force or unarmed resistance."[56]

More troubling was the use of more violent tactics—ranging from Molotov cocktails to the killing of Palestinian collaborators. These undeniably go against the grain of nonviolence. But these deplorable acts were few. (Even the Indian independence movement had a violent component, and the civil rights movement included militant groups.) Where the Palestinian leadership erred was in instances condoning or legitimizing, albeit in a limited way, the use of such violence.

However, thankfully, the use of overt violence was a small part of the Intifada. The single largest instance was in the punishment of collaborators, ironically themselves Palestinians. At the time of the First Intifada, the Israelis had a reported 18,000 Palestinians feeding them information. These Palestinians had been compromised in one way or the other. Naturally, other Palestinians viewed them as threat. Even here, the punishment was largely nonviolent through the use of ostracism and social boycotts. However, violence—ranging from beatings to murder—was used ever so often because the collaborators were seen as a threat to the Intifada and the very fabric of Palestinian society. (Interestingly, the use of guns here showed that the Palestinians had weapons that could be turned on the Israelis if they wanted to.) The killings to a good extent undermined the nonviolent nature of the Intifada and reinforced cynicism in the eyes of many Israelis.[57]

"While the number of violent incidents may seem large, when spread out over more than two years and weighed against the total activity of the Intifada, they were minimal," contends Abu-Nimer.[58] King writes, "The evidence shows conspicuous control of violence for the initial two years of the Intifada, and well into the third, and even after that, the uprising did not exhibit organized violence." The major exception was stone throwing, however, which allowed the Israelis to portray the whole exercise as bloodthirsty. Sharp cautioned repeatedly against it, warning of a disproportionate Israeli reaction. The tactic caused a huge rift within the human rights community, with some like international legal scholar Richard Falk viewing stones as symbolic, while others like Mubarak Awad took a less benign view. Palestinians contended that the stones took no lives (though one did hit a rabbi in the face). Women and educated professionals such as lawyers often joined in, erasing differences of gender and class. The stone throwing also ironically set up the whole scenario as David versus Goliath, with the stone-throwing Palestinian kids coming across as brave and plucky in standing up to the Israeli security machine. "Their actions aren't terrorism—but rather the actions of a national movement," said an Israeli general. "There were no attacks on any of a dozen Israeli resort settlements and no Israeli fatalities or even serious injuries from the several million stones that must have been tossed," notes a writer.[59]

The Israelis countered that their attempts at preventing Palestinians from acquiring weapons were successful, and that's why there wasn't more violence.

But the Palestinians did have at least some weapons and consciously chose not to employ them. The London think tank International Institute for Strategic Studies reported that even three years into the Intifada, there hadn't been the "anticipated rise in the use by the Palestinians of firearms and explosives, which remained at a very low level."[60]

Grant contends that the Palestinians could have taught nonviolence to a society that lacked a tradition of it if they had adhered more firmly to its principles, just as the U.S. civil rights movement had African Americans disseminate nonviolence to a broader population. Grant argued prophetically that unless the Palestinians managed to allay the fears of a significant part of the Israeli populace, there would never be a settlement, an analysis proven quite right by subsequent events, and that there would be more of a mobilization of international support behind the Palestinians the more nonviolent their struggle would be. Sadly, the Palestinians did not take his advice.[61]

ISLAM AND THE INTIFADA

Islam occupied an interesting place in the Intifada. Although the uprising was essentially a secular affair with both Muslim and Christian leaders, it was informed heavily by Muslim and Arab precepts. In an interesting attempt to imbue the struggle with pacifist Muslim values, Mubarak Awad and his group distributed an Arabic booklet on Ghaffar Khan, as noted above.[62]

A survey showed in the late 1980s that half of Palestinians were strongly religious and another one-fifth moderately religious. Not surprisingly, mosques played a central role in mobilizing the community. Sermons were used to exhort people to action, as were loudspeakers. (Interestingly, joint actions were sometimes undertaken by mosques and churches.) Even the ritual of fasting for Ramadan helped maintain a sense of sacrifice and discipline.[63]

"The broader influence of Islam on the Intifada, centering on the role of the mosque, the effect of ritual practices, and the promotion of traditional values and modes of interaction, was not directly linked to nonviolent resistance, but it created an atmosphere in which Palestinians could see and react to more than occupation, repression, violence and anger," writes Abu-Nimer. "It therefore helped preserve a sense of perspective, kept them from responding to provocations with violence, and helped the Intifada create the psychological and spiritual balance it needed to sustain the nonviolent resistance."[64]

Gorenberg of the *Weekly Standard* sought to find out in the context of the Intifada if there's space for nonviolence in Islam. "His name is in our hands," one Palestinian ally of Mubarak Awad, a schoolteacher, told him, spelling out Allah with the fingers of both hands. "I teach children to see Allah in everyone, even in those who are fighting you. It doesn't mean you have to give up, but you must resist nonviolently, not to hurt Allah in that human being."[65]

Gorenberg met Islam expert Gilles Kepel, who cautioned him that it is best to avoid either extreme: not to essentialize Islam as equaling violence and not to cast it as perfectly flexible. Gorenberg heard the Cain and Abel story (recounted earlier in the book) from Muslim scholar Mustafa Abu Sway as a pacifism parable and read the works of Syrian philosopher Jawdat Said, who has recast Islam as a pacifist religion. In addition, he heard from Sway that Muhammad's life itself is a shining example to Muslims wishing to practice nonviolence. "Reilluminated this way—the Mecca years in the brightly lit foreground, the Medina years of conflict in the shadows, the conquests veiled in black—the prophet's life is still not quite a paradigm of absolute pacifism," Gorenberg writes. "Self-defense is permitted, but only as a final resort for the long-suffering. Armed jihad is an allowance, not an ideal."[66]

The collective leadership of the meeting drew on Islamic symbols, such as past Muslim rebellions. One central motif was the martyr, ostensibly a religious marker but one that could easily be applied to Christian and secular Palestinians, too. Often, the leadership took care to not alienate non-Muslims by not exclusively referring to mosques and often made note of churches and Christian festivals. In fact, the Intifada welcomed Israeli Jewish and American peacemakers and supporters. Here, Islam was used in an inclusive way.[67]

Another aspect of Islam that helped in the Intifada was its nonhierarchical consultative nature. Sunni Islam has no religious chain of command and has instead the tradition of consultative councils, at least in theory (although this is most often breached in practice). In the case of the Palestinians, this tradition worked quite well, leading to a process of consensus and group leadership. The proliferation of various committees (dealing with issues ranging from food to education) showed with their cooperative models of leadership how this leads to positive outcomes.[68]

Another value the Intifada drew on is the long-held one of solidarity among all Muslims. Hence, contending factions cooperated on campuses, and rural and urban Palestinians alike participated in the uprising.[69] Similarly, the Islamic notion of forgiveness was used very effectively. For example, the Palestinian leadership proclaimed a day of forgiveness where collaborators and informants were asked to repent and join the struggle. Many did.

A related value was *sumud*, or "steadfastness." This was directly derived from Muhammad's early resilience in Mecca when faced with persecution. Suffering for your faith is a long-standing tradition in Islam. Hence, prisoners were expected to maintain total silence and often did. Although fundamentalist groups such as Hamas misused Islam during the Intifada, the main leadership utilized the positive attributes, often to good results.[70] "The Intifada's nonviolent campaign, qualified by some as nonlethal/violent resistance, was as Muslim as the civil rights movement was Christian and Gandhi's movement was Hindu," contends Abu-Nimer.[71]

INTIFADA TACTICS

"Intifada" literally means "shaking off," and that was the intent of the uprising: to shake off the Israeli occupation. This was done using a variety of tactics. One of the leadership's first acts was to call for a business strike, and henceforth they operated on their own schedule instead of what the Israelis wanted. For two years, there were regular marches, demonstrations, chanting of slogans, and raising of the illegal Palestinian flag. Of Sharp's 198 categories of nonviolent tactics, at least 87 were used in the Intifada.[72]

The leadership most often called for action by using leaflets. An analysis of a sample of the leaflets showed that the most common action called for was the strike. The second most common type was solidarity with fellow Palestinians targeted in Israeli crackdowns, expressed through financial contributions, visits, and helping till the land. The third category was asking people to demonstrate and march. And there were a huge range of other tactics mentioned, from boycotts and mock funerals to graffiti campaigns and the ringing of church bells. All the time, the coordinating committee emphasized that its goal was to coexist with Israel and to seek negotiation with it.[73]

A main strategy used was economic boycott. This was because the Occupied Territories were a big market for Israeli goods and a big source for sales taxes and license revenue. So, one of the initial acts of the resistance was to curtail shopping hours only from 8:00 A.M. to noon. The Israelis tried to force the markets open but soon failed. This was a huge victory for the Intifada.[74]

Another big economic tactic utilized was tax resistance. This consisted of refusing to pay taxes, such as automobile license fees, sales taxes, and water bills. A common tactic was to avoid registering vehicles. On a more widespread scale, this was implemented by developing a barter economy in places like Ramallah, Bethlehem, and Beit Sahour. Coupled with the economic boycott and the cost of maintaining the resistance, these tactics cost Israel a huge economic bundle. At the same time, Palestinian communities had to bear an economic cost and provide compensation for the closure of Israeli labor markets and Israeli goods.[75] A related strategy was the social boycott. So, one day a week for a period of time, there was a general social strike where all normal life was stopped weekly. Here the vast portion of the economic cost was borne by the Palestinians themselves.[76]

A common Gandhian tactic used was the hunger strike. Women did this at Red Cross offices in various cities. But most famously, prisoners used this to protest harsh desert conditions, one of the most famous moments of the uprising.[77] In fact, Abu-Nimer asserts that the Intifada was more creative than Gene Sharp's prescriptions since it used methods not enumerated by him, such as humorous skits and pranks and singing. The main tactic used, however, was a very common one: marches. These were most often marking special occasions, such as the death of a prominent figure or a national holiday. They were a profound phenomenon in that they marked the temporary liberation of a village or town from Israeli occupation for the duration of the march. Most often, they were not spontaneous but rather were in keeping with directives issued by the Intifada leadership.[78]

Symbolism was used very strongly during the Intifada. This involved most prominently the use of the Palestinian colors (black, red, white, and green) in many ways. Since Israeli authorities banned these colors, people found close substitutes to use on clothes. And the colors themselves were used in defiance, from flags to bracelets worn under shirtsleeves. Another type of incredible symbolism was the disarming of weapons. In a number of instances, villagers disabled guns that they had seized in a powerful message of the affirmation of nonviolence.[79] One interesting side effect of the Intifada was that it increased solidarity among Palestinians. Traffic altercations became less severe, and neighbors cared more for each other. The amount of social grace and harmony increased on several levels.[80]

The fate of striking shopkeepers offers a glimpse into the dynamics of nonviolent action and adaptation. When merchants in Gaza struck, the Israeli security forces smashed their locks. The Palestinians responded by forming watch committees to keep an eye on the stores. The Israelis retaliated by welding the doors shut. The Palestinians got metalworkers to volunteer to break open the shutters. This back-and-forth went on for months until the Israelis finally gave up.[81]

Alas, Palestinian stores that remained open were the targets of arson, and Palestinian collaborators often suffered severe reprisals, undermining the good work that the Intifada was doing on other fronts.[82] And good work was being done on a number of fronts. Food self-sufficiency became a goal because of a boycott of Israeli produce, and neighborhood farms sprang up. In one absurd instance, the Israelis tried to get a dairy farm closed down by getting the cows killed, until the 18 cows simply disappeared (with five additions since some of them gave birth). When Israelis shut 900 schools, the Palestinians started makeshift classrooms everywhere.[83]

The Intifada was met by massive repression. More than 1,000 Palestinians were killed in a population of less than 2 million at the time. Thousands were detained, often for as long as six months. Educational institutions of all types were closed down, including kindergartens. All this put severe pressure on the nonviolent aspect of the Intifada, leading it to become more and more violent. In addition, there was a perceived lack of effectual international support.[84]

As the Intifada succeeded, the Israelis stepped up the repression. Clubbing and the use of teargas became common. A number of soldiers began to have qualms. The head of the Israeli Defense Forces, Nehmia Dagan, admitted that his men were in a no-win situation and said that he began to hate the Arabs not because he had any personal animus but because the violence he had to use against them generated such feelings. Activists like Awad got Israelis to come to the hospitals to see injured Palestinians, knowing that this would have a profound effect. But there was no internal split in the Israeli leadership, and support from the United States, although somewhat more lukewarm than in the past, remained fairly steadfast. The Intifada did have a good-sized economic effect because of the impact of everything from the loss of Palestinian labor to the additional cost of deploying an increased number of troops. But the Israeli government did not yield. To the contrary, collective punishments such as curfews became common, with an astonishing 1 million Palestinians under curfew by the end of the first year of the Intifada.[85]

One Israeli tactic that had little effect was imprisonment since going to jail became a badge of honor for the imprisoned and their families. The fear of Israeli security personnel, who were commonly seen as "supermen," largely disappeared.

More than 29,000 people went to prison in the first year of the Intifada. Membership in a popular committee was made jailable with 10 years. Dissent inside Israel grew also, notably with Women in Black, members of which, darkly clad, appeared at busy intersections in major Israeli cities. But the repression did not relent, and home demolitions and utility cutoffs were employed commonly. And in the summer of 1988, Palestinian leaders of the uprising were deported, including Awad (over the objections of the United States). Awad's expulsion was not in vain. He went, along with Sharp, to meet the PLO leadership in Tunis and played a role in changing its minds on the efficacy of armed struggle. This was part of its larger shift away from violence and played a part in the recognition of Israel that year.[86]

THE INTIFADA COMMITTEES

As the Intifada blossomed, so did popular committees. These had their roots in the uprising of 1936 and stayed alive through the 1970s and 1980s, but it was after the start of the uprising that they really came into their own. They sprang up all over and were sometimes surprisingly democratic in their structure. A single village, Beit Sahour, with a population of 12,000, had no less than 36 committees. The sector that they were most active in was agriculture since the Israelis had massively destroyed olive and other types of trees and even wheat fields. In response, the Palestinians launched a massive campaign of tree planting and small community gardens. Although the small farms were often amateurish in execution, they helped further politicize the Palestinian population. In addition, small husbandry projects became common, as the need to grow one's own dairy and meat products became necessary because of the repeated curfews and closures. The Israelis in the summer of 1988 outlawed the committees and made membership in them punishable by jail terms of up to 10 years. The Israelis deported the heads of 25 of the most popular committees and put hundreds of members in jail, which served only to increase their prestige.[87]

What was remarkable about the uprising was not that it happened but rather the degree of organization, support structure, and leadership that came into being within less than a month. The question that Hiltermann tries to answer is how planned the uprising was. Hiltermann comes down on the side of the interpretation that "grassroots activists had been organizing and mobilizing sectors of the population for years prior to the outbreak of the uprising," as he writes.[88]

The movement began spontaneously at first, with young Palestinians gathering to march, chant slogans, throw stones, and wave the Palestinian flag. Soon the collective leadership started issuing leaflets, most often recommending nonviolent action, though some violence was sometimes suggested. So the most frequent action advised in more than 20 leaflets studied was going on strike, with support for the families of the arrested being second—ranging from financial assistance to visiting prisoners—and the staging of demonstrations being third (praying and fasting being a close fourth).[89] These and myriad other directives (no taxes, no cooperation, ringing of church bells, blocking roads, and so on) were implemented with the help of a network of resistance committees. These committees often issued their own recommendations for the local area (coordinating sometimes with the PLO leadership in Tunisia), with often more than a dozen different committees formed in each locality.

After Palestinians took to the streets in December 1987 to protest spontaneously, the collective leadership formed within a month. After this, all the actions were decided by the committee. Interestingly, this leadership saw itself as complementary to the PLO rather than as a rival, even as an extension of the PLO inside the territories. A number of factors shaped the response. The intense Israeli harassment, for example, both ensured that there would be a component of violence in the response and that it would be decentralized to escape the crackdown on the leadership.[90]

A number of committees were set up that dealt with various issues, ranging from literacy and child care to health care and looking after families of Palestinians held during the Intifada. This decentralized aspect helped perpetuate the Intifada even when much of the top leadership was imprisoned. Additionally, the efforts were helped by the underground cadre of the PLO that provided training for the effort. There was also close coordination between the PLO's leadership in exile and the activists within the territories.[91]

Carrying out all this work were popular committees. There was an all-encompassing coordinating committee. And then there were local popular committees that took care of day-to-day needs, such as food and medical needs. In addition, there were committees representing different segments of the Palestinian population, such as women, students, and labor. The Israelis especially went after the committees, which set up alternative institutions, such as schools, to make up for the closing down of the official entities. Soon, even these became targets of crackdowns.[92]

Within the first couple of months, the Palestinians had learned what to do. They consciously chose not to use weapons, and there was little political infighting. A leadership comprised of the main non-Islamist parties coalesced soon after the start of the Intifada. The "Command" suffered from several waves of arrests but learned soon and had couriers running between the various members so as to ensure that it would be hard for everyone to be compromised at the same time. It was unknown among even most Palestinians who the members of the Command were. The Command acted "as a crucible for the population's ideas rather than a leadership trying to impose its own predetermined notion," says Palestinian analyst Daoud Kuttab. So, there was a careful attention to decentralization and popular participation. "The Command's most important functions were to move the center of action from one location to another, and to distribute pressure and prevent fatigue by devising different methods for popular dissent," writes King.[93]

A number of preexisting organizations helped lay the groundwork for the Intifada. There were two groups that rose up to confront the occupation. There was the Committee Confronting the Iron Fist—comprised of both Jews and Palestinians—that worked with Palestinian prisoners in putting together hunger strikes and demonstrations to focus attention on their plight. And there was the Palestinian Center for the Study of Nonviolence, headed by Awad, which translated articles on nonviolent techniques into Arabic and disseminated them throughout the Occupied Territories. There were also a number of welfare groups formed in various fields—health, welfare, and education, for instance—that played a key role in mobilizing people and participating in the Intifada.[94]

Within a few weeks, coordination started, and an umbrella group, the Unified National Leadership of the Uprising, was formed. Even fundamentalist organizations, such as the Islamic Jihad and Hamas, cooperated with the nonviolent approach of the Intifada.[95] A significant group urging nonviolent resistance was the Committee Confronting the Iron Fist, jointly formed by a Palestinian, Feisal Husseini, and a former Israeli paratrooper who had become a journalist, Gideon Spiro. (The "iron fist" was in reference to Defense Minister Yitzhak Rabin's boast about Israeli policies.) The committee fused together several activist committees that had taken their lead from Eastern European dissident movements. Their operative notion was to show that they didn't have fear, and they soon launched a bevy of actions, including prison protests, seminars, and house demolitions. One idea that wasn't fully implemented was the advocacy of a "Gandhi-style" resistance by Spiro that involved 200,000 Palestinians forming a human wall around the Israeli settlement of Kiryat Arba in Hebron. A huge step that the organization took was that it "recognized both the state of Israel and the humanity of Israeli citizens," King observes, a breakthrough that was completely ignored by the Israeli media and citizenry. Instead, the Israeli authorities jailed Husseini for 15 months between 1987 and 1989, going the route of administrative detention because it made it easier to hold him. Israeli peace groups protested on his behalf. While in jail, "Husseini's faultlessly polite behavior toward his prison guards showed indebtedness to a Gandhian principle in which acceptance of punishment offers an opportunity to influence the adversary," writes King. But Israeli courts showed their contempt for the tactics of the likes of Husseini when they said that the absence of violence from such groups did not mean the absence of danger to Israel.[96] In June 1987, the Committee Confronting the Iron Fist staged a big demonstration—a precursor of sorts to the Intifada six months later—the first political protest in Arab East Jerusalem that the Israelis ever gave permission for.[97]

The creation and mobilization of committees soon reached a new level. The functions of the participating committees were formally laid out. A prominent one was the Palestinian Medical Relief Committee. This was comprised of doctors, nurses, and myriad health workers and built several clinics of both the traditional and the mobile variety. By 1987, several hundred mobile clinics were in existence. With the repression intensifying and Palestinian injuries escalating, these clinics became more and more useful. (A full 20,000 Palestinians were injured in the first year alone.)[98]

There was a multilevel health system set up. There were the regular hospitals that existed from before. Then there were village clinics providing basic care. In addition, medical committees roamed around giving access to mobile health service. And the exigencies of the Intifada created grassroots medical committees to cope with those injured. This parallel health system led to the establishment of independent facilities as well as empowerment of the population.[99]

An even more uphill challenge was to create a self-sufficient economy in a situation of such heavy Israeli control and dependency. Since a full delinking from the Israeli economy wasn't possible, the Palestinians acted pragmatically. They built up their own economy to the extent possible by urging people to buy local goods. Self-sufficiency in agriculture was more achievable, with the ban on Palestinian workers from crossing over into Israel proving to be an actual boon to the sector. A number of cooperatives were set up during this period. This was a change with far-reaching consequences, Abu-Nimer asserts, because it meant a radical rethinking of attitudes toward food, work patterns, land, family, and community. It also meant a change in the decision-making process with the cooperative structures. The Israelis highlighted the "danger" by arresting the leadership of the committees.[100]

An interesting aspect of the Intifada was the creation of an autonomous system of justice. The collective leadership called for a resignation of all the Palestinian police. This was followed by a campaign of social ostracism. This resulted in law enforcement almost totally collapsing. Instead, an alternative method of conflict resolution was tried where the disputing parties were encouraged to reach a settlement. Criminals were shunned, though in some cases more extreme methods, such as a high degree of violence, were used. Palestinians who were tried by the Israelis most often refused to have a lawyer as a mark of protest.[101] Such efforts were important since they channeled energy in positive ways, providing sustenance to the Intifada and "psychological support for the continuance and enlargement of its nonviolent aspects," writes Abu-Nimer.[102]

The leaflets with instructions on how to conduct the uprising "took on totemic proportions," writes King. They were the "only authority" the children listened to, said one father. People often ignored the poetic flourishes and directly went to the instructions. The leaflets were supplemented in time by radio broadcasts from Syria and Iraq. And graffiti soon started appearing frequently to supplement the leaflets. Strikes were announced, and political positions were inscribed. A Palestinian youth was killed in Nablus while scribbling graffiti. Music and poetry were added to the mix, with songs being composed in the honor of the Intifada and artists dedicating themselves to the Intifada in exhibitions and their work. An example of out-of-the-box thinking was the idea of the Palestinians setting their watches to a separate time zone. Unfortunately, the reaction of Israelis was to smash wrists and to break the offending timepieces.[103]

A pivotal action of the Intifada—one that got significant media attention—was the decision of the village of Beit Sahour not to pay any taxes. Some of the village residents had been expressing noncooperation in this way for ages, and in the summer of 1988, the entire village decided to join them. The Israeli response to what one Palestinian observer called the "almost perfect" nonviolent action by a "valiant village" was profoundly embarrassing. The Israelis laid siege to the village in the fall of 1989, first imposing a continuous curfew for five days and then dusk-to-dawn curfews for weeks more. The Israelis severed all communication, ransacked homes and businesses, arrested residents, and confiscated goods. The media and Western diplomats were barred from entering. Finally, the siege was lifted after widespread outcry. "So fearful was the Israeli administration of the economic and symbolic value of nonpayment of taxes that it went to extraordinary measures to crush the 'tax rebellion,'" states analyst Scott Atran. After this episode, the Israelis became more discreet, conducting swift raids against tax dissenters.[104]

Israel also started employing the weapon of curfews on a large scale, placing 200,000 Palestinians under curfew within a month of the start of the Intifada and more than 1 million by December 1989. The efforts boomeranged because an unprecedented sense of social solidarity was created. Food donation drives were launched outside the areas of curfew, and self-reliance in the area of food increased. Even the baking of bread became a political act, with wealthy women sometimes kneading dough for the first time in their lives. The huge effect of the curfews and closings was in the field of education, with an astounding 35 percent of the Palestinian student population affected at the peak. The closure of Bir Zeit University itself marooned 3,500 students and lasted more than four years. But even here, there was an unintended side effect, as King points out. The dispersal of so many educated youth throughout the territories actually helped propel the Intifada even more. "The happenstance of Israeli curfews and closures hastened the spread of ideas about Palestinian nonviolent resistance and contributed to an historic instance of intellectuals, academicians, and elite activists being joined with savvy young organizers in common cause," writes King. At the same time, grassroots efforts sprang up to fill the educational void, with local committees organizing classes in homes, places of worship, and community venues. Soon, the Israelis outlawed even these efforts at education, with a 10-year jail sentence and a $5,000 fine for any teacher involved with it. Finally, the Israelis gave up and reopened the schools in July 1989, especially since they realized that the parallel education system was doing them harm.[105]

The media played a huge role in the Intifada. The Palestinian intellectuals were adept at getting the message across. And, more important, reporters let an audience in Israel and abroad know what was happening. The media became the "darling of the Palestinians, and bane of the soldiers," writes analyst Joel Greenberg, and sent back dispatches on the often "pointless thuggery" of the security forces. "The sight of unarmed youths dying daily from the bullets of a vastly superior military, armed by a superpower, touched the sensibilities of viewers, who were at the same time seeing reports of the mighty Soviet Union imploding, abetted by similarly popular and unarmed civil resistance in Poland, East Germany, and the Czech and Slovak republics," writes King.[106]

WOMEN AND THE INTIFADA

Women were an essential part of the uprising from its earliest days—marching, arguing, and even throwing stones. "Women assumed a profile they had not had on such a scale in public before," writes Hiltermann. "Soon commentators were referring to the Intifada not only as a 'shaking off' of military rule, but as a social revolution in its own right, in which the younger generation was rebelling against the older one, street activists were challenging the authority of the PLO, and women were casting off the yoke of gender oppression."[107]

Women became deeply involved. They held more than 100 demonstrations, including one in Ramallah where 500 women appeared. They "confronted Israeli troops; they shared in decision-making; they . . . did what the men did, without fear or complexes," King quotes an analyst. "Perhaps it would be still more accurate to say that because of the Intifada, the role of men was altered."[108]

Hiltermann cautions that some wildly optimistic notions of the change of the status of women in Palestinian society resulting from the Intifada were vastly overblown. But there did emerge a change in women's consciousness and mobilization and in discussions about women's rights and their place in the nationalist movement. For women, long-term social trends facilitated their organizing. Since a good number of Palestinian men had to migrate in search of livelihoods, women from the 1970s on increasingly entered the labor market. These women became ripe for collective action. Often, this was done by college-educated Palestinians from places such as Bir Zeit University, from where the first network, the Women's Work Committee, came out, encompassing both professional and working-class women.[109]

"Other groups in Palestinian society shared identities and structures, and they were among the first to be mobilized: professionals (doctors, lawyers, engineers), students, women workers, merchants, artists and writers, even—to an extent— housewives," Hiltermann writes. "In all cases, organizers attempted to make a link between people's daily experiences and the military occupation, and while offering concrete services to their members, they firmly places their organizations' programs within the overall nationalist framework."[110]

Young women emerged on the streets in December 1987, challenging not only Israel but also their menfolk for being absent. ("Where are you, men of Ramallah?" was one slogan.) Women's participation was across ages and backgrounds, including in villages and refugee camps. It was so pervasive that it became almost impossible in the larger places to distinguish the women from the men in terms of their participation in key roles. In response, the Intifada established day care centers and health education classes to cope with injuries sustained in the uprising.[111]

The reaction of women did differ from town to town, with Ramallah showing a much higher level of participation than conservative Hebron. The marches often included demands for women's rights. Astonishingly, the number of women casualties remained quite low in spite of their high level of participation. Whether it was homeschooling children or boycotting Israeli goods in the marketplace, women provided a full response to the calls of the collective leadership. In perhaps their most significant achievement, a number of women's cooperatives were set up, though they lacked a clear transformative goal for Palestinian society.[112]

A positive effect of the women's participation was to bring women's groups together. Eventually, the four main women's groups were joined together in the

Higher Women's Council, later renamed the Unified Women's Council. Ironically, women benefited from an official reluctance to crack down too heavily on them. But this did not result in women taking leadership roles in the overall leadership. Their marginal role was revealed by the small amount of references to them in the leadership communiqués—and that too, often, as mothers. Women's groups tried to deal with this the best way they could, being assertive without sounding too defensive about the situation. Activists also tried to intervene in cases of domestic abuse and women being thrown out of their homes. Women's groups also faced a challenge from organizations such as Hamas, which successfully imposed its notions of women wearing head scarves on pretty much the entire movement.[113]

Hiltermann prophetically stated in 1991 that the long-term impact of the women's groups on Palestinian society would only be as lasting as the impact they made on the uprising itself.[114] He suggests that although both the women's movement and the trade unions left their mark on the Intifada, women's groups were better prepared for the uprising. This was due to a number of reasons. Workers were often constrained by their role as breadwinners. The authorities cracked down much more heavily on them. And factional rivalries hindered their effectiveness. Women's groups did not suffer from these drawbacks.[115] "In the third year of the uprising, the labor and women's movement's had proven their worth," writes Hiltermann. "Not only did they survive the changes wrought by the uprising, they deployed their considerable resources to sustain the Intifada and then were actually able to capitalize on the uprising's political accomplishments."[116]

WORKERS AND THE INTIFADA

Hiltermann says that most analyses of the Intifada miss the mark when they try to pinpoint the start of it to one particular event. Instead, it was the culmination of a decade-long effort at organizing and consciousness raising. Workers' organizations became the backbone of the uprising. These were formed through a particularly Palestinian phenomenon: the day laborer. These laborers, crossing over into Israel and forming the backbone of the Israeli economy, have been routinely exploited with negligible protection offered by Israeli unions or labor laws. This led to the formation of Palestinian labor unions linked to the Palestinian nationalist movement and in alliance with other key sectors, such as women's groups and medical organizations.[117]

The workers had such an active participation in the movement that in the first 10 months, 50 percent of the fatalities were from the workers, with the involvement being spontaneous since at this stage there wasn't an organized call for joining in by the workers' leadership. The Israelis were quick to put curbs on the activities of trade unions. Labor leaders coped with this by working informally in their individual capacities to organize the uprising.[118]

In some sense, Hiltermann says, the transition from aboveground to underground was not that surprising because the unions were constantly harassed before the uprising, too. And a few unions had begun the transformation to workers' council even before the start of the Intifada, for instance, in the village of Yatta, where it used to "discuss the current situation, raise the political conscious-ness and press for the formation of popular committees," in the words of a local activist.[119]

What happened as a result of the Intifada was that the role of the unions transformed so that "the national struggle aspect of the unions increased, while the social struggle aspect decreased proportionally." Labor leaders were well po-sitioned to play a role in the Intifada because of their earlier prominence and consequently placed themselves in the forefront, with a number of them serving as head of the collective leadership committee. One of the tasks of these workers' committees was to classify workers by occupation so that they could play useful tasks in the uprising. For instance, locksmiths were called on to repair the locks of merchants destroyed by the Israeli security forces.[120]

The main call was for workers to stop working for Israeli factories, though this was soon modified to asking workers to stay away on occasions of general strikes and requesting workers employed in the settlements to work elsewhere. The im-pact of these calls is hard to measure precisely, though there was a clear evidence of Palestinian absenteeism, partly due to the strike calls and partly due to harsh curfews. (Official numbers showed a 20 percent decrease in Palestinian workforce participation in Israel.) Many Palestinians went back to tilling their land, with the result that construction in some settlements stopped altogether. The Israeli authorities responded with mostly hollow threats to bar Palestinians from enter-ing Israel completely, though in some cases they were actually able to punish villages in this way for nationalist activity. And Israeli employers did often lay off workers who joined in the strike actions.[121]

In the second phase of the Intifada, starting in the spring of 1988, the role of the workers was more institutionalized, with the setting up of more committees. At the same time, the leadership called on Palestinian businesses to absorb the workers suffering caused by the Intifada. For example, in mid-1988, the Inti-fada coordinating committee asked "employers to refrain from dismissing work-ers, increasing their work hours, or deducting strike days from their salaries." In response to the formalization of protest, Israeli repression increased, with more arrests and deportations.[122] "Precise detention figures are not available," writes Hiltermann. "However, at least forty-four labor organizers who were members of executive councils in the three labor federations and affiliated unions were being held in the summer of 1988. At that time, the army had closed down at least thirty trade union offices in the West Bank."[123]

Some of the labor unions continued to operate in spite of the repression, even holding press conferences. Some started operating from work sites instead of union offices. They also started targeting Palestinian employers, with a strike at a Palestinian-operated TC Cola factory being the first action of its kind. While the action was partly successful in wresting concessions, the Israeli au-thorities cracked down harshly, putting the strike committee's leader in deten-tion for six months. When there was a clash between competing objectives, the workers' committees reached agreements with Palestinian-owned businesses that workers could not be penalized for striking as long as they worked 48 hours a week. In one instance, by mutual agreement, management and workers at a number of local employers drew up fresh contracts that pledged, among other things, to produce more locally made goods, no layoffs, Jordanian labor law for vacations, and continued payment of wages for absent days due to national strike campaigns.[124]

There were conflicting trends for the Palestinian labor movement. On the one hand, the International Confederation of Free Trade Unions, the world's largest trade union federation, sent a delegation to the Occupied Territories that issued a harsh denunciation of Israeli policies at its tour's conclusion. "For the first time in the history of the Palestinian labor movement, Palestinian trade unions were formally recognized as trade unions by the most powerful exponents of the international labor movement," writes Hiltermann. But at the same time, the economic situation continued to get worse. The gross domestic product in the Occupied Territories plummeted by an astonishing 12 to 15 percent during 1988–90. The jobs picture was desperate. Unions responded by negotiating collective bargaining agreements with employers to retain jobs.[125]

At a later stage of the uprising, economic troubles forced the unions to refocus their attentions to the plight of the workers. This led to a call for expanding the wages of workers and for employers not to fire workers and to form arbitration committees. Strikes proliferated in the months to come, and agreements were reached to better the wages and working conditions. The plight of the workers was worsened by the response of the Israeli authorities. For example, the Israeli Employment Service put tight restrictions on the hiring of workers from East Jerusalem and the West Bank. The Israeli National Insurance Institute stopped giving benefits to Palestinian occupants of East Jerusalem. The Israeli security forces tightly scrutinized the flow of Palestinian workers to Jerusalem. Vehicle stickers were given only to workers with "clean" records. In the summer of 1988, new identification cards were announced for Gazans under the aegis of "Operation Plastic Card." And all this was in addition to the toll exacted by the repeated curfews imposed by the Israeli authorities. But the labor actions continued, including a (mostly unsuccessful) attempt to destroy the new ID cards. More successful was the determination to continue the struggle, although unfortunately this included some violent acts, such as the bombing of a couple of Israeli labor offices.[126]

THE SUCCESSES OF THE INTIFADA

The First Intifada chalked up several accomplishments. The Intifada "exerted substantial influence on popular opinion throughout the Arab world that forced some often unresponsive regimes to take the Palestinian question seriously once again," writes Zunes. And it "forced the PLO to take such political initiatives as the declaration of independence of December 1988, which led to diplomatic successes, including recognition of the PLO as a negotiating partner by Israel and the United States."[127]

The Palestinian Intifada was somewhat undermined by its refusal to strictly abjure violence. The Israeli Defense Forces felt justified to lash out. And Western sympathy was undercut. The Palestinians fell into "the trap of shifting to fight with the opponents' chosen weaponry," says Sharp. But the Palestinians did achieve a lot. The uprising laid the groundwork for the Israelis to commit to negotiations that led eventually to the Oslo Accords. And it helped transform for a while the image of the Palestinians from armed militants to underdogs. These weren't inconsiderable achievements.[128]

The Intifada had an impact in many other ways. It aroused sympathy for the Palestinian cause as never before and made Israeli authorities look quite bad in their response. It also generated a huge amount of support and consternation in Israel for the Palestinians, an absolute first.[129] The Intifada also had profound external consequences. King Hussein of Jordan relinquished his claim to the West Bank. Yasir Arafat was pushed into renouncing terrorism and accepting the two-state solution. As part of its change, the PLO also interestingly initiated nonviolent action, such as a "Ship of Return" to return Palestinians to their homes on Haifa. (The ship was blown up by the Israelis.)[130]

But among the most important changes was within the Palestinians themselves. The newfound sense of confidence meant that the often fratricidal competition between the different groups lessened considerably. The role of women changed considerably, as noted. Children were in the forefront, causing the family dynamic to change since they became much more independent of their parents. A younger generation displaced the older entrenched leadership. And the Intifada caused great institutional changes. Rudimentary medical clinics sprang up all over to meet the challenges of the uprising. Schools and day care centers were established to counter the effects of the Israeli closures. And the boycott calls against Israeli goods made a number of Palestinians start up their own cottage industries.[131]

The Intifada affected the Israeli economy on both ends. The easy supply of cheap Palestinian labor was curtailed. The boycott of Israeli goods affected Israeli industries. Even investment in the Israeli economy was dampened because of the political backdrop of the Intifada. The growth rate of the Israeli economy dropped sharply, in good part because of the Intifada.[132]

The Intifada caused deep divisions within Israeli society because of uncertainty about how to respond to the Intifada, with sharp boundaries springing up in both the major parties between those who favored negotiations and those who wanted a harsh response. "The sooner the Palestinians return to terrorism, the better it will be for us," said an Israeli Labor Party leader. The Israeli settlers in the Occupied Territories did feel besieged because of the constant barricading of major roads, cars being attacked, and supplies and utilities being cut. They retaliated with vigilante actions, destroying Palestinian homes and fields and beating and sometimes even killing them. The Israeli authorities countered the attacks on the settlers in their own way by encouraging more and more immigrants, especially from the then Soviet Union, to gravitate toward those areas.[133] The Intifada, King contends, was in four stages lasting a total of five years, with the second stage—from 1988 to 1990—being the most effective. "Unarmed Palestinians have succeeded in exposing Israeli brutality, transforming the image of the Palestinians in the international community," said activist Daoud Kuttab."[134]

One of the principal achievements was to nudge the PLO into recognition of Israel and negotiations. The 19th Palestinian National Congress session (dubbed the "Intifada PNC"), held in Algiers in November 1988, was a watershed. Gone were the references to armed struggle. The Intifada played a pivotal role in this shift. Even Henry Kissinger said, "Israel's best hope is with Arab leaders living on the West Bank."[135]

The Intifada also showed to the Israelis the limits of their occupational strategy and consolidated international public opinion behind the Palestinians, with Palestine recognized by nearly 100 countries, as Kuttab pointed out. As King asserts, the Intifada was a leading reason for both Israelis and Palestinians to compromise. This led first to the Madrid negotiations in 1991. A number of the intellectuals who were the fountainheads of the Intifada, such as Feisal Husseini and Sari Nusseibeh, acted as interlocutors and go-betweens here and in the subsequent rounds of negotiations. Over time, this was supplanted by the Oslo Accords as a result of direct, secret negotiations between the Israeli government and the PLO.[136] The PLO's disposition toward negotiation "rested on the success achieved through the Intifada, powered by its self-discipline in the use of nonviolent strategies and belief that negotiation could be beneficial," writes King.[137]

THE FIRST INTIFADA ENDS

By the end, it became a bit much. The Palestinians had neither the stomach nor the resources for a full-fledged drawn-out nonviolent civil disobedience campaign. The PLO started interfering more and more and took over the leadership role by 1990. "This is when the uprising was aborted," Muhammad Jadallah, a local organizer, told King. "The Intifada was strangulated by Palestinians before it was strangulated by the Israelis." Soon, the exhortations to nonviolent actions disappeared. "In the end, ambivalence about the choice of nonviolent struggle helped to destroy the First Intifada," writes King.[138]

A remarkable transformation did occur where the Palestinians went from being afraid to being the feared among Israeli soldiers. "The population was kept under control because they feared the army," said Kuttab. "Since the beginning of the Intifada, this fear has evaporated." Yet the use of stones led to a certain ambiguity and fed into an Israeli defensiveness that still made them think of themselves as victims. "The stones fed Israeli fear and let antagonists criticize the uprising as inherently violent, thus diminishing its political results," writes King.[139]

"The uprising was unarmed, if arms refers to guns and not to gasoline-filled bottles," writes Gorenberg in the pro-Israel *Weekly Standard*. "The leaders of the uprising were 'opposed in principle' to using firearms and explosives, says Yaakov Pery, who was deputy chief of the Shin Bet, Israel's internal security service at the start of the Intifada and became the head of the agency soon after."[140]

Gorenberg says that the Palestinian mix of violent and nonviolent tactics helped muddy the picture while acknowledging the harsh Israeli response. "Elias Rishmawi, whose pharmacy was emptied" when Israeli soldiers ransacked Beit Sahour during the tax strike, "remembers bitterly that adopting the slogan 'no taxation without representation' did not bring American support," writes Gorenberg. "The United States vetoed a Security Council resolution condemning the Beit Sahour operation. In the Knesset, describing the operation, Yitzhak Rabin said, 'We will teach them a lesson . . . we will not allow this kind of civil disobedience.'"[141]

Yet, as Gorenberg points out, Rabin privately acknowledged the impact of the Intifada, and it pushed him toward negotiating and signing the Oslo Accords. "The uprising was a missed chance," writes Gorenberg. "It was not a Gandhian revolt, but it hinted at what a nonviolent Palestinian strategy could, and might yet, achieve, if followed strictly."[142]

In March 1989, a delegation led by Gene Sharp met with the leadership of the PLO (including Yasir Arafat) to try to convince them of the effectiveness of a purely nonviolent strategy. Sharp insisted that such an approach would cause a split in Israeli and U.S. public opinion and swing world opinion over to the Palestinian side. (Assassinated PLO leader Abu Jihad owned the entire three-volume Sharp work *The Politics of Nonviolent Action*.) Arafat and his people listened politely but gave no indications of a fundamental change in tactics. Three months later, Sharp returned to the Occupied Territories and found much to his dismay a sharp increase in Palestinian lives lost. He suggested that the Intifada become strictly nonviolent, but again to no avail.[143]

By 1990, the Intifada was running out of steam. The leadership did keep up its efforts with a delegation in January 1990 meeting with Israeli members of parliament. Perhaps the last gasp was in May 1990, when Feisal Husseini and others organized a hunger strike in response to the killing of seven Palestinians by a gunman and 15 in a subsequent protest. "This is the last chance to keep the Intifada nonviolent," said Husseini. Even the United States seemed willing to allow UN peacekeepers into the Occupied Territories.[144]

And then a PLO leader, Muhammad Abu Abbas, attempted a raid on a Tel Aviv beach. All bets were off. Husseini remarked that the Abbas action was a stab in the back worse than the "frontal wounds delivered by enemy arrows." This sort of internal infighting about what approach to adopt for liberation plagued the Palestinians throughout. While activists urged the South African model, the PLO preferred the Algerian example. At best, Fatah saw nonviolence as just one aspect of a broader struggle. In March 1988, for instance, a PLO hijacking attempt left three Israelis dead, leaving activists inside the territories in despair, with Nusseibeh denouncing the sabotage of a "revolution in which people don't use any arms." Prime Minister Shamir used the occasion to assert no difference between the hijackers and those "igniting the disturbances in the territories." Over time, it was, unfortunately, the Command that gave way to the thinking of the PLO, with Leaflet no. 65 referring to "all forms of struggle."[145]

The leadership of the Command changed, and the number of people familiar with Mubarak Awad or Gene Sharp's work declined until there was no one left after 1990. The PLO asserted full control and employed the only nonviolent tactic it knew: indiscriminate strikes, which did more harm than good. Iraq's invasion of Kuwait dealt a death blow to the Intifada since Arafat's endorsement of Saddam Hussein alienated Israeli and international public opinion so badly that it ended up hurting all Palestinians. The assertion of leadership by people like Feisal Husseini, who had wriggled free of the PLO leadership, was broken. King asserts that to a certain extent the PLO encouraged dissension in the territories-based leadership so that they could continue dominating the Palestinian community.[146]

Riven by internal contradictions and differences between the PLO and the Command leadership, the Intifada collapsed. The unhelpful attitudes of the Israelis also contributed greatly. "Although the nonviolent consensus was lost, it is significant that the uprising never became in any sense an armed rebellion, and a fundamental determination to limit violent acts and keep a popular civilian character remained in view," says King.[147]

There were dissenters from the Intifada consensus, of course, with the most prominent being the Islamist movements—Hamas and Islamic Jihad. Hamas called for the "liberation" of all of Israeli/Palestine and for the use of armed struggle. What mitigated things was the relatively cordial relationship that the group had with the Intifada Command. Not so the Islamic Jihad, which in its zeal even outdid Hamas. In December 1992, Hamas severely weakened the uprising when it killed four Israeli soldiers, giving Israel an opportunity to harshly retaliate by deporting Islamist leaders to the no-man's-land zone between Israel and Lebanon. (This had the effect, however, of increasing their popularity and visibility.) Hamas did by the early 1990s moderate its stance toward Israel a bit, perhaps under the influence of the Intifada. But much worse was to come a few years later, with the massively violent split of Fatah and Hamas, the takeover of the Gaza Strip, and Israel's 2009 assault on Gaza.[148]

Because of the interference of the PLO, there wasn't large-scale training of the Palestinians in nonviolent methods. Even the limited use of nonviolence was able to reach many of the goals. Israelis were cajoled into compromising. The Israeli security forces were not able to retaliate to the fullest extent. But the use of stone throwing ensured that the suspicions of Israelis did not go away fully. Research showed that a large portion of them saw nonviolence as not much more than a ruse to get their guard down.[149]

The Palestinian Intifada was not the only essentially nonviolent uprising to not be strictly nonviolent. King gives an entire range of examples, from South Africa to Eastern Europe to Burma. She gives a detailed account of the South African struggle, where the African National Congress always had an armed wing, the Mkhonto we Sizwe, which played a minor but significant role in the campaign to rid the country of apartheid. "Judgments against the First Intifada for its lack of scrupulosity and inability to hold unanimity after 1990 should note that nonviolent mobilizations without any act of violence are historically rare," writes King.[150] "The Intifada, had it secured uncompromising nonviolent discipline, could have changed the face of the Middle East," she adds. "One must acknowledge, however, that it would have been difficult to have a mass movement of such consistency."[151]

In the end, the First Intifada fizzled out without changing the dynamics of the region. "Official Israel's refusal to recognize the Intifada as an effort to lift the occupation through nonviolent action, not an attempt to defeat Israel with armed struggle, had the effect of weakening the very Palestinians who were working to substitute nonviolent means of contention for organized violence on a permanent basis," says King.[152]

Still, the uprising had two huge effects: first, it swayed international public opinion, and, second, it did compel the Israelis to sue for negotiations. This ultimately led to the 1993 Oslo Accords, which gave the Palestinians a measure of autonomy. This was optimistically meant to lead to Palestinian statehood, but because of reasons too complex to get into here, that never happened. And the creation of the Palestinian Authority undermined local Palestinian leaders who had believed in nonviolence.

The returning Palestinians "had not participated in the formation of civilian networks and were not conversant with the discourses of the activist intellectuals and their Israeli counterparts," writes King. "They had not read the *samizdat* of Awad, attended workshops, heard Sharp's lectures, followed the dialectics of Husseini and Nusseibeh, grappled with the concept of disengagement, nor seen the historically proved action methods of nonviolent struggle applied by Palestinians." Instead, they brought with them the rhetoric and notion of armed struggle.[153]

In 2000, the last shot at a comprehensive peace accord failed when both sides couldn't reach an agreement at Camp David. The Second Intifada started in September 2000 with Ariel Sharon's provocative visit to the Old City of Jerusalem. The initial Palestinian demonstration the day after was nonviolent but invited a harsh Israeli response, with four demonstrators killed by live ammunition. Even then, the first few weeks were essentially nonviolent, but the Israelis delivered a very tough reply. "Not since the 1967 war has Israel used such heavy weapons against Palestinians," said Daoud Kuttab. The Palestinians, for their part, formed militias that targeted settlers. And then there were the suicide bombings. Within three months, they had started and were in full earnest by the following spring, heavily tarnishing the reputation of the Palestinians and casting a pall over the entire proceedings. Although they were mainly the work of Hamas, Arafat didn't try hard enough to crack down since "it likely would have led to a Palestinian war," states analyst Glenn Robinson. Israel retaliated with extremely harsh measures. The peace process was out in hiatus, notwithstanding unofficial initiatives such as the Geneva Accord, a joint venture of Israeli and Palestinian eminences. Israel capped it all by building a separation barrier, ostensibly for security purposes, but also fulfilling the aim of incorporating Palestinian territory. The withdrawal of the Israelis from the Gaza Strip wasn't a major advance; indeed, it lead to Hamas seizing control of the territory and the massive assault on the area in December–January 2008–9 by the Israelis in response to Hamas rocket attacks.[154]

In spite of the disarray of the legacy of the First Intifada, King is still optimistic, saying that when a Palestinian state is established, the lessons of nonviolent struggle will be essential in establishing a just and equitable society and will provide a role model for the region. She is hopeful for the prospects of a long-term peace, although she cautions that it will require a complete adjustment of attitude—of the Arab countries toward Israel and of Israel toward Palestine. "Had the Palestinian leaders who accepted coexistence with Israel been offered reinforcement rather than jail and deportation . . . they could have formed the crux for acceptance of permanent citizenship for Israelis in the region," writes King. "Israeli policies instead undermined those who forged the new systems of thought that led to the First Intifada and its enunciation of acceptance of a two-state solution."[155]

THE NONVIOLENT MODE CONTINUES

In recent years, the Palestinian landscape has been dominated by violence. But even with the heavy dose of violence in the Second Intifada, there have been heartening instances of nonviolent activism, mainly against the Israeli separation barrier, which has often traversed into Palestinian territory and appropriated Palestinian land. The village of Bilin has been the most prominent site, but there have been other villages, such as Jayyus, Biddu, Deir Ballut, and Budrus. They have held regular demonstrations against the wall, often joined by Israelis and people from around the world.[156] "Some entitle this 'the Intifada of the Wall,'" King writes. "Their successes have been modest but noteworthy, as they have altered the route or slowed the progression of the wall that takes still more land and encircles them in enclaves—although they could not halt it outright."[157]

Two groups involved in nonviolent training—Middle East Nonviolence and Democracy and Holy Land Trust—claim that they are receiving more requests than they can handle.[158] In 2007, Palestinian activists scored a huge victory when the Israeli Supreme Court rerouted the Israeli separation barrier at Bilin in response to the protests and a court case. The village of Bilin, led by its local council leader, Ahmed Issa Abdullah Yassin, got a prominent Israeli human rights lawyer to file its case, saying that roughly 500 acres of village land had been appropriated by the barrier. The court agreed, saying that the wall ran a mile east of an Israeli settlement and that there was no security rationale that justified its route. About half the land confiscated because of the barrier was ordered returned to the village. "The panel of three judges ruled unanimously that a mile-long section of the barrier should be redrawn and rebuilt in a 'reasonable period of time,'" the New York Times reported. "Chief Justice Dorit Beinish wrote in the ruling, 'We were not convinced that it is necessary for security-military reasons to retain the current route that passes on Bilin's lands.'"[159]

Although this is not the first time that Israel's highest court ruled in the Palestinians' favor in a case about the barrier, this case took on a special significance as a symbol of popular resistance to the construction. But the court decision wasn't enough. The Israeli authorities refused to reroute the wall, and the protests continued. The barrier attracted weekly protests every Friday at the village. The village protest movement received a huge boost in the arm and global recognition in August 2009 when The Elders, a group of international statesmen including Jimmy Carter and Bishop Desmond Tutu, visited the village. "Just as a simple man named Gandhi led the successful nonviolent struggle in India and simple people such as Rosa Parks and Martin Luther King led the struggle for civil rights in the United States, simple people here in Bilin are leading a nonviolent struggle that will bring them their freedom," Tutu said.[160] A grandson of the Mahatma himself, Rajmohan Gandhi (someone I've interviewed a number of times), honored Bilin by also visiting the village and participating in the weekly demonstration.[161] One of the leaders of the protest in Bilin has been Abdullah Abu Rahma, a high school teacher, leading demonstrations every Friday against the wall. He estimated that 800 people were injured in the first three years by Israeli soldiers. (On the part of the demonstrators, the principal expression of violence, again, was stone throwing.) Abu Rahma cited a 1936 uprising and the First Intifada as inspirations. "Nonviolence gave Palestinians a chance to get involved in the resistance in many different ways," he told The Progressive. Abu Rahma has been arrested by the Israelis multiple times but was released quickly because of the international network that supports him. "What Gandhi achieved in his country," he added, "I want to achieve in mine."[162]

The Bilin clashes have become a national and international symbol, being embraced by the Palestinian government and receiving support from the Spanish authorities. "Bilin is no longer about the struggle for Bilin," a coordinator said. "This is part of a national struggle."[163] The Israelis, on their part, alleged that the demonstrations have been in fact violent, a charge that astonishes the leaders of the agitation. "They want to destroy our movement because it is nonviolent," said Rahma, referring to the imprisonment of some of the protest coordinators.[164]

Edith Garwood of Amnesty International emphasizes how hard it is for the Palestinians to sustain a nonviolent movement. "Israeli policies are repressive and brutal," she writes. "The use of live ammunition, beatings, destruction of property, rejection of building permits, constant threats, repeated administrative detentions, and the escalation in arrests is discouraging and has been effectively obstructive."[165]

The protests at Bilin keep on going more than half a decade after they started. They have become increasingly creative, dressing up as Avatar characters and engaging in parody of a popular Israeli ad by playing with a soccer ball. The demonstrations are an example of grassroots nonviolence, though the rock throwing by certain Palestinians is still seen by Israelis as proof that they really aren't nonviolent. Five years after they began, the Israeli government finally started implementing a Supreme Court order to move the barrier wall. But this gives back the Palestinians only one-third of the land that they claim as their own. (The International Court of Justice ruled in 2004 that the barrier was illegal on its current route since it encroached on Palestinian land.) "I feel really, very sad," exclaimed Mahmoud Samarra, a Bilin resident. "To whom can we complain? The judge and the enemy is the same." Samarra, age 64, is going to get only a fraction of his land back, which he can access only by foot, walking the 1.5 kilometers with the help of a stick.[166]

And the protests have taken their toll. Bassem Abu Rahma, who died at age 31 in 2009 when he was hit in the chest by a teargas canister during a protest, is mourned by his mother Subhiyeh every waking minute. But his brother Ahmad says that he still believes in peace and even wore a T-shirt showing the Palestinian and Israeli flag side by side. The Israelis insist that such unfortunate incidents are in response to stone throwing (even though the BBC says that video footage in the case of Bassem shows no such thing) and that Palestinians armed with rocks and fence cutters regularly attack Israeli soldiers.[167]

In their more candid moments, the Palestinians don't deny the use of rocks. "We don't have planes or tanks or rifles, all we have is the rock," says Subhiyeh. "And they are afraid of the rock." The New York Times states that 19 Palestinians have been killed since 2004 in clashes caused by the separation barrier and that an American, Tristan Anderson, was so badly injured by an Israeli tear gas canister in March 2009 that he suffered brain damage. An organizer says that 1,200 Palestinian protesters have been hurt and 85 arrested. (Roughly 100 Israeli officials have been injured in the protests, the New York Times estimates.) The demonstrators say that they still hope for a complete victory. "We hope it will be all our land," says Ratib Abu Rahman. "If the wall is destroyed, that will be a big achievement."[168] "To find the Palestinian Gandhi or MLK, the first step is to look in Israeli detention centers," writes Amnesty International's Garwood. "The next step is to let them out. A sustainable peace is only possible when it is based on respect for each other's humanity."[169]

CONCLUSION

The Palestinian struggle has been a long and difficult one and marked with a fair amount of violence. However, there has also been utilization, no matter how imperfectly, of nonviolent methods. This did yield some results before circumstances destroyed further progress. Yet even the partial use of nonviolence by the Palestinians provided the movement a huge boost, both domestically and internationally, and gave them an image globally as the underdog. It's a pity, then, that the use of nonviolence has not been more consistent or used in recent years on a broader scale. This road may be the one to yield the most results for Palestinians.

CHAPTER 11

To Topple Dictators without Force: Peaceful Protest in Modern South Asia

There have been recent nonviolent mass movements in South Asia that have for the umpteenth time demonstrated the resonance of peaceful protest in Muslim societies. They were able to achieve the seemingly undoable: getting rid of supposedly infallible dictators, one of them in power for three decades. And they did this without resorting to violence.

PAKISTAN'S AMAZING LAWYERS

A mass agitation in Pakistan—one of the world's largest Muslim countries—not too long ago confirmed yet again the global reach of civil disobedience. The amazingly defiant lawyers' stir that took on and toppled the military dictatorship of General Pervez Musharraf demonstrated that the Muslim world is as fertile for the application of nonviolence as any other part of the planet. The movement was once more an extremely effective counter to the libel that Muslims—being followers of an allegedly intrinsically aggressive and violent religion—are immune to the charms of peaceful protest.

"If we define a 'lawyers' movement' as a coherent nationwide struggle by legal professionals, sustained over time and fought primarily in the streets, Pakistan would emerge as the only case," writes analyst Daud Munir. "The problem is that while Western policymakers are ready to extend billions of dollars in military aid to subdue the extremist impulse, they seem unwilling to engage with—or even to adequately acknowledge—the secular, reformist impulse in Pakistani society that is represented by the lawyers' movement."[1]

While the lawyers' major motivation was to defend the integrity of the legal system, they were also reflecting broader complaints about the Musharraf dictatorship, which had been firmly in place since a bloodless coup in October 1999.

After a promising start, where it seemed that Musharraf perhaps presented a better alternative to the corrupt major political parties, the autocrat disappointed on various fronts. He coddled the fundamentalist religious formations, backtracked on women's rights, and compromised on legislation that would have reformed draconian blasphemy laws. And he constantly played a double game, fostering certain militant groups for use against India and in Afghanistan while cracking down on others in response to U.S. pressure.

The lawyers' protests began in March 2007, when Musharraf sacked the chief justice of Pakistan's Supreme Court, Iftikhar Muhammad Chaudhry, for having the gall to defend Pakistan's constitution. Chaudhry was an unlikely opponent of the regime. He had refused to resign unlike some other judges when Musharraf asked the judiciary to take an oath of loyalty. As a result, he was elevated to the Supreme Court in 2000 and made chief justice in 2005. But slowly in subsequent years, he started taking a more activist approach that set him on a collision course with the regime. Chaudhry's court began questioning Musharraf on a range of issues.[2]

As British-Pakistani intellectual Tariq Ali observes, this was the nub of the complaint against Chaudhry: He was too much an activist on various fronts. And it wasn't limited to the human rights of detainees picked up for suspected involvement in the country's various insurgencies, such as a separatist movement in the province of Baluchistan. He had also publicly questioned the privatization of a steel mills complex by the then–Prime Minister and Finance Minister Shaukat Aziz for a pittance to a friendly consortium. (The outgoing chairman of the enterprise complained that "the plant could have fetched more money if it were sold as scrap.") Of a bigger worry to the military regime was the worry that he might use the detainees' cases to declare the regime itself as unconstitutional.[3] "When the Supreme Court started acting like an independent institution for the first time in sixty years, they came down very hard," said Athar Minallah, a lawyer who was actually in Musharraf's cabinet for the first couple of years of his rule. "In the past, the Supreme Court had always connived with the establishment and the military."[4]

Chaudhry began testing the waters by first taking up relatively innocuous pieces of litigation: the privatization of two public parks and corruption charges against officials. But there came bolder moves. Chaudhry accepted the cases of 41 missing persons and then, even more astonishingly, of more than 100 disappeared people. The next day, on March 9, 2007, he was dismissed.[5]

The Musharraf regime saw Chaudhry as a serious threat. It used Naeem Bokhari, a progovernment lawyer, as a proxy and had him distribute a letter detailing the charges against Chaudhry. The e-mail circular accused the chief justice of "arrogance, aggression and belligerence" in his official conduct but then went on to more interesting territory: "I am pained at the wide publicity to cases taken up by My Lord in the Supreme Court under the banner of Fundamental Rights. . . . I am further pained by the media coverage of the Supreme Court on the recovery of a female [in official custody]. In the Bar Room, this is referred to as a 'media circus.'"[6]

Chaudhry was detained in solitary confinement for a number of hours, manhandled by security operatives, and paraded for television. But he refused to cave in and ignited a national movement. When his supporters sent him a text message on a cell phone he had hidden during his house arrest to ask him if he would resign, Chaudhry is said to have replied, "Question does not arise till my last breath."[7]

Initially, the protests for the restoration of the judges were confined to Pakistan's lawyers. But the demonstrators soon received enthusiastic backing from all sections of civil society. The country's television channels—difficult to control since they were transmitting into Pakistan from outside the country—covered these rallies extensively. Even political parties whose commitment to an independent judiciary was very suspect (including the country's most powerful Islamist right-wing party) joined in.[8]

"What are the objectives of our movement?" asked Muneer A. Malik, the president of the Supreme Court Bar Association, in *Dawn,* a leading Pakistani English-language daily. First, he answered, it was to change the mentality of the Pakistani public. To do so, he asserted, the movement had to achieve its second purpose—to change the workings of the Pakistani judiciary. The third objective, Malik stated, was to reinstate civilian rule in Pakistan. And, last but not the least, Malik laid down the aim of bolstering the myriad institutions in the country. To accomplish these goals, Malik said, the lawyers were willing to welcome support from all segments of society but only on one condition: their demands were nonnegotiable, and anyone who wanted to participate with them would have to recognize this.[9]

Instead of acknowledging the legitimacy of these demands, the Musharraf regime cracked down harshly. The most severe reaction took place in May 2007. That month, Chaudhry drove from Islamabad, the nation's capital, to Lahore, Pakistan's cultural center. A drive that normally takes a few hours took 26 to complete because of the massive crowds that greeted Chaudhry at every town en route. Musharraf decided that something had to be done and chose Karachi, Pakistan's largest city, as the venue.[10]

Chaudhry was meant to visit Karachi on May 12. The city's politics are controlled by an outfit called MQM, which has its support base in Urdu-speaking immigrants from India. The party chose to ally itself with the military regime. Immediately before Chaudhry's visit to the city, the party's leader, Altaf Hussain, transmitted a video to his followers from self-exile in London urging them to do anything to show solidarity with the ruling government. The cadre and leadership of the party prevented Chaudhry from leaving the Karachi airport. In attacks on his supporters (who fought back), at least 40 people were killed. And when a television network showed footage, MQM members targeted the network's local offices, shooting at it for hours and setting cars on fire.[11]

All this while, the law enforcement authorities stood by on official orders. A report by the Human Rights Commission of Pakistan is worth quoting in detail: "A matter of grave concern from the perspective of the institutional integrity of the state is the virtual withdrawal of the state's security apparatus for almost twenty hours and the actual takeover of the city by armed cadres of more than one political party. The spectacle of a disarmed police force operating on the direction of armed cadres was highly disturbing, especially since key officers of the state were reduced to expressing their helplessness."[12]

At a rally held on the same day in the capital Islamabad, Musharraf blamed the opposition movement for the violence and threatened further retaliation. "If they think they are powerful, then they should know that the people's power is with us," Musharraf said.[13] (In another, unexplained attack on the lawyers, a suicide bomber on July 17, 2007, outside a court in Islamabad killed 15 people and wounded dozens shortly before Chaudhry was to address a rally there. To date, the masterminds have not been traced.)[14]

A leader of the movement was Aitzaz Ahsan, a prominent legal luminary and former politician. Ahsan combined the talents of orator, lawyer, and politician, a particularly lethal combination for the Musharraf regime. "Aitzaz Ahsan is a hero for all who believe in pluralism, democracy and freedom of thought in South Asia," wrote Kanak Mani Dixit, the editor of *Himal Southasian* magazine.[15] Ahsan attained rock star status among the people of Pakistan. "The lawyers were overcome with excitement at greeting the mastermind of Pakistan's lawyers' movement, perhaps the most consequential outpouring of liberal, democratic energy in the Islamic world in recent years," wrote James Traub in the *New York Times Magazine*.[16]

"The response was astonishing. When, eight weeks after the drama, Ahsan drove Chaudhry from Islamabad to Lahore, tens of thousands of people lined the streets; the 150-mile trip took 26 hours, and every minute was covered live on television," Traub added. "For the next three months, he and Chaudhry crisscrossed the country by car, with Ahsan addressing the delirious crowds and the chief justice carefully limiting himself to high-minded speeches to his fellow lawyers."[17] "There have been corrupt and vile chief justices in the past, but he seemed to be a prince—the prince who challenges authority, defies his executioners and was prepared to go to the gallows holding his head up," Ahsan said of Chaudhry.[18]

The next dramatic development occurred when the Pakistani Supreme Court took the unbelievable step in July 2007 of restoring Chaudhry to his rightful post, "the first judicial ruling in the country's history directly challenging the action of a military dictator," says Munir. This further emboldened Chaudhry, who now was all set to consider a case challenging Musharraf's takeover itself.[19] But the general believed in the doctrine of preemption. On November 3, 2007, Musharraf took the fateful step of declaring a state of emergency. This included banning nongovernment television channels and jamming all cell phone networks. Musharraf successfully persuaded the government of Dubai, where the most prominent television outfit, Geo TV, was located, to stop the transmission. When the Supreme Court justices declared martial law illegal, they were all placed under house arrest. Several prominent leaders of the movement (including Ahsan, held incommunicado for four months) and other opposition leaders were jailed. Lawyers were detained in huge numbers, often held under awful conditions.[20]

But they persevered in their struggle. They were driven by a simple question, articulated by Babar Sattar, a prominent figure in the protests: "How do you function as a lawyer when the law is what the general says it is?"[21] For the temerity of asking that question, the lawyers and judges (and their civil society allies) were subject to mass arrest, beatings, and teargas. Musharraf came on television to explain his actions, but his performance was such an embarrassment that the attempt backfired. He complained that the court's "constant interference in executive functions, including but not limited to the control of terrorist activity, economic policy, price controls, downsizing of corporations and urban planning, has weakened the writ of the government." He also grumbled about "the humiliating treatment meted to government officials by some members of the judiciary on a routine basis during court proceedings."[22]

At the same time that he was jailing lawyers and judges, Musharraf was bargaining with terrorists. "Leading lawyer, U.N. special rapporteur, and chairperson of the independent Human Rights Commission of Pakistan Asma Jahangir, under house arrest at her Lahore residence since Saturday, termed it ironic that the President, who she said 'has lost his marbles,' had to clamp down on the press and the judiciary to curb terrorism," the Inter Press Service reported. "'Those he has arrested are progressive, secular-minded people while the terrorists are offered negotiations and ceasefires,' she added."[23]

Still, the lawyers carried on defiantly. For inspiration, they turned to Pakistan's own history. Pakistan's first military dictator, Ayub Khan, was forced out of office in the late 1960s by nationwide demonstrations. "Global media coverage of Pakistan suggests a country of generals, corrupt politicians, and bearded lunatics, but the struggle to reinstate the chief justice had presented a different picture," writes Tariq Ali.[24] The agitation was helped by the fact that the lawyers' associations were among the very few organizations in Pakistan to constantly choose their leadership through elections, and, democratically, the 116,000 lawyers chose to protest.[25] The lawyers received support from other segments of society, who showed their solidarity through innovative means. "Civil society activists are engaging in creative ways of protest focusing on symbolism, like taking flowers to the dissenting judges and spray-painting graffiti symbols like 'eject' and 'repeat' signs," reported the Inter Press Service. "On Wednesday, a small group of activists took several bouquets to Sabihuddin Ahmed, Chief Justice of the Sindh High Court, who is also under house arrest."[26]

The lawyers hoped to paralyze the judicial system by not having any attorneys appear before judges accepting Musharraf's emergency rule. "The campaign to defend the judiciary was the first serious nationwide mass movement against the arbitrariness of military rule since 1969," writes Ali. "The Supreme Court decisions that challenged the Musharraf regime had restored the country's self-respect. Its secular character had disproved the myth that jihadi terrorists were on the verge of taking over the country."[27]

The American media (or at least the major print outlets), in a heartening recognition of the lawyers' struggle, carried major coverage of the protests. The *New York Times*, for instance, on November 7, 2007, had a long front-page article on the genesis of the lawyers' movement and the astonishing courage it had shown.[28] Perhaps because of this, there were wonderful expressions of support from the United States. The American Bar Association wrote a letter to Musharraf voicing disapproval of his actions. The National Lawyers Guild issued a strong statement asking President Bush to suspend aid to Pakistan. State and local bar associations and legal faculties from all over the United States sent messages of support. Harvard conferred on Chaudhry a prestigious award. And the *National Law Journal* chose him as the lawyer of the year. The Carter Center urged in a December 2007 press release the immediate restoration of the judiciary. Congresswoman Zoe Lofgren of California introduced a resolution in the House in March 2008 calling for the reinstatement of the judges and commending the lawyers for their protests. The prestigious *Atlantic* magazine chose Chaudhry as one of its "brave thinkers" in 2009: "Though criticized for his temper and self-aggrandizement, Chaudhry has come to personify Pakistani hopes for an independent judiciary, the rule of law, and an end to the arbitrary authority exercised, often violently, by the country's political and military elite."[29]

But the Bush administration's reaction was another matter. In fact, the U.S. government was engaging in political maneuverings to prevent Chaudhry's return. "Behind the scenes, the United States is trying to dampen enthusiasm for Mr. Chaudhry, whom Washington sees as too much of a Musharraf opponent," reported the *New York Times*. "'The United States ambassador, Anne Patterson, met with Mr. [current Pakistan President Ali Asif] Zardari, and suggested that the Supreme Court judges except Mr. Chaudhry should be reinstated,' said Shahbaz Sharif, a senior member of the Pakistan Muslim League-N."[30]

Such U.S. moves were met with dismay by liberal segments of Pakistani society. "Expressions from the United States are taken seriously here, and I feel the United States ought to put its foot down, regardless of the consequences to Musharraf," said lawyer Hassan Aurangzeb.[31] In fact, the Bush administration's stance came in for strong criticism in Pakistan. "The Americans, the British and the Australians were always on the wrong side—they were with Musharraf and then Zardari," said Ahsan. "The West has turned a blind eye to the fact that the lawyers' movement is actually the only movement in the Islamic world that is liberal, secular, democratic, nonviolent, hugely popular, and above all, plural."[32] Tariq Mahmood, a former president of the Supreme Court Bar Association, told the U.S. ambassador, "My message was very simple: 'You love democracy, you live in a democracy, why do you want to deprive us? You are always supporting the dictator.'"[33]

The United States went along with the declaration of a state of emergency since it regarded Chaudhry as a troublemaker who was aiding militants by questioning too vocally their detention. It also feared that Pakistan's nuclear weapons could fall into the hands of fundamentalists and thought that a strong military regime was the best safeguard against that. So, no U.S. spokesperson criticized the dismissal or the arrest of the judges.[34] "People in the United States wonder why extremist militants in Pakistan are winning," Ahsan stated in a *New York Times* op-ed on December 23, 2007. "What they should ask is why does President

Musharraf have so little respect for civil society—and why does he essentially have the backing of American officials?"[35]

Chaudhry smuggled a letter out in which he detailed his arrest conditions. "Barbed-wire barricades surround the residence, and all phone lines are cut," his letter said. "Even the water connection to my residence has been periodically turned off. I am being persuaded to resign and to forego my office, which is what I am not prepared to do."[36] But he asserted that he and his supporters were steadfast. "There can be no democracy without an independent judiciary, and there can be no independent judge in Pakistan until the action of November 3 is reversed," the letter read. "Whatever the will of some desperate men, the struggle of the valiant lawyers and civil society of Pakistan will bear fruit. They are not giving up."[37] This was very true. The lawyers' movement had put Musharraf in a very tight spot, and no amount of repression was going to get him out. His heavy-handedness embarrassed and alienated the international community. The Bush administration felt compelled to guide him out of the impasse. Musharraf was persuaded to allow back in the country exiled ex–Prime Minister Benazir Bhutto and her husband, Asif Ali Zardari, and allow elections. Shortly before the elections, in midcampaign, Bhutto was assassinated. (The killing was carried out by Pakistani religious extremists, aided and abetted by glaring lapses in Bhutto's government-provided security.) The party that emerged in Parliament with the most seats from the election was Bhutto's Pakistan's People's Party, which assumed office in early 2008. Musharraf's party suffered a crushing rout, with a number of cabinet members being heavily defeated in their constituencies. "It was impossible to predict the pleasant if unexpected surprise that the country witnessed in the judicial upsurge," writes Ali. "Its impact was a renewal of hope, and the effective media coverage of the movement left Musharraf exposed."[38] Bhutto's widower Zardari assumed charge. His party formed a government with the support of the other major party, ex–Prime Minister Nawaz Sharif's Muslim League. They agreed that a top priority would be reinstating the judiciary. (In an interesting side story, the party led by Ghaffar Khan's heirs, the Awami National Party, made a huge comeback in the border region.)

The lawyers kept up the pressure after the loss of Musharraf's party in the elections, staging demonstrations in the summer of 2008 to call for Musharraf's ouster from the presidency and the restoration of the judges. In one such demonstration, 40,000 people led by lawyers converged on Islamabad, Pakistan's capital. "This is historic: civil society has established itself as an alternative source of power," said analyst Farrukh Saleem, calling the lawyer movement an alternative power center. "For sixty years, we've had executive dictatorships, whether military or civilian."[39] Musharraf stayed on as the president until August 2008, but the game was up. Isolated and humiliated, he was forced to relinquish power and made his way to England in self-exile, where he currently resides.

The lawyers were not through, however. They came out another time under Zardari to force him to keep his campaign pledge. Zardari was reluctant to reinstate the judges since he thought that they would question the deal he had done with Musharraf that promised him amnesty from his alleged corruption charges. (The dispute in the end came down to a fraction of the judges, including Chaudhry, who were less compliant to Zardari's wishes.) This was in spite of a June 2008 poll that showed that more than 8 out of 10 Pakistanis wanted the judges back.[40]

The lawyers' campaign reached a crescendo this time in March 2009 when the Musharraf-appointed Supreme Court ruled that ex–Prime Minister Sharif and his brother Shahbaz, the chief minister of Punjab, Pakistan's most populous province, could not contest elections. Following the ruling, Zardari dismissed the Punjab government. In response, lawyers appeared on the streets, demanding that Zardari keep his election pledge and reappoint the judges that Musharraf had thrown out.[41]

Initially, the Zardari government responded harshly, banning the march and arresting hundreds. Sharif was threatened with charges of sedition for allegedly calling for a revolution. Inevitably, Zardari was compared with Musharraf. Even people of Zardari's party were shaken. "I say it with a very heavy heart that the government is following the same policies that were carried out by General Musharraf," said Iqbal Haider, a human rights activist affiliated with Zardari's party.[42]

But Zardari had various forces arrayed against him. The demonstrations for the restoration of the judiciary drew an enthusiastic response. In most places, the police stood silently by in tacit support to the marchers. Police officers were actually warning Sharif's people to lie low to avoid arrest. Twenty-two police chiefs in the province of Punjab, including four in the Lahore area, were replaced because of a refusal to follow orders. "The officers had been asking us to defend, but when we saw the mob was so powerful we retreated, and the officers told us to retreat," Police Constable Mohammed Imtiaz told the *New York Times,* adding that the judges needed to be restored. "We need the rule of law." The chief magistrate of the Lahore government, Sajjad Bhutta, went further, resigning in a refusal to carry out orders to crack down on the demonstrators. He became a hero to the public, with crowds cheering him and waving flags.[43]

In response to the combined pressure from senior leaders from within his party, the Obama administration, and the Pakistan military, Zardari announced on March 21, 2009, that all the dismissed Supreme Court judges would be reinstated.[44] "I feel so proud because our long struggle for an independent judiciary has borne fruit," Shauqat Saddiq, a lawyer, told the *Washington Post.* "We fought for only one goal: the rule of law. Whoever sits in the justice's seat, this has been a victory of the principle, not the person."[45]

Analyst Munir points out that the lawyers' success was due to their truly national, nonsectarian character; they didn't represent any ethnic group or political party. And they had, for the most part, a focused agenda, whether under Musharraf or Zardari: the restoration of the judiciary, doing this with utmost bravery. "Beyond achieving the restoration of the judges to the bench and eroding the jurisprudential foundations of authoritarianism, the lawyers' movement has had a deeper structural impact on democratic politics in Pakistan," writes Munir. "Until the lawyers' movement, no one had offered 'rule of law' to the people."[46]

The one thing the lawyers' movement was unable to do, though, was to fundamentally transform Pakistani society, as commentator Ayaz Ahmad lamented later in the Pakistani newspaper *The News*, even as he acknowledged that "the declared objectives of the lawyers' movement were limited in their scope, primarily to the restoration of the pre-November 3 judiciary."[47] But Ahmad does have a point in that the judicial changes could have been institutionalized: "A logical next step after the judges' restoration could have been the insistence of the leaders of the lawyers' movement and the political forces that an independent prosecutorial body be established in order to support judicial proceedings," Ahmad contends. "Due to either limited objectives or political affiliations of certain leaders of the lawyers' movement, the drive for independence of the entire 'legal system' could not be carried forward."[48] That this couldn't be done speaks more to the larger shortcomings of Pakistani social structures, however, than of the abilities of the lawyers. The fact that they were able to achieve as much as they did was nothing short of remarkable.

THE ISLAND TYRANT OVERTHROWN

An almost unimaginable thing happened just a few years ago. A peaceful agitation overthrew one of the longest-reigning dictators in the world. This took place in the Muslim South Asian island nation of Maldives, where a former political prisoner named Mohamed Nasheed ousted from office in a free and fair election someone who had been entrenched in power for three full decades. Nasheed has "earned a place in the history books as the person who brought an end to the thirty-year rule of Maumoon Abdul Gayoom—Asia's longest-serving leader," BBC reported. "To his supporters, Mr. Nasheed is a latter-day Nelson Mandela, overcoming the hardships of prison to secure an inspirational election win against the odds."[49]

Himal Southasian magazine had an amazing beginning to a feature story detailing Nasheed's rise. "June 1990. After eighteen months in solitary confinement, [a political prisoner] was finally sentenced to a jail term of three and a half years. By the time the sentence was handed down, the damage caused by the regular torture he had endured had become overwhelming: his backbone was damaged, and he was suffering from internal bleeding," the article read. "November 2008. There, standing before the chief justice of the Maldives, was that very writer and activist [ready to be sworn in]."[50]

A truly remarkable saga, "no fairytale: this was the true story of a man's fight for rights and justice on behalf of the people against a brutal autocracy," wrote Simon Shareef. "There is little doubt that the triumph of Nasheed, or 'Anni' as he is widely known, will go down in Maldivian history as an enduring and inspirational tale."[51] But why only Maldives? This is an inspirational tale for the whole world.

A British-educated journalist, Nasheed in the early 1990s used a publication called *Sangu* for critiquing the Maldivian government, being one of the very first to take on the regime. The journal was banned. Nasheed was initially put under house arrest but was transferred to jail after he complained to the international media about how badly he was treated. Nasheed then spent a full 18 months in prison, with bouts of torture that included severe sleep and water deprivation, being fed food with crushed glass, and being chained to a chair outside for 12 days. Nasheed was later jailed again for his political writings, and Amnesty International declared him a prisoner of conscience in 1997.[52]

Astonishingly, Nasheed managed to get elected as a Member of Parliament in 1999 but was ejected from the legislative body on a trumped-up theft charge. Two years later, he attempted to register an independent political party but was unable to do so. In September 2003, Nasheed played a pivotal role in igniting antigovernment protests when a 19-year-old died in the country's largest prison. Nasheed asked an outside doctor to see the body. (Eventually, it was discovered that the teenager was tortured to death.) The incident was a milestone in the nation's history, causing the first large-scale outbreak of mass dissent against the long-standing Gayoom regime. There were street protests and a jail riot. Three prisoners were shot to death.[53]

This was the catalyst for the formation of the Maldivian Democratic Party by Nasheed while in exile in Sri Lanka. Finally in June 2005, Nasheed was able to register his party. Two months later he was arrested again, however, in response to a sit-in at the capital Male's Republican Square. Things seemed at such a stasis that some elements of Nasheed's party were close to issuing a call for armed struggle. But better sense prevailed, and Nasheed and his fellow party members persisted in their efforts for democracy and civil liberties. The party transformed under Nasheed's leadership from a mere anti-Gayoom group into a perceived government in waiting by the Maldivian populace, setting the stage for his successful presidential bid against daunting odds.[54]

The Maldivian regime did not let up, however. Nonviolence scholar Stephen Zunes documents the repression under Gayoom. For example, in October 2005, Jennifer Latheef, a young journalist and graduate of the University of San Francisco, was sentenced to a decade in prison on the false accusation of "terrorism," with Amnesty International adopting her as a prisoner of conscience. But growing unrest forced Gayoom to liberalize politically. Activists took advantage of this opening and were very creative in their dissent. Blogs and text messaging were used to circumvent restrictions on meetings. Web sites were created, and mobile music shows on sound trucks were organized in which popular local bands performed anti-Gayoom songs.[55] The Gayoom regime started cracking in 2007, when a number of ministers turned in their resignations. In 2008, Gayoom announced elections. The elections were monitored by foreign diplomatic missions and observers from the United Nations, with help from the local branch of Transparency International.[56]

Still, it seemed very unlikely that Gayoom would yield power if he lost. In the run-up to the election, the repression continued. "Gayoom's iron-fisted rule, marred by corruption, nepotism, cronyism, and stifling of any dissent, had remained unchallenged until these elections," editorialized India's *Economic and Political Weekly*.[57] Yet democracy activists bravely held large demonstrations. "In one, protesters paraded through the streets with coffins," writes Zunes. "Posters sprouted across the islands with a picture of Gayoom's head with the universal 'no' sign of a red circle with diagonal bar across it with the slogan 'Expires 28.10.2008,' the date of the election."[58]

International pressure on Gayoom forced him to allow parties such as Nasheed's to be registered and to allow the public to change the system to a presidential one. The first round of voting on October 7, 2008, had five candidates, including Nasheed and Gayoom. A report by the country's auditor general on the eve of the elections detailing government malfeasance had a negative effect on the regime's popularity, but still in the initial round of voting, Gayoom came first with 40 percent, with Nasheed getting a quarter of the electorate.[59]

The entire opposition decided to form a coalition and back Nasheed. This helped his campaign refute the charges that he was anti-Islam and a stalking horse for foreign interests. (The ruling party even alleged that he was conspiring to blow up the largest mosque in the capital.) The day of the voting, the early tally was for the Diaspora electorate. Soon, disbelief sunk in as Nasheed garnered a clear majority of the votes and held on to his lead.[60] "As the sun rose on 29 October [2008], thousands of men, women and children gathered at the eastern beach of the capital, to welcome the new day," writes Shareef. "Emotional scenes followed as more and more people appeared, many of them openly weeping. Among the crowd were victims of torture and mistreatment. Before long, Gayoom conceded his electoral defeat in a radio address. The prisoner of conscience had championed the cause of democracy, and turned on its head the political landscape of the atolls."[61]

Gayoom, amazingly, saw the writing on the wall and finally stepped down three decades after his ascension to power. "It is likely that Gayoom's decision to accept the results of the election was based in part on awareness of contingency plans by the opposition to engage in massive strikes and other forms of large-scale civil resistance if he tried to steal it," Zunes writes. "Such fraudulent efforts by the rulers of Serbia, Georgia and Ukraine earlier this decade had resulted in the massive popular outpourings that brought an ignominious end to these corrupt and semi-autocratic regimes."[62]

Zunes asserts that the downfall of Nasheed was a classic case of nonviolent activism in action. The years'-long struggle by prodemocracy campaigners, he says, demolished the notion of the country united around Gayoom, caused the international community to back away from the regime, and even caused fissures among the ruling class in the country. Soon, Maldivians had added Nasheed to the pantheon of national heroes, albeit of a very different kind. And here Maldivians took inspiration from the prophet of Islam, perpetuating the most peace-loving aspects of the religion. "During his first post-election press conference, Nasheed called on Maldivians to 'be humble in victory and courageous in defeat,'" writes Shareef. "These words marked a significant change in mood, and radio stations across the Maldives soon began talking about the benevolence and peaceful style of President-elect Nasheed. Some religious speakers even equated his words to the traditions of the Prophet Muhammad."[63]

Nasheed himself learned the most wonderful lessons possible from his religion. "Islam teaches you that there is no future if we hate," he told an interviewer, when asked how his government would treat Gayoom. "The embittered and re-vengeful cannot become agents of change." Nasheed's stints in prison gave him a remarkable opportunity to develop empathy, an advantage he enjoys over almost any other head of state. "Don't forget, some of the inmates were fellow prisoners, and I know them well!" was his amazing reply when asked about what he would do to reform the Maldivian legal system.[64]

Nasheed was quite modest when it came to claiming credit for his achieve-ment. He claimed that becoming the head of his country was not even on the agenda. Whoever was responsible, the change in the country was really profound. "Even the trees breathe freely now," an observer remarked.[65] As part of the transi-tion, Gayoom was forced to bequeath the country a new constitution, another gift of prodemocracy activists to their nation. "The new democratic constitution, for the first time, brought about a separation of powers in the Maldives, with the powers of the judiciary statutorily demarcated from those of the head of the state," stated the *Economic and Political Weekly*. "The Constitution gives impor-tance to the tenets of Islam, which is the state religion, while at the same time guaranteeing a regime of rights and freedoms."[66]

CONCLUSION

In just one region of the world, in two Muslim societies of vastly different sizes, nonviolent movements toppled two autocrats who seemed to be so firmly en-sconced that nothing could dislodge them. But the power of peaceful civil disobe-dience proved too much for Musharraf and Gayoom, and they and their repressive power were no match for the liberating power of nonviolence. These movements are truly uplifting fables for our times and are just illustrative, recent examples. Further back in time, there are other instances, though more complicated and perhaps a bit questionable for use in this book. There were massive protests in Pakistan that brought down the military dictatorship of Ayub Khan in 1969, with some attendant rioting. And in 1998, huge demonstrations brought down the long-reigning regime of General Suharto in Indonesia, albeit, in this case, the well-to-do Chinese minority was unfortunately targeted as a focus of pent-up resentment. The beauty of the lawyers' movement and the Maldives protests are that they happened in the very recent past and were accompanied by almost no violence. They're true role models for our times.

CHAPTER 12

Conclusion

THE NEW YORK CITY CONTROVERSY

Islam has become a hot-button issue in the United States. Nothing has made this more apparent than the proposed New York City mosque/interfaith center, which metamorphosed from a local issue to a raging national controversy just as this book was being completed.

Some people felt that it was insensitive for a Muslim structure to come up so near the World Trade Center and, in fact, thought it to be triumphalist in nature. Certainly, there were a few things about the proposed complex to make one pause. Some family members of September 11 victims were so traumatized by the attack that it was understandable for them to think it an insult to their loved ones to have a Muslim venture so close to the site of the tragedy. Notwithstanding the lofty, admirable professed goals of the Cordoba Initiative, the organization behind the scheme, there were some concerns about the group's ties with the Malaysian government, which has long been politically repressive and socially exclusionary of its non-Malay Muslim population (this has as much to do with ethnic chauvinism as religion, however). In addition, the head of the project, Imam Feisal Abdul Rauf, made some impolitic remarks after the September 11 tragedy.

But the objections had little to do with all this and much more to do with people's feelings about Islam. The religion here was being reduced here to one single, horrible event, which was being used to define and essentialize it. A number of national politicians helped fan the flames by coming out strongly on the issue.

Presidential aspirant and ex–House Speaker Newt Gingrich claimed that the project would be "hostile to our civilization."[1] Another potential Republican candidate, 2008 running mate and ex–Governor Sarah Palin, used Twitter to express her opposition to the structure. She first tweeted, "Ground Zero Mosque supporters: doesn't it stab you in the heart, as it does ours throughout the heartland? Peaceful Muslims, pls refudiate." Just six minutes later, she followed up with, "Peaceful New Yorkers, pls refute the Ground Zero mosque plan if you believe catastrophic pain caused @ Twin Towers site is too raw, too real."[2] Other Republican politicians also voiced their resistance to the proposal, including a couple of New York gubernatorial candidates and, bafflingly, a contender for a congressional seat in North Carolina.

Gingrich later went on to add, "Nazis don't have the right to put up a sign next to the Holocaust Museum in Washington. We would never accept the Japanese putting up a site next to Pearl Harbor. There's no reason for us to accept a mosque next to the World Trade Center."[3]

Other politicians joined the fray, and soon political lines got blurred. So, for instance, New York City Mayor Michael Bloomberg, an independent, and New Jersey governor Chris Christie, a Republican, warned against demonizing Muslims, while Senate Majority Leader Harry Reid, a Democrat up for a tough reelection in Nevada (thousands of miles from the site), uttered his disapproval of the project.

President Obama, for his part, lent his voice of affirmation but had to partly backtrack. "As a citizen, and as President," Obama initially said, "I believe that Muslims have the same right to practice their religion as everyone else in this country. And that includes the right to build a place of worship and a community center on private property in Lower Manhattan, in accordance with local laws and ordinances."[4]

His remarks ignited a firestorm. Gingrich, House Minority Leader John Boehner, and Congressman Peter King, Republican of New York, all came out in opposition. Gingrich accused Obama of "pandering to radical Islam." Boehner opined that the proposed complex was "deeply troubling, as is the President's decision to endorse it." And King declared Obama to be "wrong," charging that he had "caved in to political correctness."[5]

"I was not commenting, and I will not comment, on the wisdom of making the decision to put a mosque there," Obama backpedaled the very next day. "I was commenting very specifically on the right people have that dates back to our founding."[6]

The irony about the whole matter is that the people behind the project are Sufis, the very type of Muslims who are most eager for pluralism, peace and reconciliation. For this, they have come under assault in South Asia particularly. "Such moderate, pluralistic Sufi imams are the front line against the most violent forms of Islam," writes William Dalrymple, the author of a number of books on the region. "In the most radical parts of the Muslim world, Sufi leaders risk their lives for their tolerant beliefs, every bit as bravely as American troops on the ground in Baghdad and Kabul do."[7]

The most infamous episode has been a twin suicide bombing at a revered Sufi site, Data Darbar, in Lahore, Pakistan, that killed more than 40 people. Other prominent Sufi places of worship have been attacked throughout Pakistan. These have included the tomb of Haji Saheb of Turangzai, a mentor to Ghaffar Khan, and Rehman Baba, perhaps the most prominent Sufi saint of the frontier region of Pakistan. (I am a lover, and I deal in love," went one of his poems. "Sow flowers / so your surroundings become a garden. / . . . We are all one body. / Whoever tortures another, wounds himself.")[8]

ANTI-ISLAM SENTIMENT

But to ask that people appreciate the complexities of Islam is perhaps too much. In fact, the image of Islam is so negative that there are increasing sentiments against the religion and its places of worship not just in New York City but all throughout the country. A proposed mosque in Tennessee has met with hostility, including arson, vandalism and organized opposition. Ron Ramsey, the state's lieutenant governor and a gubernatorial candidate, stated, "You could even argue whether being a Muslim is actually a religion, or is it a nationality, a way of life or cult, whatever you want to call it?"[9] And these aren't isolated instances. "It's time to add Florence, Kentucky, to the list of controversial Islamic construction projects stretching from Temecula, California, to Murfreesboro, Tennessee, to, of course, lower Manhattan," reports the Web site Talking Points Memo.[10]

Anti-Islam feelings have been expressed in other ways, too. In Florida, a church was at loggerheads with the local authorities after the fire department ruled that its plans to incinerate copies of the Qur'an on the 2010 anniversary of the September 11 attacks would violate a law banning book burnings in public.[11] (It eventually backed down but not before igniting a global firestorm.) And a group has taken out ads on buses in Miami, New York, and San Francisco decrying Islam.[12]

All this ties into broader anxieties about the religion. A mid-August 2010 poll by *Time* magazine found that roughly 3 out of 10 Americans don't think that Muslims should be allowed to sit on the Supreme Court, while almost one-third deem them unfit to be president of the United States. Such negative feelings about the religion have undoubtedly contributed to suspicions about Obama, since one-fourth of Americans think him to be Muslim. (On the narrower question of the New York City project, more than 60 percent oppose it, with 7 out of 10 considering it an insult to the memory of September 11 victims.)[13]

ISLAM AND VIOLENCE

Much of the animus toward Islam has been caused by the constant barrage of news about violence in the Middle East (apart from the few terrorist attempts in the United States itself, of course). But this is based on a gross misunderstanding. The major impetus for the violence in the Middle East against Western troops is resentment at what is seen to be an occupation. A number of scholars have concluded that the reasons for suicide bombings and other hostility directed at foreign forces have little to do with religion. For instance, Professor Robert Pape of the University of Chicago has found in a comprehensive study of violent resistance—analyzing everyone from the Tamil Tigers in Sri Lanka to groups in the Middle East—that the major motivation is the urge to get rid of the alien occupier. Researcher Marc Sageman has discovered, on the other hand, that a main impetus is group bonding and a desire to blend in with—and show one's worth—to peers.[14]

"Most youth are radicalized by the situation on the ground: foreign occupation; killing of large numbers of civilians by American, Western, or Israeli military forces; a sense of humiliation and defeat; a thirst for revenge, sometimes for people killed within their own family," writes Graham Fuller. "These are very concrete and practical issues, quite unrelated to Islamic theology."[15] Fuller explains that someone intent on revenge will surely find religious texts—or extracts thereof—to rationalize such acts. "The rage comes first, the theological justification is an afterthought," he writes. With this mind-set, it is very easy to find something in the Qur'an to support a predetermined deed. A society that feels it is under attack will acquiesce in such violence. "Religion will always be invoked wherever it can to galvanize the public and to justify major campaigns, battles, and wars," writes Fuller. "But the causes, campaigns, battles, and wars are not about religion. Take away the religion, and there are still causes, campaigns, battles and wars."[16]

VICTIMS OF VIOLENCE

Besides, a huge misperception in the United States is that the major victims of violence in the past few years have been westerners. This is vastly in error. Professor Stephen Walt of Harvard University, a highly regarded international affairs scholar, did a study for *Foreign Policy* magazine tallying the number of victims over the past 30 years. He came out with a total of nearly 300,000 Muslims killed by the United States (a low-end estimate, he says), as opposed to the roughly 10,000 Americans the other way around. As he himself pointed out, a number of caveats apply to his study, such as that the United States was not solely responsible for all the deaths.

"Yet if you really want to know 'why they hate us,' the numbers presented above cannot be ignored," Walt writes. "Even if we view these figures with skepticism and discount the numbers *a lot,* the fact remains that the United States has killed a very large number of Arab or Muslim individuals over the past three decades. Even though we had just cause and the right intentions in some cases (as in the first Gulf War), our actions were indefensible (maybe even criminal) in others."[17] This goes a long way in explaining animosity toward the United States in these lands, not Islam, as is commonly supposed by a lot of people. "When you kill tens of thousands of people in other countries—and sometimes for no good reason—you shouldn't be surprised when people in those countries are enraged by this behavior and interested in revenge," writes Walt.[18] Yet, in an ironic twist, people are at best dimly aware of the huge human toll in these countries.

AMERICAN MUSLIMS

The other major reason for the antagonism toward Islam has been the terrorist plots in the United States in the past few years. The group that has borne the brunt of this has been the American Muslim community. As documented in this book (and as exhibited most dramatically in the controversy surrounding the New York City project), Muslims in the United States have been the objects of suspicion and derision. This is in spite of a Pew study in 2007 that showed the community as "middle class and mostly mainstream," as the title of the report stated. Most Muslim Americans have upbeat views about American society, with 71 percent saying that one can make it in American society through a willingness to work hard. They also reject extremism and violence in large proportions. At the same time, one-fourth of Muslims living here say that they have been victims of discrimination. (The Pew report tabulates the U.S. Muslim population as 2.3 million, while other estimates have had it as high as 5 million and above.)[19]

Even with the small number of Muslim Americans (barely 1 percent of the U.S. population), members of the community have been engaged on various fronts nonviolently. So, they protested against the Iraq War with vigor, joining in larger coalitions. For instance, in January 2003, in the run-up to the war, a demonstration in Pittsburgh had local Muslim groups participating. "We should stop supporting all the people who violate civil rights, whether they're Arab or Israeli," said Dr. Nadeem Iqbal, president of the Pittsburgh chapter of the American Muslim Council.[20]

On the first anniversary of the war, in March 2004, Mahdi Bray, executive director of the Muslim American Society Freedom Foundation and the president of the Coordinating Council of Muslim Organizations, spoke to a crowd of more than 100,000 in New York City. "We march to tell John Ashcroft that my little Muslim son and millions of American Muslim youth will not grow up in America where they are profiled as terrorist suspects, but rather, they will live in a free America where they can control and reach their highest prospects," Bray said. "We march to tell George Bush that that Bible that he reads . . . says, 'Blessed are the peacemakers.'"[21]

On the fifth anniversary of the war in March 2008, Muslim American groups again took part in protesting the war. "We need to pull out immediately," said Sharaf Mowjood, member of the Los Angeles Council on Islamic-American Relations. "So it's in a situation where the best viable option is to pull out because you have a lot of these internal problems you have to deal with—health care, sub-prime mortgage crisis, Katrina."[22]

Of course, the major anxiety of Americans has been terrorism, and there's been concern at the supposed lack of action on the part of American Muslims to counteract it. (Here, I'm not going to get into the various statements made by Muslim American groups condemning terrorism since this book deals with activism, not words.) But there have been various actions. More than 100 protesters demonstrated outside the Detroit courthouse, for instance, where Umar Farouk Abdulmutallab (the "underpants bomber") was being arraigned. "Islam is not a terrorist religion," Bilal Amen, vice chair of the Islamic Institute of Knowledge, proclaimed while holding an American flag. "Islam is a peaceful religion." At a press conference organized that morning by 10 imams from the state of Michigan, Imam Aly Lela of the Islamic Association of Greater Detroit said, "Al Qaida must be defeated not only militarily, but intellectually."[23]

The controversy over the New York City project has shown the American Muslim community that it needs to do more. It has been trying to reach out and allay concerns, going so far in some instances as to cancel Eid celebrations in 2010 since they fell around September 11. "They do not distinguish between a very small group of Muslim extremists, which we also fight, and the mainstream Islam and the mainstream Muslims," said Imam Seyed Ali Ghazvini of Fresno, Nevada. "This is not only un-useful, it is dangerous, it will harm our country and the name of our country and it will make us fail in the war against terrorism."[24]

This book has sought to dispel such misconceptions and increase understanding of Islam by highlighting a peaceful, pluralistic strain within it.

Notes

CHAPTER 1: INTRODUCTION

1. Pew Research Center, "Public Expresses Mixed Views of Islam, Mormonism," Pew Research Center Publications, September 25, 2007.

2. Business Wire, "Attitudes toward Muslims Mixed in Europe and the U.S.," August 23, 2007.

3. Marilyn Elias, "USA's Muslims under a Cloud," *USA Today*, August 10, 2006.

4. Ibid.

5. Jon Cohen and Jennifer Agiesta, "Most in Poll Back Outreach to Muslims," *Washington Post*, April 6, 2009.

6. Anny Bakalian and Mehdi Bozorgmehr, *Backlash 9/11: Middle Eastern and Muslim Americans Respond* (Berkeley: University of California Press, 2009), 1–31.

7. Richard Winton and Teresa Watanabe, "LAPD's Muslim Mapping Plan Killed," *Los Angeles Times*, November 15, 2007.

8. Jordy Yager, "Rep. Myrick Repeats Calls for Cutting CAIR Ties," *The Hill*, October 17, 2009.

9. Amitabh Pal, "Interview with Keith Ellison," *The Progressive*, November 2008.

10. Editorial, "Debates on Muslim Grievance Are Generating More Heat Than Light," *Economist*, April 17, 2008.

11. Peter Beaumont, "One in Four People Is Muslim, Says Study," *Guardian*, October 8, 2009.

12. Mary Frost, "Controversy Continues for Arabic-Themed School, Even with New Principal," *Brooklyn Daily Eagle*, January 9, 2008.

13. Steven Greenhouse, "Muslim Holiday at Tyson Plant Creates Furor," *New York Times*, August 5, 2008.

14. Maria J. Stephan and Erica Chenoweth, "Why Civil Resistance Works," *International Security* 33, no. 1 (Summer 2008): 7–44.

15. Ibid.

16. Ibid.

17. Amitabh Pal, "Interview with Gene Sharp," *The Progressive*, February 2007.

18. Pankaj Mishra, "Where Alaa Al Aswany Is Writing From," *New York Times Magazine*, April 27, 2008.

19. Khalid Kishtainy, "Violent and Nonviolent Struggle in Arab History," in *Arab Nonviolent Struggle in the Middle East*, ed. Ralph Crow, Philip Grant, and Saad Ibrahim (Boulder, CO: Lynne Rienner, 1990), 9–10.

20. Shirin Ebadi, *Iran Awakening: A Memoir of Revolution and Hope* (New York: Random House, 2006), 33.

21. Mohammed Abu-Nimer, *Nonviolence and Peace Building in Islam: Theory and Practice* (Gainesville: University Press of Florida, 2003), 163–79.

22. Ramin Jahanbegloo, "Is a Muslim Gandhi Possible?," *Reset*, January 20, 2009.

CHAPTER 2: INSPIRATION AT THE ROOTS: SOURCES OF NONVIOLENCE IN ISLAM

1. Mohammed Abu-Nimer, *Nonviolence and Peace Building in Islam: Theory and Practice* (Gainesville: University Press of Florida, 2003), 38.

2. Ibid., 183.

3. Ibid., 38.

4. Ibid., 182.

5. John Kelsay, *Arguing the Just War in Islam* (Cambridge, MA: Harvard University Press, 2007), 40–41.

6. Asghar Ali Engineer, *On Developing Theology of Peace in Islam* (New Delhi: Sterling, 2003), 38.

7. Ibid., 101.

8. Ibid., vii.

9. Tamizul Haque, *Islam: Prophet Muhammad as Warrior and Peace Maker* (Dhaka: Syed Farooque Azam, 1982), 15.

10. Seyyed Hossein Nasr, *The Heart of Islam: Enduring Values for Humanity* (San Francisco: HarperSanFrancisco, 2002), 210.

11. Ibid., 211.

12. Ibid., 213.

13. Ibid.

14. Ibid., 214–15.

15. Abu-Nimer, *Nonviolence and Peace Building in Islam*, 31.

16. Ibid., 2.

17. Ibid., 181.

18. Chaiwat Satha-Anand, "The Nonviolent Crescent: Eight Theses on Muslim Nonviolent Action," in *Peace and Conflict Resolution in Islam: Precept and Practice*, ed. Abdul Aziz Said, Nathan C. Funk, and Ayse Kadayifci (Lanham, MD: University Press of America, 2001), 204.

19. Ibid.

20. Ibid.

21. Abu-Nimer, *Nonviolence and Peace Building in Islam*, 47.

22. Ibid.

23. Satha-Anand, "The Nonviolent Crescent," 207–8.

24. Ibid., 209.

25. Abu-Nimer, *Nonviolence and Peace Building in Islam*, 71.

26. Ibid., 73.

27. Ibid., 72.

28. Hadith in ibid., 73.

29. Ibid., 74.

30. Ibid.

31. Satha-Anand, "The Nonviolent Crescent," 207–9.

32. Engineer, On Developing Theology of Peace in Islam, 114–15.

33. Abu-Nimer, Nonviolence and Peace Building in Islam, 69.

34. Ibid., 58.

35. Ibid., 79.

36. Ibid., 80.

37. Ibid.

38. Engineer, On Developing Theology of Peace in Islam, 121–22.

39. Meena Sharify-Funk, "Peace and the Feminine in Islam," in Said, Funk, and Kadayifci, Peace and Conflict Resolution in Islam, 279.

40. Abu-Nimer, Nonviolence and Peace Building in Islam, 67.

41. Ibid.

42. Sharify-Funk, "Peace and the Feminine in Islam," 278.

43. Ibid., 281.

44. Ibid., 282–83.

45. Ibid., 284–85.

46. Ibid.

47. Ibid., 286.

48. Ibid., 288.

49. Abu-Nimer, Nonviolence and Peace Building in Islam, 64.

50. Ibid.

51. Ibid., 65.

52. Ibid., 67.

53. Ibid., 71.

54. Nasr, The Heart of Islam, 218.

55. Engineer, On Developing Theology of Peace in Islam, 103.

56. Ali Bulac, "Jihad," in Terror and Suicide Attacks: An Islamic Perspective, ed. Ergun Capan (Somerset, NJ: The Light, 2005), 78.

57. Ergun Capan, "Suicide Attacks in Islam," in Capan, Terror and Suicide Attacks, 102–3.

58. Ahmet Gunes, "Views on the Rules of War in Islamic Law," in Capan, Terror and Suicide Attacks, 129.

59. Zahid Aziz, Islam, Peace and Tolerance (Wembley: Ahmadiyya Anjuman Lahore Publications, 2007), 79.

60. Abu-Nimer, Nonviolence and Peace Building in Islam, 39.

61. Engineer, On Developing Theology of Peace in Islam, 132.

62. Abu-Nimer, Nonviolence and Peace Building in Islam, 39.

63. Engineer, On Developing Theology of Peace in Islam, 132.

64. Abu-Nimer, Nonviolence and Peace Building in Islam, 46.

65. Ibid., 33–38.

66. Aziz, Islam, Peace and Tolerance, 82.

67. Abu-Nimer, Nonviolence and Peace Building in Islam, 63.

68. Ibid., 29.

69. Nuriye Akman, "Interview with M. Fetullah Gulen," in Capan, Terror and Suicide Attacks: An Islamic Perspective, 2–4.

70. Engineer, On Developing Theology of Peace in Islam, vi.

71. Ibid., 37.

72. Ibid., 97.

73. Ibid., 101.

74. Ibid., 120.

75. Nasr, *The Heart of Islam*, 204.

76. Abu-Nimer, *Nonviolence and Peace Building in Islam*, 37.

77. Ibid., 60.

78. Reuven Firestone, *Jihad: The Origin of Holy War in Islam* (New York: Oxford University Press, 1999), 73.

79. Asghar Ali Engineer, *Islam: Misgivings and History* (New Delhi: Vitasta Publishing Pvt. Ltd, 2007), 87.

80. Ibid., 59.

81. Abu-Nimer, *Nonviolence and Peace Building in Islam*, 42.

82. Ibid.

83. Ibid., 44.

84. Nasr, *The Heart of Islam*, 204–5.

85. Ibid., 206.

86. Kishtainy, "Violent and Nonviolent Struggle in Arab History," 18.

87. Firestone, *Jihad: The Origin of Holy War in Islam*, 51.

88. Ibid., 53.

89. Abu-Nimer, *Nonviolence and Peace Building in Islam*, 61.

90. Ibid., 58.

91. Ibid., 59.

92. Engineer, *On Developing Theology of Peace in Islam*, 121.

93. Engineer, *Islam*, 60.

94. Engineer, *On Developing Theology of Peace in Islam*, 123.

95. Ibid., 127.

96. Ibid., 36.

97. Ibid., 31.

98. Ibid., 131.

99. Rudolph Peters, *Jihad in Classical and Modern Islam: A Reader* (Princeton, NJ: Markus Wiener, 1996), 81.

100. Kishtainy, "Violent and Nonviolent Struggle in Arab History," 14.

101. Firestone, *Jihad*, 56.

102. Engineer, *On Developing Theology of Peace in Islam*, 94.

103. Ibid., 96.

104. Firestone, *Jihad*, 76.

105. Ibid., 64.

106. Rafiq Zakaria, *Muhammad and the Qur'an* (New York: Penguin, 1992), 41–42.

107. A. G. Noorani, *Islam and Jihad: Prejudice Versus Reality* (London: Zed Books, 2003), 53–54.

108. Ibid., 73–74.

109. Abu-Nimer, *Nonviolence and Peace Building in Islam*, 44–45.

110. Zakaria, *Muhammad and the Qur'an*, 30.

111. Abu-Nimer, *Nonviolence and Peace Building in Islam*, 42.

112. Firestone, *Jihad*, 107.

113. Ibid.

114. Ibid.

115. Ibid., 108.

116. Abu-Nimer, *Nonviolence and Peace Building in Islam*, 61.

117. Kishtainy, "Violent and Nonviolent Struggle in Arab History," 15.

118. Ibid., 40.

119. Ibid.

120. Engineer, *On Developing Theology of Peace in Islam*, 29.

121. Hamza Aktan, "Acts of Terror and Suicide Attacks," in Capan, *Terror and Suicide Attacks*, 29.

122. Ibid., 30.

123. Engineer, *Islam*, 59.

124. Engineer, *On Developing Theology of Peace in Islam*, 39.

125. Zakaria, *Muhammad and the Qur'an*, 37.

126. Engineer, *Islam*, 270.

127. Zakaria, *Muhammad and the Qur'an*, 30.

128. Ibid., 32.

129. Reza Aslan, *No god but God: The Origin, Evolution, and Future of Islam* (New York: Random House, 2005), 88.

130. Ibrahim Canan, "Islam as the Religion of Peace and Tolerance," in Capan, *Terror and Suicide Attacks*, 21.

131. Engineer, *Islam*, 21–22.

132. Aziz, *Islam, Peace and Tolerance*, 80–81.

133. Aslan, *No god but God*, 84.

134. Zakaria, *Muhammad and the Qur'an*, 33.

135. Ibid., 33–34.

136. Aslan, *No god but God*, 93.

137. Zakaria, *Muhammad and the Qur'an*, 36.

138. Ibid., 37.

139. Ibid.

140. Engineer, *Islam*, 22–23.

141. Engineer, *On Developing Theology of Peace in Islam*, 130.

142. Canan, "Islam as the Religion of Peace and Tolerance," 22–23.

143. Engineer, *On Developing Theology of Peace in Islam*, 130.

144. Gunes, "Views on the Rules of War in Islamic Law," 124.

145. Canan, "Islam as the Religion of Peace and Tolerance," 13.

146. Abu-Nimer, *Nonviolence and Peace Building in Islam*, 63.

147. Ibid., 67.

148. Ibid., 63.

149. Ibid., 62.

150. Aslan, *No god but God*, 91.

151. Engineer, *Islam*, 93.

152. Aktan, "Acts of Terror and Suicide Attacks," 30–31.

153. Ibid., 32–33.

154. Ibid., 39.

155. Engineer, *On Developing Theology of Peace in Islam*, 119.

156. Gunes, "Views on the Rules of War in Islamic Law," 128.

157. Engineer, *Islam*, 61.

158. Engineer, *On Developing Theology of Peace in Islam*, 120–21.

159. Ibid.

160. Kishtainy, "Violent and Nonviolent Struggle in Arab History," 15.

161. Engineer, *Islam*, 60.

CHAPTER 3: AT THE POINT OF A SWORD?
HOW ISLAM ACTUALLY SPREAD

1. Reuven Firestone, *Jihad: The Origin of Holy War in Islam* (New York: Oxford University Press, 1999), 10.

2. Richard Eaton, *Essays on Islam and Indian History* (Oxford: Oxford University Press, 2000), 9–10.

3. Ibid., 19.

4. Firestone, *Jihad,* 14.

5. Khalid Kishtainy, "Violent and Nonviolent Struggle in Arab History," in *Arab Nonviolent Struggle in the Middle East,* ed. Ralph Crow, Philip Grant, and Saad Ibrahim (Boulder, CO: Lynne Rienner, 1990), 22.

6. Zachary Karabell, *Peace Be upon You: Fourteen Centuries of Muslim, Christian, and Jewish Coexistence in the Middle East* (New York: Knopf, 2007), 39.

7. Ibid., 76–77.

8. Ibid., 52–57.

9. Kishtainy, "Violent and Nonviolent Struggle in Arab History," 10–11.

10. Ibid.

11. Karabell, *Peace Be upon You,* 22–24.

12. Ibid., 26–27.

13. Ibid.

14. Ibid., 28–29.

15. Graham Fuller, *A World without Islam* (Boston: Little, Brown, 2010), 86.

16. Karabell, *Peace Be upon You,* 29.

17. Ibid.

18. Ibid., 29–30.

19. Eaton, *Essays on Islam and Indian History,* 35.

20. Karabell, *Peace Be upon You,* 23.

21. Ibid., 31.

22. Fuller, *A World without Islam,* 84.

23. Karabell, *Peace Be upon You,* 50–51.

24. Ibid., 51.

25. Eaton, *Essays on Islam and Indian History,* 24.

26. Fuller, *A World without Islam,* 91.

27. Karabell, *Peace Be upon You,* 30.

28. Fuller, *A World without Islam,* 88.

29. Karabell, *Peace Be upon You,* 31..

30. Fuller, *A World without Islam,* 89–90.

31. Karabell, *Peace Be upon You,* 38.

32. Ibid.

33. Fuller, *A World without Islam,* 87.

34. Kishtainy, "Violent and Nonviolent Struggle in Arab History," 13.

35. Karabell, *Peace Be upon You,* 37.

36. Ibid., 162–63.

37. Ibid., 163.

38. Chaiwat Satha-Anand. "The Nonviolent Crescent: Eight Theses on Muslim Nonviolent Action," in *Peace and Conflict Resolution in Islam: Precept and Practice,* ed. Nathan C. Funk, Ayse Kadayifci, and Abdul Aziz Said (Lanham, MD: University Press of America, 2001), 199.

39. Kishtainy, "Violent and Nonviolent Struggle in Arab History," 14.

40. Karabell, *Peace Be upon You*, 62.

41. Ibid., 46.

42. Ibid., 63.

43. Ibid., 71.

44. Ibid., 74.

45. Ibid., 76.

46. Ibid., 60.

47. Ibid., 81–83.

48. Ibid., 116.

49. Ibid., 118.

50. Ibid., 126.

51. Ibid., 160–61.

52. Ibid., 163.

53. Ibid., 169.

54. Ibid., 172.

55. Ibid., 172–74.

56. Ibid., 177.

57. Ibid., 182–84.

58. Ibid., 192.

59. Ibid., 193.

60. Ibid.

61. Ibid., 285.

62. Fuller, *A World without Islam*, 94.

63. Eaton, *Essays on Islam and Indian History*, 36–37.

64. Ibid., 264.

65. Ibid., 264–65.

66. Ibid., 274–75.

67. Ibid., 126.

68. Ibid., 127.

69. Ibid., 37.

70. Ibid., 38–39.

71. Norimitsu Onishi, "Under Indonesia's Surface, an Intricate Quilt of Faiths," *New York Times*, February 17, 2010.

72. Eaton, *Essays on Islam and Indian History*, 41–42.

73. Fuller, *A World without Islam*, 230–33.

74. Eaton, *Essays on Islam and Indian History*, 42.

75. Ibid., 42–43.

76. Karabell, *Peace Be upon You*, 270–71.

77. Ibid., 279.

CHAPTER 4: IGNORED FOR NO FAULT OF THEIRS: THE SUFIS AND OTHER PACIFIST MUSLIM SECTS

1. Declan Walsh, "Of Saints and Sinners," *Economist*, December 18, 2008.

2. Ibid.

3. M.R. Bawa Muhaiyaddeen, "The Inner Jihad," in *Peace and Conflict Resolution in Islam: Precept and Practice*, ed. Nathan C. Funk, Ayse Kadayifci, and Abdul Aziz Said (Lanham, MD: University Press of America, 2001), 274.

4. Stephen Schwartz, "Getting to Know the Sufis," *Weekly Standard*, February 7, 2005.

5. Ibid.

6. A.R. Momin, "The Role of Sufis in Fostering Inter-Cultural Understanding and Conciliation in India," in *The Islamic Path: Sufism, Politics and Society in India*, ed. Saiyid Zaheer Husain Jafri and Helmut Reifeld (New Delhi: Rainbow Publishers, 2006), 260–61.

7. Schwartz, "Getting to Know the Sufis."

8. Annemarie Schimmel, *Mystical Dimensions of Islam* (Chapel Hill: University of North Carolina Press, 1978), 26–28.

9. Muhaiyaddeen, "The Inner Jihad," 274.

10. Ibid., 275.

11. Schimmel, *Mystical Dimensions of Islam*, 29.

12. Ibid., 207.

13. Ibid., 130–45.

14. Yoginder Sikand, *Sacred Spaces: Exploring Traditions of Shared Faith in India* (New Delhi: Penguin, 2004), 179.

15. Schimmel, *Mystical Dimensions of Islam*, 190–92.

16. Ibid., 178–84.

17. Ibid., 429.

18. Ibid.

19. Ibid., 434.

20. Meena Sharify-Funk, "Peace and the Feminine in Islam," in Funk, Kadayifci, and Funk, *Peace and Conflict Resolution in Islam*, 289–90.

21. Ibid., 291.

22. Ibid., 293.

23. Nathan C. Funk and Abdul Aziz Said, "Peace in the Sufi Tradition: An Ecology of the Spirit," in Funk, Kadayifci, and Said, *Peace and Conflict Resolution in Islam*, 248.

24. Ibid., 248.

25. Ibid.

26. Ibid., 248.

27. Ibid., 252.

28. Ibid., 250–51.

29. Ibid., 251.

30. Ibid., 251–52.

31. Ibid., 258–59.

32. Schimmel, *Mystical Dimensions of Islam*, 291–93.

33. Ibid., 299.

34. Ibid., 387–92.

35. A. R. Momin, "The Role of Sufis in Fostering Inter-Cultural Understanding and Conciliation in India," in Jafri and Reifeld, *The Islamic Path*, 263.

36. Nishat Manzar, "Mysticism and Humanism: Sufis as Poets, Connoisseurs of Music and Scholars of Comparative Religion and Mystic Philosophy," in Jafri and Reifeld, *The Islamic Path*, 236.

37. Momin, "The Role of Sufis in Fostering Inter-Cultural Understanding and Conciliation in India," 262–63.

38. Eaton, *Essays on Islam and Indian History*, 32.

39. Ibid., 191.

40. Ibid., 199.

41. Schimmel, *Mystical Dimensions of Islam*, 39–41.

42. Ibid., 42–43, 69–72.

43. Momin, "The Role of Sufis in Fostering Inter-Cultural Understanding and Conciliation in India," 265–67.

44. Manzar, "Mysticism and Humanism," 235–59.

45. Schimmel, *Mystical Dimensions of Islam*, 344.

46. Ibid., 344–60.

47. Ibid., 361–63.

48. Sikand, *Sacred Spaces*, 193.

49. Ibid., 193–94.

50. Ibid., 194.

51. Ibid.

52. Ibid., 8.

53. Ibid., 9.

54. Ibid., 116–19.

55. Ibid., 122.

56. Ibid., 125–26.

57. Ibid., 199–204.

58. Ibid., 182–85.

59. Ibid., 196–200.

60. Ibid., 202.

61. Ibid., 202–4.

62. Ibid., 205.

63. Ibid., 214.

64. Surinder Singh, "Islamic Mysticism in Northwest India: An Exploration of the Poetry of Khwaja Ghulam Farid," in Jafri and Reifeld, *The Islamic Path*, 86.

65. Fatima Zehra Bilgrami, "Crystallizing Punjabi Identity: A Note on the Role of the Qadiris and Their Literature," in Jafri and Reifeld, *The Islamic Path*, 143.

66. Momin, "The Role of Sufis in Fostering Inter-Cultural Understanding and Conciliation in India," 268.

67. Ibid., 269–70.

68. Ibid., 274.

69. Ibid., 274–75.

70. Paul Jackson, "Sufism's Enduring Impact: The Legacy of Sharafuddin Maneri," in Jafri and Reifeld, *The Islamic Path*, 199.

71. A.Q. Rafiqi, "Impact of Sufism in Kashmir," in Jafri and Reifeld, *The Islamic Path*, 154.

72. Sikand, *Sacred Spaces*, 207.

73. Ibid., 253–56.

74. Rafiqi, "Impact of Sufism in Kashmir," 156.

75. Sikand, *Sacred Spaces*, 256–60.

76. Ibid., 260.

77. Ibid., 261–63.

78. Rafiqi, "Impact of Sufism in Kashmir," 159.

79. Sikand, *Sacred Spaces*, 217.

80. Ibid., 224–25.

81. Ibid., 228–30.

82. Ibid., 231.

83. Ibid., 232–33.

84. Ibid., 235–37.

85. Ibid., 240.

86. Ibid., 266.

87. Valentine, *Islam and the Ahmadiyya Jama'at*, 55–76.

88. Ibid., xv.

89. Yohanan Friedmann, *Prophecy Continuous: Aspects of Ahmadi Religious Thought and Its Medieval Background* (Oxford: Oxford University Press, 2003), 178.

90. Valentine, *Islam and the Ahmadiyya Jama'at*, 201–2.

91. Friedmann, *Prophecy Continuous*, 165.

92. Ibid., 169–72.

93. Ibid.

94. Ibid., 172–73.

95. Ibid., 176.

96. Ibid., 172–74.

97. Ibid., 174–75.

98. Ibid., 177–78.

99. Valentine, *Islam and the Ahmadiyya Jama'at*, 197–98.

100. Ibid., 202–3.

101. Ibid., 200.

102. Ibid.

103. Ibid., 208.

104. Ibid., 210.

105. Ibid., 190.

106. Sabrina Tavernise, "Mystical Form of Islam Suits Sufis in Pakistan," *New York Times*, February 25, 2010.

107. Ibid.

108. Salman Ahmad, in discussion with the author, April 2010.

109. Matt Pascarella, "A Voice from Senegal: Youssou N'Dour," *The Progressive*, February 2010.

110. Shoma Chaudhury, "The Mystic Master," *Tehelka*, January 24, 2009.

111. Ibid.

CHAPTER 5: JIHAD IS NOT WAR: GRAPPLING WITH THE MOST CONTROVERSIAL ASPECT OF ISLAM

1. Chaiwat Satha-Anand, "The Nonviolent Crescent: Eight Theses on Muslim Nonviolent Action," in *Peace and Conflict Resolution in Islam: Precept and Practice*, ed. Nathan C. Funk, Ayse Kadayifci, and Abdul Aziz Said (Lanham, MD: University Press of America, 2001), 196.

2. Rudolph Peters, *Jihad in Classical and Modern Islam: A Reader* (Princeton, NJ: Markus Wiener, 1996), vi.

3. Simon Ross Valentine, *Islam and the Ahmadiyya Jama'at: History, Belief, Practice* (New York: Columbia University Press, 2008), 190.

4. A.G. Noorani, *Islam and Jihad: Prejudice versus Reality* (London: Zed Books, 2003), 47.

5. Reuven Firestone, *Jihad: The Origin of Holy War in Islam* (New York: Oxford University Press, 1999), 17.

6. Graham Fuller, *A World without Islam* (Boston: Little, Brown, 2010), 275.

7. Noorani, *Islam and Jihad*, 46.

8. Seyyed Hossein Nasr, *The Heart of Islam: Enduring Values for Humanity* (San Francisco: HarperSanFrancisco, 2002), 258.

9. Noorani, *Islam and Jihad*, 49.

10. Ibid., 47.

11. Valentine, *Islam and the Ahmadiyya Jama'at*, 192.

12. Ibid., 190–91.

13. Satha-Anand, "The Nonviolent Crescent," 200.

14. John Esposito and Dalia Mogahed, *Who Speaks For Islam? What a Billion Muslims Really Think* (New York: Gallup Press, 2008), 20–21.

15. Ibid., 21.

16. Nasr, *The Heart of Islam*, 258–59.

17. Firestone, *Jihad*, 17.

18. Nasr, *The Heart of Islam*, 270.

19. Khalid Kishtainy, "Violent and Nonviolent Struggle in Arab History," in *Arab Nonviolent Struggle in the Middle East*, ed. Ralph Crow, Philip Grant, and Saad Ibrahim (Boulder, CO: Lynne Rienner, 1990), 13–14.

20. Firestone, *Jihad*, 18.

21. John Kelsay, *Arguing the Just War in Islam* (Cambridge, MA: Harvard University Press, 2007), 173–74.

22. Ibid., 174–77.

23. Valentine, *Islam and the Ahmadiyya Jama'at*, 192.

24. Noorani, *Islam and Jihad*, 53.

25. Ibid., 55–56.

26. Ibid., 53–54.

27. Ibid., 54–55.

28. Abdulaziz Sachedina, "The Development of Jihad in Islamic Revelation and History," in *Cross, Crescent, and Sword: The Justification and Limitation of War in Western and Islamic Tradition*, ed. James Turner Johnson and John Kelsay (New York: Greenwood, 1990), 35–36.

29. Ibid., 37.

30. Ibid., 38–40.

31. Ibid., 43.

32. Ibid., 44–45.

33. Peters, *Jihad in Classical and Modern Islam*, 3–4.

34. Nasr, *The Heart of Islam*, 262–64.

35. Noorani, *Islam and Jihad*, 56–57.

36. Peters, *Jihad in Classical and Modern Islam*, 6–8, 124.

37. Ibid., 116–19.

38. Ibid., 112.

39. Ibid., 112–13.

40. Ibid., 61.

41. Ibid., 121–22.

42. Ibid., 150.

43. Ibid., 145–46.

44. Ibid., 124–26.

45. Ibid., 126–27.

46. Ibid., 132.

47. Noorani, *Islam and Jihad*, 58–59.

48. Kelsay, *Arguing the Just War in Islam*, 103.

49. Ibid., 104, 199.

50. Nasr, *The Heart of Islam*, 263–65.

51. Ibid., 267–68.

52. Ibid., 268.

53. Hamza Aktan, "Acts of Terror and Suicide Attacks," in *Terror and Suicide Attacks: An Islamic Perspective*, ed. Ergun Capan (Somerset, NJ: The Light, 2005), 40–41.

54. Tamara Sonn, "Irregular Warfare and Terrorism in Islam: Asking the Right Questions," in Johnson and Kelsay, *Cross, Crescent, and Sword*, 137.

55. Ibid.

56. Ibid., 138.

57. Kelsay, *Arguing the Just War in Islam*, 195–97.

58. Ibid., 197.

59. Sonn, "Irregular Warfare and Terrorism in Islam," 142.

60. Ibid., 145.

61. Nasr, *The Heart of Islam*, 270.

62. Ibid., 271.

63. Kelsay, *Arguing the Just War in Islam*, 198.

64. Noorani, *Islam and Jihad*, 46.

CHAPTER 6: A MOST IMPROBABLE TALE: NONVIOLENCE AMONG THE PASHTUNS OF PAKISTAN

1. Joan Bondurant, *Conquest of Violence: The Gandhian Philosophy of Conflict*, (Princeton, NJ: Princeton University Press, 1988), 143.

2. Amitabh Pal, "A Pacifist Uncovered," *The Progressive*, February 2002.

3. Ibid.

4. Mohammed Yunus, *Frontier Pathans and Freedom Struggle* (Delhi: Anmol Publications, 1985), ix.

5. Abdul Ghaffar Khan, *My Life and Struggle: Autobiography of Badshah Khan (as narrated to K. B. Narang)* (New Delhi: Hind Pocket Books, 1969), 29.

6. Ibid., 23.

7. Rajmohan Gandhi, *Ghaffar Khan: Nonviolent Badshah of the Pakhtuns* (New Delhi: Viking, 2004), 43–44.

8. Ibid., 48.

9. Pyarelal, *Thrown to the Wolves: Abdul Ghaffar* (Calcutta: Eastlight Book House, 1966), 21.

10. Khan, *My Life and Struggle*, 31–86.

11. Ibid., 96.

12. Ibid., 97.

13. Bondurant, *Conquest of Violence*, 133.

14. D. G. Tendulkar, *Abdul Ghaffar Khan: Faith is a Battle* (Mumbai: Popular Prakashan, 1967), 60.

15. M. S. Korejo, *The Frontier Gandhi: His Place in History* (Oxford: Oxford University Press, 1993), 17–18.

16. Pyarelal, *Thrown to the Wolves*, 24.

17. Pal, "A Pacifist Uncovered."

18. Ibid.

19. Tendulkar, *Abdul Ghaffar Khan*, 245.

20. Khan, *My Life and Struggle*, 142–44.

21. Pal, "A Pacifist Uncovered."

22. Yunus, *Frontier Pathans and Freedom Struggle*, xiii.

23. Attar Chand, *India, Pakistan and Afghanistan: A Study of Freedom Struggle and Abdul Ghaffar Khan* (New Delhi: Commonwealth Publishers, 1989), 41.

24. Bondurant, *Conquest of Violence*, 139–40.

25. Gandhi, *Ghaffar Khan*, 118.

26. Mukulika Banerjee, *The Pathan Unarmed: Opposition and Memory in the North West Frontier* (Santa Fe, NM: School of American Research Press, 2001), 123.

27. Ibid., 80.

28. Bondurant, *Conquest of Violence*, 143.

29. Tendulkar, *Abdul Ghaffar Khan*, 105.

30. Khan, *My Life and Struggle*, 193–95.

31. Pyarelal, *Thrown to the Wolves*, 25.

32. Pal, "A Pacifist Uncovered."

33. Bondurant, *Conquest of Violence*, 135.

34. Pyarelal, *Thrown to the Wolves*, 125.

35. N. Radhakrishnan, *Khan Abdul Ghaffar Khan: The Apostle of Nonviolence* (New Delhi: Gandhi Smriti, 1998), 45.

36. Banerjee, *The Pathan Unarmed*, 127–28.

37. Pal, "A Pacifist Uncovered."

38. Banerjee, *The Pathan Unarmed*, 154–55.

39. Chand, *India, Pakistan and Afghanistan*, 264.

40. Pal, "A Pacifist Uncovered."

41. Eknath Easwaran, *Nonviolent Soldier of Islam: Badshah Khan: A Man to Match His Mountains* (Tomales, CA: Nilgiri Press, 1999), 105.

42. Ibid., 133.

43. Bondurant, *Conquest of Violence*, 136.

44. Banerjee, *The Pathan Unarmed*, 100.

45. Ibid.

46. Ibid.

47. Pal, "A Pacifist Uncovered."

48. Ibid.

49. Tendulkar, *Abdul Ghaffar Khan*, 106.

50. Radhakrishnan, *Khan Abdul Ghaffar Khan*, 9–10.

51. Chand, *India, Pakistan and Afghanistan*, 201, 212; Tendulkar, *Abdul Ghaffar Khan*, 80.

52. Pyarelal, *Thrown to the Wolves*, 33.

53. Radhakrishnan, *Khan Abdul Ghaffar Khan*, 14.

54. B.R. Nanda, *In Search of Gandhi: Essays and Reflections* (New Delhi: Oxford University Press, 2002), 115.

55. Tendulkar, *Abdul Ghaffar Khan*, 1.

56. Chand, *India, Pakistan and Afghanistan*, 215.

57. Ibid., 175, 193.

58. Khan, *My Life and Struggle*, 193–95.

59. Pyarelal, *Thrown to the Wolves*, 127.

60. Tendulkar, *Abdul Ghaffar Khan*, 119.

61. Ibid., 75–76.

62. Ibid., 73.

63. Easwaran, *Nonviolent Soldier of Islam*, 19.

64. Khan, *My Life and Struggle*, 127.

65. Pyarelal, *Thrown to the Wolves*, 17.

66. Ibid., 18.

67. Yunus, *Frontier Pathans and Freedom Struggle*, 54.

68. Banerjee, *The Pathan Unarmed*, 59, 70, 114.

69. Korejo, *The Frontier Gandhi*, 52.

70. Tendulkar, *Abdul Ghaffar Khan*, 146.

71. Ibid., 148.

72. Ibid., 154.

73. Ibid., 161.

74. Ibid., 200.

75. Gandhi, *Ghaffar Khan*, 65.

76. Tendulkar, *Abdul Ghaffar Khan*, 207.

77. Banerjee, *The Pathan Unarmed*, 68; Khan, *My Life and Struggle*, 157–58.

78. Tendulkar, *Abdul Ghaffar Khan*, 217–26.

79. Ibid.

80. Ibid., 243–56.

81. Ibid., 262.

82. Ibid., 279.

83. Ibid., 285.

84. Ibid., 285, 288.

85. Ibid., 290.

86. Ibid.

87. Khan, *My Life and Struggle*, 157–59.

88. Tendulkar, *Abdul Ghaffar Khan*, 326–28.

89. Ibid., 336–37.

90. Khan, *My Life and Struggle*, 174–75.

91. Tendulkar, *Abdul Ghaffar Khan*, 350–60.

92. Ibid., 398.

93. Khan, *My Life and Struggle*, 183–92.

94. Tendulkar, *Abdul Ghaffar Khan*, 407.

95. Khan, *My Life and Struggle*, 196–203.

96. Tendulkar, *Abdul Ghaffar Khan*, 422.

97. Khan, *My Life and Struggle*, 203–5.

98. Ibid.

99. Tendulkar, *Abdul Ghaffar Khan*, 425.

100. Khan, *My Life and Struggle*, 178.

101. Tendulkar, *Abdul Ghaffar Khan*, 416–18.

102. Pyarelal, *Thrown to the Wolves*, 48.

103. Korejo, *The Frontier Gandhi*, 170–86.

104. Tendulkar, *Abdul Ghaffar Khan*, 427–46.

105. Korejo, *The Frontier Gandhi*, 170–86.

106. Tendulkar, *Abdul Ghaffar Khan*, 420–22.

107. Khan, *My Life and Struggle*, 179.

108. Ibid., 176–77.

109. Tendulkar, *Abdul Ghaffar Khan*, 449.

110. Gandhi, *Ghaffar Khan*, 243–47.

111. Pyarelal, *Thrown to the Wolves*, 57.

112. Ibid.

113. Tendulkar, *Abdul Ghaffar Khan*, 450–58.

114. Pyarelal, *Thrown to the Wolves*, 68–71.
115. Tendulkar, *Abdul Ghaffar Khan*, 466–72.
116. Ibid., 473–78.
117. Ibid., 482–504.
118. Ibid.
119. Ibid.
120. Ibid., 505–19.
121. Ibid.
122. Tendulkar, *Abdul Ghaffar Khan*, 521–22.
123. Ibid.
124. Korejo, *The Frontier Gandhi*, 209–12.
125. Ibid.
126. Pyarelal, *Thrown to the Wolves*, 108–12.
127. Gandhi, *Ghaffar Khan*, 254–58.
128. Ibid., 261–62.
129. Khan, *My Life and Struggle*, 207–8.
130. Gandhi, *Ghaffar Khan*, 263–64.
131. Korejo, *The Frontier Gandhi*, 233, 237–39.
132. "Hillary Clinton Hosts Iftar at State Department," *Muslim Observer*, September 17, 2009.
133. Pal, "A Pacifist Uncovered."
134. Ibid.
135. Chand, *India, Pakistan and Afghanistan*, xxxiii.
136. Radhakrishnan, *Khan Abdul Ghaffar Khan*, 2.
137. Pal, "A Pacifist Uncovered."
138. Radhakrishnan, *Khan Abdul Ghaffar Khan*, 1.
139. Banerjee, *The Pathan Unarmed*, 149.
140. Pal, "A Pacifist Uncovered."
141. Gandhi, *Ghaffar Khan*, 268.
142. Ibid., 274.
143. Ibid., 276.

CHAPTER 7: FOLLOWING IN THE MAHATMA'S FOOTSTEPS: MUSLIM GANDHIANS

1. Fred Dallmayr, "Gandhi and Islam: A Heart-and-Mind Unity?," in *The Philosophy of Mahatma Gandhi for the Twenty-First Century*, ed. Douglas Allen (New Delhi: Oxford University Press, 2009), 145.
2. Ibid., 146–47.
3. Ibid., 149.
4. Ibid., 156–57.
5. Ibid., 159.
6. John Leland, "Speaking Freely Where Fear Rules," *New York Times*, February 1, 2010.
7. Dallmayr, "Gandhi and Islam," 149.
8. Ibid., 160.
9. A.G. Noorani, *Badruddin Tyabji* (New Delhi: Publications Division, 1969), ix–x.

10. Ibid., 96.

11. Ibid., 137–38.

12. Ibid., 142–43.

13. Rahil Khan, "Abul Kalam Azad," http://www.sscnet.ucla.edu/southasia/History/Independent/Azad_indepindia.html.

14. Ramin Jahanbegloo, "Is a Muslim Gandhi Possible?," *Reset*, January 20, 2009.

15. Ramin Jahanbegloo, "Celebrating Diversity," *Seminar*, January 2007.

16. Rajmohan Gandhi, *Understanding the Muslim Mind* (New Delhi: Penguin Books India, 2000), 219–20.

17. Ibid., 220.

18. Ibid., 222.

19. Jahanbegloo, "Muslim Gandhi."

20. Gandhi, *Understanding the Muslim Mind*, 225.

21. Maulana Abul Kalam Azad, *India Wins Freedom: The Complete Version* (Hyderabad: Orient Longman, 1988), 4.

22. Ibid.

23. Gandhi, *Understanding the Muslim Mind*, 221.

24. Ibid., 225.

25. Ibid., 226.

26. Ibid., 228.

27. Ibid., 229.

28. Azad, *India Wins Freedom*, 32.

29. Ibid., 39.

30. Ibid., 144.

31. Gandhi, *Understanding the Muslim Mind*, 230.

32. Ibid.

33. Ibid., 233.

34. Mushirul Haq, "Maulana Abdul Kalam Azad," http://www.congresssandesh.com/AICC/history/presidents/maulana_abul_kalam_azad.htm.

35. Gandhi, *Understanding the Muslim Mind*, 238.

36. Jahanbegloo, "Celebrating Diversity."

37. Gandhi, *Understanding the Muslim Mind*, 238–49.

38. Ibid., 248.

39. Ibid., 250–52.

40. Ibid., 253.

41. Azad, *India Wins Freedom*, 98–99.

42. Ibid., 127.

43. Gandhi, *Understanding the Muslim Mind*, 281.

44. Ibid., 282.

45. Ibid.

46. Ibid., 283.

47. Ibid., 284.

48. Ibid., 286–87.

49. Ibid., 287–88.

50. Ibid., 288–89.

51. Ibid., 289.

52. Dallmayr, "Gandhi and Islam," 150.

53. Gandhi, *Understanding the Muslim Mind*, 290.

54. Ibid.

55. Ibid., 291–92.

56. Ibid., 292.

57. Ibid.

58. Ibid., 293–94.

59. Ibid., 294–95.

60. Ibid., 297–98.

61. Ibid., 298.

62. Ibid., 298, 300.

63. Zakir Husain, "A Day in August 1947," *Outlook*, October 29, 2004.

64. Gandhi, *Understanding the Muslim Mind*, 298, 300.

65. Ibid., 300.

66. Ibid.

67. Ibid., 301.

68. Ibid., 302.

69. Ibid., 304.

70. Ibid., 305–6.

71. Ibid., 306–8.

72. Ibid., 309–10.

CHAPTER 8: A REFUSAL TO COOPERATE: THE STRUGGLE OF THE KOSOVAR ALBANIANS

1. Howard Clark, *Civil Resistance in Kosovo* (London: Pluto Press, 2000), 39–41.

2. Alex Bellamy, *Kosovo and International Society* (New York: Palgrave Macmillan, 2002), 8–11.

3. Stephen Schwartz, *Kosovo: Background to a War* (London: Anthem, 2000), 127–31.

4. Bellamy, *Kosovo and International Society*, 9.

5. Denisa Kostovicova, "Kosovo's Parallel Society: The Successes and Failures of Nonviolence," in *Kosovo: Contending Voices on Balkan Interventions*, ed. William Joseph Buckley (Cambridge: William B. Eerdmans, 2000), 142–48.

6. Clark, *Civil Resistance in Kosovo*, 46–69.

7. Ibid.

8. Ibid.

9. Ibid.

10. Ibid.

11. Schwartz, *Kosovo*, 131.

12. Ibid., 4.

13. Clark, *Civil Resistance in Kosovo*, 46–69.

14. Ibid., 67.

15. Ibid., 71.

16. Ibid., 74–77.

17. Ibid., 80–82.

18. Ibid., 112–15.

19. Ibid., 114–17.

20. Ibid., 108–11.

21. Bellamy, *Kosovo and International Society*, 11–12.

22. Clark, *Civil Resistance in Kosovo*, 83.

23. Ibid., 95.

24. Kostovicova, "Kosovo's Parallel Society," 142–48.

25. Clark, *Civil Resistance in Kosovo*, 106–8.

26. Schwartz, *Kosovo*, 131.

27. Human Rights Watch, *Open Wounds: Human Rights Abuses in Kosovo* (New York: Human Rights Watch, 1993), xii–xiv.

28. Ibid., 1–2, 48–49.

29. Ibid., 107–34.

30. Clark, *Civil Resistance in Kosovo*, 64–65.

31. Ibid., 60–64.

32. Ibid., 96–99.

33. Denisa Kostovicova, "Albanian Schooling in Kosovo 1992–1998: 'Liberty Imprisoned,'" in *Kosovo: The Politics of Delusion*, ed. Michael Waller, Kyril Drezov, and Bulent Gokay (London: Frank Cass, 2001), 11–19.

34. Kostovicova, "Kosovo's Parallel Society," 142–48.

35. Kostovicova, "Albanian Schooling in Kosovo 1992–1998," 11–19.

36. Ibid.

37. Kostovicova, "Kosovo's Parallel Society," 142–48.

38. Kostovicova, "Albanian Schooling in Kosovo 1992–1998," 11–19.

39. Ibid.

40. Ibid.

41. Ibid.

42. Ibid.

43. Clark, *Civil Resistance in Kosovo*, 70–94.

44. Bellamy, *Kosovo and International Society*, 40–41.

45. Ibid., 24–31, 39–40, 43, 45–46, 49–51.

46. Clark, *Civil Resistance in Kosovo*, 203–5.

47. Ibid., 89–92.

48. Ibid., 117–19.

49. Ibid., 119–21.

50. Ibid., 67.

51. Ibid., 122–28.

52. Ibid., 123–24, 172–78.

53. Ibid., 162.

54. Ibid., 164–65.

55. Ibid., 151–57.

56. Ibid.

57. Bellamy, *Kosovo and International Society*, 67–94, 109–10, 204–5.

58. Schwartz, *Kosovo*, 127–43.

59. Ibid.

60. Bellamy, *Kosovo and International Society*, 135.

61. Ibid., 159–85.

62. Ibid.

63. Clark, *Civil Resistance in Kosovo*, 4–5.

64. Ibid., 122–38.

65. Ibid.

66. Ibid., 186–210.

67. Ibid., 186–87.

68. Ibid., 198–203.

69. Schwartz, *Kosovo*, 156.

70. BBC News, "Rugova: Kosovo's Political Survivor," May 2, 2002.

71. "Ibrahim Rugova," Obituary, *Economist*, January 26, 2006.

72. Harry de Queteville, "Kosovo Poll Reveals Failure of U.N. Rule," *Daily Telegraph*, October 25, 2004.

73. Julie Mertus, "Continuing Lessons in Democracy," *Chicago Tribune*, November 5, 2004.

CHAPTER 9: NOT JUST A LAND OF CONFLICT: NONVIOLENCE IN THE MIDDLE EAST

1. Ralph E. Crow and Philip Grant, "Questions and Controversies about Nonviolent Struggle in the Middle East," in *Arab Nonviolent Political Struggle in the Middle East*, ed. Ralph E. Crow, Philip Grant, and Saad E. Ibrahim (Boulder, CO: Lynne Rienner, 1990), 75–77.

2. Ibid., 85.

3. John Lichfield, "Mousavi 'under 24-Hour Guard,'" *Independent*, June 23, 2009.

4. Fred Halliday, "Iran's Tide of History: Counterrevolution and After," http://www.opendemocracy.net/author/fred-halliday, July 17, 2009.

5. Martin Fletcher, "Iranian Student Protester Neda Soltan Is Times Person of the Year," *Times*, December 26, 2009.

6. Ramin Jahanbegloo, "The Gandhian Moment," *Dissent Magazine Online*, June 20, 2009.

7. Neil MacFarquhar, "In Iran, Both Sides Seek to Carry Islam's Banner," *New York Times*, June 21, 2009.

8. Ibid.

9. Slavoj Zizek, "Iran on the Brink," *In These Times*, August 2009.

10. Ramin Jahanbegloo, e-mail message to author, June 25, 2009.

11. "Profile: Mir-Hossein Mousavi," BBC News, June 16, 2009.

12. Shiva Balaghi, "An Artist as President of the Islamic Republic of Iran?," *Middle East Report Online*, June 8, 2009.

13. Yasaman Baji, "Protesters Defy Khamenei-Sanctioned Crackdown," Inter Press Service, June 20, 2009.

14. Anonymous, "Letter from Tehran: With the Marchers," *New Yorker*, June 29, 2009.

15. David Sanger, "Understanding Iran: Repression 101," *New York Times*, June 27, 2009.

16. Rebecca Santana, "Women at the Forefront of Iran Protests," Associated Press, June 25, 2009.

17. Shirin Ebadi, "Resistance Has a Woman's Face," *The Progressive*, August 2010.

18. Benjamin Joffe-Walt, "'The Barrier Has Been Broken and Women Are Throwing Rocks,'" Media Line, June 27, 2009.

19. Ebadi, "Resistance Has a Woman's Face."

20. Sudarshan Raghavan, "Role of Women in Iran Protest Kindles Hope," *Washington Post*, June 28, 2009.

21. Anonymous, "Letter from Tehran."

22. Robert Mackey, "Updates on Iran's Disputed Election," *New York Times*, June 22, 2009.

23. Scott Peterson, "Iran Protesters: The Harvard Professor behind Their Tactics," *Christian Science Monitor*, December 29, 2009.

24. Ibid.

25. Pal, "Interview with Gene Sharp."

26. Nazenin Ansari, "Iran's Unfinished Crisis," http://www.opendemocracy.net/article/iran-s-unfinished-crisis, September 17, 2009.

27. Ibid.

28. Robert Worth and Nazila Fathi, "Police Is Said to Have Killed 10 in Protests," *New York Times*, December 27, 2009.

29. "Crackdown in Iran: Up to 12 Dead, Hundreds Arrested in Opposition Protests," *Democracy Now!*, December 28, 2009.

30. Robert Worth, "Opposition in Iran Meets a Crossroads on Strategy," *New York Times*, February 14, 2010.

31. Ibid.

32. Mehrdad Mashayekhi, "The Question of Political Strategy in Iran's Green Movement," *Frontline: Tehran Bureau (Online)*, January 12, 2010.

33. Robin Wright, "An Opposition Manifesto in Iran," *Los Angeles Times*, January 6, 2010.

34. Ibid.

35. Robert Worth, "Iran Reformist Tries to Enlist Labor and Teachers," *New York Times*, April 29, 2010.

36. Shirin Ebadi, "One Year Later, Women at Forefront of Iranian Democracy Movement," Progressive Media Project, June 7, 2010.

37. Ibid.

38. Will Yong and Michael Slackman, "Clashes and Protests Reported in Iran," *New York Times*, June 12, 2010.

39. Amnesty International, "Iran's Crackdown on Dissent Widens with Hundreds Unjustly Imprisoned," Amnesty International Web site, June 9, 2010.

40. Ibid.

41. Will Yong and Michael Slackman, "Across Iran, Anger Lies behind Face of Calm," *New York Times*, June 11, 2010.

42. Meris Lutz, "Mousavi Slams Government, Outlines Opposition's Objectives," *Los Angeles Times*, June 15, 2010.

43. Danny Postel, "The Specter Haunting Iran," *Frontline: Tehran Bureau (Online)*, February 21, 2010.

44. Shane M., "Green Movement: More about Islam Than Meets the Eye," http://www.insideiran.org/news/green-movement-more-about-islam-than-meets-the-eye/, November 10, 2009.

45. Ibid.

46. Ibid.

47. Brad Bennett, "Arab-Muslim Cases of Nonviolent Struggle," in Crow, Grant, and Ibrahim, *Arab Nonviolent Political Struggle in the Middle East*, 48.

48. Ibid., 49.

49. Ibid.

50. Ibid.

51. Ebadi, *Iran Awakening*, 33.

52. Bennett, "Arab-Muslim Cases of Nonviolent Struggle," 49–50.

53. Stephen Zunes, "Nonviolent Resistance in the Islamic World," *Nonviolent Activist*, January–February 2002.

54. Bennett, "Arab-Muslim Cases of Nonviolent Struggle," 50.

55. Bill Weinberg, "Iraq's Civil Resistance," *The Nation*, December 24, 2007.

56. Ibid.

57. Ibid.

58. Ibid.

59. Terry Rockefeller and Valerie Lucznikowska, "La'Onf Nonviolence Group: A Force for Peace in Iraq," *WIN Magazine*, Fall 2008.

60. Ibid.

61. Ibid.

62. Ibid.

63. Bennett, "Arab-Muslim Cases of Nonviolent Struggle," 42.

64. Ibid., 41–42.

65. Ibid.

66. Ibid.

67. Ibid.

68. Saad E. Ibrahim, "Introduction: Why Nonviolent Political Struggle in the Middle East?," in Crow, Grant, and Ibrahim, *Arab Nonviolent Political Struggle in the Middle East*, 7.

69. Bennett, "Arab-Muslim Cases of Nonviolent Struggle," 48.

70. Ibid.

71. Ibid., 54.

72. Ibid., 54–56.

73. Human Rights Watch, "Egypt: Calls for Reform Met With Brutality," May 25, 2005.

74. Kim Ghattas, "Lebanon Finds Unity in Street Rallies," BBC News, March 3, 2005.

CHAPTER 10: STRUGGLING AGAINST HEAVY ODDS: PALESTINIANS AND NONVIOLENCE

1. Mohammed. Abu-Nimer, *Nonviolence and Peace Building in Islam: Theory and Practice* (Gainesville: University Press of Florida, 2003), 131.

2. Ibid.

3. Joost Hiltermann, *Behind the Intifada* (Princeton, NJ: Princeton University Press, 1991), 208.

4. Ibid., 208–11.

5. Philip Grant, "Nonviolent Political Struggle in the Occupied Territories," in *Arab Nonviolent Political Struggle in the Middle East*, ed. Ralph E. Crow, Philip Grant, and Saad E. Ibrahim (Boulder, CO: Lynne Rienner, 1990), 62–64.

6. Abu-Nimer, *Nonviolence and Peace Building in Islam*, 133, 150.

7. Mary King, *A Quiet Revolution: The First Palestinian Intifada and Nonviolent Resistance* (New York: Nation Books, 2007), 128.

8. Ibid., 208.

9. Peter Ackerman and Jack Duvall, *A Force More Powerful: A Century of Nonviolent Conflict* (New York: Palgrave Macmillan, 2001), 404–6.

10. Ibid., 407.

11. King, *A Quiet Revolution*, 209–13.

12. Ibid., 213–17.

13. Ibid., 217–20.

14. Ackerman and Duvall, *A Force More Powerful*, 409–10.

15. Ibid.

16. Catherine Ingram, *In the Footsteps of Gandhi: Conversations with Spiritual Social Activists* (Berkeley, CA: Parallax Press, 1990), 54.

17. King, *A Quiet Revolution*, 128–30.

18. Ibid.

19. Gershom Gorenberg, "The Missing Mahatma," *Weekly Standard*, April 6, 2009.

20. Ibid.

21. King, *A Quiet Revolution*, 132–33.

22. Gorenberg, "The Missing Mahatma."

23. King, *A Quiet Revolution*, 141–42.

24. Ibid., 132–36.

25. Ibid.

26. Ingram, *In the Footsteps of Gandhi*, 47.

27. Ibid., 45.

28. Ibid.

29. King, *A Quiet Revolution*, 136–37.

30. Pal, "Interview with Gene Sharp."

31. King, *A Quiet Revolution*, 138–39.

32. Ibid., 142.

33. Ibid., 143–45.

34. Ibid., 146–48.

35. Ingram, *In the Footsteps of Gandhi*, 53.

36. King, *A Quiet Revolution*, 149–53.

37. Ibid., 155.

38. Ibid., 158–61.

39. Ingram, *In the Footsteps of Gandhi*, 43.

40. King, *A Quiet Revolution*, 141–42.

41. Ingram, *In the Footsteps of Gandhi*, 56–57.

42. Ralph E. Crow and Philip Grant, "Questions and Controversies about Nonviolent Struggle in the Middle East," in Crow, Grant, and Ibrahim, *Arab Nonviolent Political Struggle in the Middle East*, 77–79.

43. Ibid., 86–88.

44. Stephen Zunes, "Nonviolent Resistance in the Islamic World," *Nonviolent Activist*, January–February 2002.

45. Grant, "Nonviolent Political Struggle in the Occupied Territories," 62–63.

46. King, *A Quiet Revolution*, 9–10.

47. Ibid., 257–58.

48. Grant, "Nonviolent Political Struggle in the Occupied Territories," 65.

49. Ibid., 66.

50. Ibid., 70.

51. Ibid., 71.

52. Abu-Nimer, *Nonviolence and Peace Building in Islam*, 138–39.

53. Ibid., 163.

54. Ibid., 139.

55. Ibid., 141–45.

56. Ibid., 145.

57. Ibid., 145–48.

58. Ibid., 148.

59. King, *A Quiet Revolution,*, 259–62.
60. Ibid., 262–64.
61. Grant, "Nonviolent Political Struggle in the Occupied Territories," 70–72.
62. Abu-Nimer, *Nonviolence and Peace Building in Islam*, 163.
63. Ibid., 166–67.
64. Ibid., 168.
65. Gorenberg, "The Missing Mahatma."
66. Ibid.
67. Abu-Nimer, *Nonviolence and Peace Building in Islam*, 171.
68. Ibid., 173–78.
69. Ibid.
70. Ibid.
71. Ibid., 179–80.
72. Ibid., 149.
73. Ibid., 150.
74. Ibid., 151.
75. Ibid., 152.
76. Ibid., 153.
77. Ibid.
78. Ibid., 154.
79. Ibid., 157.
80. Ackerman and Duvall, *A Force More Powerful*, 412.
81. Ibid.
82. Ibid., 413.
83. Ibid.
84. Abu-Nimer, *Nonviolence and Peace Building in Islam*, 135.
85. Ackerman and Duvall, *A Force More Powerful*, 415–17.
86. Ibid., 417–19.
87. King, *A Quiet Revolution*, 228–32.
88. Hiltermann, *Behind the Intifada*, 174–75.
89. Grant, "Nonviolent Political Struggle in the Occupied Territories," 64.
90. Hiltermann, *Behind the Intifada*, 211–12.
91. Abu-Nimer, *Nonviolence and Peace Building in Islam*, 137.
92. Ibid., 157–58.
93. King, *A Quiet Revolution*, 205–9.
94. Grant, "Nonviolent Political Struggle in the Occupied Territories," 60.
95. Abu-Nimer, *Nonviolence and Peace Building in Islam*, 135.
96. King, *A Quiet Revolution*, 165–70.
97. Ibid., 174–75.
98. Ackerman and Duvall, *A Force More Powerful*, 412.
99. Abu-Nimer, *Nonviolence and Peace Building in Islam*, 158–59.
100. Ibid., 160.
101. Ibid.
102. Ibid., 161.
103. King, *A Quiet Revolution*, 225–30.
104. Ibid., 232–33.
105. Ibid., 233–35.
106. Ibid., 312.
107. Hiltermann, *Behind the Intifada*, 193.

108. King, *A Quiet Revolution*, 224–25.
109. Hiltermann, *Behind the Intifada*, 10.
110. Ibid., 11.
111. Ibid., 193–94.
112. Ibid., 195–96.
113. Ibid., 198–203.
114. Ibid., 205.
115. Ibid., 206–8.
116. Ibid., 207.
117. Ibid, 7.
118. Ibid., 177.
119. Ibid.
120. Ibid., 177–78.
121. Ibid., 179–80.
122. Ibid., 181.
123. Ibid.
124. Ibid., 182–83.
125. Ibid., 188–89.
126. Ibid., 184–85.
127. Zunes, "Nonviolent Resistance in the Islamic World."
128. Ackerman and Duvall, *A Force More Powerful*, 420.
129. Abu-Nimer, *Nonviolence and Peace Building in Islam*, 136.
130. Grant, "Nonviolent Political Struggle in the Occupied Territories," 66-7.
131. Ibid., 66–8.
132. Ibid., 68.
133. Ibid., 68–9.
134. King, *A Quiet Revolution*, 295–306.
135. Ibid.
136. Ibid.
137. Ibid.
138. Ibid., 239, 257.
139. Ibid., 263-64.
140. Gorenberg, "The Missing Mahatma."
141. Ibid.
142. Ibid.
143. King, *A Quiet Revolution*,, 271–76.
144. Ibid., 277–85.
145. Ibid.
146. Ibid., 286–92.
147. Ibid., 292–93.
148. Ibid., 265–71.
149. Ibid., 313–15.
150. Ibid., 315–22.
151. Ibid.
152. Ibid.
153. Ibid., 326–27.
154. Ibid., 328–35.
155. Ibid., 343–44.
156. Ibid., 335–36.

157. Ibid.

158. Robert Hirschfield, "Gandhi of the West Bank," *The Progressive*, March 2008.

159. Isabel Kershner, "Israel's Top Court Orders Separation Barrier Rerouted," *New York Times*, September 5, 2007.

160. Ethan Bronner, "In Village, Palestinians See Model for Their Cause," *New York Times*, August 27, 2009.

161. Ethan Bronner, "Palestinians Try a Less Violent Path to Resistance," *New York Times*, April 6, 2010.

162. Hirschfield, "Gandhi of the West Bank."

163. Isabel Kershner, "Israel Signals Tougher Line on West Bank Protests," *New York Times*, January 28, 2010.

164. Bronner, "In Village, Palestinians See Model for Their Cause."

165. Edith Garwood, "Palestinian Nonviolent Resistance Has Strong Roots," Amnesty International USA Web Log.

166. Heather Sharp, "Bilin Marks Five Years of West Bank Barrier Protest," BBC, February 19, 2010.

167. Ibid.

168. Ibid.; and Kershner, "Israel Signals Tougher Line on West Bank Protests."

169. Garwood, "Palestinian Nonviolent Resistance Has Strong Roots."

CHAPTER 11: TO TOPPLE DICTATORS WITHOUT FORCE: PEACEFUL PROTEST IN MODERN SOUTH ASIA

1. Daud Munir, "Struggling for the Rule of Law: The Pakistani Lawyers' Movement," *Middle East Report*, Summer 2009.

2. Tariq Ali, *The Duel: Pakistan on the Flight Path of American Power* (New York: Scribner, 2008), 8.

3. Ibid., 8–9.

4. Jane Perlez, "Pakistani Lawyers' Anger Grew as Hope for Changes Withered," *New York Times*, November 7, 2007.

5. Munir, "Struggling for the Rule of Law."

6. Ali, *The Duel*, 7.

7. Jane Perlez, "Set to Return, Chief Justice Creates a Test for Pakistan," *New York Times*, April 9, 2008.

8. Ali, *The Duel*, 9.

9. Muneer A. Malik, "Ideals and Expediency," *Dawn*, June 27, 2007.

10. Ali, *The Duel*, 9.

11. Ibid., 9–10.

12. Ibid., 10.

13. Q. Isa Daudpota, "12 May: The Bloodshed and Watershed," *Himal Southasian*, June 2007.

14. "Bomber Targets Pakistani Lawyers," BBC News, July 17, 2007.

15. Kanak Mani Dixit, "Taslima and Aitzaz," *Himal SouthAsian*, January 2008.

16. James Traub, "The Lawyers' Crusade," *New York Times Magazine*, June 1, 2008.

17. Ibid.

18. Ibid.

19. Munir, "Struggling for the Rule of Law."

20. Ali, *The Duel*, 163–64.

21. Perlez, "Pakistani Lawyers' Anger Grew as Hope for Changes Withered."

22. Zia Mian and A. H. Nayyar, "Khaki President," *Himal Southasian*, January 2008.

23. Beena Sarwar, "Hard on Civil Society, Soft on Extremists," Inter Press Service, November 5, 2007.

24. Ali, *The Duel*, 164.

25. Traub, "The Lawyers' Crusade."

26. Beena Sarwar, "Intelligentsia Finds Ways to Beat Emergency Rule," Inter Press Service, November 9, 2007.

27. Ali, *The Duel*, 274.

28. Perlez, "Pakistani Lawyers' Anger Grew as Hope for Changes Withered."

29. "Brave Thinkers," *Atlantic Magazine*, November 2009.

30. Jane Perlez, "Thousands Fill Streets for Protest in Pakistan," *New York Times*, June 14, 2008.

31. Perlez, "Pakistani Lawyers' Anger Grew as Hope for Changes Withered."

32. Matthew Wade, "Pakistan Celebrates Sweet Victory as Chief Justice Is Reinstated," *Sydney Morning Herald*, March 18, 2009.

33. Perlez, "Lawyers Demand Release of Judges in Pakistan."

34. Ali, *The Duel*, 165.

35. Aitzaz Ahsan, "Pakistan's Tyranny Continues," *New York Times*, December 23, 2007.

36. "Letter from Pakistan's Chief Justice," *New York Times*, January 31, 2008.

37. Ibid.

38. Ali, *The Duel*, 269.

39. Perlez, "Thousands Fill Streets for Protest in Pakistan."

40. Jane Perlez, "Pakistani Parties Clash over Reinstating Judge," *New York Times*, August 19, 2008.

41. Mirza A. Beg, "Civil Revolution May Usher a Constitutional Democracy in Pakistan," Countercurrents.org, March 21, 2009.

42. Jane Perlez, "Hundreds Jailed as Pakistan Bans Planned Protest," *New York Times*, March 11, 2009.

43. Jane Perlez, "Pakistan Leader Backs Down and Reinstates Top Judge," *New York Times*, March 15, 2009.

44. Beg, "Civil Revolution May Usher a Constitutional Democracy In Pakistan."

45. Pamela Constable, "In Pakistan, Elation over Restoration of Judges," *Washington Post*, March 17, 2009.

46. Munir, "Struggling for the Rule of Law."

47. Ayaz Ahmad, "The Unfulfilled Promise of the Lawyers' Movement," *The News*, July 8, 2010.

48. Ibid.

49. Olivia Lang, "'Anni' Heralds New Era in Maldives," BBC News, October, 29, 2008.

50. Simon Shareef, "Democratic Dawn," *Himal Southasian*, December 2008.

51. Ibid.

52. Lang, "'Anni' Heralds New Era in Maldives."

53. Ibid.

54. Ibid.

55. Stephen Zunes, "The Power of Protest in the Maldives," *Huffington Post*, December 9, 2008.

56. Ibid.

57. Editorial, "Transition to Multiparty Democracy," *Economic and Political Weekly*, November 24, 2008.

58. Zunes, "The Power of Protest in the Maldives."

59. Shareef, "Democratic Dawn."

60. Ibid.

61. Ibid.

62. Zunes, "The Power of Protest in the Maldives."

63. Shareef, "Democratic Dawn."

64. Dilrukshi Handunnetti, "Free Man as President," *Himal SouthAsian*, December 2008.

65. Ibid.

66. Editorial, "Transition to Multiparty Democracy."

CHAPTER 12: CONCLUSION

1. Joe Conason, "Defending the Mosque," *New York Observer*, August, 3, 2010.

2. Suzi Parker, "Sarah Palin to Muslims: Reject Ground Zero Mosque," Politics Daily, July 18, 2010.

3. Matt DeLong, "Newt Gingrich compares 'Ground Zero mosque' backers to Nazis," *Washington Post*, August 16, 2010.

4. Sheryl Gay Stolberg, "Obama Enters Debate With Mosque Remarks," *New York Times*, August 14, 2010.

5. Ibid.

6. Ibid.

7. William Dalrymple, "The Muslims in the Middle," *New York Times*, August 16, 2010.

8. Ibid.

9. Erik Schelzig, "Tennessee Gubernatorial Candidate Ramsey Criticized for Calling Islam a 'Cult,'" *Commercial Appeal*, July 27, 2010.

10. Evan McMorris-Santoro, "Another Mosque Project Comes under Fire—in Kentucky," TPM Muckraker, August 20, 2010.

11. "Fla. City, Church in Standoff Over 9/11 Koran Burning," Fox News, August 19, 2010.

12. Stephanie Rice, "'Anti-Islamic' Bus Ads Appear in Major Cities," *Christian Science Monitor*, July 28, 2010.

13. Alex Altman, "Majority Oppose Mosque, Many Distrust Muslims," *Time*, August 19, 2010.

14. Graham Fuller, *A World Without Islam* (Boston: Little, Brown, 2010), 283.

15. Ibid., 284–85.

16. Ibid., 285–86.

17. Stephen Walt, "Why They Hate Us (II): How Many Muslims Has the U.S. Killed in the Past 30 Years?," *Foreign Policy*, November 30, 2009.

18. Ibid.

19. Pew Research Center, *Muslim Americans: Middle Class and Mostly Mainstream*, May 22, 2007.

20. "Day of Action: 5,000 Protest in Pittsburgh Streets against War in Iraq," *Pittsburgh Post-Gazette*, January 27, 2003.

21. "Millions across the World Protest on Anniversary of Iraq War," *Democracy Now!*, March 22, 2004.

22. "Anti-War Protesters Rally in Los Angeles," United Press International, March 16, 2008.

23. Niraj Warikoo, "Muslim, Nigerian Leaders Rally against Terrorism," *Detroit Free Press*, January 8, 2010.

24. Mitchell Landsberg, "Muslims Fear Backlash as Festival Falls Near Sept. 11," *Los Angeles Times*, August 21, 2010.

Bibliography

Abu-Nimer, Mohammed. *Nonviolence and Peace Building in Islam: Theory and Practice*. Gainesville: University Press of Florida, 2003.

Ackerman, Peter, and Jack Duvall. *A Force More Powerful: A Century of Nonviolent Conflict*. New York: Palgrave Macmillan, 2001.

Ahmad, Ayaz. "The Unfulfilled Promise of the Lawyers' Movement." *The News*, July 8, 2010.

Ahsan, Aitzaz. "Pakistan's Tyranny Continues." *New York Times*, December 23, 2007.

Akman, Nuriye. "Interview with M. Fetullah Gulen." In *Terror and Suicide Attacks: An Islamic Perspective*, ed. Ergun Capan. Somerset, NJ: The Light, 2005.

Aktan, Hamza. "Acts of Terror and Suicide Attacks." In *Terror and Suicide Attacks: An Islamic Perspective*, ed. Ergun Capan. Somerset, NJ: The Light, 2005.

Ali, Tariq. *The Duel: Pakistan on the Flight Path of American Power*. New York: Scribner, 2008.

Altman, Alex. "Majority Oppose Mosque, Many Distrust Muslims." *Time*, August 19, 2010.

Amnesty International. "Iran's Crackdown on Dissent Widens with Hundreds Unjustly Imprisoned." Amnesty International Web site, June 9, 2010.

Ansari, Nazenin. "Iran's Unfinished Crisis." http://www.opendemocracy.net/article/iran-s-unfinished-crisis, September 17, 2009.

"Anti-War Protesters Rally in Los Angeles." United Press International, March 16, 2008.

Aslan, Reza. *No god but God: The Origin, Evolution, and Future of Islam*. New York: Random House, 2005.

Azad, Maulana Abul Kalam. *India Wins Freedom: The Complete Version*. Hyderabad: Orient Longman, 1988.

Aziz, Zahid. *Islam, Peace and Tolerance*. Wembley: Ahmadiyya Anjuman Lahore Publications, 2007.

Baji, Yasaman. "Protesters Defy Khamenei-Sanctioned Crackdown." Inter Press Service, June 20, 2009.

Bakalian, Anny, and Mehdi Bozorgmehr. *Backlash 9/11: Middle Eastern and Muslim Americans Respond.* Berkeley: University of California Press, 2009.

Balaghi, Shiva. "An Artist as President of the Islamic Republic of Iran?" *Middle East Report Online,* June 8, 2009.

Banerjee, Mukulika. *The Pathan Unarmed: Opposition and Memory in the North West Frontier.* Santa Fe, NM: School of American Research Press, 2001.

BBC News. "Bomber Targets Pakistani Lawyers." July 17, 2007.

BBC News. "Profile: Mir-Hossein Mousavi." June 16, 2009.

BBC News. "Rugova: Kosovo's Political Survivor." May 2, 2002.

Beaumont, Peter. "One in Four People Is Muslim, Says Study." *Guardian,* October 8, 2009.

Beg, Mirza A. "Civil Revolution May Usher a Constitutional Democracy in Pakistan." Countercurrents.org, March 21, 2009.

Bellamy, Alex. *Kosovo and International Society.* New York: Palgrave Macmillan, 2002.

Bennett, Brad. "Arab-Muslim Cases of Nonviolent Struggle." In *Arab Nonviolent Political Struggle in the Middle East,* ed. Ralph Crow, Philip Grant, and Saad Ibrahim. Boulder, CO: Lynne Rienner, 1990.

Bilgrami, Fatima Zehra. "Crystallizing Punjabi Identity: A Note on the Role of the Qadiris and Their Literature." In *The Islamic Path: Sufism, Politics and Society in India,* ed. Saiyid Zaheer Husain Jafri, and Helmut Reifeld. New Delhi: Rainbow Publishers, 2006.

Bondurant, Joan. *Conquest of Violence: The Gandhian Philosophy of Conflict.* Princeton, NJ: Princeton University Press, 1988.

"Brave Thinkers." *Atlantic Magazine,* November 2009.

Bronner, Ethan. "In Village, Palestinians See Model for Their Cause." *New York Times,* August 27, 2009.

Bronner, Ethan. "Palestinians Try a Less Violent Path to Resistance." *New York Times,* April 6, 2010.

Bulac, Ali. "Jihad." In *Terror and Suicide Attacks: An Islamic Perspective,* ed. Ergun Capan. Somerset, NJ: The Light, 2005.

Business Wire. "Attitudes toward Muslims Mixed in Europe and the U.S." August 23, 2007.

Canan, Ibrahim. "Islam as the Religion of Peace and Tolerance." In *Terror and Suicide Attacks: An Islamic Perspective,* ed. Ergun Capan. Somerset, NJ: The Light, 2005.

Capan, Ergun. "Suicide Attacks in Islam." In *Terror and Suicide Attacks: An Islamic Perspective,* ed. Ergun Capan. Somerset, NJ: The Light, 2005.

Chand, Attar. *India, Pakistan and Afghanistan: A Study of Freedom Struggle and Abdul Ghaffar Khan.* New Delhi: Commonwealth Publishers, 1989.

Chaudhury, Shoma. "The Mystic Master." *Tehelka,* January 24, 2009.

Clark, Howard. *Civil Resistance in Kosovo.* London: Pluto Press, 2000.

Cohen, Jon, and Jennifer Agiesta. "Most in Poll Back Outreach to Muslims." *Washington Post,* April 6, 2009.

Conason, Joe. "Defending the Mosque." *New York Observer,* August 3, 2010.

Constable, Pamela. "In Pakistan, Elation over Restoration of Judges." *Washington Post,* March 17, 2009.

"Crackdown in Iran: Up to 12 Dead, Hundreds Arrested in Opposition Protests." *Democracy Now!,* December 28, 2009.

Crow, Ralph E., and Philip Grant. "Questions and Controversies about Nonviolent Struggle in the Middle East." In *Arab Nonviolent Political Struggle in the Middle East,* ed. Ralph Crow, Philip Grant, and Saad Ibrahim. Boulder, CO: Lynne Rienner, 1990.

Dallmayr, Fred. "Gandhi and Islam: A Heart-and-Mind Unity?" In *The Philosophy of Mahatma Gandhi for the Twenty-First Century*. New Delhi: Oxford University Press, 2009.

Dalrymple, William. "The Muslims in the Middle." *New York Times*, August 16, 2010.

Daudpota, Q. Isa. "12 May: The Bloodshed and Watershed." *Himal Southasian*, June 2007.

"Day of Action: 5,000 Protest in Pittsburgh Streets against War in Iraq." *Pittsburgh Post-Gazette*, January 27, 2003.

DeLong, Matt. "Newt Gingrich Compares 'Ground Zero Mosque' Backers to Nazis." *Washington Post*, August 16, 2010.

de Queteville, Harry. "Kosovo Poll Reveals Failure of U.N. Rule." *Daily Telegraph*, October 25, 2004.

Eaton, Richard. *Essays on Islam and Indian History*. Oxford: Oxford University Press, 2000.

Ebadi, Shirin. *Iran Awakening: A Memoir of Revolution and Hope*. New York: Random House, 2006.

Ebadi, Shirin. "One Year Later, Women at Forefront of Iranian Democracy Movement." Progressive Media Project, June 7, 2010.

Ebadi, Shirin. "Resistance Has a Woman's Face." *The Progressive*, August 2010.

Editorial. "Debates on Muslim Grievance Are Generating More Heat Than Light." *Economist*, April 17, 2008.

Editorial. "Transition to Multiparty Democracy." *Economic and Political Weekly*, November 24, 2008.

Elias, Marilyn. "USA's Muslims under a Cloud." *USA Today*, August 10, 2006.

Engineer, Asghar Ali. *On Developing Theology of Peace in Islam*. New Delhi: Sterling, 2003.

Engineer, Asghar Ali. *Islam: Misgivings and History*. New Delhi: Vitasta Publishing, 2007.

Esposito, John, and Dalia Mogahed, *Who Speaks For Islam? What a Billion Muslims Really Think*. New York: Gallup Press, 2008.

Firestone, Reuven. *Jihad: The Origin of Holy War in Islam*. New York: Oxford University Press, 1999.

"Fla. City, Church in Standoff over 9/11 Koran Burning." Fox News, August 19, 2010.

Fletcher, Martin. "Iranian Student Protester Neda Soltan Is Times Person of the Year." *Times*, December 26, 2009.

Friedmann, Yohanan. *Prophecy Continuous: Aspects of Ahmadi Religious Thought and Its Medieval Background*. Oxford: Oxford University Press, 2003.

Frost, Mary. "Controversy Continues for Arabic-Themed School, Even with New Principal." *Brooklyn Daily Eagle*, January 9, 2008.

Fuller, Graham. *A World without Islam*. Boston: Little, Brown, 2010.

Funk, Nathan C., and Abdul Aziz Said, "Peace in the Sufi Spirit: An Ecology of the Spirit." In *Peace and Conflict Resolution in Islam: Precept and Practice*, ed. Nathan C. Funk, Ayse Kadayifci, and Abdul Aziz Said. Lanham, MD: University Press of America, 2001.

Gandhi, Rajmohan. *Ghaffar Khan: Nonviolent Badshah of the Pakhtuns*. New Delhi: Viking, 2004.

Gandhi, Rajmohan. *Understanding the Muslim Mind*. New Delhi: Penguin Books India, 2000.

Garwood, Edith. "Palestinian Nonviolent Resistance Has Strong Roots." Amnesty International USA Web Log.

Ghattas, Kim. "Lebanon Finds Unity in Street Rallies." BBC News, March 3, 2005.

Gorenberg, Gershom. "The Missing Mahatma." *Weekly Standard*, April 6, 2009.

Grant, Phillip. "Nonviolent Political Struggle in the Occupied Territories." In *Arab Non-violent Political Struggle in the Middle East*, ed. Ralph Crow, Philip Grant, and Saad Ibrahim. Boulder, CO: Lynne Rienner, 1990.

Greenhouse, Steven. "Muslim Holiday at Tyson Plant Creates Furor." *New York Times*, August 5, 2008.

Gunes, Ahmet. "Views on the Rules of War in Islamic Law." In *Terror and Suicide Attacks: An Islamic Perspective*, ed. Ergun Capan. Somerset, NJ: The Light, 2005.

Halliday, Fred. "Iran's Tide of History: Counterrevolution and After." http://www.open democracy.net/author/fred-halliday, July 17, 2009.

Handunnetti, Dilrukshi. "Free Man as President." *Himal SouthAsian*, December 2008.

Haq, Mushirul. "Maulana Abdul Kalam Azad." http://www.congresssandesh.com/AICC/history/presidents/maulana_abul_kalam_azad.htm.

Haque, Tamizul. *Islam: Prophet Muhammad as Warrior and Peace Maker*. Dhaka: Syed Farooque Azam, 1982.

"Hillary Clinton Hosts Iftar at State Department." *Muslim Observer*, September 17, 2009.

Hiltermann, Joost. *Behind the Intifada*. Princeton NJ: Princeton University Press, 1993.

Hirschfield, Robert. "Gandhi of the West Bank." *The Progressive*, March 2008.

Human Rights Watch. "Egypt: Calls for Reform Met With Brutality." May 25, 2005.

Husain, Zakir. "A Day in August 1947." *Outlook*, October 29, 2004.

Ibrahim, Saad. "Introduction: Why Nonviolent Political Struggle in the Middle East?" In *Arab Nonviolent Political Struggle in the Middle East*, ed. Ralph Crow, Philip Grant, and Saad Ibrahim. Boulder, CO: Lynne Rienner, 1990.

"Ibrahim Rugova." Obituary. *Economist*, January 26, 2006.

Ingram, Catherine. *In the Footsteps of Gandhi: Conversations with Spiritual Social Activists*. Berkeley, CA: Parallax Press, 1990.

Jackson, Paul. "Sufism's Enduring Impact: The Legacy of Sharafuddin Maneri." In *The Islamic Path: Sufism, Politics and Society in India*, ed. Saiyid Zaheer Husain Jafri, and Helmut Reifeld. New Delhi: Rainbow Publishers, 2006.

Jahanbegloo, Ramin. e-mail message to author, June 25, 2009.

Jahanbegloo, Ramin. "Celebrating Diversity." *Seminar*, January 2007.

Jahanbegloo, Ramin. "The Gandhian Moment." *Dissent Magazine Online*, June 20, 2009.

Jahanbegloo, Ramin. "Is a Muslim Gandhi Possible?" *Reset*, January 20, 2009.

Joffe-Walt, Benjamin. "'The Barrier Has Been Broken and Women Are Throwing Rocks.'" Media Line, June 27, 2009.

Karabell, Zachary. *Peace Be upon You: Fourteen Centuries of Muslim, Christian, and Jewish Coexistence in the Middle East*. New York: Knopf, 2007.

Kelsay, John. *Arguing the Just War in Islam*. Cambridge, MA: Harvard University Press, 2007.

Kershner, Isabel. "Israel Signals Tougher Line on West Bank Protests." *New York Times*, January 28, 2010.

Kershner, Isabel. "Israel's Top Court Orders Separation Barrier Rerouted." *New York Times*, September 5, 2007.

Khan, Abdul Ghaffar. *My Life and Struggle: Autobiography of Badshah Khan (as narrated to K.B. Narang)* New Delhi: Hind Pocket Books, 1969.

Khan, Rahil. "Abul Kalam Azad." http://www.sscnet.ucla.edu/southasia/History/Independent/Azad_indepindia.html.

King, Mary. *A Quiet Revolution: The First Palestinian Intifada and Nonviolent Resistance.* New York: Nation Books, 2007.

Kishtainy, Khalid. "Violent and Nonviolent Struggle in Arab History." In *Arab Nonviolent Struggle in the Middle East,* ed. Ralph Crow, Philip Grant, and Saad Ibrahim. Boulder, CO: Lynne Rienner, 1990.

Korejo, M. S. *The Frontier Gandhi: His Place in History.* Oxford: Oxford University Press, 1993.

Kostovicova, Denisa. "Albanian Schooling in Kosovo 1992–1998: 'Liberty Imprisoned.'" In *Kosovo: The Politics of Delusion,* ed. Michael Waller, Kyril Drezov, and Bulent Gokay. London: Frank Cass, 2001.

Kostovicova, Denisa. "Kosovo's Parallel Society: The Successes and Failures of Nonviolence." In *Kosovo: Contending Voices on Balkan Interventions,* ed. William Joseph Buckley. Cambridge, MA: William B. Eerdmans, 2000.

Landsberg, Mitchell. "Muslims Fear Backlash as Festival Falls Near Sept. 11." *Los Angeles Times,* August 21, 2010.

Lang, Olivia. "'Anni' Heralds New Era in Maldives." BBC News, October, 29, 2008.

Leland, John. "Speaking Freely Where Fear Rules." *New York Times,* February 1, 2010.

"Letter from Pakistan's Chief Justice." *New York Times,* January 31, 2008.

Lichfield, John. "Mousavi 'under 24-hour Guard.'" *Independent,* June 23, 2009.

Lutz, Meris. "Mousavi Slams Government, Outlines Opposition's Objectives." *Los Angeles Times,* June 15, 2010.

MacFarquhar, Neil. "In Iran, Both Sides Seek to Carry Islam's Banner." *New York Times,* June 21, 2009.

Mackey, Robert. "Updates on Iran's Disputed Election." *New York Times,* June 22, 2009.

Malik, Muneer. "Ideals and Expediency." *Dawn,* June 27, 2007.

Manzar, Nishat. "Mysticism and Humanism: Sufis as Poets, Connoisseurs of Music and Scholars of Comparative Religion and Mystic Philosophy." In *The Islamic Path: Sufism, Politics and Society in India,* ed. Saiyid Zaheer Husain Jafri, and Helmut Reifeld. New Delhi: Rainbow Publishers, 2006.

Mashayekhi, Mehrdad. "The Question of Political Strategy in Iran's Green Movement." *Frontline: Tehran Bureau (Online),* January 12, 2010.

McMorris-Santoro, Evan. "Another Mosque Project Comes under Fire—in Kentucky." TPM Muckraker, August 20, 2010.

Mertus, Julie. "Continuing Lessons in Democracy." *Chicago Tribune,* November 5, 2004.

Mian, Zia, and A. H. Nayyar. "Khaki President." *Himal Southasian,* January 2008.

"Millions across the World Protest on Anniversary of Iraq War." *Democracy Now!,* March 22, 2004.

Mishra, Pankaj. "Where Alaa Al Aswany Is Writing From." *New York Times Magazine,* April 27, 2008.

Momin, A. R. "The Role of Sufis in Fostering Inter-Cultural Understanding and Conciliation in India." In *The Islamic Path: Sufism, Politics and Society in India,* ed. Saiyid Zaheer Husain Jafri, and Helmut Reifeld. New Delhi: Rainbow Publishers, 2006.

Muhaiyaddeen, M. R. Bawa. "The Inner Jihad." In *Peace and Conflict Resolution in Islam: Precept and Practice,* ed. Nathan C. Funk, Ayse Kadayifci, and Abdul Aziz Said. Lanham, MD: University Press of America, 2001.

Munir, Daud. "Struggling for the Rule of Law: The Pakistani Lawyers' Movement." *Middle East Report,* Summer 2009.

Nanda, B. R. *In Search of Gandhi: Essays and Reflections.* New Delhi: Oxford University Press, 2002.

Nasr, Seyyed Hossein. *The Heart of Islam: Enduring Values for Humanity*. San Francisco: HarperSanFrancisco, 2002.

Noorani, A. G. *Badruddin Tyabji*. New Delhi: Publications Division, 1969.

Noorani, A. G. *Islam and Jihad: Prejudice versus Reality*. London: Zed Books, 2003.

Onishi, Norimitsu. "Under Indonesia's Surface, an Intricate Quilt of Faiths." *New York Times*, February 17, 2010.

Pal, Amitabh. "Interview with Gene Sharp." *The Progressive*, February 2007.

Pal, Amitabh. "Interview with Keith Ellison." *The Progressive*, November 2008.

Pal, Amitabh. "A Pacifist Uncovered." *The Progressive*, February 2002.

Parker, Suzi. "Sarah Palin to Muslims: Reject Ground Zero Mosque." Politics Daily, July 18, 2010.

Pascarella, Matt. "A Voice from Senegal: Youssou N'Dour." *The Progressive*, February 2010.

Perlez, Jane. "Hundreds Jailed as Pakistan Bans Planned Protest." *New York Times*, March 11, 2009.

Perlez, Jane. "Pakistan Leader Backs Down and Reinstates Top Judge." *New York Times*, March 15, 2009.

Perlez, Jane. "Pakistani Lawyers' Anger Grew as Hope for Changes Withered." *New York Times*, November 7, 2007.

Perlez, Jane. "Pakistani Parties Clash over Reinstating Judge." *New York Times*, August 19, 2008.

Perlez, Jane. "Thousands Fill Streets for Protest in Pakistan." *New York Times*, June 14, 2008.

Peters, Rudolph. *Jihad in Classical and Modern Islam: A Reader*. Princeton, NJ: Markus Wiener, 1996.

Peterson, Scott. "Iran Protesters: The Harvard Professor behind their Tactics." *Christian Science Monitor*, December 29, 2009.

Pew Research Center. "Muslim Americans: Middle Class and Mostly Mainstream." Pew Research Center Publications, May 22, 2007.

Pew Research Center. "Public Expresses Mixed Views of Islam, Mormonism." Pew Research Center Publications, September 25, 2007.

Postel, Danny. "The Specter Haunting Iran," *Frontline: Tehran Bureau (Online)*, February 21, 2010.

Pyarelal. *Thrown to the Wolves: Abdul Ghaffar*. Calcutta: Eastlight Book House, 1966.

Radhakrishnan, N. *Khan Abdul Ghaffar Khan: The Apostle of Nonviolence*. New Delhi: Gandhi Smriti, 1998.

Rafiqi, A. Q. "Impact of Sufism in Kashmir." In *The Islamic Path: Sufism, Politics and Society in India*, ed. Saiyid Zaheer Husain Jafri, and Helmut Reifeld. New Delhi: Rainbow Publishers, 2006.

Raghavan, Sudarshan. "Role of Women in Iran Protest Kindles Hope." *Washington Post*, June 28, 2009.

Rice, Stephanie. "'Anti-Islamic' Bus Ads Appear in Major Cities." *Christian Science Monitor*, July 28, 2010.

Rockefeller, Terry, and Valerie Lucznikowska, "La'Onf Nonviolence Group: A Force for Peace in Iraq." *WIN Magazine*, Fall 2008.

Sachedina, Abdulaziz. "The Development of Jihad in Islamic Revelation and History." In *Cross, Crescent, and Sword: The Justification and Limitation of War in Western and Islamic Tradition*, ed. James Turner Johnson and John Kelsay. New York: Greenwood, 1990.

Santana, Rebecca. "Women at the Forefront of Iran Protests." Associated Press, June 25, 2009.

Sarwar, Beena. "Hard on Civil Society, Soft on Extremists." Inter Press Service, November 5, 2007.

Sarwar, Beena. "Intelligentsia Finds Ways to Beat Emergency Rule." Inter Press Service, November 9, 2007.

Satha-Anand, Chaiwat. "The Nonviolent Crescent: Eight Theses on Muslim Nonviolent Action." In Peace and Conflict Resolution in Islam: Precept and Practice, ed. Nathan C. Funk, Ayse Kadayifci and Abdul Aziz Said. Lanham, MD: University Press of America, 2001.

Schelzig, Erik. "Tennessee Gubernatorial Candidate Ramsey Criticized for Calling Islam a 'Cult.'" Commercial Appeal, July 27, 2010.

Schimmel, Annemarie. Mystical Dimensions of Islam. Chapel Hill: University of North Carolina Press, Press, 1978.

Schwartz, Stephen. "Getting to Know the Sufis." Weekly Standard, February 7, 2005.

Schwartz, Stephen. Kosovo: Background to a War. London: Anthem, 2000.

Shane M., "Green Movement: More about Islam than Meets the Eye." http://www.inside iran.org/news/green-movement-more-about-islam-than-meets-the-eye, November 10, 2009.

Shareef, Simon. "Democratic Dawn." Himal Southasian, December 2008.

Sharify-Funk, Meena. "Peace and the Feminine in Islam." In Peace and Conflict Resolution in Islam: Precept and Practice, ed. Nathan C. Funk, Ayse Kadayifci, and Abdul Aziz Said. Lanham, MD: University Press of America, 2001.

Sharp, Heather. "Bilin Marks Five Years of West Bank Barrier Protest." BBC, February 19, 2010.

Sikand, Yoginder. Sacred Spaces: Exploring Traditions of Shared Faith in India. New Delhi: Penguin, 2004.

Singh, Surinder. "Islamic Mysticism in Northwest India: An Exploration of the Poetry of Khwaja Ghulam Farid." In The Islamic Path: Sufism, Politics and Society in India, ed. Saiyid Zaheer Husain Jafri, and Helmut Reifeld. New Delhi: Rainbow Publishers, 2006.

Sonn, Tamara. "Irregular Warfare and Terrorism in Islam: Asking the Right Questions." In Cross, Crescent, and Sword: The Justification and Limitation of War in Western and Islamic Tradition, ed. James Turner Johnson and John Kelsay. New York: Greenwood, 1990.

Stephan, Maria J., and Erica Chenoweth. "Why Civil Resistance Works." International Security 33:1 (Summer 2008): 7–44.

Stolberg, Sherly Gay. "Obama Enters Debate with Mosque Remarks." New York Times, August 14, 2010.

Tavernise, Sabrina. "Mystical Form of Islam Suits Sufis in Pakistan." New York Times, February 25, 2010.

Tendulkar, D.G. Abdul Ghaffar Khan: Faith is a Battle. Mumbai: Popular Prakashan, 1967.

Traub, James. "The Lawyers' Crusade." New York Times Magazine, June 1, 2008.

Valentine, Simon Ross. Islam and the Ahmadiyya Jama'at: History, Belief, Practice. New York: Columbia University Press, 2008.

Wade, Matthew. "Pakistan Celebrates Sweet Victory as Chief Justice is Reinstated." Sydney Morning Herald, March 18, 2009.

Walsh, Declan. "Of Saints and Sinners." Economist, December 18, 2008.

Walt, Stephen. "Why They Hate Us (II): How Many Muslims Has the U.S. Killed in the Past 30 Years?" *Foreign Policy Online*, November 30, 2009.

Warikoo, Niraj. "Muslim, Nigerian Leaders Rally against Terrorism." *Detroit Free Press*, January 8, 2010.

Weinberg, Bill. "Iraq's Civil Resistance." *The Nation*, December 24, 2007.

Winton, Richard, and Teresa Watanabe. "LAPD's Muslim Mapping Plan Killed." *Los Angeles Times*, November 15, 2007.

Worth, Robert. "Iran Reformist Tries to Enlist Labor and Teachers." *New York Times*, April, 29, 2010.

Worth, Robert. "Opposition in Iran Meets a Crossroads on Strategy." *New York Times*, February 14, 2010.

Worth, Robert, and Nazila Fathi. "Police Is Said to Have Killed 10 in Protests." *New York Times*, December 27, 2009.

Wright, Robin. "An Opposition Manifesto in Iran." *Los Angeles Times*, January 6, 2010.

Yager, Jordy. "Rep. Myrick Repeats Calls for Cutting CAIR Ties." *The Hill*, October 17, 2009.

Yong, Will, and Michael Slackman, "Across Iran, Anger Lies behind Face of Calm." *New York Times*, June 11, 2010.

Yong, Will, and Michael Slackman, "Clashes and Protests Reported in Iran." *New York Times*, June 12, 2010.

Yunus, Mohammed. *Frontier Pathans and Freedom Struggle*. Delhi: Anmol Publications, 1985.

Zakaria, Rafiq. *Muhammad and the Qur'an*. New York: Penguin, 1992.

Zizek, Slavoj. "Iran on the Brink." *In These Times*, August 2009.

Zunes, Stephen. "Nonviolent Resistance in the Islamic World." *Nonviolent Activist*, January–February 2002.

Zunes, Stephen. "The Power of Protest in the Maldives." *Huffington Post*, December 9, 2008.

Index

About the Author

AMITABH PAL is the managing editor of *The Progressive*, for which he has interviewed the Dalai Lama, Mikhail Gorbachev, Jimmy Carter, and John Kenneth Galbraith. In addition to his role as the managing editor, Pal is the coeditor of the Progressive Media Project. He lives in Madison, Wisconsin.

"Islam" Means Peace